SAINT MARY'S SEMINARY LIBRARY
9745 Memorial Drive
Houston 24, Texas

Interpretative Reading

Interpretative Reading

TECHNIQUES AND SELECTIONS

BY

SARA LOWREY
Department of Speech
Furman University

AND

GERTRUDE E. JOHNSON
Department of Speech
University of Wisconsin

REVISED  EDITION

New York

APPLETON-CENTURY-CROFTS, INC.

COPYRIGHT, 1953, BY
APPLETON-CENTURY-CROFTS, INC.

All rights reserved. This book, or parts thereof, must not be reproduced in any form without permission of the publisher.

549-11

Library of Congress Card Number: 53-6203

Copyright, 1942, by D. Appleton-Century Company, Inc.

PRINTED IN THE UNITED STATES OF AMERICA

FOREWORD

The acceleration of life in the "Atomic Age" has given impetus to a re-thinking of education in terms of human values. Effective teaching of the humanities and social sciences to develop men and women capable of using scientific invention for the benefit of man rather than for his destruction seems imperative. In his lecture titled "The Romance of Science and the Truth of Fiction" William Lyon Phelps recognized the contribution of scientific invention to the charm of modern life, but he stressed our need for realization of the truths inherent in great literature. Literature may be studied in different ways but no method is superior to that of oral interpretation. Through this kind of study the student partakes of the experiences of all humanity and becomes of necessity "a part of all that he has met." Effective oral reading demands this inner realization if the reader is to convey vital vicarious experience to his hearers. This textbook is the result of a sincere search for ways of experiencing the *reality* of literature, ways which seem as natural as the active recall of personal experience. These ways have been tested by ourselves, our students, and many others in our field and in allied fields. They adhere closely to principles of psychology and to fundamentals of all art. If followed faithfully we believe these principles will help one to develop habits of thinking and of behavior which will improve understanding and enjoyment of literature; concentration on the work in hand, thinking in terms of the material itself result in commanding the attention of the listener. Emphasis is placed upon ways of thinking that are natural to the meaning and in harmony with the literary form.

There is need for a recognition of the nature and scope of interpretative reading. The possibilities within the framework of interpretative reading are not adequately understood by educators within or outside the speech field. Even teachers and students of interpretative reading need to explore the possibilities for personal development and for educational entertainment in schools, clubs, churches, town meetings, theatre, radio, and television.

PERSONAL VALUES

Many teachers of speech have recognized the intrinsic worth of interpretative reading in its possibilities for self-realization and growth. The development of poise and the unfolding of personalities has been the magnificent obsession of teachers of interpretative speech. The thoroughness of literary study essential for adequate oral interpretation develops awareness of that human essence which distinguishes man from brute. Living with great thoughts and attempting to communicate them to others invariably results in some absorption of this greatness.

Interpretative reading should make distinct contributions to mental stability and emotional maturity. Since literature is an interpretation of life it calls for an understanding of life and contributes to living. Thus it sets up a constructive cycle quite contrary to the vicious cycles which bring maladjustment. As one learns more about literature he has better understanding of life which enables him to interpret literature more effectively. In working for abandon to emotion and while using restraint in its expression one should achieve emotional balance. Since an interpretative art requires an objective attitude toward emotion it should render one more objective toward his own emotions. Thus, through experiencing the thoughts and feelings expressed in literature and through sharing them with listeners, the student receives that which is basic to mental balance and emotional maturity.

CORE OF SPEECH TRAINING

Under various titles (elocution, oratory, expression, and declamation) historically interpretative reading was the core of speech training. The fundamental nature of interpretative reading was understood as the perfect Gestalt of the speech field. Textbooks on the training of the speaking voice still give recognition to this fundamental nature. The reading of literature expressive of various moods is the method used to cultivate flexibility of voice and the alert discriminating mind essential for all expression.

PUBLIC SPEAKING

Interpretative reading and public speaking are clearly interrelated, each one helping the other. Interpretative reading is often used within a public address and direct speech is used to introduce interpretative reading. The practice of direct speaking helps the reader to remain simple and communicative in presentation while many of the finer aspects of public speaking such as the use of vivid imagery, sense of timing, voice flexibility etc. can best be learned through interpretative study. An interesting case in point has come to our attention. In a preliminary oratorical contest, the chairman predicted the winner of the contest. His prediction was correct and upon presentation of the award the chairman said: "You have had experience in poetry reading." The winner responded, "Yes, I had a regular poetry reading program on the radio for more than a year before I began the study of public speaking. How did you know?" The chairman answered, "You had the elements one learns in interpretative reading and lacked the pattern one is likely to develop when he confines his practice to extempore speaking. You were skillful and subtle in imagery, your tones, tempo, and rhythm were varied in accord with meaning, and you had the art which conceals its artistry."

ACTING

It is an accepted premise that interpretative reading is not acting. The fact that great acting includes interpretative reading is too often overlooked. The weakness in the educational theatre is the speaking of lines. Education has made rapid strides in applying professional techniques of stage design, lighting, movement, grouping, but has neglected the study of interpretation of meaning through the reading of lines. Is it because the interpretative reading of lines is the most difficult area to teach and to learn? This fact should prove a challenge in education. This textbook gives a plan for mastering some of the lessons suggested by Boleslavsky [1] as among the first to be learned by an actor. His "Creature" worked for a year to learn the art of concentration through mental imagery. She must have been a real student to have mastered the first lesson alone. Most students of theatre need the help of an interpretative reading teacher to learn this and other speech techniques so essential to good acting.

PROFESSIONAL READING

The close relation between acting and interpretative reading is emphasized by the professional reading of actors. We are indebted to Charles Laughton for spearheading, as it were, the revival of the art of reading on the professional stage. Today Tyrone Power, Emlyn Williams, Edith Evans, Basil Rathbone, and others are contributing to the popularity of this veteran speech art. The dramatic schools of England have kept interpretative reading in its rightful place as an integral part of the training of actors. Perhaps that is why some of the finest recorded poetry reading available is done by actors. While such reading is of great worth, it should serve as a challenge to teachers of Interpretation. Can we afford to let the professional aspect of our work be taken over so completely by actors? Should not we too be *doing* as well as teaching our art? It would be a sad commentary on our attitude if we had to accept this cryptic judgment of George Bernard Shaw: "those who *can,* do; those who *can't,* teach."

The hearing of fine reading is as important to our speech students as is the hearing of fine music to the music student. Through such examples they are helped to set their own

[1] Richard Boleslavsky, *Acting, The First Six Lessons* (New York, Theatre Arts Inc.).

standards of excellence. We should bring readers of proven ability and skill to the campus. We, ourselves, should make a point of presenting programs and arrange to have our students read publicly. Opportunities are not lacking. Many schools find delight in regular Reading Hours in which the students, teachers, and others participate. Once it is known that there are readers among us, countless invitations to read come from varied sources such as men's and women's clubs, church groups, business organizations, libraries, luncheon and dinner groups and many others. Response to these invitations not only affords our students the opportunity to experience public reading in a true life situation but it gives them the satisfaction of fulfilling a social obligation to their community.

Too little has been done by interpreters in the matter of recording their readings. There is a demand for such recordings. When the album of recorded readings by Gertrude E. Johnson of the University of Wisconsin was decided upon, practically all records were sold before the album was ready for distribution. A further supply failed to satisfy the demands which came from all parts of the country. The long-playing records of Lew Sarrett of the University of Florida have met with success. For the Dartmouth recordings of the readings by teachers of Interpretation, thanks go to Albert T. Martin.

THE ELEMENTARY SCHOOL

Educators are searching for ways of developing the creative ability in children. We should recognize the contribution interpretative reading may make in the elementary school and in the training of elementary-school teachers. Suppose every elementary-school teacher could read so as to share the charm of literature and interpret the essence of truth for the children in her class room. If elementary school teachers could read effectively themselves and could direct children to read naturally (concentrating on thought rather than on expression, speaking in rhythms innate to the literature) they would succeed in fostering the creative spark that makes children responsive to beauty, eager for stories, and appreciative of the rhythm in such books as *Mother Goose* and *A Child's Garden of Verse*. Why are so many university students prejudiced against poetry? It is because somewhere they got a false concept of poetry. Students working with the principles outlined in this textbook frequently say, "Why have we not been taught to read like this before?" They are amazed at the possibilities for enjoyment, larger living, and deeper understanding through the study of literature.

Many public school teachers are recognizing the need for oral reading in the public schools. They have no wish to return to the word-calling which once characterized the so-called oral reading. They are eager for guidance. We can help them to read and to teach children to read so that history and literature are zestful experiences and not the drudgery some of them think. In a day when rapid silent reading is emphasized (and there is good reason for it) there is also need for reading in which one takes time to experience and convey meaning.

LANGUAGE STUDY

Interpretative reading may make a significant contribution to language study at any level: expanding vocabulary, refining sentence structure, improving pronunciation, enunciation and fluency. Many writers have attributed their literary style to reading Shakespeare and the Bible. If silent reading can contribute so much to one's use of language, how much can the intensification through oral interpretation contribute? We predict that when teachers of language arts and literature are trained in interpretative reading a new renaissance of literary culture will give hope to civilization.

SOCIAL RESPONSIBILITY

Are we socially responsible when we fail to recognize the great values inherent in interpretative reading? Are we socially responsible when we limit our goals to class room reading by students who happen to enroll? Does social responsibility include more effort on our part to follow the ways to effective reading, to explore its scope and to spread its usefulness?

SPEECH CORRECTION

Social responsibility includes the education of exceptional children. Teachers of speech correction should give careful consideration to the place oral interpretative reading may take in making their work more effective. Therapeutic value is gained through experiencing literature imaginatively and speaking it in natural, varied rhythms and tones. The cerebral palsied, for example, need to cease to listen to how they say words and concentrate on meaning. Experimentation has revealed that they may, through mental imagery, so abandon themselves to the idea that rhythms become natural and easy and they may even experience the joy of normal fluent speech while reading a poem. Such reading enables them, not only to communicate, but to build confidence.

A speech correctionist recently said, "I build my work in speech rehabilitation upon the Gestalt of interpretation. We work on the whole thought and then concentrate on the special difficulty that seems to hinder the particular student from realizing full expression. We have found that students learn more readily through enjoyment than through discouragement so we first enjoy a story or a poem and then get down to the drudgery of clearing out the difficulties that prevent that pleasure from becoming a complete joy."

Stutterers are usually able to sing. The step from singing to speaking a poem with concentration upon imagery is often quite easy. The fact that language is already supplied is a great relief to a stutterer. If he is able to build confidence in his ability to read fluently he may find speaking not so difficult as formerly.

RADIO

The relation of interpretative reading to radio seems too obvious to need mentioning. Much of radio is read even when it sounds like extempore speech. Perhaps this is the great contribution radio and the public address system have made to interpretative speech. After hearing the Quartette in *Don Juan in Hell,* Elsa Lanchester said to her husband, Charles Laughton, "You have learned the last thing an actor can learn—how to speak to an audience as if they were just people in a room." [1] Doubtless a fine public address system made its contribution to this ability. The "fireside chats" of Franklin Delano Roosevelt were read from a manuscript. One who holds the interest of a radio listener must have the ability to command attention and interest, speaking to an audience as if "they were just people in a room." A young woman well versed in these techniques was asked to substitute on the radio for a storyteller. The day before she was to take over the program she went to hear the regular storyteller. She saw a maid mopping the corridor. The young woman decided that the next day she would so interest that maid in the story that she would stop mopping. The storyteller succeeded. As the story began the maid paused, as it proceeded she walked to the studio door, peered in and stood, mop in hand, listening until the story ended, then proceeded with her work.

THE TEXTBOOK

A textbook cannot take the place of a teacher. Its purpose is to supplement, to reinforce, and perhaps to guide. It may contribute to a teacher's background of knowledge on the subject. It should suggest new points of view, new avenues of approach, new techniques of teaching. It must prove a valuable aid in presenting subject-matter to the students. It should support and enlarge the teacher's point of view. It may serve as a helpful check to the teacher in presenting the whole, or at least a balanced picture, and thus prevent the overemphasis of one phase to the neglect of other phases of equal importance.

This is not a book of exercises, though we have endeavored

[1] Robert Wahls, "Don Juan Raises Theatrical Cain," *Sunday News* (March 30, 1952), p. 2.

to point the way to plans and practices. Selections for practice have, after some thought, been placed in the latter portion of the book, thus avoiding the arbitrary feeling that certain selections are desirable for only *one* element of the interpreter's expression. It invites selection and decision by teacher and student, as to which material shall be used for any given idea or practice. It will be noticed that many "old favorites" (for some of the older of us) have been included. It is our experience that the younger generation too often knows little of the wider choices offered by authors not directly contemporaneous. This latter material is at hand and can be found in many places.

A NEW APPROACH?

At first glance this book may seem to offer a strange approach to the subject of interpretative reading. It is a departure from the traditional approach and organization. That very departure may be its chief value to the teacher. If the teacher is familiar with other approaches he has no need of another book treating the subject in the same way. His knowledge of other methods will furnish a background for his understanding and evaluation of the ideas presented in this book.

The basic ideas presented in this book are not new. Originality is not claimed for them. It is in the method of presentation and in the specific application that originality may be discovered. If the teacher is already familiar with these ideas in the fields of psychology, sociology, education, literature, and the philosophy of art, then he has a basis for testing them in the field of interpretative reading. If he is already using these ideas in interpretative reading, even then he may find some suggestions which will supplement, and many which will support, his teaching. This book may then prove of more value to him than if it presented a totally new approach.

Techniques and procedures here suggested have been thoroughly tested with gratifying results. If the suggestions are new to you, try them with your students. Experimentation is valued in other fields; experiment a bit in the field of creative reading and see if it does not add freshness, vitality, and even originality to your teaching. All alert teachers will supplement from their own rich experience the suggestions in any book. A textbook, however, like a key for a lock, cannot function without being put to use. Put these practices to use and see if they will unlock doors to the understanding and views of wholeness which interpretative reading represents.

CRITICISM

One of the most important aspects of effective teaching is evaluation of student work. The word *criticism* needs defining since too often it connotes mere faultfinding. Criticism, as used in our teaching, means an appraisal, an evaluation. A good criticism may consist entirely of praise. A criticism of student reading should usually include three steps. First, commendation of that which is good for the sake of encouragement, since we all need encouragement if we are to grow in the realm of artistic expression. George Matthew Adams says:

> Encouragement is oxygen to the soul. Good work can never be expected from a worker without encouragement. No one ever climbed spiritual heights without it. Note how well *you* feel after you have encouraged someone else. No other argument is necessary to suggest that you never miss the opportunity to give encouragement.[1]

It might be added, "Note how well you feel when someone encourages *you*. Are you not stimulated to finer accomplishment?"

To test the power of praise, criticism, or ignoring in the learning process an experiment was conducted on three groups of children. Although it was admitted by those conducting the experiment that any one of the methods applied alone was inadequate, the following results were given. The ignored group made least progress, the criticized group made more,

[1] George Matthew Adams, "Oxygen to the Soul," *The Reader's Digest* (February, 1941), p. 6. By permission of the author.

and the praised group made the most progress. Indiscriminate praise, however, is likely to result in a superiority complex instead of social adjustment. When the student knows he does not deserve the praise unfortunate distortions and contempt for the praise itself may result.

The *second* element in criticism should be constructive suggestion. Constructive suggestion means pointing out faults and making it clear how to correct them. Faultfinding is not constructive criticism. Anybody can find fault. Faultfinding is an attribute of little minds. A teacher should point out a fault only as a means of aiding the student to correct it. Such frankness in a teacher is appreciated by the student who realizes that he is not perfect and who quite possibly is taking the course in order to learn a better way of doing something. If his weaknesses are pointed out and the way made clear for him to gain strength, he will appreciate the suggestions.

The *third* element in criticism is to suggest no more than the student is able to take. Young teachers often err by offering too many suggestions, and as a result they give their students a feeling of defeat; the student is made to feel that so much has to be done the situation is hopeless. If the teacher selects one thing at a time, makes clear the way to improvement, progress, however slight, is sure.

THE WHOLE

The process of centering the attention of the student on one problem at a time results in the solution of many other problems at the same time. When the teacher strikes at the center of a student's needs, the whole is apt to be reached. For example, a teacher once asked the class what was the matter with a student who had read poorly. One said, "He needs to enunciate more clearly"; another said, "He needs to talk louder"; another said, "He needs to support his voice." The teacher said, "Have any of you touched the *cause* of his inadequate performance?" One student answered, "No, he needs to *realize the significance* of what he is saying and to *care* whether we get it or not." The class then discussed the meaning and significance of the material which had been read. The student was called upon to re-read so as to affect the listeners. Not only did his voice become stronger and his enunciation clearer, but he stood taller, his face became animated, his body as well as his speech became vitalized.

Development in speech, like physical development, depends upon the growth of *the whole being*. Even though emphasis is placed upon one thing at a time, the teacher should keep ever before himself and his students a vision of the whole. Each part should be considered as a part of a whole and dealt with according to its relation to the whole.

TALENT

One further thought seems important here. It is difficult to detect talent in the field of oral interpretation. Talent is frequently discovered after many have failed to discern it. Surely oral interpretation will prove of value to all students, not merely to those who are considered talented. A teacher's success may be measured both by the progress of the class as a whole and by the progress of each individual. A teacher who neglects the poorest student has missed one of the greatest satisfactions which can come to a teacher—that of seeing light gradually reflected in dull eyes and hope dawn in a discouraged soul.

On the other hand those especially endowed should become a joy to their teacher. How amazing that some teachers should be jealous of their excellent students, as if it were not a teacher's greatest accomplishment to have students excel him. As William Lyon Phelps says in his autobiography:

> The highest ambition of every good teacher is to be excelled by his pupils. The one thing he wants more than anything else is that those whom he teaches will surpass him in every respect—in brains, character, achievement. As every normal father is prouder of his

son's accomplishments than of his own independent work, so every normal teacher looks with happiness and pride on the success of those who were once his students.[1]

S. L.
G. E. J.

[1] William Lyon Phelps, *Autobiography with Letters* (New York: Oxford University Press, 1939), p. 656. By permission of the publishers and of the author.

CONTENTS

	PAGE
Foreword	v
To the Student	3

SECTION I
TECHNIQUES

CHAPTER
I.	INTERPRETATIVE READING, A CREATIVE PROCESS	13
II.	A TECHNIQUE OF THINKING FOR INTERPRETATIVE READING	26
III.	BODILY ACTION IN INTERPRETATIVE READING	46
IV.	DRAMATIC TIMING IN INTERPRETATIVE READING	77
V.	STRUCTURE IN INTERPRETATIVE READING	134
VI.	ILLUSION IN INTERPRETATIVE READING	168
VII.	VOICE IN INTERPRETATIVE READING	179
VIII.	INTERPRETATION OF MEANING	197
IX.	BACKGROUNDS, INTRODUCTIONS, AND PROGRAMS	234
X.	CHORAL READING	254
XI.	INTERPRETATIVE READING FOR THE RADIO	285

SECTION II
SELECTIONS FOR INTERPRETATION

SELECTIONS FOR INTERPRETATION	323

Appendices

A. Syllabus for a College Course in Interpretative Reading 579
B. Suggested Material for Supplementary Reading and Reference 585

Index 589

Interpretative Reading

Nothing is so absolutely secure as art; its integrity is inviolate because by the law of its nature it cannot be created save by those who comprehend and reverence it.

HAMILTON WRIGHT MABIE

TO THE STUDENT

> Not scholars, not even critics is the present need of literature, but interpreters, virtuosos in emotion; men with full orbed souls, capable of running the scale of human feeling from the bass note of self-pity to the high clear C of mystical rapture.[1]
>
> *M. M. Hedges*

A man once asked a public speaker, "What will I get out of your talk?" The speaker responded, "That depends upon what you bring to get it in." The answer indicated that the speaker believed in the value of a high intelligence quotient. In that he was in accord with the attitude prevalent in the average college today, namely, that those with special ability should excel in understanding and in accomplishment. In the arts one calls this special ability *talent*. It is frequently said that if one has talent in a certain field it will manifest itself; if not, he may as well seek another field. Now this theory may be correct, but the problem is how to measure talent in oral reading. A student who seems to be talented often proves to be a "flash in the pan," while others who are considered mere plodders succeed. You have not forgotten, I am sure, that Edison was made to sit on a dunce stool because he was considered so stupid.

Perhaps the speaker in the illustration above would have given a wiser answer if he had said, "What you get from my talk depends upon how determined you are to get it." Edi-

[1] M. M. Hedges, "Creative Teaching," *School and Society Journal,* January 27, 1918. By permission of The Science Press.

son said that genius was nine tenths hard work. Modern psychologists state that memory depends largely upon one's will to remember.

When Katherine Cornell was playing the rôle of Elizabeth Barrett in *The Barretts of Wimpole Street* at Baylor University, Waco, Texas (the home of the largest Browning collection in the world), Miss Cornell wore a topaz brooch from the collection: the one given to Elizabeth by Robert Browning on the first anniversary of their marriage. Dr. Armstrong, who has devoted his life to assembling and preserving the Browning treasures at Baylor, wished Miss Cornell also to use from the collection the first edition of *Sordello*. This was the poem from which Elizabeth Barrett was supposed to be reading when Robert made the remark, "At the time that was written only God and Robert Browning knew what it meant; now only God knows." Miss Cornell was appreciative of the honor paid her by the Browning scholar but responded, "Dr. Armstrong, I'm afraid to attempt to play with a book different from the one I'm accustomed to. You see, when we were learning the play I had my secretary type in the lines to be delivered as I held the book. Although I've played the rôle over two hundred times I've never memorized those lines." Miss Cornell had not spoken those lines with the will to remember them. She could not, therefore, depend upon her memory to repeat them accurately.

If you, as a student of interpretative reading, approach this subject with a will to learn you will be rewarded with the satisfaction which comes from achievement. If you were able to learn your a-b-c's, if you were able to pass the average high school course, then you have sufficient talent for a course in creative reading. Your progress will depend largely upon your will to learn, the sincerity of your attack, and your faithfulness in applying the underlying principles of creative reading. Some students may have the ability to go further than others as creative artists and as public performers, but any student can succeed sufficiently to realize the joy of interpreting literature for others and to appreciate the value of such an ability in his education.

You will also find this work fundamental to all other courses. The ability to read the meaning of the printed page is fundamental in every educational pursuit. Your understanding and appreciation of history, mathematics, science, and languages will be increased if you approach this subject with a will to learn and with a will to master the principles presented. The insight gained from interpreting life through literature will illumine other hours than those devoted to the study of creative reading.

If you approach this study with the attitude of merely "getting by," if you consider interpretative reading a "snap course" and give to it last-minute preparation, or if, because the teacher encourages reading from the book, you give no advance preparation but depend upon sight reading or inspiration, this course will prove a drag. You will become dissatisfied with the subject and uncomfortable about your own performance. As Emerson says, "A man is relieved and gay when he has put his heart into his work and done his best, but that which he has done otherwise shall give him no peace." Your success depends upon your mental attitude and your energy in applying the principles presented. It depends upon how determined you are to get the benefits offered.

A public speaker once explained to a group of students his conception of the difference between a genius and the average person. We are sorry we do not know his name since his idea is so fundamental to the art of interpretative reading. He gave the key to accomplishment and to the sense of well-being which comes with accomplishment. He said: "There are just two ways in which a genius differs from the average man. The genius gives his entire attention to the thing of the moment; and he makes a quick transfer, without wasted motion, from one task to another." Apply these two principles to your college course of study: Try (1) giving complete attention to the course before you and (2) making a definite and immediate transfer from one course to another. A former student admitted that while in the class in interpretative reading he spent much of his time thinking about the French class which met the next hour; during the French class his mind kept wandering to his English course and the fact that he had not prepared his theme; during his study period when he was supposed to be writing his theme, he thought of the girl he had a date with for the next prom; and so on all day long his mind roamed to something other than that which should have held his attention at the moment.

Try for one day, or for one week, the technique of complete concentration on the thing at hand and make quick and immediate transfers "when the bell rings" for another class or occupation. Your ability to concentrate will grow, and your joy in each study will increase. Furthermore, this technique will prove of value socially as well as scholastically. Complete concentration upon the activity of the moment is an excellent technique of living. It is conducive to a stable and magnetic personality.

Another important element in accomplishment is faith—faith in yourself, faith in others, and faith in the thing which you are doing. Some students defeat themselves by acquiring the mental attitude that others with more speech training, more ability, or better clothes have an advantage over them. These students complain that the class is not equal in experience, ability, or training. Of course the students in the class are not equal: they are all unequal because their grandfathers were different; they are unequal because their home environments were different. Each student in a class is an individual. You cannot be exactly like, or equal to, any other in the class; and who wants to be like or equal to another person?

Consider further and see that there is equality of opportunity. You have just as many hours in the day as any other student; it is the use you make of your time which counts in accomplishment. You have equal access to the library; it is the use you make of the library which is important to your development. You have equal opportunity to learn from the teacher, from the other students, and from the assignments; it is the use you make of these advantages which determines your progress.

Many students defeat themselves because they do not believe that knowledge is power. Nowhere except in the educational system do people think it is smart to pay for a thing and then refuse to take it. In other phases of life people pride themselves on getting more for their money. Only in education do people pride themselves on "getting by" without gaining the benefits. Knowledge is power. Skills give advantage in life competitions. Habits of concentration and industry pay big dividends in the business of living.

Give these ideas a thorough test. Do not wait for inspiration or until you "feel like it." When that time comes, go to an appointed place and buckle down to work. Robert Louis Stevenson said, "I go to my desk as a laborer goes to his work, and I work at it." A laborer does not ask whether he feels like it or not; he goes to work, and his interest grows as he works. So it is with the creative writer; so it is with the creative reader; so it is with the creative student.

As students you are urged to work at this course in oral interpretation because of what it will do for you in life. In his autobiography William Lyon Phelps discusses the strange situation in the education which specializes in everything except life. He states:

> It is curious that many people believe in the importance of what they call vocational and practical courses and regard the study of great literature as merely ornamental, a pretty accomplishment in seminaries for young ladies. As a matter of fact, nothing is more essential in the proper furnishing of a man's mind than a knowledge of the world's best literature. Literature is the immortal part of history. Literature is the interpretation of human life.[1]

A doctor once said, "If I were advising a pre-med student I'd tell him to spend more time in the English and speech departments. He will get his scientific training in medical school. He needs an understanding of human beings and

---
[1] Phelps, *Op. cit.*, p. 308. By permission of the publishers.

how to deal with them such as he should gain from a study of speech and literature. If he does not get this in his college course he is likely never to get it and to be a poor doctor because of it." Mr. Phelps supports this idea as follows:

I asked a successful engineer in Boston, a man who is at the head of enterprises with scores of young engineers working under him, this question: "What studies in college would you advise for one who intends to become a civil engineer?" He replied without hesitation, "Anything so long as it has no connection with engineering." He told me that those who came to him from technical schools with no liberal education began at first to surpass those who had studied literature and other general subjects. But in a few years the truly "educational" young men went ahead, because they had imagination, interesting minds, and a knowledge of human nature.[1]

This book, *Interpretative Reading,* is offered to you as a means by which you can learn more about life through the study of literature. It suggests techniques through which you may interpret the life depicted in literature and share that interpretation with others. It suggests techniques by which you may learn to think and to communicate thoughts to others. These techniques are offered as a key to literature, to reading (silent and oral), to life itself. A student once wrote on an examination paper at the conclusion of a course in which these principles and methods were taught: "This course teaches a student how to *live;* and I don't mean *exist.* Here a student is taught character, life—a most important course stuck off in the corner of the curriculum.

[1] Phelps, *Loc. cit.*

How many other subjects teach so much? This course should be required of every student in this college. Trig. is required; chemistry is required. How much will the college student need these when sorrow comes, when joy comes, when *life* comes? We students need to know *how to live.*"

SECTION I
TECHNIQUES

Chapter I

INTERPRETATIVE READING, A CREATIVE PROCESS

> There is creative reading as well as creative writing.
> *Ralph Waldo Emerson*

There is a question in the minds of some teachers as to whether ours is a creative or merely a recreative art. It is our belief that interpretative reading is creative when the reader follows the laws of the creative artist. The reader's materials are the literature he chooses to interpret plus the oral expression through which he reveals the author's meaning. Professor F. M. Rarig states in an article in the *Quarterly Journal of Speech:*

Only in a limited sense is the oral reader a creative artist. The writer has already done the work of observation, selection, and organization. It remains for the reader to submit himself, with all his powers of memory, imagination, and insight, to the author's organization as recorded in words.[1]

We shall do well to consider this point of view carefully. Is it not, however, as true of the actor and the musician as of the interpretative reader? The playwright has "already

---

[1] F. M. Rarig, "Some Elementary Contributions of Aesthetics to Interpretative Speech," *Quarterly Journal of Speech*, Vol. 26, No. 4, p. 527-28. Reprinted by permission.

done the work of observation, selection, and organization," and it remains for the actor "to submit himself, with all his powers of memory, imagination, and insight" both to the playwright's organization as recorded in words and often to the interpretation of a director. Is the actor, then, not to be considered a creative artist?

The musician, likewise, interprets the written symbols which the composer has recorded in musical terms. Is the musician who interprets what the composer has recorded only in a limited sense then a creative artist? It is not our purpose to present an argument as to the degree to which an interpretative reader, an actor, or a musician is a creative artist but to present some of the creative elements in the process of oral interpretation. Perhaps we may find unity in the point of view that the interpretative reader is a creative artist to the degree to which he re-creates the author's concepts in terms of living speech. Hiram Corson compares the oral study of literature to the study of music:

> How is the best response to the essential life of a poem to be secured by the teacher from the student? I answer, by the fullest interpretative vocal rendering of it. . . . Learning about poetry does not, of itself, avail any more, for poetical cultivation than lecturing about music avails of itself, for musical cultivation.[1]

Since it is the function of all creative art to present truth in forms which may be perceived by others, the interpretative reader may be said to read creatively when the content of the printed page is so vividly re-created that it gives understanding to, and gains response from, an audience.

---

[1] Hiram Corson, *The Aims of Literary Study* (New York: The Macmillan Company), pp. 99–102. By permission.

INTERPRETATIVE READING, AN ART

It is the purpose of all art to convey an idea, a mood a concept. The value of a work of art is estimated largely by its power to evoke a feeling or a response from others. This response is in ratio to the clarity with which the interpreter reveals his concept. This concept is sometimes referred to as the spirit, or the essence, of the art. The spirit is the distinguishing feature of art: it is the quality which lifts craftsmanship into the realm of art.

All art must have some medium through which this essence is revealed. For sculpture there is marble, for music there is tone, for literature there are words; and the marble, the tones, the words are the materials with which the artists express their concepts. The materials which the creative reader uses are the literature which he selects to interpret, and his voice and body, through which he conveys his concept.

This concept which the interpretative reader expresses is his own understanding of the author's meaning. His function, as has been pointed out, is that of re-creating, or giving his interpretation of, the meaning of an author. The first step, then, in creative reading is to find the meaning of the author, and the second step is to reveal that meaning through the spoken word. The reader's success will depend partly upon his ability to understand, to re-create the concept of an author, and partly upon his ability to reveal that concept to an audience.

Interpretative reading as a fine art presupposes an artist. An artist must not only have a concept and have material through which this concept is to be revealed, but he must find a way of handling his material so that it may express his concept. This way of handling his material is called technique. Technique means simply the way or the method an artist uses in handling his material. Technique is a means to an end—not an end itself. The fundamental techniques of all arts are the same. We submit in this textbook some of the techniques of art and the means of applying them to the art of interpretative reading.

Individuality in Art

An essential element of all art is individuality. There must be the personal stamp of the individual artist. There must be that subtle something by which his creation is recognized as his own. There must be a unique quality which suggests the artist's personality, that results from his own individual thinking. No one can call himself an artist if he simply copies others. This fact is as true of the creative reader as it is of the sculptor, the actor, the writer.

The recognition of the necessity for individuality in the art of speech causes many readers, speakers, and even teachers of speech to question the value of technique. The fear of being imitative, artificial, affected causes many speakers and readers to discard the ways (the techniques) of others and to look for a way of their own.

Finding one's own way without the aid of instruction from others who have achieved is likely to prove a haphazard process, with a great deal of wasted time and energy. There are, no doubt, some people of genius who find their own way, unconscious of the means by which they achieve success. Success without consciously following the experience of others is so unusual that it catches the imagination of the average person and causes him to overrate its significance. Because the average person is so willing to be deceived, the publicity department which has as its aim the building of a "star" overnight will claim that this or that actor leaped into fame by his own genius and brilliant personality when close examination of the facts will reveal a totally different explanation.

It seems foolish for one to spend his time and energy and run the risk of failure to find his own way when he can so easily profit by the experience of others. A few lessons from a good "pro" will enable one to learn techniques in golf which improve his game more in a short time than many times as much practice in finding his own way could improve it. Sportsmen know well the value of techniques; so in football, tennis, or boxing the aspirants heed eagerly the ways which have been found successful and practice diligently to make these techniques their own. Only after they have mastered the ways of experts do they feel capable of creating new ways of their own. They know that skill involves mastery and that mastery calls for practice on a way of doing a thing until that way becomes easy, habitual, natural.

PREVALENT ATTITUDES TOWARD TECHNIQUE IN INTERPRETATIVE READING

There are two very definite attitudes concerning technique in the art of interpretative reading. One is that there are definite techniques to be mastered with the meticulous care with which a golfer learns his strokes, a musician masters five-finger exercises, or a dancer learns his steps. The adherents to this point of view claim that the techniques of oral reading may be taught, just as the techniques of these other arts are taught. They admit that the mastery of techniques does not insure art, that as long as the reader's concentration is on his manner of reading he will be mechanical and ineffective. They agree that oral reading is artistic only when the spirit takes precedence over the form; yet they believe that form is essential for artistry. This group usually claim that the essence of art (that subtle something which lifts craftsmanship into the realm of art) cannot be taught but depends upon the inherent imagination, the talent, the genius of the artist. They are likely to tell an aspirant in any phase of art to master his form, promising him that if he has any talent it will speak through the medium of his carefully developed technique. In other words, they believe in the two phases of art, skill and spirit. They believe that the one can be taught and that the *other* cannot but that the one which cannot be taught will be present to the degree to which the individual possesses artistic ability.

The other attitude toward technique in the art of interpretative reading is that *form is born of spirit*. The adherents to this point of view believe in training students to think and to feel and to allow the form (or technique) more or less to take care of itself. They believe that emphasis upon technique is likely to make one mechanical, or artificial. They trust to thinking and feeling as means by which sincere expression will be created. They too admit the two phases of art, form and spirit, and they too believe that one can be taught and the other cannot. They too believe that if one of these essentials is taught the other will be present to the degree to which the individual possesses artistic ability.

One occasionally finds artistic readers from each of these schools of thought. Genius frequently leaps over established rules and finds its own form, unconsciously adhering to the rules or creating in their places new forms. Those who are opposed to teaching techniques of interpretative reading can find examples of artists who are unconscious of the means by which they have achieved their artistry. These artists will no doubt say, "I just thought it" or "I just felt it." These artists know of no techniques save thinking and feeling the content of the printed page.

There are other artists, however, who will testify that technique is a valuable means by which one may learn to reveal the author's concept. They will tell you that the mastery of technique insures the way and leaves the artist free to concentrate on ideas and moods with confidence that his way of revealing them will be adequate. To these artists skill is a means and not an end, but to them the means is important in gaining the end.

The Importance of the Whole

Is it not apparent that each of these points of view possesses some truth and that each leaves something to chance? In the one, the thing of primary importance is left to chance; and in the other, the means by which it is revealed is left to haphazard methods. Is it not clear that these two points of view may be harmonized and that the student may drill upon a way of expressing an author's concept at the same time that he is concentrating on the concept itself? Gestalt psychology stresses the importance of the whole. That philosophy of oral interpretation which stresses less than the whole is inadequate. *The whole of any art includes both form and spirit.* The whole of the art of interpretative reading involves the concept and the means by which that concept is revealed to an audience. It is nature's way for wholes to evolve as wholes. Little children are whole human beings with the capacity to think, to feel, and to express themselves. They develop in the use of language as they think new thoughts and acquire the words through which to express these thoughts. Skill in the use of the techniques of interpretative reading and habits of concentrating on the idea can both be acquired together. Artistry is a matter of growth; it is not the acquisition of a few tricks, nor is its revelation accidental or haphazard.

The First Essential in Interpretative Reading

Leland Powers, who advocated a very definite technique of impersonation, also stressed what he called "mental cause."[1] When asked his opinion of the importance of imagination in reading, he replied that it was the first essential. Stanislavski in his autobiography, *My Life In Art*, urges the danger of mechanical drills and stresses the importance of keeping words and thoughts close together in developing a technique of acting.[2] Thought and speech are necessary each for the other. We cannot conceive of developing a language except as a result of thinking, nor can we conceive of complex thinking except through the medium of language.[3] Facility in the use of language and facility in

[1] Leland Powers, *Talks on Expression* (Boston: Thomas Groom and Company, 1924), p. 8.
[2] Constantin Stanislavski, *My Life In Art* (Boston: Little, Brown & Co., 1938), p. 84.
[3] Edward Sapir, *Language* (New York: Harcourt, Brace & Co., 1921), p. 14.

thinking depend each upon the other. As thought is an essential in the use of language, imagination is the *sine qua non* of creative reading.

Originality

One may learn much from the ways of others in interpretative reading, just as in other arts, without losing his individuality. Originality consists in the new slant given to an old truth. If the reader depends upon his own creative thinking to understand and to interpret an author's idea, his reading will be individual. If he will digest the techniques of others and then, as Kipling says, "draw the thing as he sees it" his reading will be sincere, unaffected, and individual. After one has mastered the ways of capable leaders, he is then able to create new ways. One must live under the law before he attempts to be above the law. Only by accepting the rich heritage left by others can one develop understanding and insight for the creation of new and better ways.

The Natural Versus the Habitual

"But," says the student, "I feel awkward and unnatural when I attempt to do a thing someone else's way." That is true. There are two fundamental principles involved in this answer. One always feels awkward and unnatural the first time he attempts to do something a new way. Only by continued practice does he reach the place where the new way becomes the old way, the easy way, the seemingly natural way. Do you suppose the student of violin felt natural the first time he held the bow? Do you think he would have become a greater musician if, in the beginning, he had held the bow his own way instead of the way of Heifetz, Kreisler or Mischa Elman? Do not confuse the natural way with the habitual way. The natural way is the way which follows the laws of nature, the way which when mastered will prove easy and effective. One may be in the habit of doing things in an awkward manner which is in opposition to the laws of nature but which seems to him natural because it is habitual.

Self-Discipline Essential

The other fundamental principle involved in the answer to the student who wishes in the beginning to disregard the techniques of others, can best be expressed through another law of Gestalt psychology, *an organism resists the outside forces which disturb it.* It is natural for us to resist other people's ways of doing things. The stronger your character the more tempted you will be to make such an excuse. Art calls for self-mastery. If you would be strong, efficient, effective in any line of work you must learn early the lesson that he who would rule others must first rule himself.

It falls within the purpose of this book to set forth some of the techniques others have found helpful in mastering the art of interpretative reading. The term *creative reading* is frequently used because that reading which is really effective possesses the essentials of a creative art. The creative reader interprets the author: that is, the reader gives his own understanding of the author's words and creates the form of expression which will give that understanding to others. In creative reading the student must rely upon his own thinking, his own understanding, his own individual way of speaking the thoughts and the words of the author. The student's own way will be evolved as he follows the ways of others until he is sufficiently master of himself and his art to create his own way.

THE SCOPE OF INTERPRETATIVE READING

All of the techniques of interpretative reading cannot be set down in a single textbook. The student should not limit his own way by depending solely upon one author, one teacher, or one method as his guide. He should be constantly on the alert for new ways, new ideas, new attitudes which will give him understanding, fresh attacks, clearer insight into the art of interpretation. These ways may be obtained from various sources such as life, literature, the stage; books on the technique of oral reading, speech, or acting; discussions of the techniques of all other arts *ad infinitum*.

Literature is an interpretation of life. Creative reading is an interpretation of literature. So the creative reader is really an interpreter of life through the medium of literature. If he is to interpret literature adequately he must understand the life which that literature interprets as well as the ways by which it may be revealed through the spoken word.

Knowledge and skill are the two essentials which the interpretative reader must acquire. Knowledge is the basis upon which skill is developed. Skill is developed through practice. The old adage "practice makes perfect" is inadequate; careless practice, thoughtless practice, practice of faulty methods will lead the student away from perfection.

Only practice under intelligent guidance will lead the student toward perfection. If the reader is to become skillful in influencing the thinking of audiences, if he is to become a creative artist, he must rely upon his own intelligence as a guide in his practice—his own intelligence, enriched by the experience of others, fed by the knowledge and understanding of the ways others have found successful.

Let the student of interpretative reading be a *student* in the highest sense of the word; let him study for understanding and let him practice for perfection upon the basis of that understanding. Perhaps the student of interpretative reading will feel toward perfection as the little girl did who read in the Bible, "Be ye perfect." She asked her father why such a command was given when Jesus surely knew a human being could not be perfect. The wise father answered, "Yes, my child, but we must not be satisfied with less than perfection. That is an ideal toward which we must aim." Butcher points out:

> The fundamental thought in Aristotle's philosophy is *Becoming*, not *Being* . . . Becoming to him meant a process of development, an unfolding of what is already in the germ, an upward ascent ending in Being, which is the highest object of Knowledge.[1]

The very fact that the ideal cannot be completely attained is a challenge to the creative reader. As Browning says, "Man's reach should exceed his grasp, or what's a heaven for?" The interpretative reader will continually reach upward and outward toward the goal of understanding litera-

---

[1] Samuel Henry Butcher, *Aristotle's Theory of Poetry and Fine Art* (London & New York: Macmillan Company, 1898), p. 159. By permission of the publishers.

ture and perfecting his skill in conveying that understanding. He will keep ever before him the vision of the ideal as he studies for understanding and guides his practice by that understanding.

Chapter II

TECHNIQUE OF THINKING FOR INTERPRETATIVE READING

> The most important step toward getting mental power is the acquisition of a right method in work.
> *George W. Eliot*

The dictionary suggests the idea of thought in reading by the definitions of the word itself: "to go over understandingly with or without utterance; to discern by observation of signs." The signs for reading are the words, the letters, or as Woolbert puts it, "the marks on the page." [1] The reader discerns the meaning of these signs; he *thinks the meaning* of the words; so reading is a process of thinking.

The definition above suggests two kinds of reading, silent and oral. *Silent* reading may be defined as the process of perceiving the thought of the printed page. One reads to find the meaning of the written word. A child when rebuked for reading her mother's letter said, "The world isn't a secret, is it?" To that child reading was a means of finding out more about the world in which she lived. She understood the significance of the word *reading* better than many students who say, "I've read over my lesson three times and still do not have any idea what it is about." Now, has

---

[1] Woolbert and Smith, *The Fundamentals of Speech* (New York & London: Harper and Brothers, 1927), p. 380. Reprinted by permission of Harper and Brothers.

SENSATION AND IMAGINATION

the student in this case read at all? He will readily admit that while his eye followed the lines of the page his mind was on something else. What a foolish waste of time! If instead of *reading over* the lesson three times he had *read* it once, he would have known something about it, for reading is a process of understanding, of discerning, or of perceiving the meaning. It is a process of thinking.

Since silent reading is a process of thinking that which is suggested by the written word, *oral* reading may be defined as a process of thinking aloud. The purpose of silent reading is to *get* ideas; the purpose of oral reading is to *share* ideas. In silent reading there is the process of perceiving thought; in oral reading there is the *dual* process of perceiving the thought and of revealing the thought through the spoken word.

Andrew T. Weaver points out that "all reading begins with oral reading."[1] This is true in the history of mankind as well as of each individual. Language was first spoken; writing was developed to record the spoken word. Children learn to read by recognizing the printed symbols and speaking the words they represent. The modern method of teaching children to read recognizes two fundamental techniques of reading which train the child to think the meaning instead of mere words. These techniques are (1) to read by phrases (the units of thought) and (2) to look off the page while speaking the words. Thus thought reading has taken precedence over word calling even in the primary grade. Instead of reading, "I—see—a—cat," pointing out each

---

[1] Andrew Thomas Weaver, *Speech Forms and Principles* (New York, London, & Toronto: Longmans, Green and Co., Inc., 1942), p. 130. By permission of the publishers.

word as he speaks it, the modern child looks at the page, then looks off and says, "I see a cat."

DENOTATIVE AND CONNOTATIVE MEANING

Words have two types of meaning, both of which are essential for adequate thinking. There is the logical meaning which one finds recorded in a dictionary definition. This type of meaning is known as *denotative* meaning. The dictionary defines the word denotation as "a sign, an indication, a designation." The word *denote* is defined "to mark out plainly, to indicate, to signify." When one comes across an unfamiliar word in his reading he should find the meaning, but his understanding and thinking of the word is, at first, limited to the denotative meaning.

The other type of meaning is known as *connotative,* which is associative and emotional in character. The dictionary defines connotative as "implying something additional." Experience in the use of a word gives one something additional, something in one's memory which is connected with the word, something suggested or implied by the word. The connotation of a word is quite as important and more meaningful to the individual than the denotation. The word *home* for example suggests emotional associations which give something personal, something meaningful, something additional.

As we have already seen, speaking and thinking are closely allied. Each is both a cause and a result of the other. When in oral reading the speaker thinks the idea as he speaks it, he is very likely to convey the meaning. In much of what is called oral reading the speaker repeats words with little concentration on their meaning. Too many oral readers do as Hamlet said: they read "Words, words, words," instead of thoughts, ideas, concepts. It is significant that when the reader concentrates upon the idea, the concentration of the audience is held there also. When the reader calls the words, with his thought elsewhere, it is difficult for the audience to get the meaning, hence the minds of the hearers wander.

People generally read more poorly than they speak. The average person's speech may be direct, sincere, unaffected, spontaneous, earnest, interesting, and convincing because he thinks of speech as a means of communicating ideas. When a person's thoughts are clear to himself and when he desires to impart them to others, his speech is almost sure to have elements of effectiveness. Oral reading, however, is often artificial, monotonous, stumbling, uninteresting, and unconvincing because the concentration of the reader is not upon ideas and his desire to communicate them. The reader's concentration may be upon the performance, memory, or upon his own inadequacy. He may have confidence in his ability to communicate through speech, and yet lack that confidence in reading. His thinking and his speaking may be closely allied when he is "just talking," yet his thinking when reading may be far from the ideas he is supposed to be communicating.

It is the ideal of the interpretative reader to keep thought and speech as closely allied in reading as they are in effective speaking. In cultivating the habit of giving the type of reading which is a process of thinking, the student usually needs more instruction than the mere "think it." He needs a means by which he may know that he is thinking; he needs a technique of thinking.

A TECHNIQUE OF THINKING

Though the instruction, "Think the author's thought," may have proved sufficient advice for a few readers who were not self-conscious when reading aloud, and in whose experience the habit of thoughtless or mechanical reading had not been acquired, too often the reading of words with little or no realization of their significance has become habitual. The interpretative reader must find a way of thinking which will enable him to be sure he thinks the author's meaning, not merely his words. The creative reader must have a *technique* of thinking as a basis for his *habit* of thinking.

Sensation and Imagination

Someone has said that common sense is merely thinking with one's senses. That which one sees, hears, smells, touches, or tastes forms the basis for one's concepts. Sensation comes from that which is present to the senses. Imagination is the means by which one perceives that which is not present to the senses. Creative thinking is sometimes defined as the recombination in thought of that which has been perceived through the senses.[1] The creative reader perceives the meaning which the author describes by recombining sensations in his experience through the process of imagination. Concerning the significance of experience in reading Kerfoot says,

[1] Knight Dunlap, *Elements of Psychology* (St. Louis: C. V. Mosby Company, 1936), p. 290.

If there is one fact that we have grown thoroughly to understand and accept, it is the fact that we have nothing to read with except our own experience,—the seeing and hearing, the smelling and tasting and touching that we have done; the fearing and hating, and hoping and loving that has appeared in us; the intellectual and spiritual reactions that have resulted, and the assumptions, understandings, prejudices, hypocrisies, fervors, foolishnesses, finenesses, and faiths that have thereby been precipitated in us like crystals in a chemist's tube.[1]

The technique of thinking that we suggest for interpretative reading is that the student shall imagine he is experiencing with his senses the sights, sounds, odors, flavors, movements suggested by the author's words at the very moment he is speaking the words. This way of thinking when practiced sufficiently will become a habit of thinking. This habit of thinking will keep words and their significance so close together that the student will soon find himself in possession of that subtle something which commands the interest and attention of his audience. Abbé Dimnet says, "The most of our mental operations are inseparable from images or are produced by images."

Louise Dudley in her provocative book, *The Study of Literature,* says, "If an artist cannot hold his images long enough to externalize them, we do not know that he had them." [2] She is referring to the writer, but her words are equally applicable to the interpretative reader. Many a reader fails to communicate meaning because the images are not held long enough for him to externalize them, thus

[1] J. B. Kerfoot, *How to Read* (Boston & New York: Houghton Mifflin Company, 1916). By permission of the publishers.
[2] Louise Dudley, *The Study of Literature* (New York: Houghton Mifflin Company, 1928), p. 60. By permission of the publishers.

projecting them to the audience. Concerning this matter Miss Dudley says further,

> The clearness and fidelity of an author's images . . . are mirrored in his work. If the author does not have a clear or faithful image himself, he cannot leave a clear or faithful image in the mind of the reader. And since an author is remembered by the images he creates in the minds of others, the clearness and fidelity of his own images are vital to his life as an author.[1]

The interpretative *reader* is, likewise, remembered by the images he creates in the minds of others. When the reader creates in the imagination the mental images described by the author, the reader may then know that he is thinking the essence of the author's thought, and that he has a chance of projecting that essence to the audience. When he reads the author's words, creating in the imagination the sensations suggested by the words, he may be said to be projecting ideas and not to be reading merely words. He will then have a technique of thinking which will result in stimulating the thinking of the hearers.

STUDIES IN IMAGERY

Sight Images

The sense of sight is usually considered the strongest sense. To develop the habit of thinking with the senses it is perhaps best to begin with the sense of sight. As a first step in externalizing the mental image, practice reading poems and passages of prose which depend largely upon sight images. As you read create in the imagination the sight images suggested by the words. Lift your eyes from the book

[1] Dudley, *Loc. cit.*

and picture on the back wall of the room the mental pictures which the words convey. Do not allow yourself to speak a phrase until you have created the mental picture suggested by that phrase. Do not rush; take all the time you need to get the thought from the words and to create the mental pictures with your *eyes off the book*. Concentrate on the mental picture as you read. "I Wandered Lonely As a Cloud," by William Wordsworth.

Place the book before you on a table or desk. Sit in a comfortable position with the arms resting on the desk and with one or both hands holding the book at an easy angle for reading. Read at a glance the words of the author's first idea, then look off the book and imagine you see a cloud floating slowly in the sky. Concentrate on the mental picture of the cloud as you read:

> I wandered lonely as a cloud
> That floats on high o'er vales and hills.

Glance down at the book, read the next idea silently, then look up and when you have created the mental picture read:

> When all at once I saw a crowd,
> A host, of golden daffodils.

Continue the process of getting the idea at a glance and then looking off immediately to see the mental picture as you speak the words which describe it.

Be sure you exert the self-command needed to shut everything else out of your mind except the mental picture suggested by the author's lines. Do not say a single word with the eyes on the book. Hold the mental picture until you have completed the words which describe it, *then* look down at the page for the next idea. Do not worry if the periods of silence seem long. Take plenty of time to get the thought and to see the mental picture *before* and *during* the process of speaking.

Re-read the poem in this manner many times. As you become familiar with the lines do not allow yourself to become careless with your technique of thinking. Practice until you can read the entire poem with facility in this manner. In practicing for a single classroom recitation you should become sufficiently master of yourself and of the author's thought to center your attention completely upon one idea at a time, shutting everything else out of your mind but the one mental picture and the words which convey it. When you can concentrate with sufficient mastery to receive each idea from the printed page at a glance and then look off and with sight imagery repeat the words accurately and easily, and when you can go from one mental picture to another without a break in coherent thinking, you are then ready to try this experiment before the class. Students report that it is easier to concentrate in practice than before a class. A severe test in creative oral reading is met when you can concentrate as completely before an audience as you can when alone.

I WANDERED LONELY AS A CLOUD

William Wordsworth

I wandered lonely as a cloud
    That floats on high o'er vales and hills,
When all at once I saw a crowd,
    A host, of golden daffodils;
Beside the lake, beneath the trees,
    Fluttering and dancing in the breeze.

Continuous as the stars that shine
    And twinkle on the milky way,
They stretched in never-ending line
    Along the margin of a bay:
Ten thousand saw I at a glance,
    Tossing their heads in sprightly dance.

The waves beside them danced, but they
    Outdid the sparkling waves in glee:
A poet could not but be gay,
    In such a jocund company.
I gazed—and gazed—but little thought
    What wealth the show to me had brought;

For oft, when on my couch I lie
    In vacant or in pensive mood,
They flash upon that inward eye
    Which is the bliss of solitude;
And then my heart with pleasure fills,
    And dances with the daffodils.

Read the following passages with the same type of concentration on sight images.

OZYMANDIAS OF EGYPT

Percy Bysshe Shelley

I met a traveller from an antique land
Who said: Two vast and trunkless legs of stone
Stand in the desert. Near them on the sand
Half sunk, a shatter'd visage lies, whose frown
And wrinkled lip and sneer of cold command
Tell that its sculptor well those passions read
Which yet survive, stamp'd on these lifeless things,
The hand that mock'd them and the heart that fed;

And on the pedestal these words appear:
'My name is Ozymandias, king of kings:
Look on my works, ye Mighty, and despair!'
Nothing beside remains. Round the decay
Of that colossal wreck, boundless and bare,
The lone and level sands stretch far away.

From THE DESTRUCTION OF POMPEII
Edward Bulwer-Lytton

Suddenly the eyes of the crowd in the amphitheatre beheld, with ineffable dismay, a vast vapor shooting from its summit in the form of a gigantic pine-tree; the trunk, blackness,—the branches, fire—a fire that shifted and wavered in its hues with every moment, now fiercely luminous, now of a dull and dying red, that again blazed terrifically forth with intolerable glare!

From THE FIRST SNOW-FALL
James Russell Lowell

The snow had begun in the gloaming,
    And busily all the night
Had been heaping field and highway
    With a silence deep and white.

Every pine and fir and hemlock
    Wore ermine too dear for an earl,
And the poorest twig on the elm-tree
    Was ridged inch deep with pearl.

I stood and watched by the window
    The noiseless work of the sky,
And the sudden flurries of snow-birds
    Like brown leaves whirling by.

From PSALM XIX

The heavens declare the glory of God;
And the firmament sheweth his handiwork.
Day unto day uttereth speech,
And night unto night sheweth knowledge.

Auditory Images

The following passages illustrating auditory images can be as vividly sensed as any visual image. See if you can hear in the imagination the auditory images as you saw the visual images. Take plenty of time for each sound to become vividly manifest before you read the lines that describe it, then continue the attitude of listening as you continue to read.

From A CHILD'S LAUGHTER
Algernon Charles Swinburne

Sweeter far than all things heard,
Hand of harper, tone of bird,
Sound of woods at sundawn stirred,
Welling water's winsome word,
    Wind in warm, wan weather—

Soft and strong and loud and light—
Very sound of very light
Heard from morning's rosiest height—
When the soul of all delight
    Fills a child's clear laughter.

If the golden-crested wren
Were a nightingale—why, then
Something seen and heard of men
Might be half as sweet as when
    Laughs a child of seven.

From TO PERDITA, SINGING

James Russell Lowell

Thy voice is like a fountain,
  Leaping up in clear moonshine;
Silver, silver, ever mounting,
    Ever singing,
    Without thinking,
To that brimful heart of thine.
Every sad and happy feeling,
Thou hast had in bygone years,
Through thy lips comes stealing, stealing,
  Clear and low;
All thy smiles and all thy tears
  In thy voice awaken,
  And sweetness wove of joy and woe,
    From thy teaching it hath taken:
Feeling and music move together,
Like a swan and shadow ever
Floating on a sky-blue river
  In a day of cloudless weather.

From JOURNEY FOR MARGARET [1]

W. L. White

    At first I think the noise may be only a dream. Then all at once I know it isn't. To the north and coming nearer, quite a way off still, but distinct, the desynchronized motors of a Heinkel, droning like a couple of bumble bees; I hear Margaret stir in bed!

---

[1] W. L. White, *Journey for Margaret* (New York: Harcourt, Brace and Company, 1941), p. 73. By permission of the publishers.

Nearer now, but not loud. Coming down to us from twenty thousand. A noise you would never notice at night in America. Only in London, your ears can pick out that muffled hum through walls. Margaret moans in her sleep. Will it pass over us? It sounds that way, unless it alters course. If they meant to drop something on us, they would unload about half a minute before they got directly overhead. But then it would take roughly half a minute to drop from twenty thousand. If it is going to land close, the explosion will come when the sound of the motors is directly above. Margaret moans again. She sits up.

From A TEXAN IN ENGLAND [1]
J. Frank Dobie

It is as dark as the inside of a cow here in the city of Cambridge. The fog comes up from the fens, they say—the fens that the Romans were building a road across two thousand years ago. But the dark never gets heavy enough to keep people inside. I step out on the street and, except in the puddle of light made by my own flashlight, I can distinguish nothing.

But it is not lights or absence of lights in the darkness that strikes one! It is the sounds from human feet and human voices. Especially feet. Boots, boots, boots, marching all together. I linger to let five or six voices and pairs of feet, pass me. They are out in the middle of the narrow street, keeping step and keeping time. The voices and the firm but lightsome foot-plantings are of young women. They are singing a song with sadness in it—the only kind of love songs that ever were or ever will be beautiful. From the step, step, step, and from half a glimpse of a swinging arm as the voices pass me, I know that they belong

[1] J. Frank Dobie, *A Texan in England* (Boston: Little, Brown and Company, 1945), p. 75. By permission of the publishers.

to military women. There are other foot sounds without voices. Many of them. Some timid and groping, most of them direct. There are voices now and then that seem to be without feet. The Americans sometimes have louder voices, not always. Passing the mouth of a side street, I hear down it in the direction of the Red Lion, not far from the Blue Bear, "Where the Deer and the Antelope Play."

Olfactory Images

Kipling says, "Smells are surer than sounds or sights to make your heartstrings crack." A soldier returning from Iwo Jima during World War II said he might forget the sights and sounds of war, but he would never forget the stench of the beaches. His spirit quailed at that horrible odor. It took all the moral courage he could muster to go through it, and the memory seemed almost as vivid as the experience.

From THE ROMANCE OF A BUSY BROKER [1]
O. Henry

And through the window came a wandering—perhaps a lost —odor—a delicate, sweet odor of lilac that fixed the broker for a moment immovable. For this odor belonged to Miss Leslie; it was her own, and hers only.

The odor brought her vividly, almost tangibly before him. The world of finance dwindled suddenly to a speck. And she was in the next room—twenty steps away.

[1] From *The Four Million,* by O. Henry, copyright, 1905, 1933, by Doubleday, Doran and Company, Inc. By permission of the publishers.

From THE MOON AND SIXPENCE [1]

W. Somerset Maugham

When Dr. Coutras arrived at the plantation he was seized with a feeling of uneasiness. As he opened the door he smelt the sickly, sweet smell which makes the neighborhood of the leper nauseous. He stepped in. The stench that assailed him turned him horribly sick. He put his handkerchief to his nose and forced himself to go in.

From MACBETH

Shakespeare

Here's the smell of the blood still; all the perfumes of Arabia will not sweeten this little hand.

Gustatory Images

From A DISSERTATION UPON ROAST PIG

Charles Lamb

There is no flavor comparable, I will contend, to that of the crisp, tawny, well-watched, not over-roasted, crackling, as it is well called—the very teeth are invited to their share of the pleasure at this banquet in overcoming the coy, brittle resistance—with the adhesive oleaginous—O call it not fat—but an indefinable sweetness growing up to it—the tender blossoming of fat—fat cropped in the bud—taken in the shoot—in the first innocence—the cream and quintessence of the child-pig's yet pure

---

[1] W. Somerset Maugham, *The Moon and Sixpence* (Grosset and Dunlap, by arrangement with George H. Doran Company, 1919), pp. 296–299. By permission of the publishers.

food—the lean, not lean, but a kind of animal manna—or, rather, fat and lean (if it must be so) so blended and running into each other, that both together make but one ambrosian result, or common substance.

From A PECULIAR TREASURE [1]
Edna Ferber

The pantry was as fragrant as a garden with spices and fruit scents and the melting delectable perfume of brown freshly baked dough, sugar-coated. There was one giant platter devoted wholly to round plump cakes with puffy edges, in the center of each a sunken pool that was pure plum, bearing on its bosom a snowy sifting of powdered sugar. There were others whose centers were apricot, molten gold in the sunlight. There were speckled expanses of cheese kuchen, the golden-brown surface showing rich cracks through which one caught glimpses of the lemon-yellow cheese beneath. There were cakes with jelly; cinnamon kuchen, and cunning cakes with almond slices nestling side by side. And there was freshly baked bread; twisted loaf with poppy seed freckling its braid, its sides glistening with the butter that had been swabbed on just before it had been thrust into the oven.

Fanny Brandeis gazed, hypnotized. As she gazed, Bella selected a plum tart and bit into it—bit generously, so that her white little teeth met in the very middle of the oozing, red-brown juice and one heard a little squish as they closed on the luscious fruit.

Tactile Images

Images of touch are also significant for the interpretative

[1] Edna Ferber, *A Peculiar Treasure* (New York: Doubleday, Doran and Company, Inc., 1939), p. 81. By permission of the author.

reader's technique of thinking. How vivid is your sense image of the touch of velvet to your face, of sand under your foot, or a rough wall to your finger tips? Literature gives abundant material for the development of sensitivity to tactile images.

From HOW GREEN WAS MY VALLEY [1]
Richard Llewellyn

There is strange, and yet not strange, is the kiss. It is strange because it mixes silliness with tragedy, and, yet not strange because there is good reason for it. There is shaking by the hand. That should be enough. Yet a shaking of hands is not enough to give a vent to all kinds of feeling. The hand is too hard and too used to doing all things, with too little feeling and too far from the organs of taste and smell, and far from the brain, and the length of an arm from the heart. To rub a nose like the blacks, that we think is so silly, is better, but there is nothing good to taste about the nose, only a piece of old bone pushing out of the face, and a nuisance in winter, but a friend before meals and in a garden, indeed. With the eyes we can do nothing, for if we come too near, they go crossed and everything comes twice to the sight without good from one or other.

There is nothing to be done with the ear, so back we come to the mouth, and we kiss with the mouth because it is part of the head and of the organs of taste and smell. It is temple of the voice, keeper of breath and its giving out, treasurer of tastes and succulences, and home of the noble tongue. And its portals are firm, yet soft, with a warmth, of a ripeness, unlike the rest of the face, rosy, and in women with a crinkling red tenderness, to the

[1] From *How Green Was My Valley* by Richard Llewellyn, copyright, 1940, by The Macmillan Company, New York. By permission of the publishers.

taste not in compare with the wild strawberry, yet if the taste of kisses went, and strawberries came the year round, half of joy would be gone from the world. There is no wonder to me that we kiss, for when mouth comes to mouth, in all its silliness, breath joins breath, and taste joins taste, warmth is enwarmed, and tongues commune in a soundless language, and those things are said that cannot find a shape, have a name, or know a life in the pitiful faults of speech.

From JANE EYRE
Charlotte Brontë

A figure came out into the twilight and stood on the step; a man without a hat: he stretched forth his hand as if to feel whether it rained. . . . He descended the one step and advanced slowly and gropingly towards the grass-plot. He stretched forth his right hand; he seemed to wish by touch to gain an idea of what lay around him: he met but vacancy still; for the trees were some yards off where he stood. He relinquished the endeavor, folded his arms, and stood quiet and mute in the rain, now falling fast on his uncovered head.

From THE PIT AND THE PENDULUM
Edgar Allan Poe

My outstretched hands at length encountered some solid obstruction. It was a wall, seemingly of stone masonry—very smooth, slimy, and cold. . . .

Forth from the well hurried the rats in fresh troops, and leaped in hundreds upon my person. The measured movement of the pendulum disturbed them not at all. Avoiding its strokes, they pressed, they swarmed upon me in ever accumulating heaps. They writhed upon my throat; their cold lips sought my own; I was half stifled by their thronging pressure. With more than human resolution I lay still.

Mental Imagery, like other techniques in this textbook, is not a habit one masters and then discards. It will prove helpful as the first step in thinking the author's meaning, and as a means of reviving spontaneity no matter how often one may speak the words. The psychologist, David Seabury, says:

Mental imagery may seem fantastic and unreal, as queer as some of the difficulties to which it is applied; but it works. Image-making, used regularly and conscientiously, is a successful method of creating new habits after the old habits have been understood and there is a wish to discard them. It is, of course, a form of autosuggestion, but it goes deeper because it follows the psychological principle that the will obeys a picture, not words, that the person making the mental image must *experience* the new activity, not merely verbalize about it. It is based upon our idea that thoughts and ideas born in consciousness are later lodged permanently in the unconscious depths from which they will influence the mental state and the activities of the individual.[1]

[1] David Seabury, *What Makes Us So Queer* (New York: McGraw-Hill Book Company, Inc., 1934), pp. 326–27. By permission of the publishers.

Chapter III

BODILY ACTION IN INTERPRETATIVE READING

> The idea underlying, as in all art, must be the basis also in the art of movement.[1]
>
> *Romola Nijinsky*

The interpretative reader is first seen and then heard. The posture, bearing and general bodily attitude convey impressions which aid or detract from the communication. Sometimes one can overcome a false first impression, but a good start is important to the listener. A good beginning is also important to the reader. The interpretative reader's bearing has an influence on his own thinking. It may aid or hinder concentration. It may give confidence and a sense of freedom or it may rob one of confidence and give a feeling of restriction.

A student who had built a fear of audiences had not read in public since the time she left the platform crying when as a child her teacher insisted upon a public recitation even though the child thought her piece was not sufficiently memorized. Her college teacher recognized that she needed successful experience before an audience to overcome this fear. The teacher said, "Go before the audience with the physical bearing of confidence. Stand poised for a moment

---

[1] Romolo Nijinsky, *Nijinsky* (New York: Simon and Schuster, Inc., 1934), p. 149. By permission of the publishers.

looking into the eyes of your audience. Think of sharing your story with friends as you read." The student followed the instructions and experienced the exhilaration one feels when fear has been conquered.

Physical directness is recognized as important in public speaking. It is also important in interpretative reading. There is something about looking directly into the eyes of others that gives confidence. It also gives the listener confidence in the reader. Sometimes students of interpretative reading become too indirect as a result of work on offstage imagery. We should realize that there are times when a reader should look directly into the eyes of the audience and times when he should look just above them. It is not easy to say when a reader should be direct and when indirect. It depends in part upon the material. Poetry is said to be written to be overheard. Poetry is often too deeply personal to be shared with directness. The audience will concentrate with more freedom if the reader looks away, yet the reader must not lose a sense of communication, a sense of sharing images, attitudes, moods with the audience.

We like the term *mediate* to describe the reader's relation to the audience. The public speaker may be *direct;* he talks *to* the audience. The actor and impersonator are *indirect;* they perform *for* the audience. The interpretative reader may at times seem direct, at other times indirect but should *always* seem to be *sharing* experiences *with* the audience; he is a *mediator* between the material and the audience; he should keep a *mediate* relationship *with* the audience. The ideal is for the reader's technique always to be so subtle that the audience is not aware of what he is doing. Slight differences in bodily participation mean a great deal in interpretative reading. If the interpreter looks too high above the audience they may be disturbed by it. This error is easy to make if one is on a high platform or is too literal in locating the imagined scene.

Interpretative reading is a suggestive art. It reaches high levels when movements are subtle and suggestive rather than broad and literal. The interpreter's purpose is to do something *with* the audience, to cause them to imagine, to see, to feel. It is his purpose to innoculate, as it were, the imagination of the audience. Amateur and often professional interpreters sometimes try to do too much for the audience, literally demonstrating every idea. The audience is then distracted from the meaning of the literature to the behaviour of the reader. Bodily action in interpretative reading is most effective when the audience is least aware of it as such. S. S. Curry emphasized this idea when he said that the higher the art the more manifestative and the less representative the action. Charles Wesley Emerson said that a quiver of a muscle might convey more than violent gesticulation. Sarett and Foster give as a principle of effective speaking, "Impressions of the speaker are derived largely from signs of which the audience are unaware." [1]

The idea that the interpreter should do nothing which takes from the imaginative vision of the audience has caused some people to conclude that gestures should be eliminated altogether from interpretative reading. This attitude toward gestures may result in a rigidity which calls as much attention to itself as too much movement. In-action may seem as unnatural as exaggerated actions.

[1] Lew Sarett, W. T. Foster, *Basic Principles of Speech* (Boston: Houghton Mifflin Company, 1936), p. 22. By permission of the publishers.

Posture

A sense of uplift in the torso is the key to good posture. It gives strength at the center of the body where tones are supported and allows freedom of movement elsewhere. In a town hall lecture John Mason Brown suggested that the talent of an actress may be measured by the distance from the hip bone to the first rib. This cryptic remark reveals a subtle understanding of the importance of good posture. John Robert Powers says the hips should be tucked up under the torso for a pelvic tilt which takes the strain off of the back and gives a straight vertical line to the figure. As a test of good posture one may stand with the back to the wall touching heels, hips, shoulders, and head and attempting to touch the wall with the small of the back. The weight should be on the balls of the feet and the knees slightly bent. The attempt to touch the wall with the back helps to flatten the stomach. A good rule for posture is to stand tall and sit tall.

Motor Imagery

Sense imagery proves a wonderful help in solving the problems of bodily action. Sense imagery is not limited to the traditional five senses. Modern psychologists place no boundary on the number and types of images. One senses physical activity through the muscles. The same muscles are used in an emotional struggle as in a physical fight. When one recalls physical actions his muscles tend to move in a manner similar to that which characterized the original action. The more vivid one's image of action, the more response he may experience in the muscles. For example, the clearer one's image of himself running, dancing, swimming the more movement he senses in his legs, arms, and torso. This participation of the muscles is called motor imagery. Motor memory is said to be the strongest memory. One does not forget how to swim, dance, or knit.

It is through the body that we experience reality. No technique of interpretative reading is more natural than motor imagery, which is virtually thinking with the muscles. It is the way a child thinks. Observe a child as he tells of an experience, how his muscles participate in the recall of actions. Even the most reserved adult, when asked about certain vivid experiences such as a car wreck will respond freely with broad overt actions as he describes it. Perhaps this is what Demosthenes meant when he said, "Oratory is action, action, action." The language of literature is the language of action. Richard Boleslavski says, "A verb is action in itself." Kerfoot emphasizes that even silent reading is an active process and says, "Alertness, then, is the first requisite for a reader . . . and a mental readiness to act." [1]

Just as in silent reading the page disappears as the reader creates in his imagination the scenes suggested by the words so, in interpretative reading the reader should disappear as the audience creates in the imagination the scenes suggested by the spoken words. If the reader is gradually to disappear from the consciousness of the audience he must do nothing which takes from the mental vision of the audience. For this reason a mere suggestion of an action is more effective than literal and complete action. The image of an action serves a better purpose than a complete copy of the action. The reader's purpose is to suggest an action to the imagina-

---

[1] J. B. Kerfoot, *How To Read* (Boston, Houghton Mifflin Company, 1916), p. 73. By permission of the publishers.

tion of the audience. In other words, in interpretative reading covert action is of more value than overt action. The image of action results not only in subtle communicative actions but in meaningful tones, inflections and rhythms which suggest actions to the listener. That is why people experienced in radio sometimes recommend free bodily actions for the radio speaker. The radio listener cannot *see* actions but they can *hear* them.

Roland Hayes emphasized the value of bodily action in singing and goes on to say:

In transactions with untamed life, my father made an offering of his whole nature. When he called a deer, he was a buck himself. It is perfectly clear to me now that he opened the way for me to become a musician by showing me how to offer my body, in imitation of him, to receive the music which he taught me to discover in the natural world. I learned from my father how the body follows the imagination. If singing is to be a really imaginative art it must give off, on each occasion, the effect of a fresh creation in which mind and body act together. The body must respond freely and newly to the mind's momentary act of recreation.

I early learned from my father to let my imagination do fluently what many singers have learned to do only through the repetitive use of destructive vocal exercises. I am fifty-five years old now, and yet, because my father taught me that the body follows the mind without stress and strain, I am conscious of no wear and tear on my vocal equipment.[1]

---

[1] MacKinley Helm, *Angel Mo' and Her Son, Roland Hayes* (Boston, Little, Brown and Company, 1942), pp. 11, 12. By permission of the publishers. Reprinted in *The Atlantic Monthly* (Aug., 1942), p. 3.

While we recommend subtle suggestive actions as preferred to literal, representative actions, the latter will prove helpful in developing a technique of action which will bring literature to life in the reader's imagination. This technique will also aid in projecting vital experiences to listeners. There is no quality more important for the reader to develop than vitality. One of the comments audiences enjoy making is, "He was so alive." One of the worst things people can say of a reader is, "He was dull and lifeless."

Read the following selections with extreme abandon. Perform the action suggested by the verbs. Observe the *changes* of action suggested in almost every phrase. Enter into the experience with total abandon, the whole body, mind and voice coördinated in an exaggeration of the activity suggested by the words. Then, reread—restraining the impulse to act, keeping the *image* of the action only. Sense the actions in the same muscles which participated in the literal representation. In this second reading, motor imagery is used as a technique of thinking. It should be just as vital and even more compelling to an audience than the literal representation.

From SAUL
Robert Browning

Oh, our manhood's prime vigour! no spirit feels waste,
Not a muscle is stopped in its playing nor sinew unbraced.
Oh, the wild joys of living! the leaping from rock up to rock,
The strong rending of boughs from the fir-tree, the cool silver
    shock
Of the plunge in a pool's living water, the hunt of the bear,
And the sultriness showing the lion is couched in his lair,

And the meal, the rich dates yellowed over with gold dust
  divine,
And the locust-flesh steeped in the pitcher, the full draft of
  wine,
And the sleep in the dried river-channel where bulrushes tell
That the water was wont to go warbling so softly and well.
How good is man's life, the mere living! how fit to employ
All the heart and the soul and the senses forever in joy!

From A MUSICAL INSTRUMENT
Elizabeth Barrett Browning

What was he doing, the great god Pan
Down in the reeds by the river?
Spreading ruin and scattering ban,
Splashing and paddling with hoofs of a goat,
And breaking the golden lilies afloat
With the dragon-fly on the river?

He tore out a reed, the great god Pan,
From the deep cool bed of the river,
The limpid water turbidly ran,
And the broken lilies a-dying lay,
And the dragon-fly had fled away,
Ere he brought it out of the river.

High on the shore sat the great god Pan,
While turbidly flowed the river;
And hacked and hewed as a great god can,
With his hard bleak steel at the patient reed,
Till there was not a sign of a leaf indeed
To prove it fresh from the river.

THE PICKWICKIANS ON ICE

From THE PICKWICK PAPERS

Charles Dickens

Old Wardle led the way to a pretty large sheet of ice; and, the fat boy and Mr. Weller having shovelled and swept away the snow which had fallen on it during the night, Mr. Bob Sawyer adjusted his skates with a dexterity which to Mr. Winkle was perfectly marvelous, and described circles with his left leg, and cut figures of eight, and inscribed upon the ice, without once stopping for breath, a great many other pleasant and astonishing devices, to the excessive satisfaction of Mr. Pickwick, Mr. Tupman, and the ladies; which reached a pitch of positive enthusiasm when old Wardle and Benjamin Allen, assisted by the aforesaid Bob Sawyer, performed some mystic evolutions, which they called a reel.

All this time Mr. Winkle, with his face and hands blue with cold, had been forcing a gimlet into the soles of his feet, and putting his skates on with the points behind, and getting the straps into a very complicated and entangled state, with the assistance of Mr. Snodgrass, who knew rather less about skates than a Hindoo. At length, however, with the assistance of Mr. Weller, the unfortunate skates were firmly screwed and buckled on, and Mr. Winkle was raised to his feet.

"Now, then, sir," said Sam, in an encouraging tone, "Off with you, and show 'em how to do it."

"Stop, Sam, stop!" said Mr. Winkle, trembling violently, and clutching hold of Sam's arms with the grasp of a drowning man. "How slippery it is, Sam!"

"Not an uncommon thing upon ice, sir," said Mr. Weller. "Hold up, sir."

This last observation of Mr. Weller's bore reference to a demonstration Mr. Winkle made, at the instant, of a frantic desire to throw his feet in the air, and dash the back of his head on the ice.

"These—these—are very awkward skates, ain't they, Sam?" inquired Mr. Winkle, staggering.

"I'm afeered there's an orkard gen'lm'n in 'em, sir," replied Sam.

Emotion

Experiences in reading include both thought and feeling. Training in feeling is one of the most valuable products of the study of literature. Man's highest and lowest acts are motivated by feeling. Students frequently approach feeling with as much trepidation as they do action. The fear of overdoing stifles natural response to and sincere communication of the author's meaning. Feeling and bodily action are inextricably fused. The word *emotion* literally means *from motion*. The muscles of the entire body participate in strong feeling. When one experiences grief his muscles relax. So great may be the laxity of the muscles that his speech is unintelligible; sometimes one is prostrate with grief. Anger tenses; so does fear. One becomes stiff with anger, frozen with fear; the muscular tension may be so great one trembles from head to foot. Joy is a wholesome emotion; it makes the muscles firm, giving poise. The James-Lange theory of emotion clarifies these phenomena. Bodily action is so obviously a part of emotional experience it appears to be as much a cause as result of feeling. When one inhibits the muscular activity, the feeling tends to subside. One may build feeling by increasing bodily activity. We hear of nursing a grief, working up anger, or feeding hysterics. These common sayings are evidence of general understanding of the principle that psychic experiences are fused with physical activity. Feeling and muscular action are inseparable.

Max Eastman in his book, *The Enjoyment of Poetry* says something which at first glance appears odd, "Poetry is an attitude of body, both anteceding and transcending speech or idea. It is a way of experiencing reality." A paraphrase of his statement may clarify his meaning. Poetry, the essence of which is feeling, is first sensed in the body. The words, even the specific idea, come later. A poet experiences the reality of a poem through the body. Many people think that a poet starts with words or meter, others think he has an idea which he clothes in words and rhythm. Max Eastman says the essence of poetry is something within the body which takes precedence over and transcends speech or idea, but through which the poet experiences reality.

Mark Holstein in writing of A. E. Housman says:

Poetry it seems to him is more physical than intellectual. He can no more define poetry, he says, than a terrier can define a rat, but both recognize the object by the symptoms which it provokes. Experience has taught him, when he is shaving of a morning, to keep watch over his thoughts, 'Because, if a line of poetry strays into my memory, my skin bristles so that the razor ceases to act.' This particular symptom is accompanied by a shiver down the spine; there is another which consists in a constriction of the throat and a precipitation of water to the eyes; and there is a third which I can only describe by borrowing a phrase from one of Keat's last letters, where he says speaking of Fanny Brawne, 'everything that reminds me of her goes through me like a spear.' The seat of this sensation is in the pit of the stomach.[1]

[1] Mark Holstein, "A Shropshire Lad," *The Atlantic Monthly* (January 1943), Vol. 171, No. 1, p. 87. By permission of the publishers.

The reader will experience reality more easily if he begins where the poet begins, with an attitude of body. When we sense moods in the body, the idea, words, and rhythm will seem to grow out of the mood naturally and the audience, unaware of the technique, perceives the reality and is affected by it.

ORGANIC IMAGERY

The sensations which A. E. Housman experienced in poetry, and which Keats experienced when he thought of Fannie Brawne, are classified as organic. They seem to find their origin in or near the viscera. One experiences organic sensations of temperature, equilibrium, lightness, heaviness, fullness, or emptiness. They are sensed kinesthetically.

The poem "Sea Fever," by John Masefield, is rich in images of sight, hearing, and motor actions. The essence of the poem is an organic nostalgia for the sea, a yearning that tugs at the whole being, but which seems centered deep in the viscera. In speaking of organic imagery, Professor Simon states:

When we speak of imagery we usually think of five senses: sight, hearing, taste, touch, smell. And these provide a rich repertoire for the reader; the unending variety of hue and chroma, of pitch and timbre, of sweet, sour and bitter, of rough and smooth, of flowers and spices. By allowing time for imagery to pile up around a given selection, by seeking out those images and adding them to the original reaction, the student will add to his appreciation.

Although the images of these five senses, sometimes called the "distance senses," are a vital part of the aesthetic experience, he who limits his appreciation to them alone is poor indeed.

There are other sense images, some of which seem even more powerful in appreciation; images of what have been called the "intimate senses" are a vital part of the aesthetic experience. These senses are those of pain, temperature, equilibrium, organic modifications, and kinaesthesis. Aestheticians have been prone to neglect these intimate senses, frequently referring to them as the "lower senses," as though there were something base or inelegant about them. But it is not improbable that these intimate senses are the source of much more of our aesthetic appreciation than we realize. We stress the visual and ascribe to it much that really comes to us through the intimate senses. But no one who has looked at a Gothic arch and felt within his own body the lift of it, the upward surge of matter toward the infinite, can be a stranger to the kinaesthetic. Lew Sarett's poem, "Deep Wet Moss," for example, is rich in visual images, but even more vivid in temperature, organic, and kinaesthetic images. Even the title to this poem may be read with visual imagery alone, but a stronger reaction comes with attention to these intimate sense images. In the same way any poem that grips us, that seems to have a depth that we cannot analyze, may yield new vividness through attention to the organic and the kinaesthetic. The good reader is the one who feels the dancing, the running, and the galloping; the tense quietude, the agony of immobile suspense; or the slow, resistless movement of ponderous things. Depth and vividness of appreciation lie in this response, through intimate sense imagery, to the things that are about us.[1]

[1] Clarence T. Simon, "Appreciation in Reading," *Studies in the Art of Interpretation*, edited by Gertrude E. Johnson (New York, Appleton Century-Crofts, Inc., 1940), p. 26.

Organic Sense Images

From THE LOTUS EATERS
Alfred Tennyson

Why are we weigh'd upon with heaviness,
And utterly consumed with sharp distress,
While all things else have rest from weariness?
All things have rest: why should we toil alone,
We only toil, who are the first of things,
And make perpetual moan,
Still from one sorrow to another thrown:
Nor ever fold our wings,
And cease from wanderings,
Nor steep our brows in slumber's holy balm:
Nor harken what the inner spirit sings,
'There is no joy but calm!'
Why should we only toil, the roof and crown of things?

From THE HOUSE AND THE BRAIN
Edward Bulwer-Lytton

I strove to speak—my voice utterly failed me; I could only think to myself: "Is this fear? it is not fear!" I strove to rise—in vain; I felt as if weighed down by an irresistible force. Indeed, my impression was that of an immense and overwhelming power opposed to my volition—that sense of utter inadequacy to cope with a force beyond man's, which one may feel physically in a storm at sea, in a conflagration, or when confronting some terrible wild beast, or rather, perhaps, the shark of the ocean, I felt morally. Oppressed to my will was another will, as far superior to its strength as storm, fire, and shark are superior in material force to the force of man.

And now, as this impression grew on me—now came, at last, horror—horror to a degree that no words can convey. Still I retained pride, if not courage; and in my own mind I said: "This is horror, but it is not fear; unless I fear I can not be harmed; my reason rejects this thing; it is an illusion—I do not fear." With a violent effort I succeeded at last in stretching out my hand toward the weapon on the table: as I did so, on the arm and shoulder I received a strange shock, and my arm fell to my side powerless. And now, to add to my horror, the light began slowly to wane from the candles—they were not, at it were, extinguished, but their flame seemed very gradually withdrawn; it was the same with the fire—the light was extracted with the fuel; in a few minutes the room was in utter darkness. The dread that came over me, to be thus in the dark, with that dark Thing, whose power was so intensely felt, brought a reaction of nerve. In fact, terror had reached that climax, that either my senses must have deserted me, or I must have burst through the spell. I did burst through it. I found voice, though the voice was a shriek.

From SONG OF MYSELF [1]
Walt Whitman

The orchestra whirls me wider than Uranus flies,
It wrenches such ardors from me I did not know I possess'd them,
It sails me, I dab with bare feet, they are lick'd by the indolent waves,
I am cut by bitter and angry hail, I lose my breath,
Steep'd amid honey'd morphine, my windpipe throttled in fakes of death,
At length let up again to feel the puzzle of puzzles,
  And that we call Being.

[1] From *Leaves of Grass,* by Walt Whitman, copyright, 1924, by Doubleday, Doran and Company, Inc. By permission of the publishers.

From ODE TO A NIGHTINGALE
John Keats

Thou wast not born for death, immortal Bird!
  No hungry generations tread thee down;
The voice I hear this passing night was heard
  In ancient day by emperor and clown:
Perhaps the self-same song that found a path
    Through the sad heart of Ruth, when, sick for home,
      She stood in tears amid the alien corn;
        The same that oft-times hath
Charmed magic casements, opening on the foam
  Of perilous seas, in faery lands forlorn.

Forlorn! the very word is like a bell
  To toll me back from thee to my sole self!
Adieu! the fancy cannot cheat so well
  As she is famed to do, deceiving elf.
Adieu! Adieu! thy plaintive anthem fades
  Past the near meadows, over the still stream,
    Up the hill-side; and now 'tis buried deep.

Consciousness of Technique

When students begin to apply sense imagery as a technique of thinking in interpretative reading, they sometimes are more conscious of the technique than the sense image. In place of simple, direct thinking, or clear, vivid imagination there is an *effort* to see, to hear, to experience motor sensations. This consciousness of technique actually interferes with imagination. As is so frequently the case with a novice in any art, concentration is upon form instead of content, upon *how* instead of *what*. One student reported, "When I picture scenes on the back wall of the room members of my audience sometimes turn to see what I am looking at." This student's error was due not so much to the technique of sense imagery as to a consciousness of form. Perhaps a habit of creating sense images when reading was all she needed. She, however, corrected her fault by an understanding of the meaning of empathy in interpretative reading.

Empathy

The word empathy is quite familiar to the modern teacher of speech. The principle of empathy is discussed in textbooks in speech and psychology. It is defined as the "feeling in" or "inner mimicry." The manifestation of empathy is often bold and free. It is usually illustrated by the active participation of a crowd at a football game. Such an example presents a clear and vivid picture to the average American, whose joy in football is due largely to a feeling of physical participation in the game. This participation is empathy.

Empathy in an audience presents convincing evidence of a speaker's effectiveness. Authors of speech textbooks are right to emphasize its importance in effective speaking. If members of an audience lean forward eagerly as a speaker describes a situation, if people sway from side to side as a reader interprets a lyric, or if they sit on the edges of their seats during a play, empathic response gives evidence of the effectiveness of the communication. The audience is not conscious of empathy; concentration is upon the experience and not on what the actor, speaker, or reader is doing. Empathy in the audience gives evidence of the speaker's success in communicating reality.

Empathy is not limited to the experience of the audience. It is equally applicable to the experience of the speaker, reader, or actor. This "inner mimicry" is characteristic of motor and organic imagery. Surely you have while reading or speaking experienced this "inner mimicry" in response to an imaginative experience? There is a scene in A. J. Cronin's *The Green Years* where a young man's foot is trapped between the iron rails of a closing railroad switch. As the train hurtles toward him, he pulls and strains in an effort to free his foot and escape. Suppose one is reading this story. Will he not sense activity in his muscles as he reads this description? He may, then, be said to empathize with the images he is experiencing. In like manner the interpreter may sense an expansion, a stretching outward in imitation of the sea, or a prairie; may sense uplift in body as he imagines the Washington Monument or the Empire State Building. Persons in a darkened theater often actually imitate the actors; others, less overt in their expression, sense the activity, though the outward manifestation is less obvious. They experience exultation or weariness as a result of empathic response. This projection of oneself into an imaginative experience is fundamental to artistic understanding and appreciation. As Elizabeth Barrett Browning said

> . . . . When
> We gloriously forget ourselves and plunge
> Soul forward, headlong, into a book's profound
> . . . Tis then we get the right good from a book.

When actions result from empathy the whole body responds naturally. There is motor coördination. This type of motivation eliminates the tendency of the speaker to "put on" a gesture or to express with a part of the body only. Arm and hand gestures resulting from empathy may be considered an overflow of organic activity. The chief difference between actions resulting from empathy and gestures made through conscious effort to express is in the muscle tone of the whole body. From the point of view of the audience, however, it may be the difference between affectation and naturalness.

The amount of activity in interpretative reading must be at the discretion of the reader. If as he reads the *cause* of action seems to take precedence over the *actions* the gestures are likely to seem natural both to himself and to the audience. Such actions give emphasis to the meaning and do not detract from it. No one can tell a reader how much action he may use. He must be guided by the whole: the material, the occasion, his purpose and desire in communication. One should never go beyond the bounds of good taste, but even taste is related to the total situation. One's manner at a football game differs from his behavior at church. It seems well at all times to use restraint, but enthusiasm and abandon are also important. Usually the most effective bodily actions are those which result from total body tonicity. The most effective way to achieve natural and total body tonicity in reading is by empathic response to the imaginative experience. When the interpreter pictures the situation off stage, in the realm of the audience, and so concentrates on the reality that he empathizes with the imaginative experience, his bodily actions enhance the idea, and the attention of the audience is held on the experience rather than on the reader's actions.

PROJECTING THOUGHT TO AN AUDIENCE

It is said that imitation is the sincerest flattery; when audiences so forget themselves that they empathize with the interpreter there is evidence of sincere appreciation and understanding. To accomplish this it is desirable for the reader to identify himself with the experience and respond with restrained movements. As long as the reader's effort to sense motor and organic imagery is apparent his art suffers. The interpreter experiences empathy only when he so identifies himself with the author's meaning that technique is subordinated.

As soon as we are conscious of our own sensations, we are no longer contemplating the beauty of the object, for the words "our own sensations" in themselves denote that we are no longer enjoying the object, but that our aesthetic attitude has broken down under the distraction of the bodily processes. Indeed, as soon as our attention is upon such processes, there can be no identification of such movements with the lines, no fusion of the sensations with the object, and so even empathy itself is impossible.[1]

Some readers claim that the voice should be given precedence over the body as a medium for communication in interpretative reading. This point of view has merit, yet it overlooks the fact that the voice functions through the body and that motor and organic imagery are basic in any ade-

[1] Herbert Sidney Langfeld, *The Aesthetic Attitude* (New York: Harcourt, Brace and Company, Inc., 1920), p. 116. By permission of the publishers.

quate technique of voice. An apparently still body is not necessarily an inactive body. One may restrain actions yet communicate an idea of movement to an audience just as a sculptor suggests movement in a statue such as that of the disc thrower (The Discobolus). There are times when even immobility of body is compelling. Nijinsky found a technique of immobility of value even in the art of dancing.

He used immobility consciously for the first time in the history of dancing, for he knew that immobility could accentuate action often better than action itself, just as an interval of silence can be more effective than sound.[1]

In interpreting extreme emotion the reader may find it of value not only to maintain a degree of immobility but to withdraw feeling from the voice and let clear articulation be the chief medium of communication. In Robinson Jeffer's *Medea* the Nurse's story of the death of Creon and his daughter is packed with cruelty and horror. In reading this speech it appears that any attempt to project feeling through tones or body movement is excessive. Clear, crisp, rapid speech may convey a picture vivid enough for any audience. Greek drama is known for its fine balance. Murders are performed offstage giving aesthetic distance to a scene which could easily portray more agony than an audience would willingly witness. Burgess Meredith suggests a use of a "still" body in acting when, in speaking of his role in *Winterset,* he said, "I have to keep Burgess Meredith still so that Mio can emerge."

[1] Romolo Nijinsky, *Nijinsky* (New York: Simon and Schuster, Inc., 1934), p. 146. By permission of the publishers.

We desire to have a controlled but thoroughly responsive body. Control of random activity, erratic movements, habitual bodily reactions is basic to a sound technique of bodily action. Students do not find it easy to control nervous movements, mannerisms, habitual bodily responses, but he who would control others must first be self-controlled. Self-command is the first step in learning to command the attention and interest of an audience. Any movement other than that which grows out of concentration on meaning will prove distracting both to the reader and to the listener. Random movement is evidence of inadequate concentration.

Read Tennyson's poem, "Break, Break, Break," concentrating upon the attitude of a man seeking to express his feelings after the death of his dearest friend. Concentrate on imagery: sight, auditory, tactile, motor, organic.

BREAK, BREAK, BREAK
Alfred Tennyson

Break, break, break,
  On thy cold gray stones, O Sea!
And I would that my tongue could utter
  The thoughts that arise in me.

O well for the fisherman's boy,
  That he shouts with his sister at play!
O well for the sailor lad,
  That he sings in his boat on the bay!

And the stately ships go on
  To their haven under the hill;
But O for the touch of a vanish'd hand,
  And the sound of a voice that is still!

> Break, break, break,
> At the foot of thy crags, O Sea!
> But the tender grace of a day that is dead
> Will never come back to me.

Sense of Location

There are times when the creative reader will find it helpful to use a technique of location more specific than a mere matter of direct or indirect mental attitudes. This technique of location seems to be based upon a *sense of location*. One often remembers things by their location. Frequently in recalling data students say, "I remember the exact page; I can even recall the exact location on the page." A secretary may say, "Let me think—I was standing by the desk, I walked over to the door, you handed me the data—I remember now"; thus through the location, she recalls the instructions which otherwise had escaped her memory.

Directors of plays recognize this principle and place dramatic scenes in different locations on the stage so that the audience will not confuse them in memory. In a production of *Macbeth* given in the Shakespeare Memorial Theatre in Stratford-on-Avon all scenes dealing with tragedy and conflict were depicted on one side of the stage, and all scenes dealing with the home atmosphere were placed on the other side. A stairway led to an upper landing off which the murder of Duncan was supposed to have been committed. This stairway started in the center of the stage and led off on the side of the stage the director had designated for the scenes of tragic conflict. Another stairway hugged the opposite side of the stage; this stairway led to the apartment of Lord and Lady Macbeth.

The sleepwalking scene in this production began, not with the entrance of the doctor and the nurse as is found in the text of the play, but with the entrance of Lady Macbeth, walking in her sleep down the stairway from her apartment and up the stairway which led in the direction connected with the murder, as if drawn irresistibly to the very location of the crime. When she returned to the stage to speak the famous lines beginning, "Out, out damned spot—" she came from the very location to which she had gone earlier in the play when she took the dripping daggers from Macbeth and declared she would smear the faces of the grooms with blood that it might appear their crime. The consistency with which the director followed the law of association by the sense of location added much to the clarity and force of the production.

Off Stage

The interpretative reader may not be as specific in his use of the principle of location as is the actor or dramatic director, but the reader will find a technique of location a valuable aid in vivifying mental pictures for the audience. It is well here to recall some of the essential differences between reading and acting. The actor performs *for* the audience. He moves about on the stage representing the character and going through the actions of the character. The actor intends that the audience shall watch him with their physical eyes. The interpretative reader, however, usually stands in one place, making only those movements which suggest the idea to the imagination of the audience. The reader and audience visualize scenes together off stage.

The reader's scenes are in the realm of the imagination.

The creative reader and his audience see with their mental eyes, the eyes of imagination. The reader directs the attention of the audience, not to himself or what happens on the stage, but to the sights, sounds, or ideas which they (the audience and reader) create together in the imagination. You will find a fuller discussion of this matter in *Studies in the Art of Interpretation,* from which we quote:

> To me, then, there are two realms in which the interpreter may evolve his imaginary scene; the realm of the stage, a literal and objective realm whereon whatever we do will be looked *at,* whether *into* or not; and the realm of the "audience," a suggestive realm, wherein we establish scene, character, and all pertaining to the impression, as seen *in our mind's eye,* and in which we lead hearers to see with their mind's eyes, always directing them suggestively, never literally, taking care indeed, that no literal actions, gestures, or movements shall interfere with the imaginative process of the audience. They do not look on, they look in. . . .
>
> In interpretation, we never act completely, never perform characters to be looked at, never locomote or cover space "on stage." Our scene is always established in the realm of the audience, as if we saw the characters moving there, and as we see, we report like a highly sensitive photoplate all that we see plus our reactions. If our material is direct discourse, we address audiences with direct eye contacts; if it is subjective, we are not under this necessity. We are really talking aloud as to ourselves. In all cases in interpretative presentation, the ideal is to have the audience see with their own vision, create scene and characters for themselves. The interpreter must not intrude himself at any moment, *as actor,* and so break the unity of place and mood.

One last word concerning these two "realms" as they may be connected with the narrative form. To me the story offers the student, the interpreter, his finest opportunities. The story form suffers continually from the type of treatment I have referred to. The interpreter breaks unity of place and scene constantly. He addresses the audience more or less directly, and more or less indifferently in the narrative and descriptive portions, then, bringing a character to sudden and complete impersonation, with scene "on-stage," he turns to right and left addressing characters where they would be if the story were in the dramatic form of monologue or play. This jumping from a suggestive to a literal realm occurs dozens of times in the course of even a fifteen-minute reading (whether read from memory or from lines) and breaks all "unities" either of place, scene, or mood in the narration. The interpreter in narration should never become actor, nor bring his "scene" back to the acting realm, close to him "onstage." [1]

INTERPRETATION OF CHARACTERS

Interpreters are sometimes confused over techniques of bodily action in reading dialogue. How far should an interpreter go in representing characters in a story, a play or a monologue? There can be no arbitrary rule, but confusion results when one attempts to mix the arts of acting and interpretative reading. A monologue or a play may be acted; they may also be read. If acted, they are performed *on stage;* if read, the scene should be kept in the realm of the audience, or *"off stage."* When the characters are pictured "off

[1] Gertrude E. Johnson, "Impersonation, a Necessary Technique," in *Studies in the Art of Interpretation* (New York: Appleton-Century-Crofts, Inc., 1940), pp. 128–29.

stage" the reader may experience empathy, motor or organic imagery, but he does not act. In reading a story the characters should be pictured off stage as one pictures descriptions and narration. If the reader shifts from the attitude of picturing off stage to the attitude of acting on stage, the audience senses an inconsistency and feels that the reader is unnatural. Here, as elsewhere, we suggest that covert activity may communicate more than overt; manifestative movements are usually preferable to representative; suggestive actions carry more meaning than literal.

Motor and organic imagery are significant ways of sensing characters. Empathy is a means of bringing the character to life in the imagination of the reader, causing subtle movements which aid the listener. The voice may appear to be the chief vehicle for projecting the character; yet the body must be in accord if a unified whole is achieved. Unless a reader senses the muscle tone of a character, he will hardly be able to suggest the voice of the character. Body and voice are inseparable.

Character Angles

Character angles are a convention in interpretative reading. If the reader looks slightly to the right when interpreting the lines of one character and slightly to the left for another, he helps the audience to keep the characters differentiated. The interpreter must be careful to keep these angles in the realm of the suggestive, and not to turn from side to side in a representative manner. The interpreter should not be bound by angles assuming that all the lines of a certain character must be read looking to the right and the lines of another character always directed to the left. Several characters should not be lined up arbitrarily with the eyes of the reader looking to the right for one, center for another, off-center for a third, and so on. Such a literal technique makes the means become an end and robs the interpreter of flexibility and suggestiveness. There are other techniques of character delineation more important than angles. General bearing, tone, pitch range, tempo, and rhythm are more significant than the vision lines the interpreter employs. A slight turning from side to side may help the reader to delineate characters, but a too literal use of the technique of angles will destroy illusion. We suggest that the sight line angles are affected by the width and depth of the room, or hall, in which the reading takes place, size of audience and by the reader's own, individual discretion.

Read the following selections with vivid imagery, sensing the characters and the actions, keeping the scenes off stage but suggesting dialogue by use of character angles.

HOW TOM SAWYER WHITEWASHED THE FENCE [1]

Mark Twain

BEN. "Hello, old chap, you got to work, hey?"
      Tom wheeled suddenly and said:
TOM. "Why, it's you, Ben! I wasn't noticing."

---

[1] Mark Twain, *The Adventures of Tom Sawyer* (New York: Harper and Brothers). By permission of the publishers.

BEN. "Say—I'm going in a-swimming, I am. Don't you wish you could? But of course you'd druther *work*—wouldn't you? Course you would!"

Tom contemplated the boy a bit and said:

TOM. "What do you call work?"

BEN. "Why, ain't that work?"

Tom resumed his whitewashing, and answered carelessly:

TOM. "Well, maybe it is, and maybe it ain't. All I know, is, it suits Tom Sawyer."

BEN. "Oh, come, now, you don't mean to let on that you *like* it?"

The brush continued to move.

TOM. "Like it? Well, I don't see why I oughtn't to like it. Does a boy get a chance to whitewash a fence every day?"

That put the thing in a new light. Ben stopped nibbling his apple. Tom swept his brush daintily back and forth—stepped back to note the effect—added a touch here and there—criticized the effect again—Ben watching every move and getting more and more interested, more and more absorbed. Presently he said:

BEN. "Say, Tom, let me whitewash a little."

Tom considered, was about to consent; but he altered his mind.

TOM. "No—no—I reckon it wouldn't hardly do, Ben. You see, Aunt Polly's awful particular about this fence—right here on the street, you know—but if it was the back fence, I wouldn't mind and she wouldn't. Yes, she's awful particular about this fence; it's got to be done very careful; I reckon there ain't one boy in a thousand, maybe two thousand, that can do it the way it's got to be done."

BEN. "No—is that so? Oh, come, now—lemme just try. Only just a little—I'd let you, if *you* was me, Tom."

Tom. "Ben, I'd like to, honest injun; but Aunt Polly—well, Jim wanted to do it, but she wouldn't let him; Sid wanted to do it, and she wouldn't let Sid. Now, don't you see how I'm fixed? If you was to tackle this fence and anything was to happen to it—"

Ben. "Oh, shucks, I'll be just as careful. Now lemme try. Say—I'll give you the core of my apple."

Tom. "Well, here— No, Ben, now don't. I'm afeard—"

Ben. I'll give you *all* of it!"

Tom gave up the brush with reluctance in his face, but alacrity in his heart.

UP-HILL

Christina Georgina Rossetti

Does the road wind up-hill all the way?
    Yes, to the very end.
Will the day's journey take the whole long day?
    From morn to night, my friend.

But is there for the night a resting-place?
    A roof for when the slow dark hours begin.
May not the darkness hide it from my face?
    You cannot miss that inn.

Shall I meet other wayfarers at night?
    Those who have gone before.
Then must I knock, or call when just in sight?
    They will not keep you standing at the door.

Shall I find comfort, travel-sore and weak?
    Of labor you shall find the sum.

> Will there be beds for me and all who seek?
> *Yes, beds for all who come.*

Bodily action may be considered a way of thinking the reality of that which is read. As Langfeld says of empathy, "it is virtually thinking with the body." If one observes a silent reader closely he is likely to see slight muscle movements in the face, hands, arms and sometimes broad movements in the torso. "Mind affects body and body affects mind" is an axiom of interpretative reading. This interrelation of thought and body may be observed in statues, such as *The Thinker* by Rodin. The problem in interpretative reading is not to find ways of expressing ideas but to think ideas so completely that bodily action will be an integral part of the thinking. There is a *single* mental process. Bodily action is so much a part of interpretative reading we may say, paraphrasing the quote from Nijinsky which appears under the title of this chapter:

The sense of movement underlying the idea must be the basis of the reading which communicates vital experiences to an audience.

Chapter IV

DRAMATIC TIMING IN INTERPRETATIVE READING

> Be not like a stream that brawls
> Loud with shallow waterfalls,
> But in quiet self-control
> Link together soul and soul.
> *Longfellow*

Life and literature are full of situations, the effectiveness of which depends upon dramatic timing. The dastardly tactics of the Japanese in timing the attack on Pearl Harbor at the moment Kurusu was supposed to be negotiating peace in Washington shocked a world already somewhat accustomed to the surprise attacks of Nazi blitzkriegs. It was a villainous trick but excellent timing. It was excellent timing when Washington crossed the Delaware at Valley Forge on Christmas Eve and caught the British steeped in their cups. It was excellent timing when Duncan's arrival was announced to Lady Macbeth just as she completed the reading of her husband's letter concerning the witches' prophecy that he would "be king hereafter."

Dramatic timing in the interpretative reader's technique depends upon (1) *pause:* the silence between words, phrases, or sentences; (2) *tempo:* the length of time in speaking words, phrases, or other portions; (3) *rhythm:* the recurrent pattern of sound and silence dependent upon skillful control of both time and stress. Dramatic timing is frequently said to depend upon the reader's *sense of timing*. Children who simply follow the imaginative concept often surpass the skilled actor in dramatic timing. The student will profit from a close study of the nature of these techniques of timing even though imagination here as elsewhere is the determining factor.

1. THE PAUSE

The creative reader needs time to grasp the thought of the author. Students who have faithfully followed the technique of thinking given so far will no doubt realize that the pause has been emphasized over and over through such suggestions as "take time to see, take time to sense, take time to think." You have already, no doubt, held many effective pauses unconscious of the length of the period of silence. Your concentration has been upon the idea, not upon the form of expression, hence not upon the pause. It has been so evident that time is required to create a mental picture that pauses have resulted from the need of time to grasp the idea from the printed page and to create the concept in the imagination before speaking the words which convey it to the audience. It has been evident that the interpretative reader needs pauses for his technique of thinking.

Audiences need time to grasp the significance of ideas and to create concepts. Pauses are as essential for the audience as for the reader. The audience, like the reader, is unconscious of the time length of pauses when their concentration is on the idea, for audiences need pauses in which to react to ideas. When the reader fails to give pauses of sufficient duration for adequate response, listeners are likely to con template certain ideas during periods of speech. In such cases the listener misses much of what the reader wishes to convey.

During the periods of speech the audience is intent upon catching the speaker's words, but during the pause the audience has the opportunity to grasp the thought and to realize its significance. During the periods of speech the reader concentrates upon the idea and upon communicating it to the audience, but during the pause the reader may get the next thought by glancing at the page and then react to the thought while looking off the page and forming the mental picture. This digesting of the idea during the pause causes the reader to give oral expression which conveys the meaning and gives the audience time to react to the idea given.

Dramatic timing calls for judgment on the part of the reader as to the length of time desirable for a pause. Some thoughts can be quickly grasped, and their effectiveness depends upon a quick pick-up and passing on to the next thought. Other ideas call for contemplation. It is evident that the more profound the thought the longer and more frequent should be the reader's pauses; the more trivial the thought the easier it is for the reader and audience to grasp it, hence the shorter the pauses. To test this principle let the student read through the quotation which follows without pausing between ideas:

PHILIPPIANS 4:8

Whatsoever things are true, whatsoever things are honest, whatsoever things are just, whatsoever things are pure, whatsoever things are lovely, whatsoever things are of good report, if there be any virtue, and if there be any praise, think on these things.

Now let the student reread the same passage pausing long enough between phrases to think the significance of each idea before speaking the words which convey it. As a test of the effectiveness of long pauses let the periods of silence be twice as long as the periods of speech. Here, as in earlier assignments, the student should discipline himself to get the words at a glance and then look off, thinking of the significance of the idea before and during the periods of speech. As S. H. Clark says, "Get the thought, hold the thought, give the thought." [1]

The student may observe a constructive cycle in that the mood is both a cause and a result of the pause. One soon learns to sense the length of time needed for the projection of a particular mood or idea. A good technique to follow in training oneself to hold pauses is to hold the thought of a phrase sufficiently long to think through the words of the entire phrase before speaking it. The speaking of the words may then be a re-thinking for communication to the audience.

Pick-up Within the Phrase

When given the advice to hold pauses as long as the periods of speech, some students reply that it bores them to hear one speak so slowly. Such an answer reveals a lack of complete understanding of the technique. One does not of necessity speak slowly; pick-up within the phrase is an

[1] S. H. Clark, *How to Teach Reading in Public Schools* (Chicago: Scott, Foresman and Co., 1908), p. 118. By permission of the publishers.

important factor in revealing meaning. It is well for the student to practice rapid speech within the phrase, giving the entire phrase at one impulse, speaking distinctly but merging the words within the phrase as one does the syllables within the words. The phrase is the unit of thought; one thinks in groups of words, in flashes. Ideas are more easily grasped when the phrases are spoken quickly.

As has already been indicated, pause is an essential technique in carrying meaning. Pauses occur between ideas as a means of conveying the thought, the reaction of both reader and audience being more acute during the pause than during speech—the length of the pause depending upon the relative significance of the ideas. When pauses are used effectively, both reader and audience are unconscious of the length of time of the pauses, as their attention is focused upon the author's meaning and not upon the period of silence.

Often the meaning is completely lost when the reader neglects the technique of pause. This is particularly true of brief poems. Read the following, testing the value of pauses in carrying the meaning.

RELIEVING GUARD

Bret Harte

Came the relief. "What, sentry, ho!
How passed the night through thy long waking?"
"Cold, cheerless, dark,—as may befit
The hour before the dawn is breaking."

"No sight? no sound?" "No; nothing save
The plover from the marshes calling,

And in yon western sky, about
An hour ago, a star was falling."

"A star, there's nothing strange in that."
"No, nothing; but, above the thicket,
Somehow it seemed to me that God
Somewhere had just relieved a picket."

THE HARP THAT ONCE THROUGH TARA'S HALLS
Thomas Moore

The harp that once through Tara's halls
    The soul of music shed,
Now hangs as mute on Tara's walls
    As if that soul were fled.
So sleeps the pride of former days,
    So glory's thrill is o'er,
And hearts that once beat high for praise
    Now feel that pulse no more!

No more to chiefs and ladies bright
    The harp of Tara swells;
The chord alone that breaks at night
    Its tale of ruin tells.
Thus Freedom now so seldom wakes,
    The only throb she gives
Is when some heart indignant breaks,
    To show that still she lives.

TO SEA, TO SEA!
Thomas Lovell Beddoes

To sea, to sea! The calm is o'er;
    The wanton water leaps in sport,
And rattles down the pebbly shore;
    The dolphin wheels, the sea-cows snort,

An unseen Mermaid's pearly song
Comes bubbling up, the weeds among.
   Fling broad the sail, dip deep the oar:
   To sea, to sea! the calm is o'er.

To sea, to sea! our wide-winged bark
   Shall billowy cleave its sunny way,
And with its shadow, fleet and dark,
   Break the caved Triton's azure day,
Like mighty eagle soaring light
O'er antelopes on Alpine height.
   The anchor heaves, the ship swings free,
   The sails swell full. To sea, to sea!

Dramatic Pause

The pause used for the reinforcement of ideas is an arresting and dramatic technique. An abrupt pause *after* an idea strengthens the effect of the words. A long pause *before* a significant idea creates suspense. It might almost be said that the longer the pause, the greater the suspense and hence the more dramatic the effect. In some situations the pause may even be so long that the audience becomes tense with expectation. They have the desire to speak the words themselves in order to relieve the tension. The reader's sense of timing should guide him in determining how long to hold a pause in order adequately to support an idea and when is the psychological moment to relieve tension by speech.

The pauses in the following scene from *Othello* are marked off by bars, the number of bars suggesting the comparative length of the pauses. Read it, timing your pauses by the bars. If in places you sense the time differently to that suggested by the markings read it both ways. Perhaps *your* way is better for *you,* or perhaps you will find an increase in effectiveness by following our markings until you begin to think it *that* way.

From OTHELLO [1]

William Shakespeare

OTHELLO.　　　　　　Had it pleased heaven
To try me with affliction, | had he rain'd
All kinds of sores, | and shames, on my bare head, |
Steep'd me in poverty to the very lips, |
Given to captivity me and my utmost hopes, |
I should have found in some part of my soul
A drop of patience; || but, alas! | to make me
The fixed figure | for the time of scorn
To point his slow and moving finger at; ||
Yet could I bear that too; || well, || very well. |||
But there, where I have garnered up my heart, |
Where either I must live or bear no life, |
The fountain from the which my current runs
Or else dries up; | to be discarded thence! ||
Or keep it as a cistern for foul toads
To knot and gender in! ||| Turn thy complexion there, |||
Patience, |||| thou young and rose-lipp'd cherubin; ||
Ay, there, ||| look grim as hell! ||||

Pause for Comedy

The interpretative reader will find pause a helpful technique in projecting comedy. A pause just before the word or phrase which carries humor points up the meaning. This technique of pausing just before the word, phrase, or line is sometimes called "planting" the line. Such a pause cre-

[1] Act IV, Scene ii.

ates the suspense needed to make the audience alert to the idea. A pause is also frequently needed just after the word or phrase that carries meaning, in order that the audience may have time to react to the humor. The amateur is inclined to keep the humor away from the audience by going on with new ideas before the audience has had time fully to grasp preceding ideas. The creative reader holds pauses sufficiently long for the audience to catch the humor and to respond with a chuckle, a laugh, or more enthusiastic evidence of enjoyment.

Will Rogers knew the effect of the technique of pause in comedy. He used pauses before important ideas in order to plant them in the minds of the audience; he paused afterwards to give time for audience reaction. After a witty remark he would frequently just look at his audience with an amused grin, then he would begin to chew his gum or to walk about the stage as if chagrined at his own temerity in making such an audacious remark. He gave his audience plenty of time to catch the humor of his remarks and to react to the humor. He would frequently stop in the midst of a sentence, drop his head, look out shyly at the audience, twist his entire body as if ashamed to go on with his sentence. The audience sometimes started laughing in anticipation during a pause in the midst of a sentence, but, since he was a master of timing, they always laughed more heartily at the completion of the idea.

Comedy calls for subtlety. Finesse is needed in applying comedy technique. The reader must seem not to be trying at all. The pause must appear to be unpremeditated, as if occasioned only by the reader's own appreciation of the humor. Thinking in comedy must take precedence over technique, or the audience will be aware of the reader's method instead of his humor. Obvious effort blocks the flow of comedy and checks audience response. The illusion of the first time, the freshness of spontaneous reaction, must characterize the reader's performance if he is to gain a hearty response from the audience. The complete cycle of holding pauses in recognition of the value of the technique and of concentrating on the mood which causes the pause is essential in projecting humor.

Intellectual Humor

Humor is often an intellectual quality calling for quickness of perception and subtlety of projection. It takes a keen mind to perceive the subtleties of humor. Both reader and audience must be alert—on their mental toes, so to speak—to catch the delicacy of comedy. For broad comedy, however, general rapidity with few pauses proves an effective technique. No technique is of greater importance in bringing about mental alertness than the technique of well-timed pauses, whether used sparingly or frequently.

Do not deceive yourself by thinking that comedy is not worth the effort, because it is easier to be serious, especially before an audience, than it is to be funny. Students frequently mislead themselves with the excuse that they like "deeper literature." Because it takes less artistry to make the audience weep than it does to bring a spontaneous laugh, many readers do not attempt to master the technique of comedy. Such readers fail to realize that they are really in error when they claim that appreciation of the serious in literature shows more depth than appreciation of humor. They beguile themselves into believing that humor is trivial and inconsequential and that there is no need for the mastery of comedy technique.

Technique of Comedy Gives General Finesse

The creative reader will find that although the technique of comedy is difficult to master, when achieved it adds finesse to all of his reading. Because the projection of humor calls for relaxation, absolute ease (an essential of art), the mastery of the technique of humor will give the student general skill in interpretative reading. The skill developed in learning to time pauses for the projection of humor, and in so doing to maintain relaxation, ease, and spontaneous response to the mood of the moment, will serve the reader in projecting all moods.

To project comedy, the interpretative reader should often appear serious. The reader seldom laughs at the humor he projects. It is the audience which should laugh, not the reader, for he may even appear not to see the point, this pretense on his part only adding to the mirth of the audience. The reader must never give the appearance of trying to be funny; he must even seem unconcerned as to whether his remarks bring laughter or not. If he plants his lines and holds sufficiently long pauses the audience is likely to respond without any further effort on his part. The best humor appears to be accidental, spontaneous, impromptu!

Read the following, testing the effectiveness of well-timed pauses for carrying the humor.

A MODEST WIT

Anonymous

A supercilious nabob of the east, haughty, being great, purse-proud, being rich, a governor, or general, at the least, I have forgotten which, had in his family a humble youth, who went from England in his patron's suite, an unassuming boy, and in truth a lad of decent parts and good repute. This youth had sense and spirit; but yet, with all his sense, excessive diffidence obscured his merit.

One day at table, flushed with pride and wine, his honor, proudly free, severely merry, conceived it would be vastly fine to crack a joke upon his secretary. "Young man," he said, "by what art, craft, or trade did your father gain a livelihood?" "He was a saddler, sir," Modestus said, "and in his time was reckoned good." "A saddler, eh! and taught you Greek instead of teaching you to sew! Pray, why did your father not make a saddler of you?"

Each parasite then, as in duty bound, the joke applauded, and the laugh went round. At length Modestus, bowing low, said (craving pardon if too free he made), "Sir, by your leave, I fain would know your father's trade." "My father's trade! By heaven, that's too bad! My father's trade? Why, blockhead, are you mad? My father, sir, did never stoop so low, he was a gentleman, I'd have you know." "Excuse the liberty I take," Modestus said, with archness on his brow. "Pray, why did not your father make a gentleman of you?"

A Comic Sense

Many people think special talent is needed for the interpretation of comedy. They speak of "born comedians." Some people do seem to be endowed with a special gift for making others laugh. They are the life of the party, the wags, the wits who without apparent effort keep the center of attention and interest whatever the situation. They seem to be endowed with a *comic sense* which makes it easy for them to provoke laughter. One thus gifted should cherish and cultivate this talent and should learn to be discreet in its use, for as Hamlet says:

Let those that play your clowns speak no more than is set down for them; for there be of them that will themselves laugh to set on some quantity of barren spectators to laugh too, though in the mean time some necessary question of the play be then to be considered. That's villainous, and shows a most pitiful ambition in the fool that uses it.

Some people seem to possess a naturally keener appreciation of humor than others. This appreciation does not necessarily accompany the gift for making others laugh. But appreciation of humor enables one successfully to develop the technique by which he may share humor in interpretative reading, which is, itself, *a process of sharing ideas*. If one can *perceive* and *appreciate* humor he can share it with others. The reader of humor does not need to be the cause of the humor. His need is to perceive the humor and to acquire the technique by which he may project it to the audience in order that the audience may perceive the humor also. Timing is the means by which both reader and audience may perceive humor. Well-timed pauses, then, are important in the technique of projecting humor.

In the famous speech from *Cyrano de Bergerac* concerning his nose, the humor is dependent in a large measure upon well-timed pauses.

From CYRANO DE BERGERAC [1]
Edmond Rostand

    CYRANO: Ah, no young sir!
You are too simple. Why, you might have said—
Oh, a great many things! Mon dieu, why waste
Your opportunity? For example, thus:—
Aggressive: I, sir, if that nose were mine,
I'd have it amputated—on the spot!
Friendly: How do you drink with such a nose?
You ought to have a cup made specially.
Descriptive: 'Tis a rock—a crag—a cape—
A cape? say rather, a peninsula!
Inquisitive: What is that receptacle—
A razor-case or a portfolio?
Kindly: Ah, do you love the little birds
So much that when they come and sing to you,
You give them this to perch on? *Insolent:*
Sir, when you smoke, the neighbors must suppose
Your chimney is on fire. *Cautious:* Take care—
A weight like that might make you topheavy.
Thoughtful: Somebody fetch my parasol—
Those delicate colors fade so in the sun!

    It is said that Sir James M. Barrie refused for some years to have his plays printed because "the reading public would not put in the pauses" which, in his estimation, were the most important elements in his plays. It is not easy to suggest pauses on paper, timing depending so much upon the reader's spontaneous response at the moment. Besides, there is nothing arbitrary concerning the exact place for the most

---

[1] Edmond Rostand, *Cyrano de Bergerac,* prepared by Brian Hooker (New York: Henry Holt and Company, 1923), p. 40. By permission of the publishers.

effective pause. We find, however, an occasional dash in printed versions of Barrie's plays which may be taken as a suggestion for a pause.

2. TEMPO

Tempo is the rate of speed with which one speaks. As has been suggested, quick pick-up within the phrase is an aid in conveying meaning. The phrase is the unit of thought, hence there is need for continued flow within the phrase. A drawl, or a pause between words in a thought-group, causes the listeners either to lose interest or to become impatient for the reader to finish the phrase in order that they may perceive the idea. When the reader thinks the complete idea during a pause he is likely to speak the entire phrase quickly and fluently. Stark Young, realizing this need, has suggested that many, perhaps half the difficulties in the New York theatre would be avoided if actors trained for speed in enunciation, and if producers insisted upon it.

Some people are naturally fast in tempo and others slow. One keyed to a fast tempo is inclined to read rapidly; one who by temperament is slow tends to read slowly. The student who does everything rapidly will need to exert self-control to take sufficient time for pauses. The student keyed to a slow tempo will need to practice quick speech within the phrase.

One's mood influences one's tempo. When one is in a good humor, he is likely to have quick coördination and hence a relatively fast tempo. Anger tenses; it may cause fast speech or may block speech, causing long pauses but quick pick-up within the phrase. Grief relaxes and slows down one's tempo. Joy, the wholesome emotion, is conducive to balance. The interpretative reader needs to understand the nature of emotions in order that he may truly create them for his audience.

The interpretative reader is subject not to his own tendencies but to the literature he interprets. Certain types of literature call for a slow tempo, others for a fast one. Tragedy, serious drama, philosophical ideas are projected by a relatively slow tempo. Comedy, farce, trivial ideas are given in a fast tempo. As one approaches a climax in tragedy, that is, as the conflict tightens, one finds the tempo quickening. A slow drawl may prove an amusing contrast in the midst of the relatively quick tempo of farce. The creative reader should give consideration first to the general tempo which will project his author's idea, then to the portions which call for variety.

Audience interest is sustained through changes in tempo. Sharp contrast quickens interest; sameness is monotonous and decreases interest. Any tempo becomes monotonous if kept up too long. No technique is more important in preventing monotony and dullness or in preserving audience interest than the technique of tempo. Dr. Andrew T. Weaver gives clarity and force to this idea as follows:

In music, we have the terms: *largo, adagio, andante, moderato, allegro, presto,* etc. We should cultivate the same pleasing variety in the utterance of language, so that out of this variety we can select appropriately for every type of situation and material with which we may be dealing. In this matter of tempo, the besetting weakness of speakers is a uniform deliberateness which makes everything seem just as important as everything else. The characteristic drawl of certain people deprives them of any possibility of using vocal movement to stir up specific and differentiated responses in their auditors. Contrasted with these are the people who commit the offense of always being brisk, staccato, and lively, and who by their monotony of liveliness succeed in doing for themselves very much what the drawlers do for themselves, viz., obscuring all distinctions in meaning. Then there is the mistake of introducing variety for variety's sake, without reference to the values of the material to which the variety is applied. This is not much better than the monotony of the *tramp, tramp, tramp* movement of Kipling's wearied British soldier who is "sloggin' over Africa." Let us be on the lookout for opportunities to use with telling effect the slowest possible tempo, the most rapid possible tempo, and all the degrees of rate in between these two. [1]

Read the passages which follow noting first the general tempo of each, then after the general tempo is established giving attention to changes in tempo as the moods change:

AFTON WATER

Robert Burns

Flow gently, sweet Afton, among thy green braes,
Flow gently, I'll sing thee a song in thy praise;
My Mary's asleep by thy murmuring stream,
Flow gently, sweet Afton, disturb not her dream.

Thou stock-dove whose echo resounds through the glen,
Ye wild whistling blackbirds in yon thorny den,
Thou green-crested lapwing, thy screaming forbear,
I charge you disturb not my slumbering fair.

---

[1] Andrew Thomas Weaver, *Speech Forms and Principles* (New York: Longmans, Green and Co., 1942), p. 233. By permission of the publishers.

How lofty, sweet Afton, thy neighboring hills,
Farmarked with the courses of clear winding rills;
There daily I wander as noon rises high,
My flocks and my Mary's sweet cot in my eye.

How pleasant thy banks and green valleys below,
Where wild in the woodlands the primroses blow,
There oft as mild evening weeps over the lea,
The sweet-scented birk shades my Mary and me.

Thy crystal stream, Afton, how lovely it glides,
And winds by the cot where my Mary resides;
How wanton thy water her snowy feet lave,
As, gathering sweet flowerets, she stems thy clear wave.

Flow gently, sweet Afton, among thy green braes,
Flow gently, sweet river, the theme of my lays;
My Mary's asleep by thy murmuring stream,
Flow gently, sweet Afton, disturb not her dream.

THE FOUNTAIN

James Russell Lowell

Into the sunshine,
  Full of the light,
Leaping and flashing
  From morn till night!

Into the moonlight,
  Whiter than snow,
Waving so flower-like
  When the winds blow!

Into the starlight
  Rushing in spray,
Happy at midnight,
  Happy by day;

Ever in motion,
   Blithesome and cheery,
Still climbing heavenward
   Never aweary;—

Glad of all weathers;
   Still seeming best,
Upward or downward,
   Motion thy rest;—

Full of a nature
   Nothing can tame,
Changed every moment
   Ever the same;—

Ceaseless aspiring,
   Ceaseless content,
Darkness or sunshine
   Thy element;—

Glorious fountain!
   Let my heart be
Fresh, changeful, constant,
   Upward, like thee!

From L'ALLEGRO

John Milton

Haste thee, Nymph, and bring with thee
Jest and youthful Jollity,
Quips, and Cranks, and wanton Wiles,
Nods, and Becks, and wreathed Smiles,
Such as hang on Hebe's cheek,
And love to live in dimple sleek;
Sport that wrinkled Care derides,
And Laughter holding both his sides.

Come, and trip it as ye go,
On the light fantastic toe;
And in thy right hand lead with thee
The mountain Nymph, sweet Liberty;

DAY

From Pippa Passes

Robert Browning

Day!
Faster and more fast,
O'er night's brim, day boils at last:
Boils, pure gold, o'er the cloud-cup's brim
Where spurting and suppressed it lay,
For not a froth-flake touched the rim
Of yonder gap in the solid gray
Of the eastern cloud, an hour away;
But forth one wavelet, then another, curled,
Till the whole sunrise, not to be suppressed,
Rose, reddened, and its seething breast
Flickered in bounds, grew gold, then overflowed the world.

I REMEMBER, I REMEMBER

Thomas Hood

I remember, I remember
The house where I was born,
The little window where the sun
Came peeping in at morn;
He never came a wink too soon,
Nor brought too long a day;
But now, I often wish the night
Had borne my breath away.

I remember, I remember
The roses red and white,

> The violets, and the lily-cups,
> Those flowers made of light!
> The lilacs where the robin built,
> And where my brother set
> The laburnum on his birthday,—
> The tree is living yet!

3. RHYTHM

Rhythm is a fundamental principle of the universe. It is so much a part of man's everyday life that he is usually unconscious of its vital influence. Day follows night according to a definite though constantly shifting rhythmic pattern. The moon and the stars have their courses, each moving in accordance with its own rhythmic law. The winds blow, and man may mark the rhythmic beat against the window pane. We follow rhythmic laws in our daily habits of sleeping and waking, of working and resting, of eating and fasting. As Richard Boleslavsky says, "To exist is to have rhythm." The more complete our adjustment to the rhythms of life, the more harmonious, simple, and pleasant are our lives. Soldiers march to the rhythm of a band, women sing at their house work, many of us turn on the radio for a rhythmic accompaniment to everyday activities. Each individual has his habitual rhythm which, if adjusted to the specific situation, brings harmony and pleasure to the simplest experiences.

Rhythm and Speech

Rhythm is a fundamental element in speech. Fluency in speech depends to a great extent upon rhythm. The stutterer's rhythm is interfered with, or blocked; he sings with ease, but he cannot speak fluently. Let him set up a definite rhythm with a movement of hand or foot and it may carry over into his speech, breaking the lock and giving him fluency at least for the time being.

Ministers often speak in regular rhythmic patterns. Their audiences are swayed by the feeling, for as speech becomes more and more emotional, it is inclined to become more and more rhythmical. So great is the power of this rhythm that people respond with an emotional fervor which logic is powerless to explain or to check. Witness the effect of rhythm in the ceremonies of Indians and Negroes or in the religious services of almost any church or sect.

The orator swept by feeling in his peroration unconsciously follows rhythmic patterns approximating those of conventional verse. Even Abraham Lincoln in his second inaugural address expressed feeling in a rhythmic pattern which can be scanned and in which there is also rhyme.

> Fondly do we hope,
> Ferevently do we pray,
> That this mighty scourge of war
> May speedily pass away.[1]

Rhythm in Literature

There is rhythm in literature, both prose and poetry. The rhythms of prose are irregular, broken, constantly changing in pattern to fit the change in ideas. The rhythms of most poetry are somewhat regular, adhering to laws of meter and of emotion. Emotion is both a cause and a result of rhythm. The more feeling expressed in a passage, the

[1] Wayland Maxfield Parrish, *Reading Aloud* (New York: Thomas Nelson and Sons, 1932), p. 296. By permission.

more regular is the rhythmic pattern up to a certain point. Logical thinking tends to result in broken rhythms, because of the author's desire to point up or to stress specific ideas.

Rhythm is fundamental to a child's understanding and appreciation of literature. Children respond to rhythms before they can be interested in abstract ideas. The rocking, humming, soothing rhythms of the nursery are followed by the simple, regular, obvious rhythms of Mother Goose. So elemental is the appeal of rhythm in literature that it is the first appeal of literature to the child. Children gain much pleasure from chanting rhymes in the nursery and in the school room. They enjoy stories interspersed with repetitions in rhythmic patterns. They respond so much more quickly and enthusiastically to rhythm than to ideas that they instinctively chant, or read in a sing-song manner. Teachers often give children their first prejudice against poetry by discouraging sing-song reading. The teacher who stops rhythmical reading by requiring a child to read poetry "like prose" robs poetry of an essential element and robs the child of his pleasurable response to a fundamental element in appreciation.

It is interesting to find this same idea expressed by a poet. Amy Lowell states:

People have often taken issue with the proposition that poetry should not be read as if it were prose. People who have not grasped the meaning, that is. "But," they say, "surely you don't like to have poetry read in a sing-song manner." Assuredly, I do not; and yet I say, unhesitatingly, that if one must choose between these two bad traditions, I prefer to have the rhythm overaccented than to have it lost sight of altogether.

As a matter of fact, neither extreme is necessary. The good tradition, as is the way with good traditions, seeks the happy mean.[1]

Sing-song reading can be used as a first step in interpretative reading and as a first step in the appreciation of literature. The error in sing-song reading is not in rhythm but in the mechanical application of rhythm. The fundamental rhythm sensed by a child may form the basis for fluent, creative reading. As a substitute for thoughtless, monotonous, sameness in rhythm invite the child to discover changes in ideas and mood which may be expressed through subtle changes in rhythm. His discovery of variety will prove an intriguing method of increasing his appreciation of literature without the loss of his fundamental interest in rhythm.

Rhythm is as significant and as interesting to the adult as to the child. Rhythmic patterns are an aid in perceiving as well as in projecting the author's idea. As Dr. Cunningham says:

Rhythm in art—the regular or nearly regular measure by which any element in the composition is made to recur a sufficient number of times to become part of the pulse or heartbeat—can be said to be what gives the work its "character and personality." Those changes and recurrences progressively stimulate the response which is the final aim of the artist. When the rhythm is dull and monotonous, character is lacking in the art and its personality is dwarfed. It is just another picture to be glanced at, or tune to be hummed, or structure to occupy space, or specimen of commonplace verse. When the rhythm is subtle

[1] From "Poetry as a Spoken Art" in *Poetry and Poets,* copyright by Houghton Mifflin Company. By permission of the publishers.

a distinctive personality is genuinely realized. It is the quality of the rhythm which reveals and projects the inmost character of the art. Those people whose own natures are deep and rich will prefer art whose rhythm corresponds to their nature. Those people who are shallow will like best art whose rhythmic range is narrow.[1]

In prose the rhythmic pattern is suggested partly by the idea and partly by the arrangement of words. In poetry the meter forms a basis for the rhythms and the idea gives a basis for variety. In rhythm, as in tempo, variety is essential for sustained audience interest and for adequate interpretation of meaning. The interpretative reader must learn how to find the fundamental rhythm of a piece of literature and also how to give variety of expression to subtle changes in mood, idea, or rhythmic pattern. In the technique of rhythm, as with all other techniques, the idea should take precedence over the form. Rhythm in literature is not an end but an important means of projecting the author's purpose.

Read a few stanzas of the following poem in a metrical, sing-song manner. Re-read the same stanzas as if they were written in prose, stressing the idea and veering as far from the poetic form as you can. Now see if you can read the poem with the basic rhythm of the verse form but with subtle changes in tempo, tone, and rhythm suggestive of the changes in idea and mood. See if you can read in such a manner that the rhythm becomes a means of projecting your appreciation of the poem.

[1] Cornelius Carman Cunningham, *Literature as a Fine Art* (New York: Thomas Nelson and Sons, 1941), p. 35. By permission of the publishers.

From THE BROOK

Alfred Tennyson

I come from haunts of coot and hern,
   I make a sudden sally
And sparkle out among the fern,
   To bicker down a valley.

By thirty hills I hurry down,
   Or slip between the ridges,
By twenty thorps, a little town,
   And half a hundred bridges.

I chatter over stony ways,
   In little sharps and trebles,
I bubble into eddying bays,
   I babble on the pebbles.

With many a curve my banks I fret
   By many a field and fallow,
And many a fairy foreland set
   With willow-weed, and mallow.

I chatter, chatter, as I flow
   To join the brimming river,
For men may come and men may go
   But I go on forever.

Objective Methods of Finding the Rhythm

The student may realize the importance of rhythm and yet be perplexed as to how to find it and how to deal with it in interpretative reading. Here as elsewhere the student needs technique. For the development of technique in rhythm we suggest five objective ways by which the student may sense the rhythm in reading. They are (1) scansion, (2) sensing the cadence, (3) finding the objective source of the rhythm, (4) sensing the rhythm of the action, and (5) sensing the rhythm of the character. At least three of these ways may be used in the reading of prose. Consider these techniques carefully and learn when to apply each and when to use a combination of them for the most complete interpretative reading.

1. Scansion

The student of interpretative reading may find scansion a helpful means of recognizing metric patterns and thus sensing the fundamental rhythm of a poem.

Through scansion the student develops an awareness of poetic form. He becomes sensitive to the stressed and unstressed syllables in verse. He develops a recognition of the poet's form which should not be neglected in oral reading, since the poet chooses his form for a purpose. An adequate interpretation of the author's purpose, then, must take the verse pattern into consideration. The student of interpretative reading who is not acquainted with verse forms and who is not trained to recognize their importance in the author's purpose is likely to be inadequate in projecting the author's idea completely.

2. Sensing the Cadence of Poetry

The interpretative reader may find a more satisfactory method than scansion for sensing the rhythm of a poem, since scansion is usually done in a jerky, disconnected manner. The cadence of poetry may be sensed through a flowing, connected method of speech and gesture which

Elsie Fogerty calls feeling *the pulse of a poem*.[1] Try sensing the cadence of a line of poetry with a connected flow of speech and a curved, continuous gesture, accenting the stressed syllables but blending them with the unstressed so as to give a feeling of continuity and grace not found in the abrupt, jerky method of scansion. You may find this method of sensing the cadence of a poem a helpful exercise in developing the habit of response to the fundamental rhythm of a poem. In studying a poem for interpretative reading, you may find it helpful first to become familiar with the poetic form by sensing the cadence in this manner. You should not lose the sense of the fundamental cadence of a poem no matter how often you read it or to what purpose. Find the fundamental rhythm of the following poems first by scansion, then by sensing the cadence. Decide by your own experience which method gives more appreciation and effective reading.

THOSE EVENING BELLS
Thomas Moore

Those evening bells! those evening bells!
How many a tale their music tells
Of youth, and home, and that sweet time
When last I heard their soothing chime!

Those joyous hours are passed away;
And many a heart that then was gay
Within the tomb now darkly dwells,
And hears no more those evening bells!

[1] Elsie Fogerty, classroom lecture, Central School of Speech, London, 1938.

And so 'twill be when I am gone,—
That tuneful peal will still ring on;
While other bards shall walk these dells,
And sing your praise, sweet evening bells.

MY HEART'S IN THE HIGHLANDS
Robert Burns

My heart's in the Highlands, my heart is not here;
My heart's in the Highlands a-chasing the deer;
Chasing the wild deer, and following the roe,
My heart's in the Highlands wherever I go.
Farewell to the Highlands, farewell to the North,
The birthplace of valour, the country of worth;
Wherever I wander, wherever I rove,
The hills of the Highlands for ever I love.

Farewell to the mountains high covered with snow;
Farewell to the straths and green valleys below;
Farewell to the forests and wild hanging woods;
Farewell to the torrents and loud-pouring floods.
My heart's in the Highlands, my heart is not here,
My heart's in the Highlands a-chasing the deer;
Chasing the wild deer, and following the roe,
My heart's in the highlands wherever I go.

THE WIND
Robert L. Stevenson

I saw you toss the kites on high
And blow the birds about the sky;
And all around I heard you pass,
Like ladies' skirts across the grass—
  O wind, a-blowing all day long,
  O wind, that sings so loud a song!

>   I saw the different things you did,
>   But always you yourself you hid.
>   I felt you push, I heard you call,
>   I could not see yourself at all—
>   O wind, a-blowing all day long,
>   O wind, that sings so loud a song!
>
>   O you that are so strong and cold,
>   O blower, are you young or old?
>   Are you a beast of field and tree,
>   Or just a stronger child than me?
>   O wind, a-blowing all day long,
>   O wind, that sings so loud a song!

3. *Finding the Objective Source of Rhythm*

The interpretative reader may frequently find an objective source of rhythm that will give him an effective means of sensing the rhythm, for authors sometimes consciously, and often unconsciously, follow the rhythm suggested by the idea. The author may use the rhythm of that which he describes, or that from which he gets his basic idea, such as the patter of rain, the ticking of a clock, or the hoof beats of a galloping horse. When the reader senses the basic pattern of rhythm he projects an atmosphere which almost invariably brings audience response.

Try sensing the rhythm of "The Old Clock on the Stairs" by beating off the familiar rhythm of a large clock. Picture a grandfather clock and with a gesture follow the movement of the pendulum as you say, "Tick—tock, tick—tock, tick—tock." Continue the gesture as you repeat, "Forever—never, never—forever, tick—tock, tick—tock." Repeat this exercise until you have thoroughly sensed the rhythm, then read the first stanza to the rhythm you have established.

Do not worry if your reading seems mechanical. Practice this form until the rhythm takes possession of you. Then reread the poem varying the tempo, tone, and rhythm until you can express the changes in meaning. Practice until you are able to create each concept completely, giving to it the variety needed, yet keeping the fundamental rhythm of a clock. One of your problems as a creative reader is to determine how much emphasis to give to the rhythm and when to give precedence to other phases of the idea.

From THE OLD CLOCK ON THE STAIRS
Henry Wadsworth Longfellow

Somewhat back from the village street
Stands the old-fashioned country seat.
Across its antique portico
Tall poplar-trees their shadows throw.
And from its station in the hall
An ancient timepiece says to all,—
   "Forever—never!
    Never—forever!"

Halfway up the stairs it stands,
And points and beckons with its hands
From its case of massive oak,
Like a monk, who, under his cloak,
Crosses himself, and sighs, alas!
With sorrowful voice to all who pass,—
   "Forever—never!
    Never—forever!"

The fundamental rhythm of "Sweet and Low" by Tennyson is found in the rocking of a boat or of a cradle. Either idea is in keeping with the poem as the father is pictured out in his boat on the bay, and the poem itself is a lullaby in which one imagines the mother rocking the cradle as she sings. No matter how familiar this poem is to students, they read it with keen pleasure when sensing the fundamental rhythm. A class will enjoy reading it in unison swaying the bodies to the rhythm of a rocking cradle or boat. Rhythm and emotion are each so much a part of the other that one may think of them as essentially the same. They are both total bodily responses complete only when sensed through the entire body. Though his movement should be controlled and never obvious, the student should form the habit of sensing rhythm in the major muscles of torso and legs.

SWEET AND LOW

Alfred Tennyson

Sweet and low, sweet and low,
    Wind of the western sea!
Low, low, breathe and blow,
    Wind of the western sea!
Over the rolling waters go,
Come from the dying moon, and blow,
    Blow him again to me:
While my little one, while my pretty one,
    Sleeps.

Sleep and rest, sleep and rest,
    Father will come to thee soon;
Rest, rest, on mother's breast,
    Father will come to thee soon;
Father will come to his babe in the nest,
Silver sails all out of the west
    Under the silver moon;
Sleep, my little one, sleep, my pretty one,
    Sleep.

In the following poem the fundamental rhythm is that of a galloping horse. The student may quickly gain a rhythmic background for the reading of this poem by beating off with his fingers on the desk, or with coconut shells, or with plungers (as they do in radio plays). Let the class read the poem in unison while one or more students give the sound of the rhythm. The class will immediately sense a driving force which compels them in their reading as the messengers felt compelled to ride to Aix to deliver the good news. In the first few readings let the class feel swept by the rhythm without thought of any other technique than that of sensing the rhythm. After sensing the rhythm let each individual student read the poem, guiding the rhythm, tempo, and pauses by the thoughts, bringing in subtle changes. The student will find this poem an interesting study in tempo as well as in rhythm.

HOW THEY BROUGHT THE GOOD NEWS FROM GHENT TO AIX

Robert Browning

I sprang to the stirrup, and Joris, and he;
I galloped, Dirck galloped, we galloped all three;
"Good speed!" cried the watch, as the gatebolts undrew;
"Speed!" echoed the wall to us galloping through;
Behind shut the postern, the lights sank to rest,
And into the midnight we galloped abreast.

Not a word to each other; we kept the great pace
Neck by neck, stride by stride, never changing our place;
I turned in my saddle and made its girths tight,
Then shortened each stirrup, and set the pique right,
Rebuckled the cheek-strap, chained slacker the bit,
Nor galloped less steadily Roland a whit.

'Twas moonset at starting; but while we drew near
Lokeren, the cocks crew and twilight dawned clear;
At Boom, a great yellow star came out to see;
At Duffeld, 'twas morning as plain as could be;
And from Mecheln church-steeple we heard the half-chime.
So Joris broke silence with, "Yet there is time!"

At Aershot, up leaped of a sudden the sun,
And against him the cattle stood black every one,
To stare through the mist at us galloping past,
And I saw my stout galloper Roland at last,
With resolute shoulders, each butting away
The haze, as some bluff river headland its spray:

And his low head and crest, just one sharp ear bent back
For my voice, and the other pricked out on his track;
And one eye's black intelligence,—ever that glance
O'er its white edge at me, his own master, askance!
And the thick heavy spume-flakes which aye and anon
His fierce lips shook upwards in galloping on.

By Hasselt, Dirck groaned; and cried Joris, "Stay spur!
Your Roos galloped bravely, the fault's not in her.
We'll remember at Aix"—for one heard the quick wheeze
Of her chest, saw the stretched neck and staggering knees,
And sunk tail, and horrible heave of the flank,
As down on her haunches she shuddered and sank.

So, we were left galloping, Joris and I,
Past Looz and past Tongres, no cloud in the sky;
The broad sun above laughed a pitiless laugh,
'Neath our feet broke the brittle bright stubble like chaff;
Till over by Dalhem a dome-spire sprang white,
And "Gallop," gasped Joris, "for Aix is in sight!"

"How they'll greet us!"—and all in a moment his roan
Rolled neck and croup over, lay dead as a stone;

And there was my Roland to bear the whole weight
Of the news which alone could save Aix from her fate,
With his nostrils like pits full of blood to the brim,
And with circles of red for his eye-sockets' rim.

Then I cast loose my buffcoat, each holster let fall,
Shook off both my jack-boots, let go belt and all,
Stood up in the stirrup, leaned, patted his ear,
Called my Roland his pet-name, my horse without peer;
Clapped my hands, laughed and sang, any noise, bad or good,
Till at length into Aix Roland galloped and stood.

And all I remember is—friends flocking round
As I sat with his head 'twixt my knees on the ground;
And no voice but was praising this Roland of mine,
As I poured down his throat our last measure of wine,
Which (the burgesses voted by common consent)
Was no more than his due who brought good news from Ghent.

4. *The Rhythm of Action*

The interpretative reader must give attention to the rhythm of details as well as to the fundamental rhythm of the whole.

Rhythm will prove as helpful a means of projecting the meaning of individual phrases as it has proved in giving the atmosphere of the whole. A phrase or sentence may follow the rhythm of the action described or suggested by the words. For example, read, "The boy slid to third base." Picture a boy in a base-ball game sliding to a base. Make a gesture suggestive of the boy's action. As you sensed the rhythm of the action did you prolong the word *slid?* Did the rhythm of your speech correspond to the rhythm of the action? Does this not seem to you a simple and natural way of finding the rhythm which projects the idea?

Read the following lines from Robert Frost's poem, "Birches," [1] sensing the action with total motor response and reading the lines with the same rhythm as the action.

> He always kept his poise
> To the top branches, climbing carefully . . .
> Then flung outward, feet first, with a swish,
> Kicking his way down through the air to the ground.

Re-read these lines with overt action until you have so thoroughly sensed the rhythm you can read them without manifest action (still sensing movement in the muscles), maintaining the rhythm of the action in your speech.

Read the following passages, sensing the rhythm of the actions suggested by the words.

From THE WHIRLIGIG OF LIFE [2]

O. Henry

A speckled hen swaggered down the main street of the "settlement" cackling foolishly.

From CYRANO DE BERGERAC [3]

Edmond Rostand

> Your name is like a golden bell
> Hung in my heart, and when I think of you,
> I tremble, and the bell swings and rings—
> Roxane! . . . Roxane! . . . along my veins, Roxane!

---

[1] From *The Collected Poems of Robert Frost* (New York: Henry Holt and Company). By permission of the publishers.

[2] From *Whirligigs*, by O. Henry, copyright 1907, 1935, by Doubleday, Doran and Company, Inc. By permission of the publishers.

[3] Rostand, *Cyrano de Bergerac*, tr. Brian Hooker (New York: Henry Holt and Company), p. 143. By permission of the publishers.

THE EAGLE

Alfred Tennyson

He clasps the crag with crooked hands;
Close to the sun in lonely lands,
Ring'd with the azure world, he stands.

The wrinkled sea beneath him crawls;
He watches from his mountain walls,
And like a thunderbolt he falls.

INSTRUCTIONS TO THE PLAYERS

From HAMLET

William Shakespeare

Nor do not saw the air too much with your hand, thus. . . .

JAQUES' SEVEN AGES OF MAN

From AS YOU LIKE IT [1]

William Shakespeare

              All the world's a stage,
And all the men and women merely players;
They have their exits, and their entrances;
And one man in his time plays many parts,
His acts being seven ages. At first, the infant,
Mewling and puking in the nurse's arms.
And then, the whining school-boy, with his satchel,
And shining morning face, creeping, like snail,
Unwillingly to school. And then the lover,
Sighing like furnace, with a woeful ballad
Made to his mistress' eyebrow. Then the soldier,
Full of strange oaths, and bearded like a pard,

[1] Act II. Scene vii.

Jealous in honor, sudden and quick in quarrel,
Seeking the bubble reputation
Even in the cannon's mouth. And then, the justice,
In fair round belly, with good capon lin'd,
With eyes severe, and beard of formal cut,
Full of wise saws and modern instances,
And so he plays his part. The sixth age shifts
Into the lean and slipper'd pantaloon,
With spectacles on nose, and pouch on side;
His youthful hose well sav'd, a world too wide
For his shrunk shank; and his big manly voice,
Turning again toward childish treble, pipes
And whistles in his sound. Last scene of all,
That ends this strange, eventful history,
Is second childishness, and mere oblivion;
Sans teeth, sans eyes, sans taste, sans everything.

5. *Character Rhythms*

As has been stated before, each person has his own habitual rhythm which is affected by his moods and activities. The creative reader must learn to subordinate his own rhythm to that which will adequately interpret the author's idea. This is one of the problems which confronts a reader in interpreting characters. When the reader has sensed the fundamental rhythm of a character, he has gone far in interpreting him. Sensing the rhythm of a character may prove as helpful to a reader as to an actor or an impersonator. While the reader does not attempt to *act* the character, he does wish to share with the audience a vivid *concept* of the character. In the process of sharing reactions with the audience, the reader may suggest, even imitate to a degree, the actions of the character. The reader who senses the rhythm of the characters he interprets takes advantage of a subtle means of suggestion. A character, or a character's attitude, may at times be suggested through speech rhythm alone without further technique.

As a means of sensing the rhythm of a character, the reader may walk like the character, sit, stand, and gesture with the character's mannerisms as he speaks the lines. After the reader has thoroughly sensed the character's rhythm through literal actions, let him eliminate excess activity yet preserve the rhythm as he speaks. This technique will be found helpful in interpreting both direct and indirect address, both conversation and narration.

Read the selections below, experimenting with character rhythms as a means of carrying the author's purpose.

CHILD AND BOATMAN

From Songs of the Voices of Birds

Jean Ingelow

CHILD. Martin, I wonder who makes all the songs.
MARTIN. You do, sir?
CHILD. Yes, I wonder how they come.
MARTIN. Well, boy, I wonder what you'll wonder next!
CHILD. But somebody must make them?
MARTIN. Sure enough.
CHILD. Does your wife know?
MARTIN. She never said she did.
CHILD. You told me that she knew so many things.
MARTIN. I said she was a London woman, sir,
And a fine scholar, but I never said
She knew about the songs.
CHILD. I wish she did.
MARTIN. And I wish no such thing; she knows enough,
She knows too much already. Look you now,
This vessel's off the stocks, a tidy craft.

CHILD. A schooner, Martin?
MARTIN. No, boy; nó, a brig;
        Only she's schooner-rigged—a lovely craft.
CHILD. Is she for me? O thank you, Martin, dear.
        What shall I call her?
MARTIN. Well, sir, what you please.
CHILD. Then write on her "The Eagle."
MARTIN. Bless the child!
        Eagle! Why, you know naught of eagles, you.
        When we lay off the coast, up Canada way,
        And chanced to be ashore when twilight fell,
        That was the place for eagles; bald they were,
        With eyes as yellow as gold.
CHILD. O Martin, dear,
        Tell me about them.
MARTIN. Tell! there's naught to tell,
        Only they snored o'nights and frighted us.
CHILD. Snored?
MARTIN. Ay, I tell you, snored; they slept upright
        In the great oaks by scores; as true as time,
        If I'd had aught upon my mind just then,
        I wouldn't have walked that wood for unknown gold;
        It was most awful. When the moon was full,
        I've seen them fish at night, in the middle watch,
        When she got low. I've seen them plunge like stones
        And come up fighting with a fish as long,
        Ay, longer than my arm; and they would sail—
        When they had struck its life out—they would sail
        Over the deck, and show their fell, fierce eyes,
        And croon for pleasure, hug the prey, and speed
        Grand as a frigate on the wind.
CHILD. My ship,
        She must be called "The Eagle" after these.
        And, Martin, ask your wife about the songs
        When you go in at dinner-time.
MARTIN. Not I.

KINGS BOW THEIR HEADS [1]

Robert Liddell Lowe

Death's hands, fastidious and thin,
Immaculate as bone,
Do more than scrupulously ravel skin
From skeleton.
These hands, diminishing the pulse,
Do more than snap the sense
Or dry the dream within the pallid skull's
Circumference.

Such gifts of dignity they bring—
The inelastic dead,
Though strengthless now, command the proudest king
To bow his head.

AN OLD MAN TALKING IN HIS SLEEP [2]

Robert Liddell Lowe

All day his old tongue spoke
Of what was good or fair.
Vigor an ashy coal
And pride a smutty flare,
The heart was no more puzzled
Nor mind clotted with care.

But when the clock struck midnight
Two sounds frightened the air:
His tongue cried out a wisdom
By day it would not dare:
Dignity had no bridle
For weariless despair.

[1] From *The Nation*. By permission of the author and of the publishers.
[2] From *Poetry: A Magazine of Verse*. By permission of the author and of the publishers.

THE SET OF TURQUOISE

Thomas Bailey Aldrich

Scene I

CHARACTERS: Count of Lara, *a poor nobleman;* Beatrice, *his wife;* Miriam, *a maid who personates a page.*
SCENE: Count of Lara's *villa. A balcony overlooking the garden.*

LARA. The third moon of our marriage, Beatrice!
It hangs in the still twilight, large and full,
Like a ripe orange.
BEATRICE. 'Tis like some strange, rich jewel of the east,
And that reminds me—speaking of jewels—love,
There is a set of turquoise at Milan's,
Ear-drops and bracelets and a necklace—ah!
If they were mine.
LARA. And so they should be, dear,
Were I Aladdin, and had slaves o' the lamp
To fetch me ingots. Why, then, Beatrice,
All Persia's turquoise-quarries should be yours,
Although your hand is heavy now with gems
That tear my lips when I would kiss its whiteness.
BEATRICE. You love me not, or love me over-much,
Which makes you jealous of the gems I wear!
LARA. Not I.
I love you.
BEATRICE. Why, that is as easy said
As any three short words; takes no more breath
To say, "I hate you." What, sir, have I lived
Three times four weeks your wedded loyal wife,
And do not know your follies? I will wager
(If I could trap his countship into this!)
The rarest kisses I know how to give

                    Against the turquoise, that within a month
                    You'll grow so jealous—and without a cause,
                    That you will ache to kill me!
LARA.   Will you so?
                    And I—let us clasp hands and kiss on it.
BEATRICE.   Clasp hands, Sir Trustful; but not kiss—nay, nay!
                    I will not pay my forfeit till I lose.
LARA.   And I'll not lose the forfeit.
BEATRICE.   We shall see.
[*Exit* BEATRICE.]
LARA.   She has as many fancies as the wind.
                    She's no common clay,
                    But fire and dew and marble.
                    Jealous? I am not jealous. And yet,
                    I would I had not wagered; it implies
                    Doubt. And if I doubted? Pshaw! I'll walk awhile
                    And let the cool air fan me. It was not wise.
                    What if, to pique me, she should overstep
                    The pale of modesty, and give bold eyes
                    (I could not bear that, nay, not even that!)
                    To Marc or Claudian?
                    O cursèd jewels! Would that they were hung
                    About the glistening neck of some mermaid
                    A thousand fathoms underneath the sea!
[*A* PAGE *crosses the garden.*]
                    That page again! 'Tis twice within the week
                    The supple-waisted, pretty-ankled knave
                    Has crossed my garden at this self-same hour,
                    As if he owned the villa. Why, the fop!
                    He might have doffed his bonnet as he passed.
                    I'll teach him better if he comes again.
                    What does he at the villa? O! perchance
                    He comes in the evening when his master's out,
                    To lisp soft romance in the ready ear
                    Of Beatrice's dressing-maid;
                    I'll ask the Countess—no, I'll not do that;

She'd laugh at me; and vow by the Madonna
This varlet were some noble in disguise,
Seeking her favor. Then I'd let the light
Of heaven through his doublet—I would—yes,
That is, I would, were I a jealous man:
But then I'm not.
                    When he comes out again
I'll stop him, question him, and know the truth.
I cannot sit in the garden of a night
But he glides by me in his jaunty dress,
Like a fantastic phantom! never looks
To the right nor left, but passes gayly on.
                              Soft, he comes!

[*The* PAGE *enters by a gate in the villa garden and walks past the* COUNT.]

Ho! pretty page, who owns you?

PAGE.   No one now.
Once Signor Juan, but I am his no more.

LARA.   What, then, you stole from him?

PAGE.   O! no, sir, no.
He had so many intrigues on his hands,
There was no sleep for me nor night nor day.
Such carrying of love-favors and pink notes!
He's gone abroad now, to break other hearts
And so I left him.

LARA [*aside*].   A frank knave.

PAGE.   To-night
I've done his latest bidding—'twas to take
A message to a countess
In yonder villa.

LARA [*aside*]. In yonder villa?

PAGE.   Ay, sir. You can see
The portico among the mulberries,
Just to the left, there.

LARA.   Ay, I see, I see.
A pretty villa. And the lady's name?

Page.	O! that's a secret which I cannot tell.
Lara.	No? but you shall, though, or I'll strangle you!
Page.	You are choking me! O! loose your grasp, sir!
Lara.	Then the name! the name!
Page.	Countess of Lara.
Lara.	Not her dressing-maid?
Page.	No, no, I said the mistress, not the maid.
Lara.	And then you lied. Tell me you lie, and I will make you rich, I'll stuff your cap with ducats twice a year.
Page.	Well, then—I lie.
Lara.	Ay, now you lie, indeed! Here is gold. You brought a billet to the Countess—well?
Page.	Take away your hand And, by St. Mary, I will tell you all. There, now, I breathe. You will not harm me, sir? Stand six yards off, or I will not a word. It seems the Countess promised Signor Juan A set of turquoise—
Lara.	Turquoise? Ha! that's well.
Page.	Just so—wherewith my master was to pay Some gaming debts; but yester-night the cards Tumbled a golden mountain at his feet; And ere he sailed, this morning, Signor Juan Gave me a perfumed, amber-tinted note, For Countess Lara, which, with some adieus, Craved her remembrance morning, noon, and night; Her prayers while gone, her smiles when he returned; And bade her keep the jewels. That is all.
Lara.	All? Is that all? 'T has only cracked my heart! Out of my sight, thou demon of bad news!
[*Exit* Lara.]	
Page.	I did not think 't would work on him like that. How pale he grew! Alack! I fear some ill

Will come of this. I'll to the Countess now,
And warn her of his madness.

[*Exit* Page.]

Scene II

SCENE: Beatrice's *chamber*. Beatrice *sits in the attitude of listening.*

BEATRICE. Hist! that's his step. Miriam, place the lights
Farther away; keep you behind the screen. Then be still.
Move not for worlds until I touch the bell,
Then do the thing I told you. Hush! his step
Sounds in the corridor, and I'm asleep!

[Lara *enters. He approaches within a few yards of* Beatrice, *pauses, and looks at her.*]

LARA. Asleep!—and guilt can slumber!
Were I an artist, and did wish to paint
A devil to perfection, I'd paint
A woman in the glamour of her youth,
All garmented with loveliness and mystery!
How fair she is! Her beauty glides between
Me and my purpose, like a pleading angel.
She'll waken soon, and that—that must not be!
I could not kill her if she looked at me.

BEATRICE [*springing up*]. So, Lara, you are come—your dagger in your hand?
O love, you frighten me!
And you are trembling. Tell me what this means.

LARA. Countess of Lara, you are false to me!

BEATRICE. Now, by the saints—

LARA. Now, by the saints, you are!

BEATRICE. Upon my honor—

LARA. On your honor? fie!

BEATRICE. Hear me, love!

LARA. Lie to that marble there! I am sick
To the heart with lying. Beatrice,

STUDIES IN DIALECT 123

    I came to kill you.
BEATRICE. Kiss me, Count, you mean!
    Ho! come not near me with such threatening looks,
    Stand back there, if you love me, or have loved!
[*As* LARA *advances,* BEATRICE *retreats to the table and rings a small hand-bell.* MIRIAM, *in the dress of a page, enters from behind the screen and steps between them.*]
LARA [*starting back*]. The Page? now, curse him! What? no!
    Miriam?
    If this be Juan's page, why, where is Miriam?
    If this be Miriam, where's—by all the saints,
    I have been tricked!
MIRIAM [*laughing*].   By two saints, with your leave!
LARA.   The happiest fool in Italy, for my age!
    And all the damning tales you fed me with,
    You Sprite of Twilight!
MIRIAM [*bowing*]. Were arrant lies as ever woman told;
    And though not mine, I claim the price for them—
    This cap stuffed full of ducats twice a year!
LARA.   A trap! a trap that only caught a fool!
    So thin a plot, I might have seen through it.
    I've lost my reason!
MIRIAM.   And your ducats!
BEATRICE.   And
    A certain set of turquoise at Milan's!
          Arranged

Influence of Climate, Nationality, and Race

 Character rhythms are influenced by climate, nationality, and race. Peoples in warm climates are inclined through relaxation to prolong the vowel sounds and neglect the consonants. This tendency gives to their speech a musical softness which is usually considered pleasing. One hears of the beauty of southern voices, the rhythms of which are slow and legato. Northern peoples are inclined to speak with clear, distinct consonant sounds and clipped vowels. There is often admirable clarity and force, and the tendency is toward quick, staccato rhythms.

Nationality also influences speech rhythms. Concerning this Charlotte Crocker says in her splendid analysis of dialect:

> Rhythm is one of the most fascinating elements of dialect. Take for example the staccato speech of the Scot; anyone interested in exploring all the factors of dialect will readily be struck by the bare, bleak speech of the Scot and the fact that his homeland is rugged and challenging—like his speech. Again one can readily fancy a relationship between the leisurely humor of the real Irishman and his speech that is so rich in an easy, flowing, genial pace. There is, in short, an undeniable relationship between the time and pulsation factors of dialect and the temperament of the given nationality.[1]

It is not within the purpose of this book to give detailed analysis of speech dialects. There are a few authentic publications which give a study of national speech characteristics and folk dialect.[2]

The student of interpretative reading should give some attention to characteristics of dialect speech. It is evident that there are rhythmic tendencies in the speech of the British, Irish, Scotch, Australian, and American; there are characteristic rhythms in the dialects of the Swedish, Italian, French, Spanish, et cetera. In America, we have the moun-

[1] Charlotte Crocker, *Taking the Stage* (New York: Pitman Publishing Corporation, 1939), p. 212. By permission of the publishers.
[2] See Appendix A, p. 591.

tain dialect which has preserved many of the characteristics of Anglo-Saxon speech. The standard speech of the United States is usually classified into three groups, namely, Eastern, Southern, and General American. In order to sense the rhythms of any speech group the reader really needs to hear them enough for his ear to become familiar with the rhythmic patterns. When the student is unable to do this he may find radio and the movie helpful in making familiar the rhythms of dialect. He may also familiarize himself with dialects by listening to gramophone records of folk speech.

Negro dialect presents intriguing problems to the creative reader. The rhythm of Negro dialect is racial; it is not easily described nor is it easily sensed except by those who have been closely associated with the Negro. Relaxation and abandon are essential in responding to this rhythm. One distinguishing characteristic of Negro poetry and music is syncopated time in which the accent seems to fall upon the off beat. Perhaps the student can sense this rhythm by tapping off the rhythm with his fingers, reading the stressed words or syllables with the hand lifted; that is, speaking the stressed words *between* the rhythmic beats instead of *on* the beats. It may take some practice and experimentation for the reader to sense syncopation in oral reading; one is more likely to be familiar with it in music than in speech. The enjoyment of Negro dialect comes largely from this sense of rhythm which, when projected adequately, is likely to bring audience response in swaying, patting, or in some other manner giving evidence of empathic response.

A few dialect selections are given in the following pages. As you practice for adequate dialect, remember: the idea should take precedence over enunciation; the mental attitude of the character is more important than his oddities of speech.

In the introduction to a volume of Irwin Russell's poems Joel Chandler Harris writes:

> Irwin Russell was among the first—if not the very first—of Southern writers to appreciate the literary possibilities of the negro character, and of the unique relations existing between the two races before the war, and was among the first to develop them. The opinion of an uncritical mind ought not to go for much, but it seems to me that some of Irwin Russell's negro character studies rise to the level of what, in a large way, we term literature. His negro operetta, "Christmas-Night in the Quarters," is inimitable. It combines the features of a character study with a series of bold and striking plantation pictures that have never been surpassed. In this remarkable group,—if I may so term it,—the old life before the war is reproduced with a fidelity that is marvelous.

From this "group" we have selected the Negro preacher's prayer, delivered as an invocation before the dance.

From CHRISTMAS NIGHT IN THE QUARTERS [1]
Irwin Russell

O Mahsr! let dis gath'rin' fin' a blessin' in yo' sight!
Don't jedge us hard fur what we does—you know it's Chrismus-night;
An' all de balunce ob de yeah we does as right's we kin.
Ef dancin's wrong, O Mahsr! let de time excuse de sin!

---

[1] Irwin Russell, *Christmas Night in the Quarters* (New York: The Century Co.), pp. 8–12. By permission of the publishers.

We labors in de vineya'd, wukin' hard and wukin' true;
Now, shorely you won't notus, ef we eats a grape or two,
An' takes a leetle holiday,—a leetle restin'-spell,—
Bekase, nex' week, we'll start in fresh, an' labor twicet as well.

Remember, Mahsr,—min' dis now,—de sinfullness ob sin
Is 'pendin' 'pon de sperrit what we goes an' does it in:
An' in a righchis frame ob min' we's gwine to dance an' sing.
A-feelin' like King David, when he cut de pigeon wing.

It seems to me—indeed it do—I mebbe mout be wrong—
That people raly ought to dance, when Chrismus comes along;
Des dance bekase dey's happy—like de birds hops in de trees,
De pine-top fiddle soundin' to de bowin' ob de breeze.

We has no ark to dance afore, like Isrul's prophet king;
We has no harp to soun' de chords, to holp us out to sing;
But 'cordin' to de gif's we has we does de bes' we knows,
An' folks don't 'spise the vi'let-flower bekase it ain't de rose.

You bless us, please, sah, eben ef we's doin' wrong to-night;
Kase den we'll need de blessin' more'n ef we's doin' right;
An' let de blessin' stay wid us, untel we comes to die,
An' goes to keep our Chrismus wid dem sherriffs in de sky!

Yes, tell dem preshis anguls we's a-gwine to jine 'em soon:
Our voices we's a-trainin' fur to sing de glory tune;
We's ready when you wants us, an' it ain't no matter when—
O Mahsr! call yo' chillen soon, an' take 'em home! Amen.

A Scene from DAVID COPPERFIELD

Charles Dickens

CHARACTERS: OLD FISHERMAN PEGGOTTY, HAM PEGGOTTY, DAVID COPPERFIELD.

NOTE. *The scene is the interior of the Old Ark; the time is evening. The rain is falling outside, yet inside the Old Ark all is snug and comfortable. The fire is burning brightly on the hearth, and* MOTHER GUMMIDGE *sits by it knitting.* HAM *has gone out to fetch* LITTLE EM'LY *home from her work, and the old fisherman sits smoking his evening pipe by the table near the window. They are expecting* STEERFORTH *and* COPPERFIELD *in to spend the evening. Presently a knock is heard and* DAVID *enters.* OLD PEGGOTTY *gets up to greet him.*

OLD PEGGOTTY. Why! It's Mas'r Davy! Glad to see you. Mas'r Davy, you're the first of the lot! Take off that cloak of yours if it's wet and draw right up to the fire. Don't you mind Mawther Gummidge, Mas'r Davy; she's a-thinkin' of the old 'un. She allers do be thinkin' of the old 'un when ther's a storm a-comin' up, along of his havin' been drownded at sea. Well, now, I must go and light up accordin' to custom. [*He lights a candle and puts it on the table by the window.*] Theer we are! A-lighted up accordin' to custom. Now, Mas'r Davy, you're a-wonderin' what that little candle is fur, ain't yer? Well, I'll tell yer. It's for my Little Em'ly. You see, the path ain't light or cheerful arter dark, so when I'm home along the time that Little Em'ly comes home from her work, I allers lights the little candle and puts it there on the table in the winder, and it serves two purposes,—first, Em'ly sees it and she says: "Theer's home," and likewise, "Theer's Uncle," fur if I ain't here I never have no light showed. Theer! Now you're laughin' at me, Mas'r Davy! You're sayin' as how I'm a babby. Well, I don't know but I am. [*Walks toward table.*] Not a babby to look at, but a babby to consider on. A babby in the form of a Sea Porkypine.

See the candle sparkle! I can hear it say—"Em'ly's lookin' at me! Little Em'ly's comin'!" Right I am for here she is! [*He goes to the door to meet her; the door opens and* HAM *comes staggering in.*]

HAM. She's gone! Her that I'd a died fur, and will die fur even now! She's gone!
PEGGOTTY. Gone!
HAM. Gone! She's run away! And think how she's run away when I pray my good and gracious God to strike her down dead, sooner than let her come to disgrace and shame.
PEGGOTTY. Em'ly gone! I'll not believe it. I must have proof—proof.
HAM. Read that writin'.
PEGGOTTY. No! I won't read that writin'—read it you, Mas'r Davy. Slow, please. I don't know as I can understand.
DAVID [*reads*]. "When you see this I shall be far away."
PEGGOTTY. Stop theer, Mas'r Davy! Stop theer! Fur away! My Little Em'ly fur away! Well?
DAVID [*reads*]. "Never to come back again unless he brings me back a lady. Don't remember, Ham, that we were to be married, but try to think of me as if I had died long ago, and was buried somewhere. My last love and last tears for Uncle."
PEGGOTTY. Who's the man? What's his name? I want to know the man's name.
HAM. It warn't no fault of yours, Mas'r Davy, that I know.
PEGGOTTY. What! You don't mean his name's Steerforth, do you?
HAM. Yes! His name is Steerforth and he's a cursed villain!
PEGGOTTY. Where's my coat? Give me my coat! Help me on with it, Mas'r Davy. Now bear a hand theer with my hat.
DAVID. Where are you going, Mr. Peggotty?
PEGGOTTY. I'm a goin' to seek fur my Little Em'ly. First I'm going to stave in that theer boat and sink it where I'd a drownded him, as I'm a livin' soul, if I'd a known what he had in him! I'd a drownded him, and thought I was doin' right! Now I'm going to seek fur my Little Em'ly throughout the wide wurreld!

Abridged

BONIE DOON
Robert Burns

Ye flowery banks o' bonie Doon,
    How can ye blume sae fair?
How can ye chant, ye little birds,
    And I sae fu' o' care?

Thou'll break my heart, thou bonie bird,
    That sings upon the bough;
Thou minds me o' the happy days,
    When my fause luve was true.

Thou'll break my heart, thou bonie bird,
    That sings beside thy mate;
For sae I sat, and sae I sang,
    And wist na o' my fate.

Aft hae I rov'd by bonie Doon
    To see the wood-bine twine,
And ilka bird sang o' its luve,
    And sae I did o' mine.

Wi' lightsome heart I pu'd a rose
    Frae aff its thorny tree;
And my fause luver staw my rose
    But left the thorn wi' me.

TOMORROW
Alfred Tennyson

Her, that yer Honor was spakin' to? Whin, yer Honor? last
    year—
Standin' here be the bridge, when last yer Honor was here?
An' yer Honor ye gev her the top of the mornin', "Tomorra,"
    says she.

What did they call her, yer Honor? They called her Molly
    Magee. . . .

Shure, an' meself remimbers wan night comin' down be the
    sthrame,
An' it seems to me now like a bit of histher-day in a dhrame—
Here where yer Honor seen her—there was but a slip of a moon,
But I heard thim—Molly Magee wid her batchelor, Danny
    O'Roon—
"You've been takin' a dhrop o' the crathur," an' Danny says,
    "Troth, an' I been
Dhrinkin' yer health wid Shamus O'Shea at Katty's shebeen;
But I must be lavin' ye soon." "Ochone are ye goin' away?"
"Goin' to cut the Sassenach whate," he says, "over the say"—
"An' whin will ye meet me agin?" an' I heard him "Molly
    asthore,
I'll meet you agin tomorra," says he, "be the chapel-door."
"An' whin are ye goin' to lave me?" "O' Monday mornin'," says
    he;
"An' shure thin ye'll met me tomorra?" "Tomorra, tomorra,
    Machree!"
Thin Molly's ould mother, yer Honor, that had no likin' for
    Dan,
Call'd from her cabin an' tould her to come away from the man,
An' Molly Magee kem flyin' acrass me, as light as a lark,
An' Dan stood there for a minute, an' thin wint into the dark.
But wirrah! the storm that night—the tundher, an' rain that fell,
An' the sthrames runnin' down at the back o' the glin 'ud 'a
    dhrownded Hell.

But airth was at pace nixth mornin', an' Hiven in its glory
    smiled,
As the Holy Mother o' Glory that smiles at her sleepin' child—
Ethen—she stept on the chapel-green, an' she turn'd herself
    roun'
Wid a diamond dhrop in her eye, for Danny was not to be foun',

An' many's the time that I watch'd her at mass lettin' down the tear,
For the Divil a Danny was there, yer Honor, for forty year.

Och, Molly Magee, wid the red o' the rose an' the white o' the May,
An' yer hair as black as the night, an' yer eyes as bright as the day! . . .
An' sorra the queen wid her scepter in sich an illigant han',
An' the fall of yer foot in the dance was as light as snow on the lan' . . .
An' the boys wor about her agin whin Dan didn't come to the fore,
An' Shamus along wid the rest, but she put thim all to the door.
An', afther, I thried her meself av the bird 'ud come to me call,
But Molly, begorrah, 'ud listen to naither at all, at all. . . .

An' afther her paärints had inter'd glory, an' both in wan day,
She began to spake to herself, the crathur, an' whisper, an' say
"Tomorra, tomorra!" an' Father Malowny he tuk her in han',
"Molly, you're manin'," he says, "me dear, av I undherstan',
That ye'll meet your paärints agin an' yer Danny O'Roon afore God
Wid his blest Mathyrs an' Saints"; an' she gev him a friendly nod,
"Tomorra, tomorra," she says, an' she didn't intend to desave,
But her wits wor dead, an' her hair was as white as the snow on a grave.

Arrah now, here last month they wor diggin' the bog, an' they foun'
Dhrownded in black bog-wather a corp lyin' undher groun' . . . .
An' they laid this body they foun' on the grass
Be the chapel-door, an' the people 'ud see it that wint into mass—

But a frish gineration had riz, an' most of the ould was few,
An' I didn't know him meself, an' none of the parish knew.

But Molly kem limpin' up wid her stick, she was lamed iv a knee,
Thin a slip of a gossoon call'd, "Div ye know him, Molly Magee?"
An' she stood up straight as the Queen of the world—she lifted her head—
"He said he would meet me tomorra!" an' dhropt down dead on the dead.

Och, Molly, we thought, machree, ye would start back agin into life,
Whin we laid yez, aich be aich, at yer wake like husban' an' wife,
Sorra the dhry eye thin but was wet for the friends that was gone!
Sorra the silent throat but we hard it cryin' "Ochone!"
An' Shamus O'Shea that has now ten childr' han'some an' tall,
Him an' his childr' wor keenin' as if he had lost thim all.

Thin his Riverence buried thim both in wan grave be the dead boor-tree,
The young man Danny O'Roon wid his ould woman, Molly Magee. . . .
An' now that I tould yer Honor whatever I hard an' seen,
Yer Honor 'll give me a thrifle to dhrink yer health in potheen.

Chapter V

STRUCTURE IN INTERPRETATIVE READING

Art is feeling passed through thought and fixed in form.
Delsarte

The need of a technique of thinking for interpretative reading was emphasized in Chapter I. In Chapters II and III techniques of thinking in relation to sensation and dramatic timing were suggested as a means of conveying concepts to an audience. The student is now invited to consider carefully the structural elements in the art of interpretative reading.

In one of her well-known sonnets Edna St. Vincent Millay says, "Euclid alone has looked on beauty bare." Miss Millay gives recognition here to the principle that back of all beauty there is geometric form. According to her statement, Euclid, who discovered the laws of geometry, is the only one who has looked upon beauty stripped of all ornamentation. Miss Millay suggests by this statement that others have looked upon the coverings of beauty, but Euclid *alone* has looked on beauty *bare*.

The purpose of art is to create illusion; the artist wishes to cover his form, for the best art conceals its artistry. The twisted smile of the Mona Lisa baffles the onlooker. It is said that to achieve this effect Leonardo da Vinci painted the lines on one side of her face with a downward, and on the other side with an upward trend. The artist has covered his technique so well that the observer finds it difficult to perceive the direction of the lines; he sees only the mocking, teasing, baffling smile of the woman with the folded hands. The *illusion* is for the spectator; the *form* is for the artist.

As was suggested in Chapter I, the fear of artificiality has frequently prevented the reader's looking frankly at the form of oral reading. The result has been inadequate structure for the art of interpretative reading. The creative reader, like other creative artists, has need to build upon a stable structural form. He must not be afraid to look upon beauty *bare*.

CLIMAX

A technique of climax is an important phase of interpretative reading. The word *climax* comes from a Greek word meaning *ladder*. The comparison of the principles of climax to a ladder should help the student of creative reading to understand the nature of climax. The term *climax* is usually understood to mean the highest peak of interest, or the turning point in a play, story, or poem. *The climax* is reached by a series of lesser climaxes and is often followed by other lesser climaxes. The process of reaching a climax may be compared to climbing a ladder. The process of going from one climax to another may be compared to descending a ladder and ascending another. The writer uses the principle of climax to climb to or to descend from points of special interest. The reader, to interpret adequately, must give oral expression to the mounting and descending of these ladders.

The principle of climax may be said to characterize a

piece of literature as a whole and also each separate part. Each act of a play, each chapter of a book, or each stanza of a poem may have its climax which forms a step to or from the climax of the whole. The principle of climax may be discerned in sentences, even in phrases. For example, Hamlet says:

> O! that this too too solid flesh would melt,
> Thaw and resolve itself into a dew;
> Or that the Everlasting had not fix'd
> His canon 'gainst self-slaughter.

Shakespeare has given the words in a climactic order: *melt, thaw, resolve itself into a dew*. The reader's technique of climax should be commensurate with that of the writer. An increase in emphasis is the natural means of giving the climax in this phrase.

Build

The word *build* (a term familiar to actors) suggests the process of ascending climaxes and may be applied in interpretative reading. One builds in intensity, tempo, and volume as one senses the need of climbing to a peak of interest. The creative reader should sense the build in a piece of literature as a whole and also in the various parts. Each portion may be built in proportion to the climax of the whole. In some plays, novels, or poems the climax is toward the end. Sometimes, however, the author places the climax much earlier in order that there may be a descent in intensity as the problem is solved, or the plot unraveled.

Shakespeare's plays, consisting of five acts with the climax usually occurring in the third act, present an interesting study in climax. One explanation for his placing the climax so early in the play is that the play may end with a more normal emotion than that which characterizes the climax. For example, in *The Merchant of Venice* it is much more pleasant for the play to end with the charm and humor of the ring scene than with the conflict of the trial scene. This play builds in intensity until Portia pronounces the sentence upon the Jew. There is a moment of intense emotion as Portia delivers the verdict upon Shylock. The relief from this tension is almost immediate as the sub-plot is resumed and the minor climax is built concerning the rings.

Planes

The creative reader may find it helpful in building climaxes to think of the phrases as spoken on different planes of pitch. Diagrams of the relative position of phrases in building a climax may help the student to sense builds. Practice in building his oral expression according to a diagram of planes may aid him in breaking up habits of monotony in reading.

For example, let us make a diagram of Pippa's song, "The Year's At the Spring," from "Pippa Passes" by Browning.

> The year's at the spring
> And the day's at the morn;
> Morning's at seven;
> The hillside's dew-pearled;
> The lark's on the wing;
> The snail's on the thorn:
> God's in his heaven—
> All's right with the world!

This lyric suggests a division of two builds of four lines each. We may read each of these portions with each succeeding line on a slightly higher plane than the line preceding. What about the relation of the two portions to each other? It seems evident to us that the climax is in one of the last two lines. Let us say the last line is the climax. Our second portion would then build higher than our first portion, but the first line of the second portion would not be quite so high as the last line of the first portion. Consider the diagram below and test its adequacy by reading the lyric according to this form.

                                        8. All's right with the world!
                            7. God's in his heaven—
            4. The hillside's dew-pearled;
                    6. The snail's on the thorn:
        3. Morning's at seven
              5. The lark's on the wing;
    2. And the day's at the morn;
1. The year's at the spring

How would you build the following excerpt?
In the Cathedral of Lübeck, Germany, is this inscription:

        Thus speaketh Christ our Lord to us:
        Ye call me Master, and obey me not;
        Ye call me Light, and seek me not;
        Ye call me Way, and walk me not;
        Ye call me Life, and desire me not;
        Ye call me Wise, and follow me not;
        Ye call me Fair, and love me not;
        Ye call me Rich, and ask me not;
        Ye call me Eternal, and seek me not;
        Ye call me Gracious, and trust me not;
        Ye call me Noble, and serve me not;
        Ye call me Mighty, and honor me not;

Ye call me Just, and hear me not;
If I condemn you, blame me not.

Crescendo and Diminuendo

In music the ascent and descent in climax is called crescendo and diminuendo. "The Volga Boatman" is a song the popularity of which is probably due to this principle. The song starts very softly as if the boatman were far away down the river. The song gradually builds in volume and intensity as if the boatman were coming nearer and nearer. When the climax (the turning point) is reached, the volume and intensity begin to diminish as gradually as they were built. The song seems finally to fade away as if the boatman had disappeared in the distance with the last few notes of the song floating back to the listeners.

The student of interpretative reading will find many places in literature where the technique of crescendo and diminuendo may be used effectively. In Vachel Lindsay's "The Santa Fe Trail" the coming and receding of auto horns may be suggested by this technique. In the stanza which follows, from "The Explorer" by Rudyard Kipling, hope may be built and despair suggested by the technique of crescendo and diminuendo.

Till the snow ran out in flowers, and the flowers turned to aloes,
And the aloes sprung to thickets and a brimming stream ran by;
But the thickets dwined to thorn-scrub, and the water drained to shallows,
And I dropped again on desert—blasted earth, and blasting sky. . . .[1]

[1] Rudyard Kipling, "The Explorer," from *The Five Nations*, London, A. P. Watt & Son; New York, Doubleday, Doran and Company, Inc., 1903, 1931. Reprinted by permission.

DIAGRAM
```
                4. and a brimming stream ran by;
                     5. But the thickets dwined to thorn-scrub,
    3. And the aloes sprung to thickets
                          6. and the water drained to shallows,
   2. and the flowers turned to aloes,
                               7. And I dropped again on desert—
1. Till the snow ran out in flowers,
                                    8. blasted earth,
                                       9. and blasting
                                         10. sky. . . .
```

Topping

When in dialogue two or more characters build a climax together, they are said to *top* each other, the technique being known as *topping*. The student of interpretative reading may be wise to spend some time practicing this technique. Students may sense the interplay of characters if they are cast in the rôles of the characters and build a scene together, topping each other as they ascend to the climax. After gaining some proficiency in topping others, the student may then be able to suggest the various characters and also to apply the technique of topping as he reads the scene alone.

The technique of topping is of value in building scenes in tragedy and in comedy. In tragedy the student is more likely to sense the builds due to the compelling power of the emotion.

Topping is almost a sure technique for gaining laughs in comedy. Even a simple dialogue will prove amusing if built by topping. For example, apply the technique of topping in the following dialogue. Suggest a man's and a woman's voice each topping the other as you build to the woman's final "no" which should be given on a very high pitch with a feeling of finality in the tone.

He. Yes!
She. No!
He. Yes!
She. No!
He. Yes!
She. No!
He. Yes!
She. No!

Relief

In mastering a technique of climax it is important for the student to realize the need of relief as well as of tension. The descent is as important as the ascent. Relief may often be given within a general build. For example, within a speech of a character the topping may be achieved with the first phrase, the rest of the speech being given on other levels. To keep one level too long results in monotony whether that level is too low or too high. When the level is too high it gives the effect of ranting, when too low, of indifference or boredom.

The School for Scandal offers enjoyable scenes for the technique of topping. Lady Teazle and Sir Peter both seem to enjoy their quarrels. Humor can be projected by keeping Lady Teazle good humored as she provokes Sir Peter almost to the point of exasperation. Comedy is heightened in a quarrel scene by allowing only one character at a time to become tense. The one who feels himself winning is often relaxed and good humored. High comedy may be attained by a quick shift as the one who has seemed defeated turns tables and gets on top.

From THE SCHOOL FOR SCANDAL [1]
Richard Sheridan

SCENE.—*A room in* SIR PETER TEAZLE's *house.*

[*Enter* SIR PETER *and* LADY TEAZLE.]

SIR PETER. Lady Teazle, Lady Teazle, I'll not bear it!

LADY TEAZLE. Sir Peter, Sir Peter, you may bear it or not, as you please; but I ought to have my own way in everything, and what's more, I will too. What though I was educated in the country, I know very well that women of fashion in London are accountable to nobody after they are married.

SIR PETER. Very well, ma'am, very well; so a husband is to have no influence, no authority.

LADY TEAZLE. Authority! No, to be sure; if you wanted authority over me, you should have adopted me, and not married me; I am sure you were old enough.

SIR PETER. Old enough! ay—there it is. Well, well, Lady Teazle, though my life may be made unhappy by your temper, I'll not be ruined by your extravagance.

LADY TEAZLE. My extravagance! I'm sure I'm not more extravagant than a woman ought to be.

SIR PETER. No, no, madam, you shall throw away no more sums on such unmeaning luxury. 'Slife! to spend as much to furnish your dressing-room with flowers in winter as would suffice to turn the Pantheon into a green-house.

LADY TEAZLE. Lud, Sir Peter, am I to blame, because flowers are dear in cold weather? You should find fault with the climate, and not with me. For my part, I'm sure, I wish it

[1] Act II, Scene i.

was spring all the year round, and that roses grew under our feet!

SIR PETER. Zounds! madam—if you had been born to this, I shouldn't wonder at your talking thus; but you forget what your situation was when I married you.

LADY TEAZLE. No, no, I don't; 'twas a very disagreeable one, or I should never have married you.

SIR PETER. Yes, yes, madam, you were then in somewhat a humbler style,—the daughter of a plain country squire. Recollect, Lady Teazle, when I saw you first sitting at your tamber, in a pretty figured linen gown, with a bunch of keys at your side; your hair combed smooth over a roll, and your apartment hung around with fruits in worsted of your own working.

LADY TEAZLE. Oh, yes! I remember it very well, and a curious life I led,—my daily occupation to inspect the dairy, superintend the poultry, make extracts from the family receipt-book, and comb my Aunt Deborah's lap dog.

SIR PETER. Yes, yes, ma'am, 'twas so indeed.

LADY TEAZLE. And then, you know, my evening amusements; —to draw patterns for ruffles, which I had not materials to make up; to play Pope Joan with the curate; to read a novel to my aunt; or to be stuck down to an old spinnet to strum my father to sleep after a fox-chase.

SIR PETER. I am glad you have so good a memory. Yes, madam, these were the recreations I took you from; but now you must have your coach—vis-à-vis and in summer, a pair of white cats to draw you to Kensington Gardens. No recollection, I suppose, when you were content to ride double, behind the butler, on a docked coach-horse.

LADY TEAZLE. No—I never did that: I deny the butler and the coach horse.

Sir Peter. This, madam, was your situation; and what have I done for you? I have made you a woman of fashion, of fortune, of rank; in short I have made you my wife.

Lady Teazle. Well, then; and there is but one thing more you can make me add to the obligation, and that is—

Sir Peter. My widow, I suppose?

Lady Teazle. Hem. Hem!

Sir Peter. I thank you, madam; but don't flatter yourelf; for though your ill conduct may disturb my peace of mind, it shall never break my heart, I promise you: however, I am equally obliged to you for the hint.

Lady Teazle. Then why will you endeavor to make yourself so disagreeable to me, and thwart me in every little elegant expense?

Sir Peter. 'Slife, madam, I say, had you any of these little elegant expenses when you married me?

Lady Teazle. Lud, Sir Peter! Would you have me be out of the fashion?

Sir Peter. The fashion, indeed. What had you to do with the fashion before you married me?

Lady Teazle. For my part, I should think you would like to have your wife thought a woman of taste.

Sir Peter. Ay; there again—taste. Zounds! Madam, you had no taste when you married me!

Lady Teazle. That's very true indeed, Sir Peter; and after having married you, I should never pretend to taste again, I allow. But now, Sir Peter, since we have finished our daily jangle I presume I may go to my engagement at Lady Sneerwell's?

Sir Peter. Ay, there's another precious circumstance—a charming set of acquaintance you have made there.

Lady Teazle. Nay, Sir Peter, they are all people of rank and fortune, and remarkably tenacious of reputation.

Sir Peter. Yes, egad, they are tenacious of reputation with a vengeance; for they don't choose anybody should have a character but themselves!—such a crew! Ah! many a wretch had rid on a hurdle who has done less mischief than these utterers of forged tales, coiners of scandal, and clippers of reputation.

Lady Teazle. What! would you restrain the freedom of speech?

Sir Peter. Ah! they have made you just as bad as any one of the society.

Lady Teazle. Why, I believe I do bear a part with a tolerable grace.

Sir Peter. Grace, indeed!

Lady Teazle. But I vow I bear no malice against the people I abuse. When I say an ill-natured thing, 'tis out of pure good humor; and I take it for granted, they deal exactly in the same manner with me. But, Sir Peter, you know you promised to come to Lady Sneerwell's too.

Sir Peter. Well, well, I'll call in just to look after my character.

Lady Teazle. Then indeed you must make haste after me, or you'll be too late. So, good-by to you. [*Exit.*]

Sir Peter. So—I have gained much by my intended expostulation; yet, with what a charming air she contradicts everything I say, and how pleasingly she shows her contempt for my authority. Well, though I can't make her love me, there is great satisfaction in quarrelling with her; and I think she never appears to such advantage, as when she is doing everything in her power to plague me.

Reserve

One of the secrets of effectiveness in climax is for the reader to save intensity, force, and volume for the climax. This principle is called *reserve*. One needs to reserve one's power for peaks of interest. The creative reader usually needs to reserve his energy at the beginning of every portion in order that he may build. He must also keep a sense of proportion in order not to build too high in the early climaxes and thus lack the ability to ascend higher as he reaches *the climax*. A good rule is never to use more intensity than is essential for the projection of the idea. Actors sometimes find that they have been unable to build a climax effectively because they have started on too high a plane. The excitement of public occasions often causes speakers to start on too high a pitch, and it becomes increasingly difficult for them to come down, which results in ranting.

Contrast

Contrast is an essential element of art for which the student of interpretative reading should be constantly on the alert. A certain student won a declamation contest with a rendition of Kipling's "Recessional." He read the entire poem in one mood, in a high sounding manner, as it were. It sounded good to two of the judges but the third judge, feeling that the student had misinterpreted the poem from the viewpoint of contrast, voted against him. The student's rendition showed dramatic power and he might have won all three votes if he had used the principle of contrast. Portions of "The Recessional" depict the pomp and grandeur of the successful reign of Queen Victoria. Although the student's high sounding tones were fitting for these portions, they should have been contrasted with the attitude of humility which the poet felt to be essential on such an occasion.

Read the following poems, observing the principle of contrast.

LOVE AMONG THE RUINS
Robert Browning

Where the quiet-colored end of evening smiles
    Miles and miles
On the solitary pastures where our sheep
    Half-asleep
Tinkle homeward through the twilight, stray or stop
    As they crop—
Was the site once of a city great and gay
    (So they say)
Of our country's very capital, its prince
    Ages since
Held his court in, gathered councils, wielding far
    Peace or war.

Now,—the country does not even boast a tree,
    As you see,
To distinguish slopes of verdure, certain rills
    From the hills
Intersect and give a name to (else they run
    Into one,)
Where the domed and daring palace shot its spires
    Up like fires
O'er the hundred-gated circuit of a wall
    Bounding all,
Made of marble, men might march on nor be pressed,
    Twelve abreast.

And such plenty and perfection, see, of grass
    Never was!

Such a carpet as, this summer-time, o'er-spreads
    And embeds
Every vestige of the city, guessed alone,
    Stock or stone—
Where a multitude of men breathed joy and woe
    Long ago;
Lust of glory pricked their hearts up, dread of shame
    Struck them tame;
And that glory and that shame alike, the gold
    Bought and sold.

Now,—the single little turret that remains
    On the plains
By the caper overrooted, by the gourd
    Overscored,
While the patching houseleek's head of blossom winks
    Through the chinks—
Marks the basement whence a tower in ancient time
    Sprang sublime,
And a burning ring, all round, the chariots traced
    As they raced,
And the monarch and his minions and his dames
    Viewed the games.

And I know—while thus the quiet-colored eve
    Smiles to leave
To their folding, all our many tinkling fleece
    In such peace,
And the slopes and rills in undistinguished gray
    Melt away—
That a girl with eager eyes and yellow hair
    Waits me there
In the turret whence the charioteers caught soul
    For the goal,
When the king looked, where she looks now, breathless, dumb
    Till I come.

But he looked upon the city, every side,
   Far and wide,
All the mountains topped with temples, all the glades'
   Colonnades,
All the causeys, bridges, aqueducts,—and then,
   All the men!
When I do come, she will speak not, she will stand,
   Either hand
On my shoulder, give her eyes the first embrace
   Of my face,
Ere we rush, ere we extinguish sight and speech
   Each on each.

In one year they sent a million fighters forth
   South and north,
And they built their gods a brazen pillar high
   As the sky,
Yet reserved a thousand chariots in full force—
   Gold, of course.
Oh heart! Oh blood that freezes, blood that burns!
   Earth's returns
For whole centuries of folly, noise and sin!
   Shut them in,
With their triumphs and their glories and the rest!!
   Love is best.

YOUNG AND OLD

Charles Kingsley

When all the world is young, lad,
   And all the trees are green;
And every goose a swan, lad,
   And every lass a queen;
Then hey for boot and horse, lad,
   And round the world away;

>   Young blood must have its course, lad,
>   And every dog his day.
>
> When all the world is old, lad,
>   And all the trees are brown;
> And all the sport is stale, lad,
>   And all the wheels run down:
> Creep home, and take your place there,
>   The spent and maimed among:
> God grant you find one face there,
>   You loved when all was young.

Polarity

Sometimes the contrasted elements seem so far apart that the term *polarity* may be used effectively signifying "as far apart as the poles." Literature is filled with contrasts, such as life and death, kings and clowns, black and white. The mood in one portion may be very different to that of another. Witness how Shakespeare follows tragic scenes with comic, how Longfellow contrasts the peace of the Arcadian village life with the ruthless separations which follow, how Browning contrasts the sweet innocence of Pompilia with the brutal character of Guido Franceschini. Polarity makes the writer's ideas bold and vivid. The creative reader must match the writer's technique with bold tones, bold rhythms, bold changes in pitch, with *polarity*.

Any sudden change in pitch is arresting because it gives contrast. An idea may be intensified by a sudden leap instead of a gradual climb. Octave leaps and octave drops give dramatic, startling effects conducive to an increase in audience interest. For example, *The Taming of the Shrew* offers interesting scenes for the study of polarity. The reader is likely to sense octave leaps from the voice of Petruchio to the voice of Katharine, the shrew, and sometimes in the midst of the speeches of each. Read the lines which follow, testing the effectiveness of octave leaps and drops.[1]

PETRUCHIO. Good morrow, Kate; for that's your name, I hear.
KATHARINE. Well have you heard, but something hard of hearing:
They call me Katharine that do talk of me.
PETRUCHIO. You lie, in faith; for you are called plain Kate.

Read the following speech of Katharine's, observing the effectiveness of an octave leap between the last two words.

KATHARINE. I chafe you, if I tarry: let me *go.*

Read the next speech of Katharine's with a leap on the second word and a quick drop on the phrase which follows:

KATHARINE. Go, *fool,* and whom thou keep'st command.

SPEECH PATTERNS

One frequently hears a speaker criticized for having a *speech pattern*. The suggestion is that he says everything in the same intonation (or with the same geometric form). One speaks of a "ministerial tone" in which every phrase seems to turn up at the end. The pattern might be diagramed as follows:

[1] From Act II, Scene i.

A rather typical reading pattern seems to go like this:

Debaters are said to develop a pattern with a strong downward inflection somewhat the reverse of the ministers:

Speech patterns are gained through environment from many sources, social and professional. The smooth salesman, the gossipy housewife, the giggling girl are all likely to have speech patterns indicative of their modes of life and habits of thinking. The weakness in these modes of speech is due largely to their sameness.

It is easy for all of us to fall into ruts of thinking, speaking, or living. The creative artist puts forth real effort not to fall into such ruts but to keep a creative attitude and to approach each new situation with a childlike freshness of interest. The interpretative reader avoids a speech pattern by creating a *variety of speech patterns*. Changes in speech patterns suggest changes in ideas, it being the ideal of the creative reader to approach the infinite mind which creates a different pattern for every snowflake.

An objective means of breaking up a monotonous pattern in reading and an aid in creating varied patterns expressive of varied ideas is for the student to draw patterns which he conceives adequate for the expression of the ideas in a given piece of literature. These patterns may be drawn for brief phrases only or for portions long enough to show interclausal relations, as was suggested by the diagram of builds for the lyric, "The Year's At the Spring."

A possible pattern for the first sentence of Hamlet's famous soliloquy is as follows:

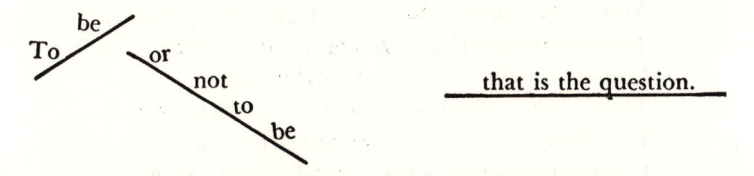

```
        be
To   /    \ or
    /      \  not                    that is the question.
              \ to
                 \ be
```

Draw diagrams for patterns which will express the ideas of the following poems. Practice reading according to your patterns until your voice follows them.

FROM A RAILWAY CARRIAGE
Robert L. Stevenson

Faster than fairies, faster than witches,
Bridges and houses, hedges and ditches;
And charging along like troups in battle,
All through the meadows the horses and cattle:
All of the sights of the hill and the plain
Fly as thick as driving rain;
And ever again, in the wink of an eye,
Painted stations whistle by.

Here is a child who clambers and scrambles,
All by himself and gathering brambles;
Here is a tramp who stands and gazes;
And there is the green for stringing the daisies!
Here is a cart run away in the road
Lumping along with man and load;
And here is a mill and there is a river:
Each a glimpse and gone forever!

ABNEGATION
Christina Rossetti

If there be any one can take my place
And make you happy whom I grieve to grieve,
Think not that I can grudge it, but believe
I do commend you to that nobler grace,
That readier wit than mine, that sweeter face;
Yea, since your riches make me rich, conceive
I too am crowned, while bridal crowns I weave,
And thread the bridal dance with jocund pace.
For if I did not love you, it might be
That I should grudge you some one dear delight;
But since the heart is yours that was mine own,
Your pleasure is my pleasure, right my right,
Your honorable freedom makes me free,
And you companioned I am not alone.

TO A SKYLARK
William Wordsworth

Ethereal minstrel! pilgrim of the sky!
Dost thou despise the earth where cares abound?
Or while the wings aspire, are heart and eye
Both with thy nest upon the dewy ground?
Thy nest which thou canst drop into at will,
Those quivering wings composed, that music still!

To the last point of vision, and beyond
Mount, daring warbler!—that love-promoted strain
—'Twixt thee and thine a never-failing bond—
Thrills not the less the bosom of the plain:
Yet might'st thou seem, proud privilege! to sing
All independent of the leafy Spring.

Leave to the nightingale her shady wood;
A privacy of glorious light is thine,
Whence thou dost pour upon the world a flood
Of harmony, with instinct more divine;
Type of the wise, who soar, but never roam—
True to the kindred points of Heaven and Home.

EMPHASIS AND SUBORDINATION

The interpretative reader needs not only to be aware of general trends and emphasis but to be discreet in perceiving portions to be subordinated. Interpretative reading is like the art of painting in that for adequate perspective most of the picture should be in the background. If the painter tried to emphasize every detail by bringing it into the focus of attention (into the foreground) he would produce a very unnatural effect. This same situation exists when the reader attempts to emphasize every word or attempts to bring every phase of every idea into the foreground of his word picture. Most of the words should be spoken in a subordinate manner providing background and perspective for the comparatively few words or ideas the reader wishes to make emphatic.

The amateur reader may either drone along without emphasizing anything or he may attempt to emphasize too much. Let us take the emphasis of words, for example. One word in a phrase will usually carry the meaning. The other words may be given without stress or even slurred without marring the sense. This principle is illustrated in the scene from *Othello* which follows. For clarity we have italicized the emphatic words. Read the scene aloud, giving emphasis to the words which are italicized.

From OTHELLO [1]

William Shakespeare

IAGO. My noble *lord*,—
OTHELLO. *What* dost thou say, Iago?
IAGO. Did Michael *Cassio,* when you woo'd my lady *Know* of your love?
OTHELLO. He *did,* from the first to last: *why* dost thou ask?
IAGO. But for a satisfaction of my *thought;* No further harm.
OTHELLO. Why of thy *thought,* Iago?
IAGO. I did not think he had been *acquainted* with her.
OTHELLO. O! *Yes;* and went between us very oft.
IAGO. *Indeed!*
OTHELLO. *Indeed!* ay, *indeed; discern'st* thou aught in that? Is he not *honest?*
IAGO. *Honest,* my lord?
OTHELLO. *Honest!* ay, *honest.*
IAGO. My lord, for aught I *know.*
OTHELLO. What dost thou *think?*
IAGO. *Think,* my lord!
OTHELLO. *Think,* my lord!
By heaven, he *echoes* me,
As if there were some *monster* in his thought
Too *hideous* to be shown. Thou dost *mean* something.

To illustrate further the fact that one word often carries the meaning of a phrase, we have reduced the speeches of this scene to key words. Read the dialogue below, thinking the meaning you have found in the author's phrases but uttering the key words only.

[1] Act III, Scene iii.

IAGO.	M'lord.
OTHELLO.	What?
IAGO.	Cassio—know?
OTHELLO.	Yes—why?
IAGO.	Thought.
OTHELLO.	Thought?
IAGO.	Acquainted?
OTHELLO.	Yes.
IAGO.	Indeed?
OTHELLO.	Indeed—honest?
IAGO.	Honest?
OTHELLO.	Honest!
IAGO.	Perhaps.
OTHELLO.	Think?
IAGO.	Think!
OTHELLO.	Think! Echoes—monster—hideous—meaning?

An interesting example of this principle is found in the dialogue *In a Garden* by Frank C. Egan.[1] This dialogue is made up of the emphatic words which might have emerged from sentences or phrases. The words in this dialogue grew out of ideas, the essence of which is expressed not in the usual sentence or phrase but in key words. In order to interpret these key words the reader must think what the character does not say that causes the words which he does say.

Emphasis

Emphasis may be defined as the prominence given to words, syllables, and ideas. The prominence given to the emphatic syllable of a word is called accent. The promi-

[1] Gertrude E. Johnson, *Modern Literature for Oral Interpretation* (New York: D. Appleton–Century Co., Inc., 1920), pp. 190–95.

nence given to a word (in order that emphasis may be given to the meaning of the phrase) is called *sense stress,* which is often referred to merely as *emphasis.* Sense stress usually falls upon one syllable of a phrase only. The accented syllable of the emphatic word carries the stress; the rest of the word is subordinate as is the rest of the phrase. The emphatic word carries the meaning as was illustrated by the dialogue composed entirely of emphatic words.

Read aloud the following sentences emphasizing the syllables written in capitals. Observe how these emphatic syllables carry the meaning and how the subordinate parts give perspective. After testing this principle read the sentences, emphasizing several words or every word and observe how meaning is distorted. One should always end such an experiment with a repetition of the better form, in order that he may cultivate the habit of good form.

> What COLor shall I take upon my brush?
> It led me with its INnocence.
> There's wild aZALea on the hill.
> What was he DOing, the great god Pan?
> They are dragged to the withered BRACKen.

Occasionally for the sake of direct contrast the unaccented syllable is stressed, as,

> I said Apartment, not DEpartment.

Sense Stress and Meter

In reading poetry one finds it necessary to merge sense stress with meter or to discriminate as to which is more important in conveying the author's purpose. In poetry the accented syllable of the word usually carries the metric stress as well as the sense stress.

Whither is fled the visionary gleam.
                              Wordsworth

She was as safe as in a sanctuary.
                            Spencer

Kind solace in a dying hour.
                        Poe

When there is conflict in these various forms of emphasis, the reader's emphasis must be guided by his own discrimination. Some readers place accepted forms of pronunciation above meter in poetry reading; others think meter should take precedence; and others decide in favor of meaning. For example in *As You Like It* the duke says:

Firm and irrevocable is my decree.

The dictionary indicates the pronunciation *irrĕ'vŏcăble* with the accent on the second syllable of the word. Try scanning the line with a metrical stress on that syllable.

Firm and irrevocable is my decree.

Now scan the line with a stress on the third syllable of that word.

Firm and irrevocable is my decree.

Which manner of scansion seems more rhythmical to you? Now give the line the *sense* test. Which accent makes the meaning stronger? Does the force given by emphasis on the third syllable of the word take precedence, in your judgment, over the dictionary pronunciation of the word? This line is read differently by different actors. We have come to appreciate the force in the pronunciation with the emphasis on the third syllable, *ĭrrĕvō'cáble*. The creative reader who assumes the responsibility of interpreter must decide these matters for himself. He may be guided, in emphasis, by his understanding of the meaning and by his judgment of the relative importance of meaning, pronunciation, and meter.

New Ideas Versus Old

It should be observed that the word which gives the new idea is usually the word to be emphasized. For example, in the following series of phrases the emphasis shifts to the new word which brings out a new phase of the idea.

> I have ridden the *wind*.
> I have ridden the *sea*.
> I have ridden the *moon* and *stars*.
> Cale Young Rice

That is an attractive *dress*. It is a *new* dress, a *blue* dress, a *silk* dress.

Echo

When the emphasis shifts to the new idea, the old idea (the idea already in the mind of the reader and audience) is given somewhat in the form of an echo of its first enunciation. In the example given above the word *dress* was stressed the first time and merely echoed the other three times. Effectiveness is often gained by repeating phrases or a portion of a phrase as an echo. Test the effectiveness of echo in the following examples:

LEST WE FORGET, lest we forget.
Rudyard Kipling [1]

IF WE HAD THE TIME, if we had the time.

Read the following poems, testing the effect of the technique of *echo*.

THE OWL
Alfred Tennyson

When cats run home and light is come,
   And dew is cold upon the ground,
And the far-off stream is dumb,
   And the whirring sail goes round;
   And the whirring sail goes round;
     Alone and warming his five wits,
     The white owl in the belfry sits.

When merry milkmaids click the latch,
   And rarely smells the new-mown hay,
And the cock hath sung beneath the thatch
   Twice or thrice his roundelay;
   Twice or thrice his roundelay;
     Alone and warming his five wits,
     The white owl in the belfy sits.

[1] Rudyard Kipling, "Recessional" from *The Five Nations,* London, A. P. Watt & Son; New York, Doubleday, Doran and Company, Inc., 1903, 1931. Reprinted by permission.

LITTLE MAN AND LITTLE SOUL

A Ballad to the Tune of "There was a little man, and he wooed a little maid"

Thomas Moore

There was a little Man and he had a little Soul,
And he said, "Little Soul, let us try, try, try,
Whether it's within our reach
To make up a little Speech,
Just between little you and little I, I, I,
Just between little you and little I!"

Then said his little Soul,
Peeping from her little hole,
I protest, little Man, you are stout, stout, **stout**,
But, if it's not uncivil,
Pray tell me what the devil,
Must our little, little speech be about, 'bout, 'bout,
Must our little, little speech be about?"

. . . . .

The little Man then spoke,
Little Soul, it is no joke,
For as sure as Jacky Fuller loves a sup, sup, sup,
I will tell the Prince and People
What I think of Church and Steeple,
And my little patent plan to prop them up, up, **up**,
And my little patent plan to prop them up."

Away then, cheek by jowl,
Little Man and little Soul
Went and spoke their little speech to a tittle, tittle, tittle,
And the world all declare
That this priggish little pair
Never yet in all their lies lookt so little, little, little,
Never yet in all their lives lookt so little!

THE SONG OF THE SHIRT
Thomas Hood

With fingers weary and worn,
  With eyelids heavy and red,
A woman sat, in unwomanly rags,
  Plying her needle and thread—
Stitch! stitch! stitch!
  In poverty, hunger, and dirt,
And still with a voice of dolorous pitch
  She sang the 'Song of the Shirt.'

'Work! work! work!
  While the cock is crowing aloof!
And work—work—work,
  Till the stars shine through the roof!
It's Oh! to be a slave
  Along with the barbarous Turk,
Where woman has never a soul to save,
  If this is Christian work!

'Work—work—work,
  Till the brain begins to swim;
Work—work—work,
  Till the eyes are heavy and dim!
Seam, and gusset, and band.
  Band, and gusset, and seam,
Till over the buttons I fall asleep.
  And sew them on in a dream!

'Oh, Men with Sisters dear!
  Oh, Men with Mothers and Wives!
It is not linen you're wearing out
  But human creatures' lives!
Stitch—stitch—stitch,
  In poverty, hunger, and dirt,

Sewing at once, with a double thread,
A Shroud as well as a Shirt.

'Work—work—work!
My labor never flags;
And what are its wages? A bed of straw,
A crust of bread—and rags.
That shattered roof—this naked floor—
A table—a broken chair—
And a wall so blank, my shadow I thank
For sometimes falling there!

'Work—work—work!
From weary chime to chime,
Work—work—work,
As prisoners work for crime!
Band, and gusset, and seam,
Seam, and gusset, and band,
Till the heart is sick, and the brain benumbed,
As well as the weary hand.'

With fingers weary and worn,
With eyelids heavy and red,
A woman sat, in unwomanly rags,
Plying her needle and thread—
Stitch! stitch! stitch!
In poverty, hunger, and dirt,
And still with a voice of dolorous pitch—
Would that its tone could reach the Rich!—
She sang this 'Song of the Shirt!'

Unity and Emphasis

The interpretative reader's understanding of the principle of emphasis should not be limited to stress given to syllables, words, or even to phrases. Emphasis and subordination have a larger significance. The creative artist sees every portion of his work in relation to every other portion. The reader must have a grasp of his material as a whole. Every piece of literature should have a central thought, a theme, an idea which should be emphasized above all other ideas. Through subordinating other thoughts to the central thought the reader achieves a perspective, or unity in emphasis.

The Central Thought

The painter gives emphasis to his central figure by various devices, such as placing it in the foreground, and through such media as light and shade, lines, and color. The creative reader gives emphasis to the central thought by similar devices, such as changes in tempo, rhythm, pitch, pause, force, and climax. Through balance, harmony and contrast the painter brings his central figure into the focus of attention. Through balance, harmony, and contrast the reader gives emphasis to the central thought and relative subordination to all other ideas.

One of the first steps in interpretative reading is to decide what is the author's central thought. Have you observed that the central thought of this textbook is that interpretative reading must have both form and spirit, with the spirit predominant? The student should train himself to perceive the author's central thought and to keep it in mind as he prepares his reading. It is well for the student to state the central thought of various types of literature in a single sentence. What is the central thought in "To a Waterfowl," the scene from *The School for Scandal,* and "The Eagle"?

The Dominant Unity

We have borrowed the term *dominant unity* from Professor Mallory because it expresses so clearly an important phase of the interpretative reader's analysis. We cannot do better, here, than to quote somewhat at length Professor Mallory's explanation.

Every well-written composition has a dominant unity, a single, main impression which the author wishes to establish, or a purpose which he wishes to serve and to which everything else is subordinate. As quickly as possible, the reader should determine what this dominant unity is, for it is only by recognizing it that he can evaluate the whole. The dominant unity may be a general idea or theme. It may consist of a specific, logical proposition. It may be a mood, an attitude, or an emotion. Sometimes it is a character. It may be nothing more than a situation. Whatever it is, the reader should recognize it and respond to it constantly as he reads. If it is explicitly stated by the author himself, its recognition is, of course, easy. Frequently the problem is more complex. The dominant unity must be inferred from what the characters say or do, or from the general organization and structure of the material. The reader must be alert for every sign that points to the single response which the author wants the reader to carry away with him as the most important element of the composition.

The reader must recognize, too, just what the nature of that response should be. Sometimes the central idea or the main proposition must be explicitly stated in its logical entirety before it can be adequately grasped. Sometimes the chief characteristics of the mood, attitude, atmosphere, feeling, character, or situation can only be described. It is an error to attempt to reduce every type of material to the logical exactness of a legal brief. Much imaginative literature may be ruined if this approach is used. It is also an error to be vague about what the author is driving at merely because the main element of the whole composition has been missed. The reader should check his grasp of the dominant unity by expressing it in writing. State it in a logical proposition if the nature of the material permits. Give a succinct description of its essential characteristics if it cannot be reduced to logical expression. The proposition or description should include all the essential elements contained in the dominant unity.[1]

Means of Emphasis

As suggested several times in our discussions, there are various devices for emphasis. The most obvious is loudness, and it is, perhaps, the least subtle; a soft tone may prove quite as emphatic as a loud one. If one has been talking in a loud voice, a sudden change to softness may prove an effective means of giving emphasis. This suggestion indicates contrast, which has been mentioned before as a means of emphasis, as have changes in pitch, rhythm, tempo, and pause. At a later time we shall discuss changes in tone. It is important for the interpretative reader to use many devices and thus to present a more colorful picture than he would give should he think of emphasis in terms of mere loudness or force.

[1] Louis A. Mallory, "Reading Aloud" in *Foundations of Speech,* ed. James M. O'Neill (New York: Prentice-Hall, Inc., 1941), pp. 271–72. By permission.

Chapter VI

ILLUSION IN INTERPRETATIVE READING

The attempt at high adventure brings reward undreamt.[1]
John Masefield

How far should one go in perfecting his form for interpretative reading? Perfection of form is an ideal toward which most artists work. Opinions differ, however, as to whether it is desirable for a reader to develop a fixed form. Spontaneity is certainly an essential for creative reading. Flashes of insight come to the reader out of the environment of the specific occasion, lending impressiveness which studied form could not achieve. But is it necessary for a carefully developed form to appear studied?

As long as form demands a portion of a reader's thinking it is likely to be within the consciousness of the audience also. Audience consciousness of the means by which the reader achieves his effect is usually considered objectionable. When, however, the form becomes so familiar, so habitual, so *crystallized* that the reader may devote his thinking to the concept, then is not the reader free to react with spontaneity, trusting to the illumination of the moment? Professor Lyman compares the skilled reader's freedom to that of the musician.

[1] John Masefield, "The Ending," in *The Wanderer of Liverpool* (New York: The Macmillan Company). By permission of the publishers.

We can use a parallel in learning to read music. A pretty painful process it is, that laborious picking out of the proper keys when one first begins! Gradually the difficulty disappears. Finally the musician sits at his instrument and runs his hands lightly over the keyboard, unconsciously performing with rapidity and skill acts which were once painfully slow. He now reads mere notes and phrases without effort and executes them with ease. His mind is free to dwell upon what the composer is saying, what the music means. In other words, the skilled performer's mind goes beyond the mechanics, into the realm of interpretation. He thinks, feels, lives his music. In a somewhat similar way, a skilled reader goes beyond symbols, and thinks, feels, and lives the meanings of the printed page.[1]

CRYSTALLIZATION

Let us consider carefully the significance of crystallization in the interpretative reader's technique. According to Webster's dictionary crystallization means the "process of assuming a fixed and definite form." Since there is some question as to the desirability of a fixed form in interpretative reading let us look further into the definition. We find "to assume a crystalline character." Now, crystalline is defined as "transparent." If the reader's form by becoming fixed becomes transparent, so that through it the thought is revealed with clarity, then surely crystallization is desirable for the reader's technique.

It seems apparent that mechanical reading results not so much from crystallization of form as from the reader's concentration on form. According to Amy Lowell, "Art becomes

[1] R. L. Lyman, *The Mind at Work* (Chicago: Scott, Foresman and Co., 1924), p. 15. By permission of the publishers.

artificial only when form takes precedence over spirit."[1] When a reader has practiced upon his form until he is sure of it, he may be more free to concentrate upon the spirit. Crystallization may then be a means by which he achieves spontaneity in his reading.

Let us consider certain elements of form concerning which there is little doubt of the value of crystallization. Take, for example, the pronunciation of difficult words. As long as the reader's concentration is upon vowel or consonant sounds, accent, or syllabification, the word is weakened as a carrier of meaning. When pronunciation becomes crystallized, the reader's concentration can be focused upon the significance of the word. When words and phrases have become so much a part of a reader's thinking that his manner of speaking them is habitual, then they should be transparent so far as audience attention upon the reader's manner of saying them is concerned. This transparency permits awareness of content for both reader and audience, relieving both of consciousness of form.

The need of crystallization is obvious for the reading of dialect. In learning a dialect one must drill upon speech sounds, accent, and rhythm. As the dialect becomes crystallized the reader may concentrate more upon the mental and emotional attitudes of the character. The character, with his thoughts, feelings, reactions, is of primary importance in dialect reading. The dialect is a means of revealing the character—his background and processes of thinking. When the reader's technique of speaking the dialect becomes crystallized then the dialect becomes a

[1] Amy Lowell, *Tendencies in Modern Poetry* (Boston: Houghton Mifflin Company), p. 7. By permission of the publishers.

medium for revealing the thoughts and feelings of the character.

Let the student test the value of crystallization further by reviewing his experience with some of the techniques already presented in this book. Have the techniques that have been suggested served to free the imagination? Have they stimulated your thinking? Does the fact that your form has, to some extent, become crystallized add freedom in revealing the spirit of literature? As the form has become easier, more habitual, more crystallized has concentration upon the essence become easier, more habitual? Your *process of thinking* will determine whether crystallization results in mechanical reading or in transparency through which the essence is made more clear and your reading made more spontaneous.

THE ILLUSION OF THE FIRST TIME

The student may achieve spontaneity in creative oral reading by keeping in mind the ideal of dramatic art known as the illusion of the first time. It is the ideal of the actor to give each movement, each word, each idea as if it had occurred to him for the first time at the moment of delivery. He wishes to react to each idea with such freshness of appreciation that he gives the illusion that the significance of the idea has just flashed upon him. The spontaneous reaction which remains with the artist after the form has become crystallized is known as *the illusion of the first time*.

Walter Hampden says that at times while playing a scene on which he has worked for perfection of form he is tempted to think of how he is doing it. This, he says, is bad. He casts aside the temptation and trusts to "the illumination of the moment." "The illumination which comes to the actor in moments of creative expression is," he states, "worth all the self-discipline, all the privations, which great art demands from its creator."[1]

As the student of interpretative reading drills upon elements of technique and works for crystallization of form let him also, *at the same time,* work to retain the illumination which gives the illusion of the first time. Let him realize that *form is born of spirit,* that adequate form and spontaneous response grow together, and that each is incomplete without the other. Let him not be satisfied with less than the finest art of reading, which is achieved by perfection of form coördinated with sincere, spontaneous response.

The student of interpretative reading should resolve that each time he reads he will capture, or recapture, that spontaneity which gives the illusion of the first time. Let him realize the truth of art, that the most carefully planned techniques may appear accidental; the most studied effects must appear careless. The interpretative reader's effects should be comparable to that of the thrush as described by Robert Browning:

> . . . he sings each song twice over,
> Lest you should think he never could recapture
> That first fine careless rapture!

RESTRAINT

Restraint has been suggested many times already as an essential in interpretative reading. When asked his opinion

[1] Phonetic Transcription of Walter Hampden, Windsor P. Daggett, *The Spoken Word Course* (New York: The Daggett Studio Publications, 1936), p. 43. By permission.

of the art of acting, John Galsworthy said that all he knew could be summed up in the one word, restraint. Shakespeare suggests the need for restraint when, in the speech to the players, Hamlet says,

> Nor do not saw the air too much with your hand, thus; but use all gently: for in the very torrent, tempest, and, as I may say, whirlwind of passion, you must acquire and beget a temperance that may give it smoothness. O! it offends me to the soul to hear a robustious periwig-pated fellow tear a passion to tatters, to very rags, to split the ears of the groundlings, who for the most part are capable of nothing but inexplicable dumb show and noise. I would have such a fellow whipped for o'er-doing Termagant. It out-herods Herod. Pray you, avoid it.

It is the purpose of art to awaken feeling in others—not to make a display of itself. When an emotion is overdone it is likely to call the attention of the audience to the performance rather than to arouse feeling in the audience. The student is no doubt familiar with a certain type of religious worker who weeps over his story of unfortunates, causing the audience to pity him instead of being moved by the story itself. The audience feels sorry for such a speaker because he does not have more control over his own emotions. Occasionally, however, one hears a speaker whose voice and manner are quiet and controlled but who so projects feeling to the audience that they are moved to weep. Such a speaker uses restraint, or what Hamilton Wright Mabie calls "noble balance."

The Classical writers, with their delicate sense of proportion, harmony, and form, never attempted to pass beyond the limits of a sound art; they were sometimes formal and cold, but they were never tumultuous, unbalanced, and lawless. In Sophocles, for instance, one never loses consciousness of the presence of a genius which, dealing with the most perplexing and terrible questions of destiny, is never tempted to pass the bounds of clear and definite artistic expression, but sustains the theme to the end with a masterful self-restraint and majesty of repose. In that noble balance, based on the harmony, not on the subjection of the heart and mind of the artist, one gets a glimpse of one of the great ends of art; which is not to express but to suggest that which transcends human thought and speech. For the great play, statue, picture, speech are prophetic, and find their fulfilment, not in themselves, but in the imagination which comes under their spell; the more complete their beauty, therefore, the more powerfully do they affirm the existence of a beauty beyond themselves. The definiteness of Greek art was not a limitation; it was a source of transcendent power.[1]

The old problem of whether an actor should feel or should merely pretend to feel his part is still argued. Actors usually agree that one should not feel to the extent that he loses control and allows feeling to run away with him; he must not go on an emotional debauch. So must the creative reader develop discretion as to the amount of feeling in which he indulges. The highest compliment the public can pay an artist is that he performed with ease. Controlled, effortless performance invites admiration. *The maximum of effect with the minimum of effort* is the ideal of the creative reader as it is of the actor, the champion golfer, the painter, or the musician.

Restraint does not mean a lack of feeling. Some students

[1] From *My Study Fire,* by Hamilton Wright Mabie. Reprinted by permission of the publishers, Dodd, Mead & Company, Inc.

claim that they are using restraint when they are impassive, even cold or indifferent. The word itself suggests otherwise; restraint means to hold back. The race horse needs to be restrained; when a horse is running away he is in need of restraint. So with emotion: the greater the feeling the more need for restraint. When the reader so controls the evidence of feeling that the feeling appears to be stronger than the expression, he may be said to use restraint. When the audience senses that the feeling is greater than the means by which it is projected, they feel that there is restraint.

Restraint might be called the "art which conceals art." It is most needed when there is the greatest amount of abandon, just as control is essential where there is most freedom. Freedom and control pulling against each other give proportion. Strong feeling held in check by restraint gives balance.

Abandon

Students of interpretative reading usually need to work for abandon before they can understand the nature of restraint; they need first to develop something to be restrained. Until one has vitalized his concepts and abandoned himself to feeling, he is hardly ready for a technique of restraint. It is often advisable, in the beginning, for the student of interpretative reading to overdo, even to exaggerate feeling. When he has experienced abandon he is then ready to draw in the feeling, or at least the expression of the feeling. Effective restraint might be compared with the effect of keeping a cap on a bottle when the contents within are seeking to push it out. That is the feeling one has in creative reading when the feeling is so strong it requires utmost control for the reader to restrain it. After such reading members of the audience may express the intensity of their own reactions by saying to the reader, "But you were so calm, I don't see how you did it."

Reread some of the material you have worked on and see how effectively you can use restraint. Bear in mind that feeling is one's greatest power in influencing others; when held in check by restraint it becomes power under control.

AESTHETIC DISTANCE

Aesthetic distance suggests a detachment which characterizes great art. The painter frames his picture to set it off from its surroundings and give to it a certain distance. For the same reason the sculptor places his statue on a pedestal. In the theater the proscenium frames the stage picture. Distance between the stage and the audience adds to the illusion by giving perspective. What, then, of aesthetic distance in creative oral reading? Dolman says that the essential difference between acting and reading is a matter of aesthetic distance. In the theater the distance is between the audience and the stage, or the actor.

In reading, the audience and reader are one, enjoying the book together. There is aesthetic distance, but the reader and the audience are on the same end of it; the book is on the other. The reader is really one of the audience, in constant communication with the rest and sharing his enjoyment of the reading with them. Being in possession of the book—or of the memorized text—he is in a situation of leadership, but he is in no sense a part of the book himself; there is no pretense or illusion about his identity, and no detachment in his audience's attitude toward him. He may go very far in enlivening his reading by play of voice, gesture, and facial expression, so long as what he does is clearly suggestion; but he must avoid an attitude of exhibition.[1]

This statement of Dolman's seems to us to uphold the technique suggested throughout this textbook, namely: that the reader should think of his material, not as being *on* the stage with him as does the actor, but *off* stage, perhaps on or beyond the back wall of the room. Both reader and audience should picture the scenes before them. They are not a part of the scene, but they share the scene: they react to the scene *together*. For the reader to objectify the experiences of the literature he interprets by placing mental pictures as far away from him as the back wall of the room establishes with certainty a distance between the reader and his material. It gives him freedom to share his reactions with the audience but never to become a part of the scene itself.

Contrast the effect of this technique with the effect of readers you have heard who thought of their material as on the stage with them and considered themselves a part of the performance. Were they not continually in the consciousness of the audience, blocking at times the audience's visualization of the concepts of the literature? Did you ever feel that a reader was constantly getting between you and the imaginative concept, taking your mind off of the author's concept and focusing attention on himself, as reader?

Some readers seem to have a mixed point of view, giving descriptions and narration with off-stage technique (visualizing with definite distance), but giving characterizations

---

[1] John Dolman, Jr., *The Art of Play Production* (New York: Harper and Brothers, 1928), pp. 41–2. Reprinted by permission of Harper and Brothers.

on-stage. They continually shift their point of view from reader to actor and back and forth to their own confusion and to that of the audience. It is little wonder that the art of oral reading has come into bad repute and caused so many to say they abhor the word *recitation*.

As a first requisite in maintaining aesthetic distance in interpretative reading we suggest the off-stage point of view. Let the student keep an objective attitude toward his material reacting to the sights, sounds, and characters, but never acting them; visualizing scenes as far away as the back wall, but *never on* the stage with him. Let him keep the point of view of the reader, the storyteller, the narrator, but never the actor. He may go as far as his own temperament, enthusiasm, or discretion dictates in suggesting characters and actions and in empathizing with them just so long as he keeps the point of view of sharing reactions *with* the audience and not of performing them *for* the audience.

Chapter VII

VOICE IN INTERPRETATIVE READING

> Surely whoever speaks to me in the right voice, him or her I shall follow, as the waters follow the moon silently with fluid steps, anywhere around the globe.
> *Walt Whitman*

Interpretative reading implies a speaking voice which attracts the listener as a magnet attracts a needle. It may seem strange that a book on interpretative reading should delay so long in introducing the subject of voice, since voice is so utterly essential in conveying moods, ideas, concepts. There are several reasons for this delay, the chief one of which is that it is presupposed that students of interpretative reading will have had some elementary training in voice and diction. It was suggested in the Foreword that no textbook is adequate without supplementary work from the teacher. It was expected that the teacher would build the course of study around the individual students, strengthening them here and there as special needs were made evident. One problem in presenting techniques of an art is that many techniques must be applied simultaneously if the student is to develop naturally, that is, as a whole. Interpretative reading infers the coördinated use of body, voice, and language guided by the thought content of the literature one chooses to read.

Interpretative reading presents an interesting and constructive cycle for the speaking voice. A good voice is essential for adequate oral interpretation of literature, and the oral expression of moods, and universal thoughts expressed in choice language refines the speaking voice. So while the student is challenged to use the voice which adequately expresses his concept, at the same time he improves his voice as a medium for the expression of concepts. While a good voice is needed through which to interpret noble thoughts, the expression of noble thoughts in turn tends to purify the tones.

Since vocal quality is an index to a speaker's total, or emotional, response, it follows that the reader's first necessity is a voice of good timbre. Such a voice depends first upon an adequate voice instrument and second upon a magnetic personality. Some of the attributes of a magnetic personality are kindness, tolerance, appreciation, and unselfish interest in others. Interpretative reading presents a very practical way of developing such a personality as each step deals with the process of sharing an appreciation of literature with others. Interpretative reading focuses attention upon percepts and concepts and upon the projection of these to others.

Let us think of some types of voice and of how they reflect the personality of the individual. What type of voice, for example, would you create for Xantippe, the scolding wife of Socrates, or for Maggie, who upbraids Jiggs on the funny page? It is obvious that the voice of a scold is high pitched, shrill and rasping. What type of voice would you create for Iago, the fawning hypocrite of Shakespeare's *Othello?* What kind of voice would you use to suggest Romeo, or Juliet, or Portia? A little contemplation on the character of each gives an idea of the type of voice which would suggest the personality.

In thinking of your own voice, then, you naturally desire a good voice expressive of your best yet suggestive of the personality which is essentially *you*. Each person has a normal voice quality which is suggestive of his individuality. It is by this individual quality that his voice is recognized on the telephone, the radio, or in the next room. This quality is *unique;* it sets one apart as an individual; at its optimum it is desirable and distinctive in interpretative reading. No amount of training should take from you that individuality, that complex arrangement of personal attributes which is *you*. In fact, training in interpretative reading, and specifically training in voice, should increase the difference between your voice and that of others; training should release and build the individuality of a voice.

An adequate voice instrument depends first upon the instrument itself and second upon one's use of the instrument. One's voice instrument depends first upon the bodily structure and psychical tendencies given him by his forebears and second upon what he does with this body and these tendencies. Most of us have inherited normal bodies and hence normal voice instruments; we can do much to keep them so and to improve them by proper use. Children often have beautiful voices which carry like the tinkle of a silver bell, and the secrets of good voice technique can be found in the use normal children make of their voices. Breath comes from the center of the body, their throats are relaxed, their tones are well placed, and overtones are formed in open resonant cavities until the inhibitions of life upset these normal conditions. It is the ideal of the creative artist to keep the childlike attitude, and it is the desire of the creative reader to keep or to regain the normal, natural, use of the speaking voice.

The interpretative reader's voice technique should consist of a coördinated adjustment of the phases of voice control. Dr. Weaver gives a clear summation of the factors of voice control as follows:

> It would be impossible to give a complete inventory of all the factors which affect vocalization. However, there are four principal psychological and physiological elements involved in the control of the mechanism: *hearing, intelligence, emotional sensitivity, and neuro-muscular co-ordination.*[1]

It has for some time been recognized that the ear guides the voice. One speaks of "a good ear" for music—of "perfect pitch." The interpretative reader must become sensitive to tone quality for its own value (whether pleasing or not) and its value in projecting meaning.

Flexibility of tone is as essential as a good normal tone for interpretative reading. Flexibility has already been suggested in connection with changes of pitch and volume for climax and with variety for speech patterns. We now come to a consideration of tone *quality* in influencing the thinking of others. Many readers seem to depend largely upon words to carry meaning, underestimating the significance of tone. Words are important and when rightly used go far in communicating ideas, but when words and tones denote different feeling, the listener is inclined to believe the tone. One may say, "I'll pay you next week" and receive the

---

[1] Andrew Thomas Weaver, *Speech, Forms and Principles* (New York: Longmans, Green and Co., 1942), p. 192. By permission of the publishers.

answer, "Oh, yeah!" The second speaker suggests meaning contrary to that implied by the words. A boy may chuckle with pleasure when a girl says to him, "You mean thing. I just hate you." His pleasure is in response to her tone which undoubtedly suggests a friendly rather than an antagonistic attitude. Literature is rife with examples of feminine sagacity in which "no" really signifies "yes." The proverb, "A soft answer turneth away wrath, but grievous words stir up anger" may well be considered as referring to tone, for it is the tone of anger more than words which really provokes wrath.

When tones and words suggest the same mood speech becomes truly effective. There is a natural coördination between tone and words, though people occasionally develop the habit of habitual tones which do not express their exact meaning. One may occasionally say, "Oh, he sounds hard but he really is not. Underneath that gruff exterior he has a warm heart."

TONE COLOR

The interpretative reader should cultivate the habit of speaking in tones which express the exact mood of the words. When a reader's tones convey the feeling of the words, they may be said to have tone color. Tone color is to the reader what onomatopoeia (sound suggestive of sense) is to poetry. By thinking the significance of the word as he speaks it, the creative reader may give to the tone the quality, or color, which conveys the exact meaning. The tone in which one says the word *hard* should suggest hardness; the tone used in saying *soft* should suggest softness.

Winston Churchill gave an excellent example of the

projection of meaning through tone color when in his speech before the Congress of the United States he spoke of Mussolini. Surely none who heard him failed to get the contempt in the tone as he said the word "Mussolini." The quick audience response was due not to the word, but to the expressive tone through which the word was uttered.

The secret of tone color is found in sincere and earnest thinking coupled with good psycho-physical coördination. Through the practice of the technique of tone color together with a technique of good tone production the reader may develop a voice of sufficient flexibility and warmth to express delicate shades of meaning. The creative reader may develop the *habit* of expressing meaning by tone color with a voice which responds quickly and with discrimination to the exact atmosphere which the word is intended to convey.

Read the following passages, seeking to give tones which express the exact moods the words convey. Be on the alert for tone contrasts even within the phrase.

SONNET

William Shakespeare

When in disgrace with fortune and men's eyes
I all alone beweep my outcast state,
And trouble deaf heaven with my bootless cries,
And look upon myself, and curse my fate,
Wishing me like to one more rich in hope,
Featur'd like him, like him with friends possess'd,
Desiring this man's art, and that man's scope,
With what I most enjoy contented least;
Yet in these thoughts myself almost despising,
Haply I think on thee,—and then my state,
Like to the lark at break of day arising

From sullen earth, sings hymns at heaven's gate;
  For thy sweet love remember'd such wealth brings
That then I scorn to change my state with kings.

THE BEE AND THE FLOWER
Alfred Tennyson

The bee buzz'd up in the heat.
'I am faint for your honey, my sweet.'
The flower said 'Take it, my dear,
For now is the spring of the year.
    So come, come!'
      'Hum!'
And the bee buzz'd down from the heat.

And the bee buzz'd up in the cold
When the flower was wither'd and old.
'Have you still any honey, my dear?'
She said 'It's the fall of the year,
    But come, come!'
      'Hum!'
And the bee buzz'd off in the cold.

From I WAS BORN AN AMERICAN
Daniel Webster

I was born an American; I live an American; I shall die an American; and I intend to perform the duties incumbent upon me in that character to the end of my career. I mean to do this with absolute disregard of personal consequences. What are the personal consequences? What is the individual man, with all the good or evil that may betide him, in comparison with the good or evil which may befall a great country, and in the midst of great transactions which concern that country's fate?

Let the consequences be what they will, I am careless. No man can suffer too much, and no man can fall too soon, if he suffer or if he fall in the defense of the liberties and constitution of his country.

A VOICE SPOKE OUT OF THE SKIES
Alfred Tennyson

A voice spoke out of the skies
To a just man and a wise—
'The world and all within it
Will only last a minute!'
And a beggar began to cry
'Food, food or I die!'
Is it worth his while to eat,
Or mine to give him meat,
If the world and all within it
Were nothing the next minute?

KING LEAR'S DEFIANCE
From KING LEAR [1]
William Shakespeare

Rumble thy bellyful! Spit, fire! Spout, rain!
Nor rain, wind, thunder, fire, are my daughters:
I tax not you, you elements, with unkindness;
I never gave you kingdom, call'd you children,
You owe me no subscription: then let fall
Your horrible pleasure; here I stand, your slave,
A poor, infirm, weak, and despised old man:
But yet I call you servile ministers,
That have with two pernicious daughters joined
Your high engender'd battles 'gainst a head
So old and white as this. O! O! 'tis foul!

[1] Act III, Scene ii.

MELODY

The interpretative reader needs not only a good, normal voice quality, a voice sufficiently flexible for tone color, but also a communicative and pleasing speech melody. The so-called reading tone which is monotonous, whether high or low in pitch, will never adequately convey the meaning of literature. This reading tone is the result of an artificial mental attitude. The student of interpretative reading who has followed the techniques thus far has, no doubt, already overcome tendencies toward such an unnatural tone, for the reading tone indicates a lack of clear and creative thinking, and creative thinking breaks down monotonous vocal tendencies.

Speech melody may be defined as the modulation of the voice from one pitch to another. The ideal of the interpretative reader is that his voice shall be modulated in response to the idea the written form conveys. In normal conversation the voice is inclined to move up and down the scale in response to the ideas or moods one wishes to communicate. The interpretative reader frequently wishes his melody to resemble that of simple, normal, everyday conversation; but sometimes he desires his melody to suggest idealized conversation such as is suggested in the balcony scenes from *Romeo and Juliet* and *Cyrano de Bergerac*. For such scenes the reader may wish a song-like melody which lifts speech above the plane of everyday life into the realm of idealization. A song-like melody is often used in the reading of poetry, especially the lyric.

Speech melody seldom follows as definite a pattern as song, and hence the tune is not as easy to represent. It is sometimes helpful, however, for the student to trace speech melody with drawings or with body movements. As a means of developing flexibility of voice and sensitivity to melody it is advisable that students experiment with diagrams suggestive of the voice modulation they think adequate for the expression of specific ideas. The sinuous line should be used for diagrams of speech melody. In the diagrams for climax and emphasis we used straight lines to suggest the general direction. A more complete suggestion of the voice movement would have called for sinuous lines. The student will recall that the curved line was used to suggest the melody of the minister's and debater's patterns, the modulation of which may not be bad except for the sameness of pattern.[1]

Inflection

Inflection may be defined as the modulation on a sustained tone within a syllable or as *vocal slide*. There are two general classifications of inflection, the upward and downward. Upward inflections suggest that the thought is incomplete, indefinite, or indecisive. The downward suggests that the thought is complete, or final. Inflection is caused by a state of mind, either specific or general. There is a characteristic tendency of individuals, localities, and languages. The modern American is said to overdo the downward inflection. Poetry usually calls for much upward inflection, or a general trend upward. It is advisable for the student to give some thought to inflection, but let him be sure to work from the cause to the effect. Inflection like all of these other techniques is a natural way of expressing intellectual and emotional attitudes. We used inflection and

[1] See pp. 151–152.

tone to express our meaning before we had a vocabulary of words. Language is acquired, but inflections are natural.

Punctuation and Inflections

Punctuation marks are an aid in finding the meaning and hence in guiding inflections. Punctuation, however, must not be depended upon as an infallible guide. For example, students are sometimes told to lift their voices at interrogation marks and to drop them at periods. Now the interrogation mark does indicate incompleteness of thought, but the question may be in the first portion and the last word before the interrogation mark may suggest a positive mental attitude. The words *where, who, what, why* may at times be given with an upward and at other times with a downward inflection. Likewise a period may indicate that the sentence is complete, yet the general mental attitude may be one of indecision and incompleteness. Much of poetry should be read with an upward inflection. Some people like the chanting of poetry. It is partly a matter of taste and partly a matter of discrimination as to the poet's meaning. Punctuation is for grammatical construction, which is to be observed by the eye, and inflection is for the ear; they differ just enough for the reader to need to be on the alert for more significant cues to the author's meaning.

For example, read the lines from the poem "Whoa" by an anonymous author:

> Whoa, confound ye! Can't ye give
> Me a peek at that there wren
> Fussin' underneath the eaves—
> Goin' t' build her nest again?

The interrogation mark is placed after the word *again*, though it is rather clear that the last line of this stanza is a statement rather than a question. The question comes earlier in the stanza. There may be an upward trend in the voice through the word *eaves*, but there should be a downward trend on the last line.

TONE COPYING

Tone copying is a helpful device in interpretative reading when the reader has difficulty in deciding upon the tone or inflection for the author's meaning. In tone copying the reader translates the meaning of the passage into familiar words, then while speaking his own words he listens to the tone and inflection he uses to express the meaning. When he has expressed the meaning adequately in his own words he then reads the author's words, copying the tone he used when he expressed the thought in familiar words. By copying the tones and inflections used when speaking familiar words, the reader may make the use of the author's language appear natural. Eventually, through tone copying, the author's language may become quite as natural as, and even more meaningful than, one's own words. Let the student observe that the technique of tone copying is not the copying of another's tone or inflection but the copying of one's own when one expresses the author's meaning in more familiar words than the author's language.

No textbook can give much more than a general idea of voice. Voice training calls for a patient teacher with a good ear and a background of knowledge and experience. Voice recording proves an objective aid in procuring adequate voice and in detecting vocal flaws. A mirror is helpful in detecting faults in the manipulation of tongue, lips, et cetera.

VOICES [1]

Walt Whitman

Now I make a leaf of Voices—for I have found nothing mightier than they are,
And I have found that no word spoken, but is beautiful, in its place.

O what is it in me that makes me tremble so at voices?

Surely, whoever speaks to me in the right voice, him or her I shall follow, as the water follows the moon, silently, with fluid steps, any where around the globe.

Now I believe that all waits for the right voices;
Where is the practis'd and perfect organ? Where is the develop'd Soul?
For I see every word utter'd thence has deeper, sweeter, new sounds, impossible on less terms.

I see brains and lips closed—I see tympans and temples unstruck,
Until that comes which has the quality to strike and to unclose,
Until that comes which has the quality to bring forth what lies slumbering, forever ready, in all words.

What am I after all, but a child, pleased with the sound of my own name? repeating it over and over,
I cannot tell why it affects me so much, when I hear it from women's voices, and from men's voices, or from my own voice,
I stand apart to hear—it never tires me.

[1] From *Leaves of Grass* (Philadelphia: David McKay Company, 1900). By permission.

To you, your name also,
Did you think there was nothing but two or three pronuncia
tions in the sound of your name?

ORATOR PUFF

Thomas Moore

Mr. Orator Puff had two tones to his voice,
The one squeaking *thus*, and the other down *so;*
In each sentence he uttered he gave you your choice,
For one half was B alt, and the rest G below.
    Oh! Oh! Orator Puff,
One voice for an orator's surely enough!

But he still talked away, spite of coughs and of frowns,
So distracting all ears with his *ups* and his *downs,*
That a wag once, on hearing the orator say,
"My voice is for war"; asked him "Which of them, pray?"
    Oh! Oh! Orator Puff,
One voice for an orator's surely enough!

Reeling homeward one evening, top-heavy with gin,
And rehearsing his speech on the weight of the crown,
He tripped near a saw-pit, and tumbled right in,—
"Sinking fund," his last words as his noddle came down.
    Oh! Oh! Orator Puff!
One voice for an orator's surely enough!

"Oh, save!" he exclaimed in his he-and-she tones,
"Help me out! help me out!—I have broken my bones!"
"Help you out!" said a Paddy who passed, "what a bother!
Why, there's two of you there; can't you help one another?"
    Oh! Oh! Orator Puff,
One voice for an orator's surely enough!

ON THE LIFE OF MAN
Francis Beaumont

Like to the falling of a star,
Or as the flights of eagles are,
Or like the fresh spring's gaudy hue,
Or silver drops of morning dew,
Or like a wind that chafes the flood,
Or bubbles which on water stood:
Even such is Man, whose borrowed light
Is straight called in and paid tonight.
The wind blows out, the bubble dies,
The spring entombed in autumn lies;
The dew's dried up, the star is shot,
The flight is past,—and man forgot.

DICTION

The term *diction* used in its broadest sense may include both choice of word and phrase and the speech sounds which one uses in uttering words and phrases. The dictionary recognizes two meanings in its definitions: "choice of words for the expression of ideas" and "mode of verbal expression." In the speech field we use the term *diction* in its oral sense and oftentimes limit it to the choice of speech sounds. One's diction, then, in interpretative reading may mean the manner of speech as regards pronunciation and articulation.

In considering diction, the thought of speech standards naturally arises. Is there a standard for spoken English? If so is it desirable for students of interpretative reading to adhere to that standard? A group of British scholars at one time decided upon a speech which they called Standard English. This speech was that of the educated people of southern England. It is recorded, as far as words are concerned, in *An English Pronouncing Dictionary* by Daniel Jones.[1] Some interpretative readers have thought it advisable to adopt this speech for the platform, and some have chosen it for general communication.

American speech differs in so many respects from the speech of southern England that many students and teachers have preferred to use the speech of their own locality. Dr. Wise divides America into three speech regions: Eastern, Southern, and General American. Concerning the problem in the teaching of speech Dr. Wise states:

> We may summarize the point of view taken in this discussion by saying that for the current years in the United States, regional standards are likely to prevail.[2] Speech teaching, instead of trying the impossible task of moving the pronunciation of a whole population toward the dialect of some very small area, will busy itself with the improvement of the speech of the various regions, continually aiding those who use substandard regional speech to achieve the level of standard regional speech.[3]

This position appears rational for the student of interpretative reading. If he should wish to develop the art

---

[1] New York: E. P. Dutton and Company, Inc.

[2] For a detailed outline of the sound systems of eastern, southern, and general American speech, see G. W. Gray and C. M. Wise, *The Bases of Speech* (New York: Harper and Brothers, 1934).

[3] C. M. Wise, in *Foundations of Speech,* edited by James M. O'Neill (New York: Prentice-Hall, Inc., 1941), p. 19. By permission of the publishers.

for the platform or stage he would wish to investigate the trends of stage speech and, at least, emphasize universal elements and reduce colloquial elements. Dr. Wise sums up the situation with a rather comprehensive statement:

> In summary, it may be said of the speech of the stage and of the platform that the actor, interpretative reader, and director should be conscious of the problem of dialect, should think the problem through wisely, and in each instance should make a choice on the basis of all of the merits of the given case.[1]

There are at least two general criteria for acceptable diction other than the matter of standardization. The first of these is clarity. Every interpretative reader should speak clearly so as to be heard and understood with ease. Clarity calls for distinct enunciation of both vowel and consonant sounds. Enunciation comes from a Latin word meaning "to set forth." An important phase of the interpreter's technique is to "set forth" his words with clarity. He must speak loud enough to be heard and clearly enough to be understood.

The other criteria for acceptable diction is that of beauty, or a speech which is pleasing to hear. There is nothing innately ugly or beautiful in the speech sounds themselves—a "broad a" is neither less nor more pleasing than a "short a." Beauty depends upon the manner of articulation. So whatever speech the student may choose as his criteria, let him remember that there may be music in vowel sounds and in sonorant consonants and that clarity in enunciation goes far in projecting meaning and in commanding the interest and attention of an audience.

---

[1] Wise; *Loc. cit.*

LANGUAGE

From Poems of a Few Greatnesses [1]

Walt Whitman

Great is Language—it is the mightiest of the sciences,
It is the fulness, color, form, diversity of the earth, and of men and women, and of all qualities and processes,
It is greater than wealth—it is greater than buildings, ships, religions, paintings, music.

Great is the English speech—what speech is so great as the English?
Great is the English brood—what brood has so vast a destiny as the English?
It is the mother of the brood that must rule the earth with the new rule,
The new rule shall rule as the Soul rules, and as the love, justice, equality in the Soul, rule.

[1] From *Leaves of Grass* (Philadelphia: David McKay Company, 1900). By permission.

Chapter VIII

INTERPRETATION OF MEANING

> When observation has passed into meditation, and meditation has transformed knowledge into truth, and the brooding imagination has incorporated truth into the nature of the artist, then comes the creative moment.[1]
>
> *Hamilton Wright Mabie*

Creative reading calls for a careful and authoritative interpretation of the meaning in literature. In considering the significance of the word *interpretation* it will prove helpful for the student to give attention to dictionary definitions. According to Webster the word *interpret* means, "to translate; to elucidate; to construe or give force or meaning to, as in the light of individual belief or judgment, as, to interpret a poem." Synonyms given are "solve, render, unfold, or unravel." The interpretative reader, therefore, attempts to *translate* into the spoken word the meaning *implied* in the written word. It is the reader's purpose to *elucidate* for the audience the meaning of the author's language; it is the reader's purpose to *construe,* to *give force to,* or to *give meaning to* the words of the author according to the light of the reader's *individual belief* or *judgment.*

The student of interpretative reading should give careful consideration to the significance of the word *judgment.*

[1] From *My Study Fire,* by Hamilton Wright Mabie. Reprinted by permission of the publishers, Dodd, Mead and Company, Inc.

Readers differ in their judgment as to the author's meaning and hence they differ in their interpretation. The judgment of two or more readers may result in very different interpretations of the same poem, leaving decidedly different impressions on the audience. As has been suggested before, we understand with our experience. Readers with widely different lives are likely to differ in their judgment as to the meaning of a piece of literature.

Two readers were discussing the poem, "The Day," by Grace Noll Crowell.[1] One reader interpreted the poem as if the words were spoken by a carefree girl who had formed the habit of looking for the lovely things of life, even to the silver lining of gray clouds. The mood created by this reader was light, bright, and charmingly gay. Another reader having felt the weight of life's dark clouds found in this poem a poignancy which revealed loveliness through a veil of tears, as it were; her reading was half glad, half sad but caused a catch in the throats of those who heard.

These two readers gave their interpretations to the author, Mrs. Crowell, who listened graciously and with characteristic generosity said she could understand the very different interpretations resulting from the different lives of the two readers. When urged to give her own interpretation Mrs. Crowell said that what she felt in writing the poem was more nearly expressed by the reader whose interpretation was half sad, half glad. The poet was quick to encourage the other reader to continue to give her own interpretation of a gay, carefree mood. Mrs. Crowell stated that although she, the author, had never thought of the

[1] Grace Noll Crowell, *Silver in the Sun* (Dallas: The Turner Company, revised edition, 1934), p. 5.

poem in that way, she was happy to hear it interpreted in such a manner.

This difference in interpretation is found in all of the arts. Two musicians may play a Beethoven sonata and one may leave the audience transfixed with emotion, while the other commands a sort of intellectual interest in his skill. Katharine Cornell and Norma Shearer both interpreted the rôle of Elizabeth Barrett Browning and presented very different characterizations. One person who heard them both said that Miss Cornell *was* Elizabeth Barrett and that Miss Shearer was "a dream of loveliness." To this person the one seemed real and the other ideal. Raphael and Leonardo da Vinci both painted Madonnas. A connoisseur sees distinct differences in the paintings of each artist and quickly recognizes which Madonnas are the creation of each.

The individuality of the interpretative artist is always significant, his interpretation being valued by the particular slant he gives to his material. Without the stamp of the reader's personality the interpretation lacks authenticity, vitality, originality. One understands, hence interprets in the light of his own experience. The value of one's interpretation is in proportion to one's worth as an individual, plus one's insight into the life he depicts, plus his skill in presentation. The value of originality is suggested by another of the dictionary definitions of the word *interpretation:* "an artist's way of expressing his thought or conception of a subject."

It is essential for the creative reader to develop discrimination as a basis for his interpretation. A reader's opinion is a determining factor in the individuality of his interpretation. As a basis for discrimination the reader must develop insight into the intent of the author. Novices sometimes express their own ideas in reading a piece of literature, regardless of the author's meaning, claiming that self-expression is their purpose. If so they should write their own poetry. Interpretative art involves loyalty to the author of the concept one is interpreting. The creative reader should become a medium through which the author's concept is revealed with clarity and force. He is truest to himself when he is true to the author. As the actor projects a feeling of oneness with the character, the creative reader should give a feeling of oneness with the author. The first problem of interpreting meaning is for us to discern the meaning implied by the author's words.

THE MEANING OF WORDS

It is obvious that we cannot understand the meaning of lines if we do not know the meaning of the words; yet students of interpretative reading are often careless in this regard. We should form the habit of checking our knowledge of words by the definitions given in dictionaries and encyclopedias. A hazy or inaccurate idea of the denotative meaning of a word may cause a reader to go completely astray in his judgment of what the author intended to imply. While the reader is checking the meaning of a word he should also give attention to the pronunciation, for he must be discriminating in pronunciation, also, if his oral art is to be adequate.

WORD CONNOTATIONS

While the dictionary meaning of a word is important in revealing the author's intention, it is not always adequate for a clear understanding of his meaning. As was suggested in Chapter II, word connotation (the association of ideas) is also important for understanding an author's purpose. Literature is often made vivid and colorful by allusions to mythology, to history, to ideas which the author takes for granted are within the experience of the reader. An understanding of such allusions is essential for adequate discrimination as to the author's meaning. Sometimes the significance of an allusion is clarified by data given in an encyclopedia; sometimes much research is essential for a clear understanding of the significance of a single word or phrase. The interpretative reader does not hesitate to spend as much time as is needed to trace allusions to a satisfactory source.

"The World is Too Much with Us" is a sonnet in which allusions are made to mythology. In order to understand the meaning of the last two lines, and hence the author's conclusion to his idea, the student must know something about *Proteus* and the significance of *Old Triton*. One is fortunate if he possesses a colorful background in Greek mythology and as a consequence has happy memories of childhood wonder and pleasure in such myths. For those to whom these words carry no such connotations, an encyclopedia, or preferably *The Classic Myths in English Literature* by Gayley,[1] will aid in gaining a basis for understanding and appreciation.

[1] Charles Mills Gayley, *The Classic Myths in English Literature,* new edition, revised and enlarged (Boston: Ginn and Company, 1911).

THE WORLD IS TOO MUCH WITH US
William Wordsworth

The world is too much with us; late and soon,
Getting and spending, we lay waste our powers:
Little we see in Nature that is ours;
We have given our hearts away, a sordid boon!
The sea that bares her bosom to the moon;
The winds that will be howling at all hours,
And are up gathered now like sleeping flowers;
For this, for everything, we are out of tune;
It moves us not.—Great God! I'd rather be
A pagan suckled in a creed outworn;
So might I, standing on this pleasant lea,
Have glimpses that would make me less forlorn;
Have sight of Proteus rising from the sea;
Or hear old Triton blow his wreathed horn.

THE AUTHOR'S MEANING

It is not always easy to find an author's meaning even when one understands the denotative and connotative meaning of words. For example, much of the poetry of Robert Browning is obscure. It is difficult to determine, with any degree of accuracy, just what he meant to imply in certain lines. In "Prospice" we find the lines:

> Bear the brunt, in a minute pay glad life's arrears
> Of pain, darkness and cold.

One's interpretation of these lines depends largely upon one's judgment concerning the use of the word *glad*. Is *glad* an adjective modifying life? Some students interpret it so and find support for their interpretation in the gladness of the life of Robert Browning. Read the lines suggesting the close relationship of the noun and the adjective by pausing after *pay* and grouping the word *glad* with the word *life*.

> In a minute pay———glad life's arrears
> Of pain, darkness and cold.

Does this reading satisfy you as an adequate interpretation of the author's meaning?

Other students consider the word *glad* an adverb modifying *pay*. In such an interpretation one admits both the adjective form of *glad* instead of the adverb form, *gladly*, and the use of inversion, which today is not considered good form in poetry. A close study of Browning reveals that the poet was often indifferent to form and that inversions were frequent in the poetry of his day. Read the lines again implying the meaning *gladly pay* by pausing after *glad*, indicating the close relation of *pay* and *glad*.

> In a minute pay glad———life's arrears
> Of pain, darkness and cold.

Which of the two interpretations do you like better? Which seems to you more expressive of the poet's attitude in the poem as a whole?

PROSPICE

Robert Browning

Fear death?—to feel the fog in my throat,
    The mist in my face,
When the snows begin, and blasts denote
    I am nearing the place,
The power of the night, the press of the storm,
    The post of the foe;
Where he stands, the Arch Fear in a visible form,

Yet the strong man must go:
For the journey is done and the summit attained,
    And the barriers fall,
Though a battle's to fight ere the guerdon be gained,
    The reward of it all.
I was ever a fighter, so—one fight more,
    The best and the last!
I would hate that death bandaged my eyes, and forebore,
    And bade me creep past.
No! let me taste the whole of it, fare like my peers
    The heroes of old,
Bear the brunt, in a minute pay glad life's arrears
    Of pain, darkness and cold.
For sudden the worst turns the best to the brave,
    The black minute's at end,
And the elements' rage, the fiend-voices that rave,
    Shall dwindle, shall blend,
Shall change, shall become first a peace out of pain,
    Then a light, then thy breast,
O thou soul of my soul! I shall clasp thee again,
    And with God be the rest!

Read the passages which follow, giving through your oral form your judgment as to the author's intent.

MEETING AT NIGHT
Robert Browning

The gray sea and the long black land;
And the yellow half-moon large and low;
And the startled little waves that leap
In fiery ringlets from their sleep,
As I gain the cove with pushing prow,
And quench its speed i' the slushy sand.

And a mile of warm sea-scented beach;
Three fields to cross till a farm appears;

A tap at the pane, the quick sharp scratch
And blue spurt of a lighted match,
And a voice less loud, through its joys and fears,
Than the two hearts beating each to each!

PARTING AT MORNING [1]

Robert Browning

Round the cape of a sudden came the sea,
And the sun looked over the mountain's rim:
And straight was a path of gold for him,
And the need of a world of men for me.

LADY MACBETH'S PREPARATION

From MACBETH [2]

William Shakespeare

[MACBETH *has been deliberating about the murder of* DUNCAN; LADY MACBETH *enters as he is meditating.*]

MACB. Now now! What news?
LADY M. He has almost supp'd. Why have you left the chamber?
MACB. Hath he asked for me?
LADY M.   Know you not he has?
MACB. We will proceed no further in this business.
He hath honour'd me of late; and I have sought
Golden opinion from all sorts of people,
Which would be worn now in their newest gloss,
Nor cast aside so soon.
LADY M.   Was the hope drunk
Wherein you dress'd yourself? Hath it slept since

---

[1] One commentator interprets this poem as spoken by a woman, the pronoun in the third line referring to the man and the pronoun in the fourth line to the woman. Another thinks the speaker in this poem is a man, the pronoun in the third line referring to the sun and the pronoun in the fourth line to himself.

[2] Act I, Scene vii.

                 And wakes it now. to look so green and pale
                 At what it did so freely? From this time
                 Such I account thy love. Art thou afeard
                 To be the same in thine own act and valour
                 As thou art in desire? Wouldst thou have that
                 Which thou esteemst the ornament of life,
                 And live a coward in thine own esteem,
                 Letting "I dare not" wait upon "I would,"
                 Like the poor cat i' the adage?
MACB.   Prithee, peace. I dare do all that may become a man;
                 Who dares do more is none.
LADY M.   What beast was't, then,
                 That made you break this enterprise to me?
                 When you durst do it, then you were a man;
                 And, to be more than what you were, you would
                 Be so much more the man. Nor time nor place
                 Did then adhere, and yet you would make both.
                 They have made themselves, and that their fitness now
                 Does unmake you. I have given suck, and know
                 How tender 'tis to love the babe that milks me;
                 I would, while it was smiling in my face,
                 Have pluck'd my nipple from his boneless gums
                 And dash'd the brains out, had I sworn as you
                 Have done to this.
MACB.   If we should fail?
LADY M. We fail! [1]

[1] This line is found punctuated differently in various versions. It is interpreted differently by various actors, critics, and readers. In a certain college, English and Speech teachers were preparing students for the enjoyment of Walter Hampden's production of *Macbeth*. One teacher read the line with emphasis on *we,* and as if the line were punctuated with a question mark, *"We* fail?" Another read it as an emphatic statement, *"We fail."* The students listened eagerly for the interpretation given by Mabel Moore who was playing Lady Macbeth in Mr. Hampden's production. She gave an easy glide on the word fail and grouped it quickly with the following phrase as if the word were followed by a comma.

> But screw your courage to the sticking-place
> And we'll not fail. When Duncan is asleep—
> Whereto the rather shall this day's hard journey
> Soundly invite him—his two chamberlains
> Will I with wine and wassail so convince
> That memory, the warder of the brain,
> Shall be a fume, and the receipt of reason
> A limbeck only. When in swinish sleep
> Their drenched natures lie as in a death,
> What cannot you and I perform upon
> That unguarded Duncan? What not put upon
> The spongy officers, who shall bear the guilt
> Of our great quell?
>
> MACB. Bring forth men-children only;
> For thy undaunted mettle should compose
> Nothing but males. . . . I am settled, and bend up
> Each corporal agent to this terrible feat.
> Away, and mock the time with fairest show;
> False face must hide what false heart doth know.

INTERCLAUSAL RELATIONS

The student of interpretative reading must give due consideration to interclausal relations. Ideas in literature are often interdependent. The meaning of one sentence may depend upon the meaning conveyed by another sentence. Likewise, clauses are interdependent, limiting, explaining, or amplifying each other. A portion of a sentence taken out of its context may carry an entirely different meaning from that intended by the author or from that which would be understood if the entire sentence were given. Authors are frequently misquoted in this manner by well-meaning advocates. Let us consider what is frequently called Wordsworth's definition of poetry. Have we not often heard that Wordsworth defined poetry as "emotion recollected in tranquillity"? Let us consider his entire sentence with its interclausal relations.

I have said that poetry is the spontaneous overflow of powerful feelings; it takes its origin from emotion recollected in tranquillity; the emotion is contemplated, till, by a species of reaction, the tranquillity gradually disappears, and an emotion, kindred to that which was before the subject of contemplation, is gradually produced, and does itself actually exist in the mind.[1]

Now does Wordsworth say that poetry is "emotion recollected in tranquillity," or does he say that "tranquillity disappears" and emotion actually exists as one creates a poem? To interpret a sentence fairly the reader must keep in mind the meaning of the sentence as a whole, the relation of all parts to each other, and the relation of parts to the whole.

In interpreting the meaning of lines the reader needs to go beyond the sentence and consider the relation of the whole piece of literature, or even of the whole works of an author or of a period. Sometimes the clause which gives understanding to another clause is found in a separate stanza or paragraph. Let us consider, for example, some lines of Robert Browning the meaning of which is dependent upon lines in another stanza. In "Rabbi Ben Ezra" the poet states:

> To man, propose this test—
> Thy body at its best,
> How far can that project thy soul on its lone way?

[1] William Wordsworth, Preface to *Lyrical Ballads*.

The line which follows immediately in the next stanza is frequently interpreted as indicating that the poet thought the body had little to do with the soul's development.

> Yet gifts should prove their use.

When one reads further he finds the lines:

> Let us not always say,
> "Spite of this flesh today
> I strove, made head, gained
> Ground upon the whole!"

Still further on the poet states:

> Nor soul helps flesh more, now,
> Than flesh helps soul.

These last lines suggest that Browning thought the body had much to do with projecting "the soul on its lone way." The reader must consider the interclausal relations of five stanzas in order not to misinterpret the poet's question:

> Thy body at its best,
> How far can that project thy soul on its lone way?

The five stanzas which include the author's discussion of the relation of soul to flesh are quoted below:

What is he but a brute
Whose flesh has soul to suit,
Whose spirit works lest arms and legs want play?
To man, propose this test—
Thy body at its best,
How far can that project thy soul on its lone way?

Yet gifts should prove their use:
I own the Past profuse

Of power each side, perfection every turn:
Eyes, ears took in their dole,
Brain treasured up the whole;
Should not the heart beat once "How good to live and learn?"

Not once beat "praise be thine!
I see the whole design,
I, who saw power, see how Love perfect too:
Perfect I call thy plan:
Thanks that I was a man!
Maker, remake, complete,—I trust what thou shalt do!"

For pleasant is this flesh:
Our soul, in its rose-mesh
Pulled ever to the earth, still yearns for rest:
Would we some prize might hold
To match those manifold
Possessions of the brute,—gain most, as we did best!

Let us not always say,
"Spite of this flesh today
I strove, made head, gained ground upon the whole!"
As the bird wings and sings,
Let us cry, "All good things
Are ours, nor soul helps flesh more, now, than flesh helps soul!"

SUGGESTIVENESS

The interpretative reader has need of a technique of suggestiveness, the pointing up of details which indicate (or suggest) the dénouement. Suggestiveness is a technique which is used by writers and should be emphasized by the reader. Let us emphasize the fact that for an adequate interpretation of a piece of literature the reader must keep before him the whole, the relation of parts to the whole, and the relation of the parts to each other. Each part must be interpreted in the light of that which goes before and that which is to come afterwards. In an interpretation of a short story, for example, the reader knows the dénouement and guides his reading, from the introduction, in the light of the author's conclusion. O. Henry is known for his surprise endings. The quick turn which his stories take at the conclusion gives his audience a delightful surprise. When one re-reads an O. Henry story, he may observe that the author has hinted the conclusion all the way through and that his stories really come to logical conclusions. The reader's technique of suggestion should be in accord with this technique of the author, and although the dénouement may surprise the audience, it will not disappoint them or make them feel that they have been led astray either by the author or by the reader.

When the author has skillfully built his story for a surprise ending, the reader may actually point up the lines which suggest the dénouement and add to the interest and suspense at the end. If the reader has interpreted each detail in the light of the conclusion, the audience will have been prepared for the dénouement, and will feel that the dénouement is logical even though they had not suspected the author's solution. In looking back over the story the audience will recall the details which pointed to the author's ending and will wonder why they did not catch on sooner.

Read the following story and note how many times the author suggests the conclusion. This is done more by what he omits to say than by what he actually says. Observe how with a pause, a tone, or an inflection the reader may add to the suggestiveness of the author.

THE DIAMOND NECKLACE
Guy De Maupassant

The girl was one of those pretty and charming young creatures who sometimes are born, as if by a mistake of destiny, in a family of clerks. She had no dowry, no expectations, no way of being known, understood, loved, married, by any rich and distinguished man; so she let herself be married to a little clerk at the Ministry of Public Instruction.

She had no gowns, no jewels, and she loved nothing else. She felt made for that alone. She was filled with a desire to please, to be envied, to be bewitching, to be sought after.

She had a friend, a former school mate at the convent, who was rich and whom she did not like to see any more, because she suffered so much when she came home.

One evening her husband came home with a triumphant air, holding a large envelope in his hand.

"There, there is something for you."

She tore the paper quickly, and drew out a printed card which bore these words: "The minister of Public Instruction and Madame Georges Rampouneau request the honor of Madame Loisel's company at the palace of the Ministry on Monday evening, January 18th."

Instead of being delighted, as her husband had hoped, she threw the invitation on the table with disdain, murmuring: "What do you wish me to do with that?"

"Why, my dear, I thought you would be glad. You never go out, and this is such a fine opportunity."

"And what do you wish me to wear?"

"Why the gown you go to the theater in. It looks very well to me." He stopped stupefied, distracted, on seeing that his wife was crying. "Why, what is the matter?"

"Nothing, only I have no gown, and therefore cannot go to this ball. Give your card to some colleague whose wife is better equipped than I."

"Come, let us see, Mathilde. How much would it cost, a suitable gown, which you could use on other occasions?"

She reflected several seconds, making her calculations and wondering also what sum she could ask without drawing on herself an immediate refusal. Finally she replied: "I don't know exactly, but I think I could manage it with four hundred francs."

He turned a trifle pale, for he had been saving just that sum to buy a gun and treat himself to a little hunting trip. However, he said, "Very well, I will give you four hundred francs. And try to have a pretty gown."

The day of the ball drew near, and Madame Loisel seemed sad, uneasy, anxious. Her husband said to her one evening: "What is the matter? Come, you have seemed very queer these last three days."

"It annoys me not to have jewels, not a single stone. I shall look poverty-stricken. I should almost rather not go at all."

"How stupid you are! Go look up your friend Madame Forestier, and ask her to lend you some jewels. You're intimate enough with her to do that."

"True! I never thought of it."

The next day she went to her friend and told of her distress.

Madame Forestier went to a wardrobe with a glass door, took out a large jewel box, brought it back, opened it, and said to Madame Loisel: "Choose, my dear."

She tried on the ornaments before the mirror, hesitated, and suddenly she discovered, in a black satin box, a superb diamond necklace, and her heart throbbed with an immoderate desire. Her hands trembled as she took it. She fastened it around her throat, outside her high-necked waist, and was lost in ecstasy at the sight of herself. Then she asked: "Will you lend me this, only this?"

"Why, yes, certainly."

The night of the ball arrived. Madame Loisel made a great success. She was prettier than any other woman present, elegant, graceful, smiling, and intoxicated with joy. All the men looked at her, asked her name, endeavoured to be introduced.

She danced with rapture, with passion, made drunk by pleasure, forgetting all, in the triumph of her beauty, in the glory of her success.

She left the ball about four o'clock in the morning. Her husband had been sleeping since midnight, in a little deserted anteroom with three other gentlemen whose wives were enjoying the ball.

He threw over her shoulders the wraps he had brought, the modest wraps of common life, the poverty of which contrasted with the elegance of the ball dress. She felt this, and wished to escape so as not to be remarked by the other women, who were enveloping themselves in costly furs.

Loisel held her back saying: "Wait a bit. You will catch cold outside. I will call a cab."

But she did not listen to him and rapidly descended the stairs. When they reached the street they could not find a carriage, and began to look for one, shouting after the cabmen passing at a distance.

They went toward the Seine, in despair, shivering with cold. At last they found on the quay one of those ancient night cabs which, as if they were ashamed to show their shabbiness during the day, are never seen round Paris until after dark.

It took them to their dwelling, and sadly they climbed up to their apartment. He reflected that he must be at the Ministry at ten o'clock that morning.

She removed her wraps before the glass so as to see herself

once more in all her glory. But suddenly she uttered a cry. The necklace was no longer around her neck!

They looked among the folds of her skirt, of her cloak, in her pockets, everywhere, but did not find it. They looked, thunderstruck, at each other. At last Loisel went out. She sat waiting on a chair in her ball-dress, without strength to go to bed, overwhelmed, without fire, without a thought.

Her husband returned about seven o'clock. He had found nothing. He went to police headquarters, to the newspaper offices, to offer a reward; he went to the cab companies—everywhere, in fact, whither he was urged by the least spark of hope.

Loisel returned at night with a hollow, pale face; he had discovered nothing.

At the end of the week they had lost all hope. Loisel declared: "We must consider how to replace the ornament."

The next day they took the box that had contained it, and went to the jeweler whose name was found within. He consulted his books. "It is not I, Madame, who sold that necklace; I must simply have furnished the case."

Then they went from jeweler to jeweler, searching for a necklace like the other, consulting their memories, both sick with chagrin and anguish.

They found in a shop at the Palais Royal, a string of diamonds that seemed to them exactly like the one they had lost. It was worth forty thousand francs.

They begged the jeweler not to sell it for three days yet.

Loisel possessed eighteen thousand francs which his father had left him. He would borrow the rest. He did borrow, asking a thousand francs of one, five hundred of another, five louis here, three louis there. He gave notes, took up ruinous obligations, dealt with usurers and all the race of lenders. He compromised all the rest of his life, risked his signature without even knowing whether he could honour it; and frightened by the trouble yet to come, by the black misery that was about to fall upon him, by the prospect of all the physical privations and moral tortures that he was to face, he went to get the new necklace, laying upon the jeweler's counter the forty thousand francs.

When Madame Loisel took back the necklace, Madame Forestier said to her in a chilly manner: "You should have returned it sooner; I might have needed it."

She did not open the case, as her friend had so much feared. If she had detected the substitution, what would she have thought, what would she have said? Would she not have taken Madame Loisel for a thief?

Thereafter Madame Loisel knew the horrible existence of the needy. She bore her part, however, with sudden heroism. That dreadful debt must be paid. She would pay it off. They dismissed their servant; they changed their lodgings; they rented a garret under the roof.

Every month they met some notes, renewed others, obtained more time.

At the end of ten years they had paid everything, everything, with the rates of usury and accumulations of the compound interest.

Madame Loisel looked old now. She had become the woman of impoverished households—strong, and hard, and rough. With frowsy hair, skirts askew, and red hands, she talked loudly while washing the floor with a great swish of water. But sometimes, when her husband was at the office, she sat down near the window, and thought of that gay evening long ago, of that ball where she had been so beautiful and so admired.

What would have happened if she had not lost that necklace? Who knows? Who knows? How strange and changeful is life! How little a thing is needed for us to be lost or saved!

But, one Sunday, having gone to take a walk to refresh herself from the labours of the week, she suddenly perceived a woman who was leading a child. It was Madame Forestier, still young, still beautiful, still charming.

Madame Loisel felt moved. Should she speak to her? Yes certainly, and now that she had paid, she would tell her all about it. Why not?

She went up. "Good day, Jeanne."

The other, astonished to be thus familiarly addressed, did not recognize her at all and stammered: "But—Madame—I do not know— You must be mistaken."

"No. I am Mathilde Loisel."

"Oh, my poor Mathilde! How you are changed!"

"Yes, I have had days hard enough since I have seen you, days wretched enough—and that because of you!"

"Of me! How so?"

"Do you remember that diamond necklace you lent me to wear at the Ministerial ball?"

"Yes, well?"

"Well, I lost it."

"How can that be? You returned it to me."

"I returned you another exactly like it. And for this we have been ten years paying. You can understand that it was not easy for us, us who had nothing. At last it is ended and I am very glad."

"You say that you bought a necklace of diamonds to replace mine?"

"Yes. You never noticed then! They were very like."

"Oh, my poor Mathilde! Why, my necklace was paste! It was worth at most only five hundred francs."

ATTITUDES

The interpretation of attitudes is important, in that the meaning may frequently depend upon the attitude suggested—the attitude of the author, of the character, or of the reader. The attitude of the reader, of course, is guided by that of the author or the character. As was suggested before, an understanding of the author's meaning may depend upon a knowledge of the author's works in general or of the period in which it was written. The work itself usually gives a rather clear indication of the attitude; hence the interpretative reader should maintain an unbiased attitude on his own part. It is inexcusable for a reader to superimpose upon a piece of literature his own pet ideas, theories, prejudices, or attitudes.

In his book, *Reading Aloud,* Maxfield Parrish devotes a chapter to the interpretation of attitude. He states:

> There is a third factor in reading which is necessary for a complete understanding of meaning, and that is the *attitude* of the reader toward what he says. A given phrase or sentence may mean several quite different things depending upon the mood or attitude of the speaker. He may be joking or in earnest, ironical or matter-of-fact, sarcastic or sympathetic. Unless you understand your author's attitude, and communicate it to your hearers, you are giving them only an imperfect understanding of his meaning. . . .
>
> When listening to a speaker's voice we generally have no difficulty in recognizing these shades of meaning, but they are nearly always too subtle for analysis. They consist partly of emphasis, partly of voice-glide, or of changes in quality or rate, but we cannot define the exact combination of expres-

sional elements involved. We must still depend upon the "natural" method, assuming that a correct perception of the writer's attitude will prompt a correct expression of it.[1]

Sometimes in a poem, a story, or an essay a character is implied. For example, Louis Untermeyer wrote a poem called "Caliban in the Coal Mines." An understanding of the attitude in this poem depends upon the reader's understanding of the nature or character of Caliban, but even more upon an understanding of Mr. Untermeyer's social attitudes. Edna St. Vincent Millay wrote a number of children's poems under the caption, *From a Very Little Sphinx*. In one of them the child says, "I know a hundred ways to die." [2] The reader's problem is to decide what is the attitude of a "very little sphinx" as she contemplates the various modes of death her imagination can contrive. We are inclined to interpret the attitude in this poem as that of "innocent pleasure." There is no fear, no horror, nor dread suggested; the innocence of the child forms a charming and somewhat amusing contrast to that of adults who contemplate such things.

Read the following scene from *Romeo and Juliet* observing the contrast in the attitudes of Juliet and of the Nurse. Juliet's general attitude is one of eagerness and impatience. The nurse evades her questions in order to tease her. The effect upon the audience is one of humor. Be on the alert for quick changes in attitude.

[1] Wayland Maxfield Parrish, *Reading Aloud* (New York: Thomas Nelson and Sons, 1932), p. 69.
[2] Edna St. Vincent Millay, *Poems* (New York: Harper and Brothers, 1929).

JULIET'S DILEMMA

From Romeo and Juliet [1]

William Shakespeare

Juliet. The clock struck nine when I did send the nurse;
In half an hour she promised to return.
Perchance she cannot meet him: that's not so.
O, she is lame! love's heralds should be thoughts,
Which ten times faster glide than the sun's beams,
Driving back shadows over lowering hills

. . . . .

Now is the sun upon the high most hill
Of this day's journey, and from nine till twelve
Is three long hours; yet she is not come.

. . . . .

But old folks, many feign as they were dead;
Unwieldy, slow, heavy and pale as lead.
[*Enter* Nurse *with* Peter.]
O God, she comes! O honey nurse, what news?
Hast thou met with him? Send thy man away.
Nurse. Peter, stay at the gate.
[*Exit* Peter.]
Juliet. Now, good sweet nurse,—O lord, why look'st thou sad?
Though news be sad, yet tell them merrily;
If good, thou shamest the music of sweet news
By playing it to me with so sour a face.
Nurse. I am a-weary; give me leave a while.
Fie, how my bones ache! what a jaunce have I had!
Juliet. I would thou hadst my bones and I thy news:
Nay, come, I pray thee, speak; good, good nurse, speak.
Nurse. Jesu, what haste? Can you not stay a while?
Do you not see that I am out of breath?

[1] Act II, Scene v.

ATTITUDES

JULIET. How art thou out of breath, when thou hast breath
To say to me that thou art out of breath?
The excuse that thou dost make in this delay
Is longer than the tale thou dost excuse.
Is thy news good, or bad? answer to that;
Say either, and I'll stay the circumstance:
Let me be satisfied, is't good or bad?

NURSE. Well, you have made a simple choice; you
know not how to choose a man: Romeo! no, not he;
though his face be better than any man's, yet his
leg excels all men's; and for a hand, and a foot,
and a body, though they be not to be talked on, yet
they are past compare: he is not the flower of
courtesy, but, I'll warrant him as gentle as a
lamb. Go thy ways, wench; serve God. What, have
you dined at home?

JULIET. No, no: but all this did I know before.
What says he of our marriage? what of that?

NURSE. Lord, how my head aches! What a head have I!
It beats as it would fall in twenty pieces.
My back o' t'other side,—ah, my back, my back!
Beshrew your heart for sending me about,
To catch my death with jauncing up and down!

JULIET. I' faith, I am sorry that thou art not well.
Sweet, sweet, sweet nurse, tell me, what says my love?

NURSE. Your love says, like an honest gentleman,
and a courteous, and a kind, and a handsome, and I
warrant, virtuous,— Where is your mother?

JULIET. Where is my mother! Why, she is within;
Where should she be? How oddly thou repliest!
'Your love says, like an honest gentleman,
Where is your mother?'

NURSE. O God's lady dear!
Are you so hot? marry, come up, I trow;
Is this the poultice for my aching bones?
Henceforward do your messages yourself.

JULIET. Here's such a coil! Come, what says Romeo?
NURSE. Have you got leave to go to shrift today?
JULIET. I have.
NURSE. Then hie you hence to Friar Laurence' cell;
There stays a husband to make you a wife:
Now comes a wanton blood up in your cheeks,
They'll be in scarlet straight at any news.
Hie you to church; I must another way,
To fetch a ladder, by the which your love
Must climb a bird's nest soon when it is dark;
I am the drudge, and toil in your delight;
But you shall bear the burthen soon at night.
Go; I'll to dinner; hie you to the cell.
JULIET. Hie to high fortune! Honest nurse, farewell.

Acting, a Helpful Device

A helpful device for finding the attitude expressed in a piece of literature is for the student to act it out with informal posture, bearing, or movement. To be sure, we have emphasized that reading is not acting—yet acting may prove a means of experiencing the reality; it may prove a *device* for finding the attitude. As Max Eastman says, "Poetry is an attitude of body," and, as we have suggested, through motor imagery the student may find an understanding of the essence which might be obscure to him if he approached the poem from a purely logical or intellectual point of view. A teacher once said, "Oral interpretation is difficult to teach because the reader cannot *do* anything with his *body*." We would say that something *does* happen in the body if one interprets adequately. We would go a step further and say one may "do" something with one's body as a means of experiencing the reality of literature. There are times when definite and positive action is the surest means of experiencing the reality, sensing the meaning, and finding the attitude.

A group of students staged "My Last Duchess" with a girl posing as the Duchess of the portrait, another acting out the rôle of the Duke, and a third pantomiming the envoy. A member of the audience said it was a fine show but completely concealed Browning's idea. To that observer the acting concealed rather than revealed the author's meaning. Suppose, however, such a performance had been given as a classroom project only, as a means of experiencing realities in preparation for an interpretative reading. Do you think those participating would have had a clearer understanding of the Duke's attitude? We suggest that as a classroom project you act out this monologue as completely as you wish, even letting the envoy put in a few lines where they seem natural. After this experiment let one or more members of the class read it interpretatively, with no representative actions and with "off-stage" technique. The results will probably justify the time spent in such a realistic performance.

MY LAST DUCHESS

Robert Browning

That's my last Duchess painted on the wall,
Looking as if she were alive. I call
That piece a wonder, now: Fra Pandolf's hands
Worked busily a day, and there she stands.
Will 't please you sit and look at her? I said
"Fra Pandolf" by design, for never read
Strangers like you that pictured countenance,
The depth and passion of its earnest glance,
But to myself they turned (since none puts by

The curtain I have drawn for you, but I)
And seemed as they would ask me, if they durst,
How such a glance came there; so, not the first
Are you to turn and ask thus. Sir, 'twas not
Her husband's presence only, called that spot
Of joy into the Duchess' cheek; perhaps
Fra Pandolf chanced to say, "Her mantle laps
Over my lady's wrist too much," or "Paint
Must never hope to reproduce the faint
Half-flush that dies along her throat:" such stuff
Was courtesy, she thought, and cause enough
For calling up that spot of joy. She had
A heart—how shall I say?—too soon made glad.
Too easily impressed: she liked whate'er
She looked on, and her looks went everywhere.
Sir, 't was all one! My favor at her breast,
The dropping of the daylight in the West,
The bough of cherries some officious fool
Broke in the orchard for her, the white mule
She rode with round the terrace—all and each
Would draw from her alike the approving speech.
Or blush, at least. She thanked men,—good! but thanked
Somehow—I know not how—as if she ranked
My gift of a nine-hundred-years-old name
With anybody's gift. Who'd stoop to blame
This sort of trifling? Even had you skill
In speech—(which I have not)—to make your will
Quite clear to such an one, and say, "Just this
Or that in you disgust me: here you miss,
Or there exceed the mark"—and if she let
Herself be lessoned so, nor plainly set
Her wits to yours, forsooth, and made excuse,
—E'en then would be some stooping; and I choose
Never to stoop. Oh sir, she smiled, no doubt,
Whene'er I passed her; but who passed without
Much the same smile? This grew; I gave commands;

Then all smiles stopped together. There she stands
As if alive. Will 't please you rise? We'll meet
The company below, then. I repeat
The Count your master's known munificence
Is ample warrant that no just pretence
Of mine for dowery will be disallowed;
Though his fair daughter's self, as I avowed
At starting, is my object. Nay, we'll go
Together down, sir. Notice Neptune, though,
Taming a sea-horse, thought a rarity,
Which Claus of Innsbruck cast in bronze for me!

A student once brought to a speech class the poem, "A Sailor Boy" by Alfred Tennyson. Because the teacher encouraged informal delivery, the student sat at the teacher's desk and read the poem to the class. He made a definite effort to "think aloud" the author's ideas. The delivery was cramped and the communication inadequate. In the classroom were some steps left by a group of drama students. It was suggested that the reader place one foot on a step and assume the easy informal posture of a boy contemplating the life of a sailor. With this pose his body became vital and as he read bodily changes suggested each mood naturally and vividly. At one point he took his foot off of the step and with both feet planted firmly on the floor concluded the reading with a sense of reality which brought empathic response from the class.

A SAILOR BOY

Alfred Tennyson

He rose at dawn and, fired with hope,
Shot o'er the seething harbor-bar,

And reach'd the ship and caught the rope,
And whistled to the morning star.

And while he whistled long and loud
He heard a fierce mermaiden cry,
"O boy, tho' thou art young and proud,
I see the place where thou wilt lie.

"The sands and yeasty surges mix
In caves about the dreary bay,
And on thy ribs the limpet sticks,
And in thy heart the scrawl shall play."

"Fool," he answer'd, "death is sure
To those that stay and those that roam,
But I will nevermore endure
To sit with empty hands at home.

"My mother clings about my neck,
My sisters crying, 'Stay for shame;'
My father raves of death and wreck,
They are all to blame, they are all to blame.

"God help me! save I take my part
Of danger on the roaring sea,
A devil rises in my heart,
Far worse than any death to me."

These suggestions concerning the acting of poetry are made largely as a means to an end. But, after all, why should the interpretative reader of necessity stand in a certain definite place on a platform? If he can communicate the author's purpose better by sitting, by leaning against a column, or by moving about—why should he not do so? Readers at one time, it appears, thought they must stand stiffly erect, give the title and author, then move two steps forward before reciting the first line of their "piece." While such a convention may no longer exist, unnatural stiffness has often resulted from the instruction that interpretative readers must beware of actions which are too literal or movements which call attention to themselves and interfere with the mental concept. While we agree with Dr. Curry that the higher the art the more manifestative and less representative the form; still, we insist that flexibility of form and spontaneity of expression may at times justify informal bearing and literal actions.

Read Browning's "Home Thoughts from Abroad." Could you sense the reality better sitting in an armchair than standing in the center of a platform? Would a yellow flower held in the hand aid you in relating these thoughts concerning spring in England? Experiment a bit with this idea of natural, informal bearing and see if you are aided in finding and in projecting the author's attitude.

HOME-THOUGHTS FROM ABROAD
Robert Browning

Oh, to be in England
Now that April's there,
And whoever wakes in England
Sees, some morning, unaware,
That the lowest boughs and the brushwood sheaf
Round the elm-tree bole are in tiny leaf,
While the chaffinch sings on the orchard bough
In England—now!

And after April, when May follows,
And the whitethroat builds, and all the swallows!

Hark, where my blossomed pear-tree in the hedge
Leans to the field and scatters on the clover
Blossoms and dewdrops—at the bent spray's edge—
That's the wise thrush; he sings each song twice over,
Lest you should think he never could recapture
The first fine careless rapture!
And though the fields look rough with hoary dew,
All will be gay when noontide wakes anew
The buttercups, the little children's dower
—Far brighter than this gaudy melonflower!

APPRECIATION

The reader's own enjoyment, the reader's own appreciation of literature are essential for adequate interpretation. How can one share with an audience that which he does not possess? How can one cause an audience to enjoy that to which he is indifferent? How can a reader project an appreciation in which he does not share? Interpretative reading is a process of sharing with others the moods, attitudes, ideas one finds suggested on the printed page. Enthusiasm is contagious, and so are enjoyment and appreciation. A positive attitude of appreciation on the part of the reader invites a positive reaction from the audience. A negative attitude from the reader engenders a negative response from the audience. The reader's own appreciation is the *sine qua non* of audience appreciation.

Rapport between reader and listener is achieved through the reader's active appreciation at the moment he is reading. No amount of advance preparation can take the place of the reader's response at the moment he is reading aloud to others. Communication of ideas involves concentration upon ideas and something more—the reader's own reaction, his own enjoyment, his own appreciation plus his desire to share with others.

If the mood involves humor the reader must perceive the humor and enjoy sharing it with the audience. The laugh may be for the audience only, but the appreciation which occasions the laugh is as essential for the reader as it is for the hearer. If the material is tragic the reader must understand and sympathize with the conditions which cause the tragedy and share his understanding with the audience. If the material is deeply philosophical, thought provoking, the reader's appreciation of the significance of the ideas is his means of creating the expression which will stimulate the thinking of the audience. Vagueness in the reader's comprehension engenders vagueness in his interpretation; a casual or indifferent attitude in the reader is very likely to result in indifference on the part of the audience.

The reader must not expect audience appreciation necessarily to equal his own. Factors other than a response to the reader's appreciation will enter into the understanding and appreciation of the audience. The probability is that the appreciation of the majority in any audience will fall far below the appreciation of the reader. A few listeners with unusual background and astuteness may go beyond the reader in appreciation. The appreciation of listeners will depend upon their own capacity and receptivity plus the reader's projection of the idea or mood. A reader teeming with enthusiasm for his material and eager to share his appreciation with others may overcome obstacles in the hearer's background and turn attitudes of indifference, even antagonism, into enthusiasm. We are all subject to the influence of that which causes enthusiasm in others.

HOW TO DEVELOP APPRECIATION

The student may say, "But suppose I don't like the literature assigned to me to read? How can I share with an audience an appreciation I don't have?" The answer is obviously, "You can't." One of the first steps in developing appreciation and the ability to project appreciation is to read that which you *do* enjoy. You may be wise to omit, for a while, that to which you do not respond with immediate enjoyment. As a beginning in the art of sharing appreciation with others, choose that which you like and stay with it until you like it tremendously, then read it to an audience with a will to make them like it too. It may be wise for you to ignore what you do not like until you have developed confidence in your ability to project appreciation to others. You must avoid making your prejudices deep-rooted by developing your *capacity* for appreciation.

Open-Mindedness

Prejudices are indications of a limited point of view; one dislikes what he does not understand. You may dislike a poem because the idea it suggests is more profound than your understanding. You may be wise to keep quiet about your prejudices until you have developed a capacity for broader enjoyment. To express your dislike may be to admit that you are not big enough to appreciate it. Instead of rejecting it and building reasons for your dislike try facing the matter honestly and asking yourself why you do not like it. Are some of the words unfamiliar? The dictionary may care for that. Are the allusions obscure? Perhaps the encyclopedia or other reference works will disclose their significance. Is the phase of life outside your experience? Perhaps you've been missing something thrilling: why not investigate? Maybe your prejudice is due to your ignorance. Surely you do not wish to close your mind to that which great minds create and respond to, so why not remedy the situation by substituting knowledge for ignorance?

Dr. Frank Crane says, "The great soul makes sure he is right and is then firm; the small soul is first firm and then casts about for reasons for being so." [1] There is no place for a small soul in the field of interpretative reading. Do not take the first step towards making or keeping yourself so by closing your mind to that which you do not understand. If you would be really big, pay the price for bigness by investigating the life which you do not understand, for wisdom comes from understanding, and understanding is based upon information. Until you have spent due time in investigation you are not ready to pronounce judgment.

One of the most tragic scenes in literature is depicted in Tennyson's *The Idylls of the King* when Queen Guinevere realized where her happiness lay—too late. Read her words thoughtfully:

> I thought I could not breathe in that fine air,
> That pure severity of perfect light—
> I yearned for warmth and color which I found
> In Lancelot—now I see thee what thou art,
> Thou art the highest and most human too,
> . . . Ah my God,
> What might I not have made of thy fair world,
> Had I but loved thy highest creature here?
> It was my duty to have loved the highest:

[1] Dr. Frank Crane, *Four Minute Essays* (New York: Wm. H. Wise & Co., Inc., 1919), Vol. VII, p. 77. Reprinted by permission.

> It surely was my profit had I known:
> It would have been my pleasure had I seen.
> We needs must love the highest when we see it.

Many students go through college missing the best because they think they cannot live in that "fine air." Many never discover that "the highest is the most human too."

A wise teacher explained to his students the difference between firmness and stubborness as follows. The stubborn person says, "Right or wrong I keep my opinion." The firm person says, "I keep my opinion as long as I believe it is right but I will remain open minded, and if I am convinced that I am wrong I will change and be just as firm on the other side. I am seeking the truth and will stand firmly by what I consider true."

The student has a right to his opinion about literature; he has a right to decide what is worthy of his appreciation. Passive acceptance is not appreciation: appreciation is positive; it is dynamic; it is individual. Appreciation is a result of one's own response and not something superimposed by a teacher or textbook. It is important for the student to work for a sense of values and not to close his mind to any literature which others of more experience than he consider worth while.

Yet appreciation cannot be forced; it is partly a matter of growth. There is an Eastern proverb which states, "My children know me when I pass by." One recognizes truth when he has the knowledge or the experience to understand and to appreciate it. One feels a kinship for a poet or a philosopher who interprets for him his own experience. We have all had the experience of suddenly becoming aware of the truth of a familiar quotation. The truth flashes upon us with astounding clarity when knowledge and experience enable us to say, "I see, I understand, I know that is true."

Significance of Imagination

Should one wait, then, to interpret certain literature until he has had the experience which will clarify it for him? No, everyone has the power to understand and to appreciate experiences he has not participated in. Through imagination he can put together odd bits of his own past and create new experiences revealed to him in literature. There is a kinship in all nature by which understanding comes. Experience clarifies, it vivifies, it is revealing, but it is not the only revealing force in nature.

Every student has asked himself after a startling experience, "How did I know the truth before this happened to me?" For example, a young girl after a bereavement felt the comforting power of words of sympathy, flowers, the presence of friends. Their meaning came with such clarity she wondered how she had known, before this happened to her, to write notes of sympathy, to send flowers, or to attend the funeral services when her friends were bereaved. The answer is simple; she possessed a sympathetic nature. By the power of imagination, she could place herself in the situation of others. Jane Addams has said, "The person of the highest culture is the one who can put himself in the place of the greatest number of other persons." Interpretative reading gives one vicarious experiences which aid in developing this power.

Chapter IX

BACKGROUNDS, INTRODUCTIONS, AND PROGRAMS

> I am a part of all that I have met.
>
> . . . . .
>
> All experience is an arch wherethro'
> Gleams that untravell'd world.
> *Tennyson*

Backgrounds for interpretative reading may be considered from two points of view: (1) the reader's general background of knowledge and experience, and (2) the specific background concerning the author and the literature to be interpreted. Let us consider first the background of the reader's own experience, direct or vicarious, which is so clearly stated in the two quotations above from Alfred Tennyson's "Ulysses." As suggested by these words, we are what we are as a result of our experiences, and experience enables us to see "gleams" of the world we have not traveled. We create new concepts out of old experiences. J. B. Kerfoot suggests this idea when he says:

The living we ourselves do is never really comprehended by us until we have read and reread it into other lives; and the infinitely various livingness of others is never really grasped by us until we have read and reread it into as many as may be of those potential selves that life has denied us the chance to be.[1]

We have heard much of a similar nature in modern education since Dr. Watson announced, as something more or less new, "To every stimulus the organism receives from without, it makes a definite response, the nature of which depends upon both the *stimulus* and the *past experience* of the organism." But even in "the gay nineties" Dr. S. S. Curry was stating, "A man cannot express that he does not possess." Surely this last is just another way of stating that the response of the individual depends upon his experience.[2]

Background for interpretative reading is gained directly through experience and indirectly through reading and all forms of listening. Sound films offer opportunity for experiences in lands and periods of time which would otherwise be less realistic and vivid. A group of people were invited to a home to see color films of Hawaii. One member of the group testified that her appreciation of the beauty of that land of charm was vivified, she believed, more than the actual experience would have afforded. Another who had been to Hawaii said her experience was made more meaningful by the films.

Indirect experiences, however, are not usually as vivid as direct experiences. One may have an imaginative picture of the Grand Canyon of Arizona, but that picture is vivified and one's appreciation is increased by seeing the Canyon itself especially at sunrise or sunset when the crags reflect

---

[1] J. B. Kerfoot, *How to Read* (Boston and New York: Houghton Mifflin Company, 1916), p. 3. By permission of the publishers.
[2] Gertrude E. Johnson, *Studies in the Art of Interpretation* (New York: D. Appleton-Century Co., Inc., 1940), p. 3.

the colors of the sky. Travel, reading, human contacts, and the theater are means one may employ to increase a general background.

The value of experience, however, for creative art is determined largely by one's *response* to experience. Concerning this important aspect Hamilton Wright Mabie states:

> Great art of any kind involves a great temperament even more than a great intellect; since the essence of art is never intellectual, but always the complete expression of the whole nature. A great temperament is a rarer gift than a great mind; and it is the distinctive gift of the artist. Browning had the vitality, the freshness of feeling, the eagerness of interest, the energy of spirit, which witness this temperament. He had an intense joy in life, in nature simply as nature, without reference to what lay behind. For one must feel freshly and powerfully through the senses before one can represent the inner meaning of life and nature in art.[1]

The *use* one makes of experience, as Mr. Mabie suggests, is significant in determining its value as background. To the poetic, a sunset, moonlight on a lake, or cleaning a pasture spring is sufficient motivation for a poem, a painting, or a creative response which gives meaning and fullness to life. Mr. Frost aptly expresses this idea in his poem, "The Pasture," in which the farmer so simply sums up the whole cycle of life in the words, "You come too." [2] Literature and experience set up a constructive cycle for the interpreter by which experience gives appreciation for literature and

---

[1] From *My Study Fire,* by Hamilton Wright Mabie, pp. 51–2. Reprinted by permission of Dodd, Mead and Company, Inc.
[2] Robert Frost, *The Collected Poems of Robert Frost* (New York: Halcyon House, 1936).

literature in turn interprets life. Yet there are those who "having eyes, see not; and having ears, hear not." The student of interpretative reading must develop the habit of reacting positively to experience and of translating experience into creative reading. A constructive cycle is thus formed, giving color and interest to life and in turn understanding and appreciation to literature.

This principle is developed in the writings of John Ruskin whose art principle Agnes Knox Black applies to interpretative reading in her discussion of *Speech as a Fine Art,* wherein she points out the relation of oral interpretation to creative writing in the lives of well-known authors:

Each one of the great prose writers of the Nineteenth Century has left on record—in letters or biography—his indebtedness to vocal interpretation as a means of *liberating the creative impulse,* and each one of the far-flung band was himself an interpreter of literature through vocal rendering. De Quincey never wearied of declaiming the impassioned prose of Hooker and Sir Thomas Browne; Macaulay was not more effective as a writer than as a speaker; Carlyle and Ruskin were most impressive lecturers and readers. Mr. Mallock of the *New Republic* has said: "I have heard him (Ruskin) lecture several times, and that singular voice of his, which would often hold all the theater breathless, haunts me still. He read magnificently. Passages came with new force and meaning when recited with appropriate emphasis and intonation." Surely every reader of this magazine knows of the marvelous tones of Emerson's voice as described by Lowell and Dr. Ames, or Newman's as described by Shairp and Matthew Arnold. What magnificent readers and interpreters were the three latest of the great novelists of England—Dickens, Thackeray, and George Eliot! The principle informing these significant facts is that intelligent, sympathetic reading aloud gives us the true vision of a writer's meaning, and thereby are stirred into activity those ideas which respond to the ideas enshrined in great books. It is from the power of true appreciation—the appreciation which can be developed only by contact with the great—that good and noble expression comes.[1]

SPECIFIC BACKGROUND

No matter how adequate our general background may be there is need also for special background for the understanding and appreciation of specific literature. What this background is to consist of depends largely upon the literature itself. Much literature is an expression of the point of view of the author, so knowledge of his life is often significant. One cannot always segregate those elements in an author's life which contribute to an appreciation of his writing, but a knowledge of his experience, his struggles, and his attainments as influenced by his environment usually adds insight and thus gives a specific background for interpretative reading. A student gave a lecture-recital on Lord Byron, using as the basis for her program the biography of Byron by André Maurois. She interspersed her program with poetry connected with experiences related in the biography. At the conclusion of the program a young man remarked, "Isn't it interesting how an understanding of a man's life affects your reaction to his works? I'd never liked Byron before. Now I believe I'll read his poetry with interest and understanding."

Sometimes a background is needed concerning the char-

[1] Agnes Knox Black, "Speech as a Fine Art," in *Studies in the Art of Interpretation*, edited by Gertrude E. Johnson (New York: D. Appleton-Century Co., Inc., 1940), pp. 68–9. By permission of the author.

acter which the author interprets. A young woman was preparing a review of *Mary of Scotland* by Maxwell Anderson. She asked her teacher just what Mary's attitude was towards Queen Elizabeth, and Elizabeth's attitude towards Mary, Queen of Scots. The teacher answered, "I do not know, but if I were going to review the book I would find out." "How?" asked the student. "Well," responded the teacher, "I would draw out of the library every biography listed of both Mary and of Elizabeth. I would read some of them carefully and read portions of others. When I had a sufficient basis of knowledge I would compare Maxwell Anderson's interpretation of the two queens with that of other biographers." A few days later the student came back for another conference with the teacher. She had followed the suggestions and was eager to share her knowledge of these queens and the varied interpretations biographers had given. A few weeks later this student gave her review of the play, and afterwards a guest remarked, "You show a remarkable understanding; there is so much *back* of your interpretation."

A knowledge of the circumstances under which a piece of literature is written is helpful. The working conditions for children in England at the time Elizabeth Barrett wrote motivated her poem, "The Cry of the Children." One who reads this poem needs similar motivation gained from knowledge of those conditions. A knowledge of the historical significance of Gettysbury is needed as background for an interpretative reading of Lincoln's Gettysburg Address. A knowledge of the fact that Robert Browning wrote "Prospice" (*looking forward*) after the death of his wife and that the line, "I shall clasp thee again," refers to her, gives understanding to Browning's attitude towards death as expressed in this poem.

It is sometimes essential for the reader to become familiar with an author's works as a whole in order to understand his philosophy, grasp his style, and do justice to him in interpretative reading. One reader said that before she attempted to give an interpretative reading of a certain poem by Archibald MacLeish, she read a number of his books and found that understanding came gradually but surely as she became more familiar with his general philosophy and style. One of the most helpful sources she found was *A Note on Verse* written as a preface to his poetic play *Panic*. In this preface Mr. MacLeish explains his method of developing his verse form.

Many things in that preface should prove helpful to an actor, a director, or an interpretative reader in giving an authentic interpretation, for Mr. MacLeish explains his attempt to find "a verse form capable of catching and carrying the rhythm of the spoken language of his time and place." A further statement strikes a responsive chord for every interpretative reader:

> Verse, after all, is not an arrangement upon the page: it is a pattern for the ear. If it does not exist in the ear, it does not exist.[1]

In a similar fashion, the preface which Maxwell Anderson wrote for *Winterset* gives insight into his thought for poetic creation and expression; Mr. Anderson considers the stage a cathedral for the unfolding of mysteries and the building

---

[1] Archibald MacLeish, Preface to *Panic* (Boston: Houghton Mifflin Company, 1935), p. ix. By permission.

of faith. He considers poetry a necessary medium in the theater.

A written analysis of the background and its relation to a piece of literature will prove helpful to the student in assimilating his material. Written analyses clarify one's thinking; they insure thorough study in preparation for an interpretative reading. They help one to overcome careless and superficial habits.

INTRODUCTIONS

All art involves selection. From the background one has accumulated he may select certain important elements to be given to his audience in an introduction in order that the audience may also have a background for understanding and appreciation. Someone has said that a speaker's wastebasket should contain more material than his notebook. Even if the reader discards most of the notes he has accumulated as background, the effect of his study will remain with him. Out of his scope of knowledge he will evolve understanding which will give authority to his interpretation. He should select from this background only the choicest, most fitting information for his introduction. Only that which is needed for a clear understanding of the author's ideas and moods should be included in the introduction.

Consideration should also be given to the length of an introduction. In general, introductions should be brief. One who has given sufficient preparation to a background for interpretation will be tempted to make his introduction too lengthy. Remember—the background will be revealed in the interpretation of the lines; only the most significant ideas should be included in the introduction. Five minutes or less should be sufficient time for an introduction to almost any piece of literature. One well-developed, carefully phrased sentence is frequently sufficient.

The audience and occasion also serve to guide the reader in selecting material for introductions. He may supplement this planned introduction at the last minute with spontaneous remarks which grow out of the occasion. One should be alert for incidents which occur just prior to his reading and to the value of such in giving interest, understanding, freshness, and direct contact to his material. How well Will Rogers understood that principle! He not only read the daily papers but he was constantly on the alert for data concerning local interests. In a college town during football season he inquired naïvely if the college had a Dean or a President. He said that he had heard of the coach and of the football team but he wasn't sure whether the college had a faculty or administrative officials. The delighted audience called for the President, who was loved as much as the coach; then Will Rogers showed his further knowledge of the local situation by remarking facetiously, "Mr. President, I want to give you some advice. Don't you teach those Baptists out there too much; if you do they won't be Baptists." When the audience laughed, Will Rogers added, "Oh, you Methodists needn't laugh!"

A reader's introduction should lead naturally into the interpretation of the first line of the literature he is to interpret. Natural transitions are important for sustained interest and coherent thinking. The introduction must create atmosphere which will prepare for, or blend with, the first line of the literature. This transition from the introduction to the material is partly a matter of writing and partly a matter of reading technique.

PROGRAMS

As in the case of introductions, so also in selecting material for a program, questions of occasion, time of day, place of program, type of audience, must always be considered. The reader is likely to have certain tendencies, likes and dislikes, some types of material he "does best," but care should always be exerted to check the impulse to do those things one "does best" to the exclusion of other necessary considerations. One's taste must be catholic. In an hour's general program to be given by one person there should be a balance in elements of humor, drama, prose, poetry, scene, sketch, monologue. But not all these in one hour!

The opening number in a general program is an important consideration. It should not be overlong: better under ten minutes than over. It should have a fairly simple and direct appeal, preferably with an element of humor though not in excess. An audience is not prepared upon our first appearance to give as good a response to our "appeals" as later when they are "settled" and have had a chance to become acquainted, as it were, with the interpreter. The mistake in opening with selections which are in monologue form is that the audience does not know us yet, so why ask them to meet a character other than ourselves? The mistake in opening with dialect is that the audience should know *our* speech and enjoy it ere we ask them to enjoy another speech form. And the mistake in opening with poetry is that while some may enjoy it, certainly others will not, since prose forms are nearer the general life and daily ways of most of humanity. These forms all offer hindrances as opening numbers. Be simple, direct, easy, with normal humor and no attempt to run the gamut of emotion or bedazzle with an array of characters or your *acting* ability; give the hearers a chance to meet *you* as a normal human being like themselves. Your ability and versatility, your artistry, will grow upon them as you progress.

One of the chief concerns in arrangement of selections chosen for a program should be to place them so that the audience will be prepared to give to every number as favorable a response as possible. Our general reactions do not go abruptly from grave to gay and back to grave, nor from sublime to ridiculous. Arranging selections in too great or too regular contrast is not likely to gain the best possible response. Shading, leading away from the mood just presented and on towards another definitely different mood, offers a better basic plan. One prose narrative following another, even if in a different vein, is not desirable, for the fact of the identical form tends to dull the reception. There is the possibility of shorter numbers intervening, probably poetry which may be grouped into "a" and "b" numbers, which will help to form a break and lend the possibility of the melding of mood, mentioned earlier.

A word or two as to "grouping." There should be some basic reason for this, and since poetry is most likely to fall into the grouping idea we might mention that mood, and idea or theme, are two reasons for grouping. Selections by the same author may be grouped, though the fact that it *is* the same author should not be the primary reason; theme and mood would still supersede. Seldom if ever should prose and poetry form an "a" and "b," as unity of mood and idea does not usually appear in these two forms. Prose is usually long, and the difference in the forms of the writing does not make for unity. A number long enough to form a whole unit, such as an eight or ten minute selection, usually should stand alone. A scene from a play or a one-act play should not be included as an "a" and "b" number. There might be exceptions in the case of scenes from plays but seldom in the case of the one-act play. This latter in particular would overshadow any other number in the group.

There is also the question of climax. Some advocate moving in a steadily rising intensity with the crescendo at the close, while others contend that the hearers are likely to be best prepared to react favorably to the most intense number (not necessarily tragedy) about half or two-thirds of the way through the program. The latter seems definitely more sound, psychologically speaking.

Sometimes it is necessary or desirable to break the program into parts, as *Part One* and *Part Two,* in which case there may be some selection desirable to include which is in the nature of an exit, a monologue perhaps, in which the character in the monologue is making his or her exit from the scene and hence concludes a part. Preferably one should use this to end *Part One* rather than making it the closing number of an entire program.

In giving a program from the works of one author, the reader should always have as a primary objective not only the pleasure and profit of the audience but the various facets of approach and interests of the *author*. This is frequently overlooked. The reader too often seems to have chosen *his* favorites or those selections which have "dramatic" possibilities or, and here we must be guarded, those in which his talents or idiosyncratic style will shine. None of these reasons should stand foremost in any program selection, but when the reader is presenting the work of one author he must in his selections, and as far as possible, do justice to that author.

The following examples are offered as suggestions observing many of the principles set forth. They are intended for general audiences.

RECITAL FROM THE POETRY OF JOHN MASEFIELD

Part I

A Consecration
Ships

WANDERLUST

Roadways
The West Wind
Vagabond
A Wanderer's Song

SAILORS

Sea Change
Cape Horn Gospel
Mother Cary
The Port of Many Ships
D'Avalo's Prayer

Part II

Reynard the Fox

(Introduction: Mr. Masefield says that he wrote this story of a fox hunt because the events have been for many centuries the deepest pleasure in English country life, bringing together on terms of equality all sorts and conditions of the English people. He adds that he felt that a fox hunt made a frame in which many of the more permanent types of English character might be portrayed. The fox hunt means and will always mean more to the English people than to any other.)

RECITAL

SELECTED READINGS
Prose and Poetry

Part I

The Check-Book (Prose)   *Geoffrey Kerr*
  (Truth or fiction?)

POETRY   *Robert Frost*

Blueberries
Wild Grapes
A Servant to Servants

LYRICS

The Telephone
The Rose Family
Into My Own

Part II

The Butterfly That Stamped   *Rudyard Kipling*
  (A Fable in Prose)

RHYTHMS

The Potatoes Dance   *Vachel Lindsay*
Tarantella   *Hilaire Belloc*
When I Danced with the Great
  King of Spain   *Anna Hempstead Branch*

DRAMATIC RECITAL

Part I

The First Act of
CALL IT A DAY
By
C. L. Anthony

CHARACTERS

Roger Hilton
Dorothy Hilton (his wife)
Ann (aged 15)
Martin (aged 17)
Catherine (aged 19)
Vera (the maid)

SCENE

Early morning in Roger and Dorothy's bedroom.

Part II

POETRY

The Poodle and the Pug	*H. H. Herbert*
Miss Busy	*H. H. Herbert*
Lilacs	*Amy Lowell*
The Passing Strange	*John Masefield*

We turn rather too easily and often to the play for our hour's reading, but the royalty question makes the use of the play for reading increasingly difficult, and in a final analysis the ultimate values for the interpreter's growth in the use of the play are too closely connected with characterization. Arranging a play offers some problems, but they are not too difficult. The main theme can usually be followed, care being taken not to destroy balance in moods and situations. Keep the play "whole" as to its central idea whatever is done. An hour and fifteen minutes should ordinarily be an outside limit for time.

No discussion of program materials is complete without considering the values of the book-length novel for interpretative purposes. Oddly enough it is not so generally used as are drama and poetry. The prose form itself doesn't receive the attention from many teachers that it deserves as a training for the interpreter. It contains many teaching "devices," both in content and form, which no other type of material offers. Says W. H. Crawshaw in his book, *The Interpretation of Literature:*

> The novel deals principally with humanity. In the treatment of individual character, it is dealing mostly with man; and in the treatment of character relations, it is dealing with human life. We have seen that drama, being chiefly concerned with human action, is more likely to emphasize the latter. In the novel, however, man is likely to be more prominent; for action is not so important, and there is more opportunity for psychological analysis. Another important difference between drama and novel is that the latter deals with the common man and emphasizes the worth of the individual soul. The novel holds closely to the human centre; but it is very free in showing the relation of humanity to the other great subjects.
>
> The novel is practically a combination of the drama and the romance. It is like the drama in substance and in purpose, and is therefore to be regarded as dramatic literature. It is like the romance in form and method; for it presents its characters and its plot by means of direct prose narration. Even more than the prose drama, the novel is the typical prose representative of the dramatic impulse; for the true realm of the drama is poetry, and the novel has made good its position as

the most appropriate literary form for the representation of life in its more prosaic aspects.[1]

Many further direct values must be admitted as valid justification for more comprehensive use of the novel for interpretative purposes. Historical significance as in *The Sea of Grass, Show Boat, Suns Go Down,* and *Gone With the Wind;* the lure of foreign lands in *Listen! The Wind, North to the Orient,* and *Keys of the Kingdom;* character studies as in *The Bridge of San Luis Rey, My Antonia, One More Spring, One Foot in Heaven,* and *Grandma Called It Carnal;* animals holding the center of interest as in *The Voice of Bugle Ann, Flush,* and *The Ugly Dachshund;* families and their doings, as in *Life With Father, Time at Her Heels, Jalna,* and *Oh, Promise Me.* These are but a few examples chosen as they come to mind, and the list can be extended indefinitely in every direction.

Nor is the arrangement so difficult as might at first be supposed. Usually it will be desirable to condense and arrange to occupy not over an hour or a little more, the time varying somewhat according to the nature of the novel chosen for arrangement. Much may be condensed and told in part in the reader's own words, or portions of material omitted may be woven into brief connecting statements.

The arranging of the novel may call for a reduction in the number of characters, for too many will make for confusion and by involving too much dialogue will retard the dramatic progress of events or climaxes. Minor characters may be omitted as in a play. If drama and comedy or contrasting moods of any sort are present, these should be kept in proper proportion and balance. In all cases the inherent

[1] W. H. Crawshaw, *The Interpretation of Literature* (New York: Macmillan Company, 1908), Chapter V, p. 87. By permission of the publishers.

ideas and intention of the author must be thoroughly understood and adhered to for a truthful and artistic result.

The Lecture-Recital

The lecture-recital offers opportunity for the reader to combine the values of public speaking and reading in a unified and effective manner. In the lecture portion the reader may give information and explanations which clarify the selections of literature he chooses to read. The vividness and color of interpretative reading should keep audience interest at a high peak of enjoyment. A lecture-recital, like a well developed speech, should be built upon a single theme from which unity is derived. Variety may be attained through choice of material and techniques of delivery. Personal comment from the reader aids appreciation; it seems to be an integral part of a lecture-recital.

The development of a lecture-recital follows basic principles of both public speaking and interpretative reading. The introduction should win the good will of the audience to the speaker and to the theme. It is usually advisable for the speaker to state the theme clearly, evoking audience interest in its development through explanations and illustrations. Introductions are usually more effective when given extemporaneously than when read.

Due credit should be given to authors for material quoted. One may state the sources from which material is taken in the introduction, before or after specific portions, or at the end of the program. Frequently in radio, data such as titles, authors, *et cetera* are given by an announcer at the end of the program. In the lecture-recital these data often seem an essential part of the lecture and hence are given as introductory to the reading of specific selections. Clear statements concerning the source give authenticity, a part of the scholarly work expected of both readers and lecturers. No reader of integrity would wish to claim as his own any quoted material. Due credit to the author seems always desirable.

Selections should be arranged in sequence following the principles of composition. This sequence may be chronological, according to time. It may be logical according to cause and effect. It may be psychological: according to the effect the reader wishes to produce upon the audience. For example, one may start a program with an amusing anecdote, fable, or poem in order to catch the interest of the audience and establish rapport between speaker and audience. It is usually considered wise to give the more intellectual portions toward the beginning while the audience is fresh. Interest may be sustained by emotion or material that is varied and vital. The principle of climax is important. It may be applied in many ways. Sometimes it is a climax of feeling, sometimes of spectacular or novel elements. Sometimes there is the climax, or turning point, of a plot, such as the lecture-recital built upon the correspondence of Robert Browning and Elizabeth Barrett Barrett printed in the second section of this book. It is entitled, *Love's Courage*.

Continuity is sustained through well planned transitions from one portion to another. Transitions which grow out of the idea or mood of one portion should lead into the next portion. This continuity should seem to rise naturally and spontaneously and should lead progressively to the climax. Transitions may be read or spoken extemporaneously. The directness of extempore speech gives the audience a feeling of intimacy and informality that is often highly desirable. The conclusion, whether spoken or read, should give a sense of completeness, though it is always good to leave an audience wanting more.

If a program lasts more than twenty or thirty minutes the audience is likely to have restless moments. No matter how interesting the material may be individuals must shift position occasionally. An effective reader may, by pausing and shifting his own position, cause the audience to make these shifts between ideas or portions, and prevent distracting shifts during important moments. A speaker who had held the audience virtually spellbound for twenty minutes said with disarming charm, "Now I think we'd better have a squirming pause." The audience laughed, relaxed and was ready for more of the intense concentration for which that occasion called. Squirming pauses do not have to be labeled to be effective. In fact they are usually more effective without the audience even being aware of them. Yet the reader should be aware and may even mark his manuscript to remind him to give the audience time to relax before he takes up a new idea, mood or situation.

Chapter X

CHORAL READING

> Choric speech as a method of teaching has proved itself worthy of consideration. As a method of artistic expression it contains possibilities of renewing and vivifying the whole art of poetry.
>
> Dr. Gordon Bottomly

A modern book on interpretative reading would hardly be complete without some word concerning the communal approach known as choral reading. This form of reading has been used continually through the ages in religious services and, to a certain extent, in drama, notably that of the Greeks. The twentieth century revival of choral reading has spread from religion and the theater into radio and education. Its forms now include not only the rituals of the church and the choral parts of plays but the reading of lyrics, ballads, essays, narration, of prose and poetry *ad infinitum.* Some verse speaking choirs have been organized to give public performances with a view to entertainment or for the promotion of an art form. Choral speaking has flourished in radio because, no doubt, of its heightening of dramatic effect not only for plays but for current events, historical episodes, narration, and announcements even to a football game given in duo instead of by the more usual single voice of a sports reporter.

Concerning the value of a revival of choral reading Cécile de Banke says:

> The value of a revival of any form of art lies not so much in the emulation of past achievement as in the fact that, once the standard of that achievement is recognized and accepted as a challenge, the artists evolve a new expression of the art, which has the further value of being creative, vital, and contemporaneous. So with the revival of choral speaking, we find, after fourteen years' study of its history and past achievement, and after experimental work in all its phases, that a form is beginning to emerge which, carrying the dignity and impress of its splendid past, yet expresses the virile rhythm and tone of its immediate environment. A rapid survey of the growth of choral speaking from its earliest forms to the latest expression of the modern revival, and ending with conjecture as to its future expansion, will serve, perhaps, to clarify our own objective in studying and teaching what is at the same time the oldest and the newest manifestation of the spoken word.[1]

Students of interpretation may approach choral reading from one of two distinct points of view neither wholly precluding the other but each having ultimate aims quite widely divergent. These two approaches are (1) as an educational device, with the ultimate aim of improving the individual's understanding, appreciation, and skill in the interpretation of literature; and (2) as an art form for public presentation. This book is dedicated to the stabilizing influence of interpretative reading upon the individual. This phase of interpretation will therefore be considered from the educational point of view, and choral speaking as a

[1] Cécile de Banke, *The Art of Choral Speaking* (Boston: Walter H. Baker Co., 1937), p. 15. By permission of the publishers.

public performance will be left entirely to the discretion of the individual students or teachers.

As a teaching function, group reading has usually been a part of the procedure of classes in interpretative reading. Voice drills and exercises are given chorally with the teacher serving as director. It is a short step, then, from a choral exercise, in which good tone quality is the goal, to an art form in which tone is achieved as a means of expressing the mood, the idea, and the effect intended by the author. The starting point in choral reading is adequate tone quality for the expression of an idea. The danger is that the group will lose sight of the idea and work for tone alone. This is no uncommon fault in individual reading, but it is more likely to occur with a group due to the necessity of preserving harmony with other voices.

Some advocates of choral speaking claim that there is such a thing as "group thinking" and that choral reading can therefore be as spontaneous as individual interpretation. Others claim that the members of the group think as individuals but that through a process of crystallization the form becomes sufficiently stable for harmony and spontaneity to be preserved together. Elsie Fogerty solved this problem with the chorus for the London production of T. S. Eliot's *Murder in the Cathedral* by directing each individual in the chorus to create a character as individual as if he were acting alone. The chorus then spoke not as a single voice but as a group of individuals voicing similar sentiments and reacting to the same stimuli.

In choral speaking a consideration of tempo and rhythm follows closely upon that of tone. Herein lies an excellent opportunity for developing flexibility and for breaking up an individual's habit of superimposing his own tempo and rhythm upon whatever he may read. The necessity of "keeping in step" with the group causes the slow ones to speed up, the fast ones to slow down, and the inflexible ones to work for variation. One perhaps learns to sense rhythms better by group reading than by individual interpretation; at least he must submit to the discipline of the rhythm established by the group and in this discipline may learn to sense other rhythms than his own habitual ones.

The same possibilities may be recognized for other techniques, such as change of pitch, inflection, pause, emphasis, and climax. The chief danger in choral reading is that the concentration may be too much upon effects and the very essence of art, the revelation of an idea, may be lost. This tendency must be counterbalanced by the stimulation that a group gives to the individual to sense, to create, to imagine the oral expression which will adequately interpret the author's purpose. When the interpretation of a selection is shared by a group, interesting aspects are sometimes disclosed. To one a line means this, to another it suggests that. Through sharing ideas a broader, more thorough approach may be gained and individual thinking stimulated.

In her conclusion to a discussion of the art of choral speaking, Louise Abney says:

> Its classroom value in the appreciation and enjoyment of poetry, and its constructive contribution to better speech and better reading, far surpass its auditorium value. On the other hand, the bringing together of many groups of boys and girls in a great co-operative experience has brought much inspira-

tion to both participants and audience, especially at the Christmas and Easter seasons. "I hear America singing" is coming true in the music of speech as well as in that of song.[1]

DIRECTING CHORAL READING

The amount of direction a group should be given by the director (or leader) is an important problem in choral reading. Some authors take it for granted that the director is the artist and the choir the instrument and that the director plays upon this human instrument as a musician plays upon an organ. The education viewpoint may call for the reverse of this attitude. Since our purpose is the development of the individuals in the group, we might favor an interpretation which grows out of the thinking of the members of the group. One schoolteacher encourages small children to plan (to create) the interpretation and to lead the group in their interpretation. A child may be allowed to go to the cloakroom "to think aloud" and upon his return to the schoolroom lead the group in the interpretation he worked out while alone. A piece may be led by several different boys or girls with others in the chorus offering suggestions here and there, the group then selecting the interpretation or the phases of interpretation which the majority like best. Such a plan encourages individual initiative, creativeness, and coöperation. Such a plan helps to prevent regimentation by the director with a form superimposed upon the group.

There is a difference of opinion as to how many should

[1] Louise Abney, *Choral Speaking Arrangements for the Junior High* (Boston: Expression Company, 1939), p. 21. By permission of the publishers.

compose the group for choral reading. One writer suggests that the group consist of not less than ten, while another suggests that seven and nine are ideal for choral groups. It would seem that the number would depend upon the total situation and in a large measure upon the material the group is reading, the purpose of the performance (whether as a schoolroom exercise, for a public reading, or for radio), and upon the age, ability, and organization of the group. For instance, in public performance for a seen or unseen audience the group speaking in unison should not be so large that the voices sound muddled and the enunciation indistinct. The leader may break up a large group into small units for the reading of certain portions of a selection and thus handle the situation of giving many people something to do without having too many speak in unison.

There are various methods of arranging material for choral interpretation, such as unison reading, antiphonal reading, three part divisions, an echo chorus for refrains, a line around, solo and chorus, adding and subtracting voices and so forth. Some of these will be illustrated in the following pages.

UNISON READING

In unison reading there is little attempt to direct the voice pitch of the group except in the matter of interpretation. That is, each member of the chorus speaks in his own normal key, allowing his voice to move up and down the scale in response to the idea. Harmony results from the blend of voices, and unity is gained by an agreement as to the meaning. It is important that tempo and rhythm be agreed upon in order that all may keep together. The rhythm of a passage may be sensed by the individuals by feeling the pulse of the rhythm as was suggested in Chapter III. It is always essential at first to follow a leader (the teacher or some member of the group). Some advocates of choral reading claim that a group soon learns to sense the rhythm and may keep together without a director. Modulations must be agreed upon, although they may grow gradually, out of an attempt to express the meaning rather than from being accepted *a priori* from a teacher or leader.

The following lyrics lend themselves nicely to unison reading. The three stanzas of the first poem suggest three definite moods which give variety to the whole. The words *answer echoes* and *dying, dying, dying* may be given with an echo effect either by the entire chorus or by a selected group of voices.

THE SPLENDOUR FALLS
From THE PRINCESS
Alfred Tennyson

The splendour falls on castle walls
   And snowy summits old in story:
The long light shakes across the lakes,
   And the wild cataract leaps in glory.
Blow, bugle, blow, set the wild echoes flying,
Blow, bugle; answer, echoes, dying, dying, dying.

O hark, O hear! how thin and clear,
   And thinner, clearer, farther going!
O sweet and far from cliff and scar
   The horns of Elfland faintly blowing!
Blow, let us hear the purple glens replying:
Blow, bugle; answer, echoes, dying, dying, dying.

O love, they die in yon rich sky,
   They faint on hill or field or river:
Our echoes roll from soul to soul,
   And grow for ever and for ever.
Blow, bugle, blow, set the wild echoes flying,
And answer, echoes, answer, dying, dying, **dying**.

CLEAR AND COOL

Charles Kingsley

Clear and cool, clear and cool,
By laughing and shallow and dreaming pool;
   Cool and clear, cool and clear,
By shining shingle and foaming weir;
Under the crag where the ousel sings,
And the ivied wall where the church-bell rings,
     Undefiled, for the undefiled;
   Play by me, bathe in me, mother and child.

   Dank and foul, dank and foul
By the smoky town in its murky cowl;
   Foul and dank, foul and dank,
By wharf and sewer and slimy bank;
Darker and darker the farther I go,
     Who dare sport with the sin-defiled?
   Shrink from me, turn from me, mother and child.

   Strong and free, strong and free,
The flood gates are open, away to the sea,
   Free and strong, free and strong,
Cleansing my streams as I hurry along,
To the golden sands, and the leaping bar,
And the taintless tide that awaits me afar,
As I lose myself in the infinite main,
Like a soul that has sinned and is pardoned **again**,
     Undefiled, for the undefiled;
   Play by me, bathe in me, mother and child.

ANTIPHONAL READING

The Psalms and other portions of the Bible are used for antiphonal reading in religious worship. Sometimes the minister reads a line (or verse) and the congregation or choir responds with the next line. Sometimes antiphonal reading is given by two choirs (speaking, singing, or chanting) or sometimes by one choir, with the congregation being led by the minister. The popular Negro radio singers who give the program *Wings over Jordan* read antiphonally, with the leader reading a line and the choir repeating the same portion. This technique gives opportunity for individual interpretation on the part of the leader and restatement by the chorus of voices.

PSALM XXIV [1]

First Choir.   The earth is the Lord's, and the fulness thereof;
　　　　　　　　The world, and they that dwell therein.
　　　　　　　For he hath founded it upon the seas,
　　　　　　　　And established it upon the floods.
　　　　　　　Who shall ascend into the hill of the Lord?
　　　　　　　　Or who shall stand in his holy place?
Second Choir. He that hath clean hands, and a pure heart;
　　　　　　　　Who hath not lifted up his soul unto vanity,
　　　　　　　　Nor sworn deceitfully.
　　　　　　　He shall receive the blessing from the Lord,
　　　　　　　　And righteousness from the God of his salvation.
　　　　　　　This is the generation of them that seek him,
　　　　　　　　That seek thy face, O Jacob. Selah.
First Choir.   Lift up your heads, O ye gates;
　　　　　　　　And be ye lifted up, ye everlasting doors:

[1] Arranged by Sara Lowrey.

	And the King of Glory shall come in.
Second Choir.	Who is the King of Glory?
First Choir.	The Lord strong and mighty,
	The Lord mighty in battle.
	Lift up your heads, O ye gates;
	Even, lift them up, ye everlasting **doors**:
	And the King of Glory shall come in.
Second Choir.	Who is this King of Glory?
First Choir.	The Lord of Hosts,
All.	He is the King of Glory. Selah.

The technique of rhythm suggested for the interpretation of "The Old Clock on the Stairs" carries over effectively into choral reading. A number of the chorus may be designated to give the rhythm of the clock while others speak the narrative lines of the poem. For example, a group may start the rhythm with "Tick-tock, tick-tock, tick-tock," and after a line or two the other group may start reading the lines of the poem to the accompaniment of the chorus of "tick-tocks." In "The Kitchen Clock" the two groups may speak together lines such as those from "Seconds reckoned" through "nickety-knock." The two groups may thus alternately speak separately or together according to the ingenuity and plan of the director or by group agreement.

THE KITCHEN CLOCK

John Vance Cheney

Knitting is the maid o' the kitchen, Milly;
Doing nothing, sits the chore boy, Billy;
"Seconds reckoned,
Seconds reckoned;
Every minute,
Sixty in it,

Milly, Billy,
Billy, Milly,
Tick-tock, tock-tick,
Nick-knock, knock-nick,
Knockety-nick, nickety-knock,"
   Goes the kitchen clock.

Close to the fire is rosy Milly,
Every whit as close and cosy, Billy;
"Time's a-flying,
Worth your trying;
Pretty Milly—
Kiss her, Billy!
Milly, Billy!
Billy, Milly,
Tick-tock, tock-tick,
Now—now, quick—quick!
Knockety-nick, nickety-knock,"
   Goes the kitchen clock.

Something's happened, very red is Milly;
Billy boy is looking very silly;
"Pretty misses,
Plenty kisses;
Make it twenty,
Take a plenty,
Billy, Milly,
Milly, Billy,
Right—left, left—right,
That's right, all right,
Knockety-nick, nickety-knock,"
   Goes the kitchen clock.

Weeks gone, still they're sitting, Milly, Billy;
Oh, the winter winds are wondrous chilly;
"Winter weather,

Close together;
Wouldn't tarry,
Better marry,
Milly, Billy,
Billy, Milly,
Two—one, one—two,
Don't wait, 'twon't do,
Knockety-nick, nickety-knock,"
   Goes the kitchen clock.

Winters two are gone, and where is Milly?
Spring has come again, and where is Billy?
"Give me credit,
For I did it;
Treat me kindly.
Mind you wind me,
Mister Billy, Mistress Milly,
My-o, O-my,
By-by, by-by,
Nickety-knock, cradle rock,"—
   Goes the kitchen clock.

REFRAINS

"The Rhyme of the Duchess May" by Elizabeth Barrett Browning offers an interesting opportunity for a group of choral readers. When read by a single voice the refrain, *toll slowly,* which occurs in every stanza may interfere with the story or become somewhat monotonous. When given by a chorus it may create a mood and preserve unity for the interpretation. There are a number of arrangements which may prove effective for a choral rendition, one of which is for the chorus of voices to intone the refrain and the story to be told by a cast consisting of a narrator, an old bell ringer, the Duchess May, the Lord of Leigh, the Lord of Linteged, and so on.

From THE RHYME OF THE DUCHESS MAY
Elizabeth Barrett Browning

To the belfrey, one by one, went the ringers from the sun,—
  Toll slowly.
And the oldest ringer said, "Ours is music for the Dead,
  When the rebecks are all done."

There I sate beneath the tree, and the bell tolled solemnly,—
  Toll slowly.
While the trees' and river's voices flowed between the solemn noises,—
  Yet death seemed more loud to me.

There, I read this ancient rhyme, while the bell did all the time
  Toll slowly.
And the solemn knell fell in with the tale of life and sin,
  Like a rhythmic fate sublime.

Broad the forest stood (I read) on the hills of Linteged,—
  Toll slowly.
And three hundred years had stood, mute adown each hoary wood,
  Like a full heart, having prayed.

And the little birds sang east, and the little birds sang west,—
  Toll slowly.
And but little thought was theirs, of the silent antique years,
  In the building of their nest.

Down the sun dropt, large and red, on the towers of Linteged,—

> *Toll slowly.*

Lance and spear upon the height, bristling strange in fiery light,
> While the castle stood in shade.

There, the castle stood up black, with the red sun at its back,—
> *Toll slowly,*

Like a sullen smouldering pyre, with a top that flickers fire,
> When the wind is on its track.

And five hundred archers tall did besiege the castle wall,—
> *Toll slowly,*

And the castle, seethed in blood, fourteen days and nights had stood,
> And to-night was near its fall.

Yet thereunto, blind to doom, three months since, a bride did come,—
> *Toll slowly.*

One who proudly trod the floors, and softly whispered in the doors,
> "May good angels bless our home."

'Twas a Duke's fair orphan-girl, and her uncle's ward, the Earl
> *Toll slowly.*

Who betrothed her twelve years old, for the sake of dowry gold,
> To his son Lord Leigh, the churl.

But what time she had made good all her years of womanhood,—
> *Toll slowly.*

Unto both these Lords of Leigh spake she out right sovranly,
> "My will runneth as my blood.

"And while this same blood makes red this same right hand's veins," she said,—
Toll slowly,
" 'Tis my will, as lady free, not to wed a Lord of Leigh,
But Sir Guy of Linteged."

The old Earl he smiled smooth, then he sighed for wilful youth,—
Toll slowly.
"Good my niece, that hand withal looketh somewhat soft and small
For so large a will, in sooth."

She too smiled by that same sign,—but her smile was cold and fine,—
Toll slowly.
"Little hand clasps muckle gold; or it were not worth the hold
Of thy son, good uncle mine!"

Unto each she bowed her head, and swept past with lofty tread,—
Toll slowly.
Ere the midnight-bell had ceased, in the chapel had the priest
Blessed her, bride of Linteged.

Fast and fain the bridal train along the night-storm rode amain:—
Toll slowly.
Hard the steeds of lord and serf struck their hoofs out on the turf,
In the pauses of the rain.

Fast and fain the kinsmen's train along the storm pursued amain,—

    Toll slowly,—
Steed on steed-track, dashing off—thickening, doubling, hoof
 on hoof,
    In the pauses of the rain.

And the bridegroom led the flight, on his red-roan steed of
 might,—
    Toll slowly.
And the bride lay on his arm, still, as if she feared no harm,
    Smiling out into the night.

"Dost thou fear?" he said at last;—"Nay!" she answered him
 in haste,—
    Toll slowly.
"Not such death as we could find—only life with one behind—
    Ride on fast as fear—ride fast!"

Up the mountain wheeled the steed—girth to ground, and
 fetlocks spread,—
    Toll slowly.
Headlong bounds, and rocking flanks,—down he staggered—
 down the banks,
    To the towers of Linteged.

High and low the serfs looked out, red the flambeaus tossed
 about,—
    Toll slowly.
In the courtyard rose the cry—"Live the Duchess and Sir Guy!"
    But she never heard them shout.

On the steed she dropped her cheek, kissed his mane and kissed
 his neck,—
    Toll slowly.
"I had happier died by thee, than lived on as Lady Leigh,"
    Were the first words she did speak.

But a three months' joyaunce lay 'twixt that moment and to-day,—
   Toll slowly.
When five hundred archers tall stand beside the castle wall,
 To recapture Duchess May.

And the castle standeth black, with the red sun at its back,—
   Toll slowly.
And a fortnight's siege is done—and, except the Duchess, none
 Can misdoubt the coming wrack.

Oh, the little birds sang east, and the little birds sang west,—
   Toll slowly.
On the tower the castle's lord leant in silence on his sword,
 With an anguish in his breast.

With a spirit-laden weight did he lean down passionate,—
   Toll slowly.
They have almost sapped the wall,—they will enter there withal,
 With no knocking at the gate.

Then the sword he leant upon, shivered—snapped upon the stone,—
   Toll slowly.
"Sword," he thought, with inward laugh, "ill thou servest for a staff,
 When thy nobler use is done!

"Sword, thy nobler use is done!—tower is lost, and shame begun:"—
   Toll slowly.
"If we met them in the breach, hilt to hilt or speech to speech,
 We should die there, each for one.

"If we met them at the wall, we should singly, vainly fall,"—
   Toll slowly.
"But if I die here alone,—then I die, who am but one,
 And die nobly for them all.

"Five true friends lie for my sake—in the moat and in the
    brake;"—
                Toll slowly.
"Thirteen warriors lie at rest, with a black wound in the breast,
        And not one of these will wake.

"So no more of this shall be!—heart-blood weights too
    heavily,"—
                Toll slowly.
"And I could not sleep in grave, with the faithful and the brave
        Heaped around and over me.

"Since young Clare a mother hath, and young Ralph a plighted
    faith,"—
                Toll slowly.
"Since my pale young sister's cheeks blush like rose when
    Ronald speaks,
        Albeit never a word she saith—

"These shall never die for me—life-blood falls too heavily:"—
                Toll slowly.
"And if I die here apart,—o'er my dead and silent heart
        They shall pass out safe and free.

"When the foe hath heard it said—'Death holds Guy of Lin-
    teged,' "—
                Toll slowly.
"That new corse new peace shall bring; and a blessed, blessed
    thing
        Shall the stone be at its head.

"Then my friends shall pass out free, and shall bear my mem-
    ory,"—
                Toll slowly.
"Then my foes shall sleek their pride, soothing fair my widowed
    bride,
        Whose sole sin was love of me.

"She will weep her woman's tears, she will pray her woman's
    prayers,"—
          Toll slowly.
"But her heart is young in pain, and her hopes will spring again
    By the suntime of her years."

All these silent thoughts did swim o'er his eyes grown strange
    and dim,—
          Toll slowly.
Till his true men in the place wished they stood there face to face
    With the foe instead of him.

"One last oath, my friends, that wear faithful hearts to do and
    dare!"
          Toll slowly.
"Tower must fall, and bride be lost!—swear me service worth
    the cost,"
      —Bold they stood around to swear.

"Each man clasp my hand, and swear, by the deed we failed in
    there,"—
          Toll slowly.
"Not for vengeance, not for right, will ye strike one blow to-
    night!"—
      Pale they stood around—to swear.

"One last boon, young Ralph and Clare! faithful hearts to do
    and dare!"
          Toll slowly.
"Bring that steed up from his stall, which she kissed before you
    all,—
      Guide him up the turret-stair.

"Ye shall harness him aright, and lead upward to this
    height!"—

Toll slowly.

"Once in love and twice in war, hath he borne me strong and
    far,—
He shall bear me far to-night."

They have fetched the steed with care, in the harness he did
    wear,—
Toll slowly.
Past the court and through the doors, across the rushes of the
    floors;
But they goad him up the stair.

Then from out her bower chambère did the Duchess May re-
    pair,—
Toll slowly.
"Tell me now what is your need," said the lady, "of this steed,
That ye goad him up the stair?"

"Get thee back, sweet Duchess May! hope is gone like yester-
    day,"—
Toll slowly.
"One half-hour completes the breach; and thy lord grows wild
    of speech.—
Get thee in, sweet lady, and pray.

"In the east tower, high'st of all,—loud he cries for steed from
    stall,"—
Toll slowly.
" 'He would ride as far,' quoth he, 'as for love and victory,
Though he rides the castle-wall.'

"And we fetch the steed from stall, up where never a hoof did
    fall."—
Toll slowly.
"Wifely prayer meets deathly need! may the sweet Heavens
    hear thee plead,
If he rides the castle-wall."

She stood up in bitter case, with a pale yet steady face,—
>   *Toll slowly.*

Like a statue thunderstruck, which, though quivering, seems to look
>   Right against the thunder-place.

Then the good steed's rein she took, and his neck did kiss and stroke:—
>   *Toll slowly.*

Soft he neighed to answer her; and then followed up the stair,
>   For the love of her sweet look.

Oh, and steeply, steeply wound up the narrow stair around,—
>   *Toll slowly.*

Oh, and closely, closely speeding, step by step beside her treading,
>   Did he follow, meek as hound.

On the east tower, high'st of all,—there, where never a hoof did fall,—
>   *Toll slowly.*

Out they swept, a vision steady,—noble steed and lovely lady,
>   Calm as if in bower or stall.

Down she knelt at her lord's knee, and she looked up silently,—
>   *Toll slowly.*

And he kissed her twice and thrice, for that look within her eyes,
>   Which he could not bear to see.

Quoth he, "Get thee from this strife,—and the sweet saints bless thy life!"—
>   *Toll slowly.*

"In this hour, I stand in need of my noble red-roan steed—
>   But no more of my noble wife."

Quoth she, "Meekly have I done all thy biddings under sun:"—
> *Toll slowly.*
"But by all my womanhood,—which is proved so, true and good,
> I will never do this one.

"Now, by womanhood's degree, and by wifehood's verity,"—
> *Toll slowly.*
"In this hour if thou hast need of thy noble red-roan steed,
> Thou hast also need of me."

Oh, he sprang up in the selle, and he laughed out bitter well,—
> *Toll slowly.*
"Wouldst thou ride among the leaves, as we used on other eves,
> To hear chime a vesper-bell?"

She clang closer to his knee—"Ay, beneath the cypress-tree!"—
> *Toll slowly.*
"Mock me not; for otherwhere, than along the greenwood fair,
> Have I ridden fast with thee!

"Fast I rode with new-made vows, from my angry kinsman's house!"
> *Toll slowly.*
"What! and would you men should reck, that I dared more for love's sake,
> As a bride than as a spouse?

"What, and would you it should fall, as a proverb, before all,"—
> *Toll slowly,*
"That a bride may keep your side, while through castle-gate you ride,
> Yet eschew the castle-wall?"

Twice he wrung her hands in twain,—but the small hands closed again,—

Toll slowly.

Back he reined the steed—back, back! but she trailed along his track,
    With a frantic clasp and strain.

And his heel did press and goad on the quivering flank bestrode,—
Toll slowly.
"Friends, and brothers! save my wife!—Pardon, sweet, in change for life,—
    But I ride alone to God."

Straight as if the Holy Name had upbreathed her like a flame,—
Toll slowly.
She unsprang, she rose upright—in his selle she sate in sight;
    By her love she overcame.

And, "Ring, ring, thou passing-bell," still she cried, "i' the old chapelle!"—
Toll slowly.
Then back-toppling, crashing back—a dead weight flung out to wrack,
    Horse and riders overfell.

Oh, the little birds sang east, and the little birds sang west,—
Toll slowly.
And I read this ancient Rhyme, in the kirkyard, while the chime
    Slowly tolled for one at rest.

Oh, the little birds sang east, and the little birds sang west,—
Toll slowly.
And I said in underbreath,—All our life is mixed with death,
    And who knoweth which is best?

Oh, the little birds sang east, and the little birds sang west.—
>> *Toll slowly.*
And I smiled to think God's greatness flowed around our incompleteness,—
>> Round our restlessness, His rest.

A LINE AROUND

"The Drinking Song" by Sheridan presents a charming chorus for a group of men or boys. It may be read by a line around, with the entire group repeating the refrain. The last stanza may be read by the entire group or by divisions according to some arrangement whereby the speakers seem to be agreed upon the idea that all women are worthy of a toast.

DRINKING SONG

Richard Brinsley Sheridan

Here's to the maiden of bashful fifteen,
>> Here's to the widow of fifty;
Here's to the flaunting extravagant queen,
>> And here's to the housewife that's thrifty;

Chorus. Let the toast pass,
>> *Drink to the lass,*
I'll warrant she'll prove an excuse for the glass.

Here's to the charmer, whose dimples we prize,
>> And now to the maid who has none, sir,
Here's to the girl with a pair of blue eyes,
>> And here's to the nymph with but one, sir.
>>> *Let the toast pass, etc.*

Here's to the maid with a bosom of snow,
    And to her that's as brown as a berry;
Here's to the wife with a face full of woe,
    And now to her that is merry:
        Let the toast pass, etc.

For let 'em be clumsy, or let 'em be slim,
    Young or ancient, I care not a feather;
So fill a pint bumper quite up to the brim,
    And let us e'en toast them together.

Chorus. Let the toast pass,
    Drink to the lass,
I'll warrant she'll prove an excuse for the glass.

THREE-PART DIVISION

The reading chorus is sometimes divided into three groups, high, medium, and low, according to the normal key of the voices. The selection is then divided as seems fitting for the various voice groups. The following poem may be read in such a manner.

A SONG FOR ST. CECILIA'S DAY
John Dryden

Medium. From Harmony, from heavenly Harmony
    This universal frame began:
    When Nature underneath a heap
      Of jarring atoms lay
    And could not heave her head,
    The tuneful voice was heard from high,
      'Arise, ye more than dead!'
    Then cold, and hot, and moist, and dry
    In order to their stations leap,
      And Music's power obey.

THREE-PART DIVISION

Low.   From harmony, from heavenly harmony
        This universal frame began:
        From harmony to harmony
    Through all the compass of the notes it ran,
    The diapason closing full in Man.

Medium. What passion cannot Music raise and quell?
        When Jubal struck the chorded shell
        His listening brethren stood around,
        And, wondering, on their faces fell
        To worship that celestial sound.
    Less than a god they thought there could not **dwell**
        Within the hollow of that shell
        That spoke so sweetly and so well.
    What passion cannot Music raise and quell?

Low.   The trumpet's loud clangor
        Excites us to arms,
    With shrill notes of anger
    And mortal alarms.
Medium. The double double double beat
        Of the thundering drum
High.   Cries 'Hark! the foes come;
Low.   Charge, charge, 'tis too late to **retreat!'**

High.   The soft complaining flute
        In dying notes discovers
Medium. The woes of hopeless lovers,
Low.   Whose dirge is whisper'd by the **warbling lute.**

High.   Sharp violins proclaim
    Their jealous pangs and desperation,
    Fury, frantic indignation,
    Depth of pains, and height of passion
        For the fair disdainful dame.

Medium. But oh! what art can teach,
          What human voice can reach
             The sacred organ's praise?
          Notes inspiring holy love,
          Notes that wing their heavenly ways
             To mend the choirs above.

Low. Orpheus could lead the savage race,
          And trees unrooted left their place
             Sequacious of the lyre:
Medium. But bright Cecilia raised the wonder higher;
          When to her Organ vocal breath was given
High. An Angel heard, and straight appear'd—
          Mistaking Earth for Heaven.

Grand Chorus

ALL. As from the power of sacred lays
            The spheres began to move,
          And sung the great Creator's praise
            To all the blest above;
Low. So when the last and dreadful hour
          This crumbling pageant shall devour,
Medium. The trumpet shall be heard on high,
High The dead shall live, the living die,
ALL. And Music shall untune the sky.

ADDING AND SUBTRACTING VOICES

The crescendo and diminuendo effect frequently **needed in the interpretation of literature may be gained in choral reading by adding and subtracting voices as the climax is built or diminished. The following poem, suggesting a mystical mood which may be interpreted in a chanting tone with marked rhythm and changes in tempo, lends itself well to the choral technique of adding and subtracting voices.**

ADDING AND SUBTRACTING VOICES

The arrangement suggested below calls for a small chorus to set the mood from which other moods may be built by adding or subtracting voices. The exact number of voices is left to the discretion of the group. Five would be an acceptable number for the small chorus. Two voices could be added or subtracted each time that such a suggestion is made by the marginal notation. This matter must, in the final analysis, depend upon the total number of speakers who are to participate in the reading.

SONG OF SLAVES IN THE DESERT
John Greenleaf Whittier

Small Chorus.	Where are we going? [*add voices*] Where are we going,
Add Voices.	Where are we going, Rubee?
Small Chorus.	Lord of peoples, lords of lands,
Add Voices.	Look across these shining sands,
Add Voices.	Through the furnace of the noon.
Add Voices.	Through the white light of the moon,
Add Voices.	Strong the Ghiblee wind is blowing,
	Strange and large the world is growing!
Subtract Voices.	Speak and tell us where we are going,
Subtract Voices.	Where are we going, Rubee?
Add Voices.	Bornou land was rich and good,
Add Voices.	Wells of water, fields of food,
Add Voices.	Dourra fields, and bloom of bean,
	And the palm-tree cool and green:
Subtract Voices.	Bornou land we see no longer,
Subtract Voices.	Here we thirst and here we hunger,
Subtract Voices.	Here the Moor-man smites in anger:
Small Chorus.	Where are we going, Rubee?

Add Voices.	When we went from Bornou land,
Add Voices.	We were like the leaves and sand,
Add Voices.	We were many, [*small chorus*] we are few;
Small Chorus.	Life has one, and death has two:
Add Voices.	Whiten'd bones our path are showing.
Add Voices.	Thou all-seeing, thou all-knowing!
Add Voices.	Hear us, tell us, where are we going,
Small Chorus.	Where are we going, Rubee?
Add Voices.	Moons of marches from our eyes
	Bornou land behind us lies;
Add Voices.	Stranger round us day by day
	Bends the desert circle grey;
Add Voices.	Wild the waves of sand are flowing,
Add Voices.	Hot the winds above them blowing,
Add Voices.	Lord of all things! where are we going?
Small Chorus.	Where are we going, Rubee?
Small Chorus.	We are weak, [*add voices*] but thou art strong;
Add Voices.	Short our lives, but Thine is long:
Small Chorus.	We are blind, [*add voices*] but Thou hast eyes;
Small Chorus.	We are fools, [*add voices*] but Thou art wise!
Large Chorus.	Thou, our morrow's pathway knowing
	Through the strange world round us growing,
	Hear us, tell us where are we going?
Small Chorus.	Where are we going, Rubee?

A LIST OF SELECTIONS FOR VARIOUS CHORAL ARRANGEMENTS

FOR REFRAIN WORK

"The Pirate Don Durke of Dowdee"	Mildred Plew Meigs
"Sir Eglamare"	English Ballad
"Robin-A-Thrush"	English Ballad
"In Come de Animals"	Negro Rhyme
"Leave Her, Johnny, Leave Her"	Traditional
"Jessie James"	William Rose Benét

LISTS FOR CHORAL ARRANGEMENTS

"Pioneers! O Pioneers!" . . . . . Walt Whitman
"Our Drums" . . . . Carrie Rasmussen
"It Was a Lover and his Lass" . . . Shakespeare
"The Lobster Quadrille" . . . . . Lewis Carroll
"Blow, Blow, Thou Winter Wind" . . Shakespeare
"The Wind" . . . . Robert L. Stevenson
"The Old Clock on the Stairs" . . . Henry W. Longfellow

FOR ANTIPHONAL WORK

"Lord Randal" . . . . English Ballad
"An Apple Orchard in the Spring" . . William Martin
"The Throstle" . . . . . . Alfred Lord Tennyson
"Tarantella" . . . . Hilaire Belloc
Father William . . . . . . Lewis Carroll
"Psalm Twenty Four" . . . . . King James version of *Bible*
"When All the World Is Young" . . Charles Kingsley
Psalm One Hundred and Forty-seven . *Bible*
Psalm One Hundred and Forty-eight . *Bible*
Psalm One Hundred and Fifty . . . *Bible*
The Beatitudes . . . . . . *Matthew 5:3–11*
"Whistle, Whistle" . . . . . . Traditional Verse
"Friday Street" . . . . Elenn Farjean

FOR SEQUENCE WORK
(Line around)

"I Hear America Singing" . . . . Walt Whitman
"Give Me the Splendid Silent Sun" . . Walt Whitman
"Chicago" . . . . Carl Sandburg
"The Sugar Plum Tree" . . . . . Eugene Field
"Sweet Is the Rose" . . . . . . Edmund Spenser
"The Owl and the Pussy Cat" . . . Edward Lear
"Pioneers! O Pioneers!" . . . . . Walt Whitman
"When Icicles Hang" . . . . . . Shakespeare
"A Tract for Autos" . . . . . . Arthur Ginterman
"Thanksgiving Hymn" . . . . . Ralph Waldo Emerson
"Boots" . . . . Rudyard Kipling
"The Year's at the Spring" . . . . Robert Browning
"Elephant Song" . . . . Don Blanding
"Barter" . . . . Sara Teasdale
"Dirge for a Righteous Kitten" . . . Vachel Lindsay

CHORAL READING

FOR CUMULATIVE WORK OR PART SPEAKING

"The Judgment Day"	James Weldon Johnson
"Daniel"	Vachel Lindsay
"The Sands of Dee"	Charles Kingsley
"The Squaw Dance"	Lew Sarett
"Four Little Foxes"	Lew Sarett
"The Mysterious Cat"	Vachel Lindsay
"Boot and Saddle"	Robert Browning
"A Tragic Tale"	Thackeray
"Foreboding"	Don Blanding
"Marching Along"	Robert Browning
"Drake's Drum"	Sir Henry Newbolt
"Lochinvar"	Sir Walter Scott

FOR UNISON SPEAKING

"Oh Captain! My Captain!"	Walt Whitman
"Allen-A-Dale"	Sir Walter Scott
"Harp Song of the Dane Women"	Rudyard Kipling
"Sea Fever"	John Masefield
"The Music Makers"	O'Shaughnessy
Psalm One Hundred	*Bible*
"Sunrise" from "Pippa Passes"	Robert Browning
"The World Is Too Much with Us"	Wordsworth
"Love of Country"	Sir Walter Scott
"Fairy Land"	Shakespeare
"Shoes and Stockings"	A. A. Milne

Chapter XI

INTERPRETATIVE READING FOR RADIO

> As broadcasts become better, their execution seems easier. In fact the success of a broadcast may be said to to be in inverse ratio to the amount of strain it reveals.
> *John S. Carlile*

Radio has increased the scope of the art of interpretative reading. It has given recognition and emphasis to effective, natural, and creative reading. Much of broadcasting is through reading, even though the *effect* may suggest spontaneous, informal, and even impromptu speech. Speeches, plays, poetry, stories, announcements, and news reports are in a large measure read from scripts. This close adherence to scripts is due to the demands for accurate adjustment of time allotment and the need for adequate use of every second on the air. Oral reading usually seems to be the most satisfactory means by which the broadcaster may give the maximum of effect with a minimum of error.

The style of reading desirable for the radio is similar to the style we have recommended for reading to a seen audience. As yet the radio speaker is not seen except when such an audience is provided for the purpose of stimulating interest. In radio reading, technique for the ear must be emphasized and eye appeals must not be depended upon. The *voice* of the radio reader must carry the mental pictures, the concepts, the reactions suggested by the words of the script. Does this mean, then, that the reader need use no body movement while on the air? Quite the contrary, for while movement is not *seen* "on the air" it is, in a measure, *heard*. The suggestion of movement in the voice can hardly be made without a sense of movement in the body. Concerning this fact Professor Abbot says:

> Psychological experiment has shown that the muscles of the body respond in perfect accord with speech efforts. If one were to record in waves, on a strip of paper, the voice of a speaker and also the subconscious movements of any part of his body, for instance, the arm, one would find that these two curves agree.[1]

Motor sense images are fundamental to effective reading for radio as are all other types of imagery. Live bodies produce live voices. Bodily activity, both overt and covert, contributes to vitalized thinking, to vibrant tones, accurate timing, and a sense of unity, climax, and emphasis. Abandoned body movements are the surest means of gaining convincing tones and persuasive rhythms. Professor Abbot makes a similar suggestion:

> If the use of quiet gestures will help your delivery, by all means use them. Point your finger at an imaginary listener. Shake your fist. A smile is heard over the radio because it changes the quality of your voice. A person a thousand miles away will "hear" you lift your eyebrows. Do not neglect these aids to speech. Make no gesture or movement, however, which might cause extraneous sound. Do not shake the hand that holds the manuscript paper. Do not rub an unshaven chin. Do

---

[1] Waldo Abbot, *Handbook of Broadcasting* (New York: McGraw-Hill Book Company, Inc., 1941), p. 25. By permission of the publishers.

not smack your lips or snap your fingers. Do not sigh or pound the desk, for these sounds will not be understood by the distant listener.[1]

The interpretative reader needs to project less volume on the air than when reading to a seen audience. Volume in radio is controlled to a large degree by the technician at the broadcasting station, by the wave length and power of the station, and by the individuals who happen to turn the dials of the various radios. Furthermore the microphone is a very sensitive instrument which picks up slight sounds often unheard even in small rooms. The individual reader needs to learn something concerning his relation to the microphone, techniques of tone production, and the control of breath and articulation for the best effect on the air.

Intimacy is considered important in radio reading. One is often instructed to think of a radio audience as a small group in the home—a family consisting of father, mother, and child gathered about the proverbial "fireside" which in modern life may be the radio. The "fireside chats" of President Franklin Delano Roosevelt hold a high place in the annals of radio lore. The clarity, force, and apparently unstudied effects of his radio speeches have successfully projected the illusion of intimate conversation.

Radio demands the art which commands the interest and attention of its audience. Will Rogers used to say that he felt sorry for the person who was too lazy to turn a dial when he was bored. It is easy for one to turn a radio dial and to find other programs which appeal to his taste. It is therefore important for the radio reader to find the art which commands the interest and attention of listeners.

[1] Abbot; *Op cit.,* p. 26.

The techniques given in this book should result in that art. The *first* requisite to the art of commanding attention and interest is imagination and the *second* is adequate technique for the projection of ideas. The technique of thinking with the senses should result in tones vibrant with the essence of meaning, tones which catch the imagination of the hearer and hold his interest. The techniques of timing, climax, and illusion should result in the variety, force, and subtlety essential for sustained interest. We offer the techniques of interpretative reading as techniques of effective radio reading.

A former student, having gained progressively better positions in radio, passed an audition test of the National Broadcasting Company for a position with one of the largest clear channel stations in America. This student testified that his success in radio, and specifically on the audition test, was due in a large measure to a course in interpretative reading. Through interpretative reading he learned the essentials for commanding the interest and attention of listeners. He said that as he approached each phase of the audition he thought, "I can do this. I had experiences similar to this in that course in interpretative reading."

Dr. Mallory, of Brooklyn College, emphasized this fact in an address before the Convention of the National Association of Teachers of Speech:

> The basic problems encountered in oral interpretation for the radio and for the platform are identical. The radio reader's initial concern, like that of the platform reader, must be the understanding, appreciation, and assimilation of his material. After meaning has been as fully as possible mastered, the reader must then have general speech skill sufficient to enable

him to express that meaning effectively. The microphone may introduce new factors and special problems, but microphone technique offers no short cut to the basic reading skills.[1]

Concerning the value of techniques of tempo, rhythm, and pause in radio Mr. McGill states in his authentic book on *Radio Directing:*

Life is geared to rational tempi; when any one of them is interpolated into a situation in which it does not belong the result is an incongruous violation of all our normal expectations. Consequently a director should remember that scenes should be played at tempi that are consistent with their emotional and ideational content, and transitions from one scene to another, from one pace to another, should be arrived at without a violent rhythmic wrench. Perfectly integrated drama has the beat and cadence of music. The flow of words and music and sound and ideas is actuated by its own inner compulsion and should always obey the canons of harmony and rhythm. The pause between two words can often demand a little eternity of its own, and the sensitive director will supply it at the cost of cutting a page of dialogue. That awareness of the need for speed or slow time should be part of a director's equipment, and if he has none of it there is no way to supply him with it any more than a monotone can be equipped with absolute pitch.[2]

There is one kind of reading for radio which we have not yet emphasized in this book. Frequently on the air, especially in a broadcast in a radio station, it is essential for one

[1] Louis A. Mallory, *Oral Interpretation for the Radio and for the Platform* (Detroit, 1941). By permission.
[2] Earle McGill, *Radio Directing* (New York: McGraw-Hill Book Company, Inc., 1940), pp. 113–14. By permission of the publishers.

to be able to read effectively at sight. The broadcaster may be handed announcements, bulletins, or corrections while he is at the microphone and be expected to read these convincingly. He may develop a technique of sight reading which will serve him well on such occasions. As has been mentioned before, one thinks in groups of words; the phrase is the unit of thought. Since this is the natural way to think, even in sight reading one may develop the habit of thinking the idea as he reads the word-group which expresses it. In sight reading one should read for information and at the same time share that information with others. This method offers a striking contrast to that of calling words with little thought of the meaning conveyed by the words.

It is not easy in sight reading to perceive interclausal relations and to project a sense of unity, but it can be done. One may discipline oneself even in sight reading to grasp the essentials of a paragraph almost instantly and to perceive the relationship of thoughts during the brief pauses essential for carrying the meaning. Sight reading may be as spontaneous, clear, and convincing as carefully prepared reading if the reader concentrates upon the meaning and significance of the words and the relation of thoughts to the whole. Even sight reading may be creative if the reader makes it so—if he creates in the imagination the concepts, and shares with his listeners the essence, of the material he reads.

Pauses, as pointed out by Mr. McGill, are essential in radio reading. We would emphasize this matter because some people seem to think that since sound is the medium in radio there must be a continuous flow of sound. Effective reading always demands the adequate timing of periods of silence. The *listeners* must have time to grasp ideas and time to react to moods. The *reader* must use pauses for the spacing of thoughts and for the reinforcement of ideas. He must take time to create and time to react to concepts. The chief difference between pauses on the air and pauses in reading to a seen audience is that in the latter case audience reaction may aid in guiding the reader in timing his pauses whereas on the air the reader must be guided entirely by the meaning and his own discretion as to the time needed for audience reaction.

So the radio reader's problem and method are very much the same as those of any other interpretative reader: he must so vivify the imaginative concept that the reality is projected to the listener. The radio reader must share ideas with listeners who are not there, communicating as much as he would if they were in the studio with him. Indeed the radio reader must at times create even his audience in his imagination. The radio reader is expected to be so direct, spontaneous, interesting, and communicative that a man will put down his newspaper, a woman will refrain from conversation, and a child will listen with rapt attention in preference to any other occupation or amusement!

Can interpretative reading meet these demands? We believe that at times it does. People in general are interested in stories, ideas, and philosophy couched in simple, unaffected speech and projected by varied tones and rhythms. Sometimes it is advisable to supplement these simpler forms with music, special sound effects, group speaking, or a cast of readers. Even then creative reading may be the essential medium by which the essence of the script is projected. Even acting, in radio, is essentially the interpretative reading of the lines of a script, and its technique is more akin to the technique of reading than that of acting in the theater.

Radio reading as a profession, and certainly as an art, presupposes a good voice. Milton Cross suggests, "An announcer's voice must be healthy, well dressed, and cheerful." Mr. Carlile of the Columbia Broadcasting System says:

Proper voice production is more important in radio broadcasting than in conversation or platform address because, on the air, the voice becomes the full medium of expression of the man; and the microphone picks up every variation in sound. Radio and telephone engineers refer to the microphone in this connection as "a device for converting the energy of sound waves which a speaker produces into electrical energy that has similar vibrational characteristics." The sound of the voice is translated into electrical energy and back into sound without distortion. Improperly produced voice sounds become more noticeable; faults in speech more apparent. The necessity for the improvement of vocal production is obvious.[1]

Does radio reading call for more striking vocal effects or closer identification with the characters than other creative reading? This question cannot be answered arbitrarily. The student of interpretative reading should not draw lines around himself saying, "This is good art and that, bad." Anything done well may be called good and anything done poorly is bad. What should be done depends to a great extent upon the one who is doing it—his interpretation, his individual slant, or his purpose. Many a person has succeeded by doing the thing which others said could not or should not be done. As creative artists let us keep open,

---

[1] John S. Carlile, *Production and Direction of Radio Programs* (New York: Prentice-Hall, Inc., 1940), p. 269.

alert minds to respond with appreciation to that which is done well, to catch a vision of that which we may do, and to work on forms until we find ways which adequately express our ideas.

Radio invites experimentation, although it demands that experimentation succeed, if success can be measured by listener response through fan mail or by increase in sales of the product advertised. It has not yet been proved that spectacular forms meet with greater success than simple forms of direct, communicative speech. Reading with musical backgrounds, dramatizations, and variety shows have at times seemed to take the spotlight in radio. How long they will hold it and what other forms will be developed one can hardly predict. The one certainty is that there will be change within the forms now in vogue and that new forms will be developed. There is no progress without change, though the student must not conclude that all change is progress. *Ideas* are the most important things in radio now and probably will continue to be, as ideas are the determining factors in progress. Some forms, however, are universal and permanent and hence always acceptable. Among the permanent forms are simple, sincere, and unaffected speech, and vivid, imaginative, creative oral reading.

A RADIO READING CLUB

There have been many successful radio programs based specifically upon the art of interpretative reading. Ken Peters,[1] who developed such a program, has given us permission to quote a portion of his report concerning the success of his experiment:

[1] "Ken Peters," Radio Station WLW, Cincinnati, Ohio.

The reading club experiment in oral interpretation by radio, as conducted over station WMFG at Hibbing, Minnesota.

I. Its inception.
   A. Although seen from the start as an experiment in adult education, it was presented throughout as primarily an entertainment feature.
   B. Introductory program.

   The program was introduced as a half hour to be set aside each week-day afternoon as a time to read together from different works of literature. By writing in and expressing approval of the idea the audience became reading club members and as such were free to comment on works read, and to suggest works to be used. We were free to delve into all forms of literature: short story, poetry, drama, novels, biographies, etc.

   The first two weeks were devoted to short stories, during which time a very encouraging number of listeners responded enthusiastically. An active audience once established, we felt free to start with reading of a longer work which would be continued from day to day. This proved most popular and novels became the primary vehicle of the club, with short stories and poetry being used between the longer works.

II. Audience response.
   A. Its interest was general from the start.
   B. Listeners felt "in," and soon were referring to the program as "our reading club."
   C. A general comment was that they could "just see everything that was read, and many expressed it "just like seeing a movie."
   D. Letters came in from literary clubs of the various

towns expressing appreciation. At the same time a large number of people of foreign birth, of little or no formal education, professed that they "never missed a single program."

III. Its educational value.
  A. Made available to many an appreciation and understanding of works which they were unable to absorb for themselves. While they could not "get into" certain books when they tried to read them, themselves, they were able to when read to them by one who had prepared them for oral presentation.
  B. Libraries of the range reported that there was a demand for each book which had been or was being used on the reading club. They also reported inquiries for other books by authors featured.
  C. Listening demanded an active play of the imagination, and many who said they had no time to read for themselves were regular members.

IV. The job is more than reading "a chapter a day."
  A. Judicious cutting is essential.
    1. The usual procedure was to spend two-week, or 10 half-hour, periods on each of the longer works. Cutting was guided by an attempt to retain description and dialogue which was a vital part of the underlying theme and mood of the story.
    2. A carefully planned synopsis of what had gone before was essential.
  B. Knowledge of the technique of interpretation is necessary.
  C. Choice of material is an important factor.
    1. Certain authors "read aloud" well.

D. All success depends upon establishing rapport with the audience.
  1. The approach throughout was one of the reader and the listener uniting in quest of mutual entertainment and enlightenment.
  2. A feeling of sincere friendship and common interest arose.
     (*a*) Received regular weekly letters from certain listeners discussing the work being read, and making suggestions for the future. Still receive letters from some of these unseen friends.
     (*b*) Faithful and enthusiastic listening I would attribute largely to the fact that the half hour was in no respect just a half hour's job each day, but rather something in which I was vitally interested heart and soul. I personally had absorbed the work much more completely after presenting it orally than I ever could from silent reading.

V. Novels and other continued works read.
  A. The starting of each new work was prefaced with a brief discussion of the author, and any pertinent facts concerned with the writing, or with the reason for the choice. I always attempted to make each day's reading a unit as much as possible.
  B. A listing of works used.
    So Big—Ferber
    Cimarron—Ferber
    If Winter Comes—Hutchinson
    Years of Achievement—Starett
    A Lantern in Her Hand—Aldrich
    Spring Came on Forever—Aldrich

A RADIO READING CLUB

Flush—Woolf
Lost Horizon—Hilton
We Are Not Alone—Hilton
Life with Father—Day
The Exile—Buck
East Wind, West Wind—Buck
Ethan Frome—Wharton
Jeremy—Walpole
Jeremy and Hamlet—Walpole
A Prayer for My Son—Walpole
Beyond Sing the Woods—Gulbranssen
Wind from the Mountain—Gulbranssen
The Man of Property—Galsworthy
Suns Go Down—Lewis (Flannery)
Turmoil—Tarkington
Gone with the Wind—Mitchell
Green Gates—Sheriff
The Homemaker—Canfield
The Sea of Grass—Richter
Midnight on the Desert—Priestley
Years of Grace—Barnes
Sorrell and Son—Deeping
A Man for the Ages—Bacheller
Growing Pains—Touhey

C. Conclusions.
1. Looking back over the more than two years' existence of the reading club, I would not be able to cite one particular type of story which was most popular. I believe that with careful consideration to variety, all types were well received. Once the proper listening spirit is instilled, the listeners are in a responsive mood to whatever work is chosen.
2. The most general response was gained by the read-

ing of works which had not been previously read by the listeners.
3. A large number of listeners expressed appreciation of works which they had previously read. The usual comment was that they had gained a deeper appreciation of the work through its reading club.
4. The question arises—"Would works popular in this particular locale be given equal approval elsewhere, or for nationwide audience?" Since the listeners represented people of all degrees of schooling, people in all walks of life, it would seem that its response could be duplicated elsewhere.

VI. The use of poetry.
  A. I found that I was able from time to time to devote a half hour to the reading of poetry and call forth general response on it.
    1. A half hour with the poetry of Robert Frost. (Read introduction.)
    2. Two lives—William Ellery Leonard
    3. Readings from *John Brown's Body*.
  B. Additional evening program of poetry with organ music reached another audience, and developed a regular group of listeners.
    1. Usual procedure was to select a theme—autumn, hills, gardens, home, portraits, friendship, and to select poems expressive of the theme. The organist selected music in the mood of the poem.

VII. Programs for special days and seasons.
  A. Whenever possible we sought to add to the appreciation and significance of different holidays with appropriate readings.

VIII. Consideration of "rights" for broadcasting books and published writings.
    A. After consulting with different people, I felt free to use locally any works which did not contain specific restrictions against dramatic and radio use.
    B. If such programs become general the problem of copyrights will be a real one which must be met.

IX. General Conclusions.
    A. Radio is an effective medium for the oral interpretation of literature and could conceivably restore it as a popular art.
    B. Such oral interpretation has effective possibilities as a medium of radio education.
    C. Radio might conceivably become a medium for "first publication" of literary works.

Concerning general training for radio speaking Mr. Peters says:

    A. Microphone technique is incidental to a thorough training in the fundamentals of speech.
        1. Primary purpose is still to win response and the problems are essentially the same as that of the platform.
        2. Proper bodily action is still necessary, though unseen.
    B. The successful speaker will see himself as speaking not to a mass audience, but to individuals.
        1. To many successful performers, the microphone possesses a personality and itself becomes the audience.
    C. Work in Oral Interpretation provides effective training for radio performance.

1. Radio performing is dependent upon the ability to speak effectively from a manuscript.

Concerning the reader's technique Mr. Peters observes:

A. Reader should use voice as if what he was saying were being said for the first time.
B. Over-dramatic emphasis is just as bad as monotony. The eloquent variation of pitch and tone must not attempt to mimic the persons of the tale; it must be, if it is to be warmly received, the expression of the reader's own emotion.
C. A great deal must depend upon the rapport between the reader and the listener.

THE SELECTION AND ARRANGEMENT OF LITERATURE FOR RADIO

Whether there is need for a special type of literature for radio is a debatable question. Some writers have experimented with poetry and drama written especially for radio. Notable among these is Archibald MacLeish and his *The Fall of the City, Air Raid,* and *America Was Promises.*[1] Various types of literature have been adapted or arranged for radio with evident success. A turn of the dial has brought us Shakespeare, fairy tales, poetry, novels, short stories, history, and current events. The requisites which have seemed to be of primary importance are universality of appeal, timeliness, appeal to the ear, and adaptability to the time allotment.

[1] Duell, Sloan and Pierce, Publishers, New York, 1941.

Universality

Great literature is suitable for radio, since its requirements are universality and permanence. Literature which lasts does so because it expresses truth which is true for all men at all times; it is not limited to a certain group nor to the period in which it was written. The characters of Shakespeare are as human today as when the Bard of Avon produced them; his philosophy is as true and his plots as conceivable in spite of the fact that we no longer believe in witches and that few governments are ruled by kings and queens. Literary merit was the first item given by Max Wylie in selecting a short story adaptation for his *Best Broadcasts*. Concerning the criteria upon which choice was made he states:

Determining the best broadcast in the classification of serious short story adaptations presented one of the severest problems met with in the preparation of this anthology. The short story adaptation is one of radio's most common dramatic types, and it has been estimated with reasonable accuracy that over thirty thousand programs for this division alone are broadcast every year. Four hundred and fifty were examined for this book. Many fine pieces were rejected as candidates for inclusion and the final choice was arrived at only by making the criteria of qualification so severe as to render ineligible, on one claim or another, most of the disputed properties. In the final judgment the following factors were taken into account:

1. Literary merit of the original.
2. Difficulty of the adaptation problem.
3. Artistic integrity of the adapter's inventions.
4. Adherence to the pattern, mood, and intention of the original.

5. Recognition and use of expansible suggestion.
6. Playing power.

In the degree to which each story adaptation met these tests, it was given its independent rating.[1]

Timeliness

Current events give special force and meaning to certain pieces of literature. For example, Hitler's rise to power gave motivation for the Orson Welles interpretation of *Julius Caesar*. The world again understood the significance of the lines of Brutus:

> Had you rather Caesar were living,
> And die all slaves, than that
> Caesar were dead, to live all free men?

So, whether presented on the stage or over the air, Shakespeare's *Julius Caesar* was especially timely before and during the second World War.

The Trojan Women, by Euripides, likewise became timely and meaningful with the subjugation of Europe by the Nazis and the rumors of Japanese atrocities in the Far East. The heroism and effective fighting of the small group of Americans on Wake Island gave understanding to stories of Thermopylae, Bunker Hill, and The Alamo.

The timeliness of great literature may often be made evident by the adaptation, especially by the introduction. The adaptation of a radio script should bring the literature into the lives, the personal experience of the audience. Arthur Edward Phillips gives "reference to experience" as

[1] Max Wylie, *Best Broadcasts of 1938–39* (New York: McGraw-Hill Book Company, Inc., 1939), p. 22. By permission of the publishers.

a basic principle of effective speaking. His explanation of the principle emphasizes the need of bringing an idea into the experience of an audience by linking it with that which is vivid in audience experience. As criteria for evaluating audience experiences he suggests that which is recent, frequent, and originally intense.[1]

Appeal to the Ear

Since radio calls for adaptations principally for the ear, should the script call for more varied tones and vocal devices than in other interpretative reading? Should the radio script emphasize character parts and special sounds which the reader may reproduce in a realistic manner? The answer to these questions will depend upon a number of things such as the material, the reader, and the purpose. Some literature lends itself to vocal tricks. Some readers can visualize and imitate a wide number of characters and can project through the voice convincing and realistic characterizations and imitations. Some listeners like to hear vocal stunts, and they admire the reader or actor who can change his voice so as to present realistic imitations. Tricks and stunts, however, are not necessary to the most convincing interpretative reading. The radio reader like other readers or speakers should be careful not to go off on tangents and gain a reputation for tricks when he has the ability for a fine artistic technique. Mr. Carlile suggests the force of sincere interpretative reading in setting the scene for radio drama.

In writing legitimate drama, tradition has the author commence each scene and act with description of the set. This is

[1] Arthur Edward Phillips, *Effective Speaking* (Chicago: The Newton Company, 1926), pp. 28–35.

later constructed to his specifications. In the script for a radio play, the author sometimes does the same. If intelligently read by the actor or narrator, he can help the listener construct the scene better than any group of architects, carpenters, and painters. A vivid description of Johnny the Priest's saloon, or the stern of Old Chris' Barge at once transports the audience into a scene of "Anna Christie" with such suggested realism as would gratify O'Neill. New times, new devices! The swing of the pendulum carries us forward, but it swings back to do so. If the dramatist renews his acquaintance with the ancient Greek theatre, he may find in the messenger who trod the stage erected beside the temple of Dionysus, and in the chorus which chanted tragedies unseen, the prototypes of announcers, narrators, and formal voices of radio.[1]

The same point of view may be taken toward background music, special sound effects, and group reading. Radio has brought an increase in group reading as well as in reading with musical background. Music gives atmosphere and in the opinion of many is a needed supplement for poetry reading on the air. Mr. Whipple suggests that musical background may be overdone for radio drama:

Music which is used for background or mood requires careful thought on the part of the writer. In the author's opinion there is little excuse for introducing music as a background to the ordinary dramatic scene to enhance its emotional value. The motion picture producers often have done this unintelligently to the detriment of the picture. The audience cannot help being conscious of the fact that in certain situations music has no logical reason for expression, and is used merely to aid emotional reactions. It is an old device used on the stage in

[1] Carlile; *Op. cit.,* p. 173.

sentimental melodramas, and is not good modern technique.

The true aim of a dramatic presentation is to make the listener unaware of the medium of expression—to make him, as nearly as possible, a participant in the lives and emotions of the actors. Any false or illogical device makes him aware of an attempt to create an emotional response, and the illusion of actual participation in the play is destroyed. Many in the audience resent this use of music to stimulate their emotions.[1]

Group reading, cast reading, and duo voices for announcements and advertisements are sometimes thought to be more effective than a single voice in getting and holding the attention of the listener. While these supplements and innovations have frequently proved effective, they too may be overdone. The reader must not lose proportion in his evaluation of them or neglect the use of individual interpretative reading as a medium for radio. Poetry, stories, monologues, and plays have been read effectively on the air without such supplements.

Adapting to the Time Allotment

The three essentials emphasized for effective radio adaptation are (1) an arresting introduction, (2) sustained interest throughout the script, and (3) a satisfying conclusion.

The introduction should gain attention and interest. It may do so by a striking comparison to that which already holds the listener's interest or by the use of the unusual. The introduction may be so simple and subtle that it slips into the listener's attention without his awareness, or it may

---

[1] James Whipple, *How to Write for Radio* (New York: McGraw-Hill Book Company, Inc., 1938), p. 50. By permission of the publishers.

be so novel, so striking, so unusual that his curiosity will not allow him to turn from that frequency. Whatever the methods, the introduction must lend itself to immediate interest on the part of the listener.

This interest must not be lost during the body of the script. Easy and natural transitions are needed. The word *continuity* suggests coherence in writing as well as in delivery. Variety is needed for sustained interest; climax is essential to a build in interest. Irrelevant material must be eliminated and essential details should be emphasized by varied devices of writing and delivery. Since conversation often gives a better opportunity for vividness, stories may be adapted so as to emphasize characterization. Two or more characters may be kept before the minds of the listeners by having each call the name of the other more often than would be necessary in print. Actions should be described either in the conversation of characters or in the narrative portions.

It is always the purpose of a conclusion to give a sense of completeness. This may be done by a clear and vivid summation of the idea in a forceful concluding paragraph or sentence or by climactic effect in sound, in feeling, or in concept. An effective conclusion will depend, like all other portions, partly upon the effectiveness of the writing and partly upon the force of delivery.

When George W. Fithian [1] was with Radio Station WKRC in Cincinnati he found radio an interesting medium for the projection of the art of interpretative reading. "What interested me most," he says, "was a series of adap-

[1] Formerly with WKRC, the *Times Star* Station, Cincinnati, Ohio; now with United States Signal Corps Depot, Avon, Kentucky.

tations for a sustaining feature. I set about applying my theories and ideals of oral interpretation to radio and I surely ran into a good many aesthetic as well as practical problems. The public response was surprisingly encouraging." Mr. Fithian read the following script over the radio just before the fall of France.

(Short-Story Series) [1]

"Remember This One?"

"The Last Lesson" by Alphonse Daudet

ANNOUNCER. [*Cold.*] Remember This One?
MUSIC—THEME, UP FIVE SECONDS AND UNDER
ANNOUNCER. Can you remember a time, ever, when you were forbidden to speak your native tongue? Stop and reflect a moment. What does it mean to you—your native tongue? The rhythm of your speech falters or quickens with the rhythm of your heart beat, with the movement of the tide, the moon and the sun, perhaps with the very pulse of the heart of God. Is one language, then, any more than another, the language of freedom, of liberty?—Today we bring you a story of war-torn France written seventy years ago, yet as timely and pertinent today as it was then.
MUSIC—OUT
ANNOUNCER. And here's your narrator.
READER. Good afternoon. If you or I were a native of Alsace-Lorraine, how would we feel today?—Alsace-Lorraine, for two thousand years shuttle-cocked back and forth between France and Germany. Perhaps just like the man who tells this story. He's an old man talking to a younger, maybe his son.

[1] George W. Fithian, by permission.

MUSIC—IN VERY SOFTLY AND UNDER FOR TWENTY SECONDS, WHEN IT FADES OUT ALMOST IMPERCEPTIBLY

You hear those guns? They're coming nearer now, nearer and nearer. Oh, God! It's coming again—the time when this land of ours will not be ours. Oh, I can remember another time when it happened. I was just a little kid then.

I started to school very late that morning and was in great dread of scolding, especially because M. Hamel had said that he would question us on participles, and I did not know the first word about them. For a moment I thought of running away and spending the day out of doors. It was so warm, so bright! The birds were chirping at the edge of the woods; and in the open field back of the sawmill the German soldiers were drilling. It was all much more tempting than the rules of participles, but I had the strength to resist, and hurried off to school.

When I passed the town hall, there was a crowd in front of the bulletin board. For the past two years all our bad news had come from there—the lost battles, the draft, the orders of the commanding officer. And I thought to myself, without stopping: What can be the matter now?

Then, as I hurried by as fast as I could go, the blacksmith, Wachter, who was there, with his apprentice, reading the bulletin, called after me, "Don't go so fast, bub; you'll get to school in plenty of time!"

I thought he was making fun of me, and reached M. Hamel's little garden all out of breath. Usually, when school began, there was a great hustle, which could be heard out in the street, the opening and closing of desks, lessons repeated in unison, very loud, with our hands over our ears to understand better, and the teacher's great ruler rapping on the table. But now it was all so still; I had counted on the commotion to get to my desk without being seen; but, of course, that day everything had to be as quiet as Sunday morning. Through the window I saw my class-mates, already in their places, and M. Hamel walking up and down with his terrible iron ruler under his arm. I had to open the door and go in before everybody. You can imagine how I blushed and how frightened I was. But nothing happened. M. Hamel saw me and said (very kindly): "Go to your place quickly, little Franz. We were beginning without you."

I jumped over the bench and sat down at my desk. Not till then, when I had got a little over my fright, did I see that our teacher had on his beautiful green coat, his frilled shirt, and the little embroidered black cap, that he never wore except on inspection and prize days. Besides, the whole school seemed so strange and solemn; but the thing that surprised me most was to see, on the back benches that were always empty, the village people sitting quietly like ourselves; old Houser with his three-cornered hat, the former mayor, the former postmaster, and several others besides. Everybody looked sad; and Houser had brought his old primer, thumbed at the edges; and he held it open on his knees with great spectacles lying across the pages. While I was wondering about it all, M. Hamel mounted his chair, and in the same grave manner and gentle tone which he had used to me, he said:

"My poor children, this is the last lesson I shall give you. The order has come from Berlin to teach only German in the schools of Alsace-Lorraine. The new master comes tomorrow. This is your last French lesson. I want you to be attentive."

What a thunder-clap those words were to me!

Oh, the wretches; that was what they had put up at the town hall! My last French lesson! Why, I hardly knew how to write! I should never learn any more! I must stop there, then! Oh, how sorry I was for not learning my lessons, for hunting bird's eggs, or going sliding on the Soar! My books, that had seemed such a nuisance a while ago, were old friends now, that I couldn't give up. And M. Hamel, too; the idea that he was going away, that I should not see him again, made me forget all about how cranky he was.

Poor man! It was in honor of the last lesson that he had put on his fine Sunday clothes, and now I understood why the old men of the village were sitting there in the back of the room. It was because they too were sorry that they had not gone to school more. It was their way of showing the master how they appreciated his forty years of service, and of showing their respect for the country that was theirs no more.

While I was thinking of all this, I heard my name called. It was my turn to recite. What would I not have given to be able to say that dreadful rule for the participle all through, very loud and clear, and without one mistake? But I got mixed up on the first words and stood there, holding on to my desk, my heart beating, and not daring to look up. I heard M. Hamel say to me:

"I won't scold you, little Franz; you must feel bad enough. See how it is? Every day we have said to ourselves: 'Bah, I've plenty time. I'll learn it tomorrow.' Now, you see where we've come to! Ah, there's great trouble in Alsace; she *puts off learning until tomorrow*. And now those fellows out there will have the right to say to you: (scorn) 'How is it? You pretend to be Frenchmen! And yet you can't even speak or write the language!' But you are not the worst, little Franz. We've all a great deal to reproach ourselves with.

"Your parents weren't anxious enough to have you learn.

They preferred to put you to work on the farm or at the mills, so as to have a little money. And I? I've been to blame also. Have I not often sent you to water my flowers instead of learning your lessons? And when I wanted to go fishing, did I not just give you a holiday?"

Then from one thing to another, M. Hamel went on to talk of the French language, saying that it was the most beautiful language in the world, and the cleverest, the most logical; that we must guard it among us and never forget it, because when people are enslaved, as long as they hold fast to their language it is as if they had a key to their prison. Then he opened a grammar and read us our lesson. I was amazed to see how well I understood it. All he said seemed easy, so easy! I think, too, that I never listened so carefully, and that he had never explained everything with so much patience. It seemed almost as if the poor man wanted to give us all he knew before going away, and to put it all into our heads at one stroke.

After the grammar, we had a lesson in writing. That day M. Hamel had new copies for us, written in a beautiful round hand; "France, Alsace; Alsace, France." They looked like little flags floating everywhere in the school-room. How everyone set to work! And how quiet it was! The only sounds were the scratching of the pens on the paper and the cooing of the pigeons on the roof. I thought to myself: Will they make them sing in German, even the pigeons?

When I looked up from my writing, I saw M. Hamel sitting motionless in his chair and gazing first at one thing, then at another, as if he wanted to fix in his mind just how everything looked in that little school-room. Fancy! For forty years he had been there in the same place, with his garden outside the window and his class in front of him, just like that. Only the desks and benches had been worn smooth; the walnut trees in the garden had grown taller; and the hop-vine that he had planted himself twined about the windows to the roof. It must have broken his heart to leave it all, poor man; and to hear his sister moving about in the room above, packing their trunks. For they must leave the country the next day.

But he had the courage to hear every lesson to the very last, history, spelling. At the back of the room old Houser had put on his spectacles, and, holding his primer in both hands, spelled out the letters. He was crying: his voice trembled with emotion; and it was so funny to hear him that we all wanted to laugh and cry at the same time. Oh, how well I remember it—that last lesson!

All at once the church clock struck twelve. Then the Angelus. At the same time the trumpets of the Germans, returning from drill

MUSIC—IN VERY SOFTLY

sounded under our windows. M. Hamel stood up, very pale, in his chair. I never saw him look so tall.

"My friends," he said, "I—I—" but something choked him. He could not go on. Then he turned to the blackboard, took a piece of chalk, and, bearing down with all his might, he wrote as large as he could:

"Vive la France!"

Then he stopped and leaned his head against the wall, and, without a word, he made a gesture to us with his hand, as if to say:

"School is dismissed—you may go."

MUSIC—FADE OUT

I'll never forget it—that last lesson. It's hard to talk about . . . and to think, it's coming again—with those guns, and all the dead! Oh, there are *other* lessons we never learned, but not the last! I pray to God, not the last!

READER.
    The last lesson. IS YOUR LANGUAGE, more than another's, THE KEY TO LIBERTY, AND RIGHT, AND JUSTICE: Is it the key to THE GREATER LIBERTY? There must be one somewhere. Good afternoon.

MUSIC—THEME, UP AND UNDER

ANNOUNCER. We have read for you Alphonse Daudet's story "The Last Lesson" taken from the volume *Monday Tales* [*etc.*].

(Short-Story Series) [1]

"Remember This One?"

"The Snow Man" by Hans Christian Andersen

ANNOUNCER. [*Cold.*] Remember This One?

MUSIC—THEME, UP FIVE SECONDS AND UNDER

ANNOUNCER. Do you remember the time when snows fell heavier and the drifts were deeper? the time when hearts seemed warmer and affections keener?—so that even a man of ice and snow felt love within his breast? . . .

    This afternoon we bring you a love story for the Valentine season.

MUSIC—FADE OUT

ANNOUNCER. Okay, here goes! And hearts are trumps.

READER. Thanks [*etc.*]. And good afternoon. Yes, hearts are trumps in this story—and there's a spade in it too. But I can't call it a spade; to be exact, I'll have to call it a shovel. And remember that shovel.

    The emotions, I'm told, depend on what the heart is

---

[1] George W. Fithian, by permission.

made of. Sometimes I doubt that adage; because today, like the man in this story, I love nothing so much as a good warm stove. For there's snow outside, even though it's not so deep as I remember its being years ago, when it was fun to make a snow man. Do you remember any one snow man that you made, who, when your back was turned, fell in love? I remember one that did, on Valentine's Day. But he had a very special kind of heart that might have caused it. And not only did he have a heart but he talked. He said:

(*Snow Man.*) It's so *crisp* and *cold* I'm really crackling. That North wind just bites life into me. And that round bright thing going down! how she does blaze! But she can't make me blink; I'll hold on to my parts tight enough.

He was talking about the sun, and his "parts" were two big three-cornered pieces of slate shingle that he had for eyes; his mouth was a piece of old rake, so that he had some teeth . . . he was born amid the cheering of the boys and the cracking of whips from the sleighs.

The sun went down and the full moon rose, big and bright and beautiful, in the sky.

(*Snow.*) There she comes up again from another direction.

He mistook the moon for the sun showing itself again.

(*Snow.*) But I've taught her to quit that blazing. But she can hang up there and light up, so I can look at myself . . . I wish I knew how to go about moving myself. I'd like to shift myself: why, if I could do that, I'd go down and slide on the ice like the boys, but I don't know how to run.

(*Dog.*) Off! Off! . . .

It was the watchdog; he had been rather hoarse ever since he had been a house dog and lay under the stove.

(*Dog.*) The sun will teach you to *run* all right. [*Cynical.*] Off! Off! Oh yes, you'll run *off!*

(*Snow.*) That bright thing up there can't teach me to run. Why, she ran when I looked hard at her, and now she comes creeping up from another direction.

(*Dog.*) [*Scornful.*] You've just been put together; so you don't know anything. That one up there is called the moon; the one that went off just now is the sun. She'll come up again tomorrow, and she'll teach you to run—down into the moat!

(*Snow.*) The way you say that sounds rather uncomfortable, friend.

(*Dog.*) Off! Off!

And the watchdog turned himself round three times and lay down in his kennel to sleep. . . . Early next morning, a mist, all thick and damp, spread itself over the whole neighborhood. At dawn a breeze sprang up, so icy that the frost took a tight hold; but what a sight there was when the sun rose! Every tree and bush was covered with hoar-frost, like a whole forest of white coral. It was as though every branch was loaded with dazzling white flowers. Every tiny twig came into view, and formed a lace-work so brilliantly white that a white radiance seemed to flow from every branch. The weeping birch waved in the wind; and when the sun came out, how it sparkled, as if it were powdered with diamond dust. And all about over the earth's snow coverlet big diamonds shone out.

A young girl, with a young man, came into the garden.

(*Girl.*) It is very beautiful; a lovelier sight one doesn't get even in summer.

(*Man.*) And such a fellow as that Snow Man isn't to be seen either. He's in his prime.

The Girl laughed and nodded to the Snow Man, and danced off with her friend, over the snow, which crunched under their feet as if they were walking on starch.

(*Snow.*) Who were those two, Dog? You've been here longer than I. Do you know them?

(*Dog.*) Off with them! Of course I do. She's often patted me, and he's given me many a bone. I don't bite them though.

(*Snow.*) But what are they doing here?

(*Dog.*) Sweet-hear-r-rt-ing. They're to move off into another kennel and gnaw the same bone. Off! Off!

(*Snow.*) Do those two matter as much as you and me?

(*Dog.*) Why, they belong to the quality! Foh! people don't know much that were born only yesterday. That's you. I'm old, and know everybody about this place; I've known the time when I didn't stand out here in the cold. [*Shiver.*] Uff! Uff!

(*Snow.*) Why, the cold is lovely. But tell me all about it. And please don't rattle your chain, it makes me crackle.

(*Dog.*) [*Mournful.*] Uff! Uff! I was a puppy—cute little thing, they said. I lay on a soft chair there in the house, and, yes, in the lap of the best of the quality, was kissed on the mouth and had my paws wiped with a handkerchief. They called me "sweet thing" and "poochkins." But I got too big for them, so they gave me to the housekeeper. It was a lower situation than upstairs, but it was comfortabler. I had just as good food and lots more of it. I had my own pillow, and then there was the *stove;* in weather like this it was the finest thing in the world. I used to crawl right under it and hide. I dream about it still. Uff! Uff! You can see it from where you stand, down there in the basement.

(*Snow.*) Is a stove beautiful to look at, like me?

(*Dog.*) Umph! Nothing like you! It's coal black, has a long neck with a tin pipe. It eats coal, and that makes fire come out of its mouth. And when you hug the stove or get underneath it, there's nothing so comfortable. You can see it in there through the window.

And the Snow Man looked, and he saw a black polished object with fire burning underneath. The Snow Man felt very queer; he couldn't explain the sensation. Something came over him that he knew nothing about; but all human beings know it if they are not Snow Men.

(*Snow.*) And why did you forsake her then?

He felt the stove must be a female.

(*Snow.*) How could you leave such a place as that?

(*Dog.*) I had to go; they pushed me out, and tied me here on a chain. I bit the youngest one of them in the leg, because he kicked away the bone I was gnawing; and I thought "bone for bone," and from that time I have been chained up—and lost my clear voice. [*Clearing his throat.*] Uff! Off! Hear how hoarse I am?

But the Snow Man wasn't listening: he was gazing into the housekeeper's window, into *her* room,—where stood the stove on four iron legs, looking about as big as the Snow Man himself.

(*Snow.*) There's a strange crackling inside me here. . . . Oh, if I could only get in there! I *must* get in there; I must nestle up against her, even if I have to break the window.

(*Dog.*) You'll never get in. And if you get to the stove, [*laugh*] you'll be off! off!

(*Snow.*) I might as well be off, the way I feel. I'm all to pieces, I think.

All day long the Snow Man stood and looked in the window. When night came the room looked still more attractive; from the stove there shone a light so kindly that neither the moon nor the sun can equal it—a light such as only a stove can give. When the door was opened, a glow poured forth, so that the Snow Man blushed red from the waist up.

(*Snow*.) I can't stand it! How beautiful she looks when she sticks her tongue out!

All night long the Snow Man was absorbed in his wonderful thoughts; and it froze so, that they crackled inside him. In the early hours the windows of her room bloomed with the loveliest ice-flowers that any Snow Man could wish for. Oh, but they hid the stove! The panes would not thaw! He could not see her! . . . It crackled, it crunched; it was just such weather as ought to delight a Snow Man; but he was not delighted. He was exceedingly unhappy: he had stove-sickness.

(*Dog*.) [*Apprehensively*.] Unf! Unf! that's a bad complaint for a Snow Man. I've had it myself, but I got over it. . . . Off! Off! Now the weather is going to change.

The weather did change; it turned to a thaw. The thaw came on; the Snow Man went off. He didn't say anything, he didn't complain; and that is the plainest of symptoms. . . . One morning he tumbled down. Something that looked like a broomstick remained sticking up where he had stood. The boys had built him up around it. The Dog looked at it.

(*Dog*.) Humph! Now I understand that yearning of his. The Snow Man had a shovel in his body! that's what stirred itself in him, but now it's all over and done with: Off! Off!

And soon winter was over and done with too. "It's gone off, off!" barked the watch-dog. The little girls in the house sang:

> Bloom, pussy-willow, little wooly kittens!
> Come, bloom! Hang out your mittens!
> Lark, cuckoo! come and sing;

February's here, so we must have spring.
Chwee-chwee! Cuckoo; I'll sing too.
Shine out, Sun! Make haste with you!

And nobody thought about the Snow Man any more. He'd gone off, off. And nothing was left of him but his heart, a heart that was a spade.

MUSIC—THEME UP AND UNDER

ANNOUNCER. The story read for you was Hans Christian Andersen's "The Snow Man" [*etc.*].

SECTION II

SELECTIONS FOR INTERPRETATION

THE DEFENCE OF POETRY
Percy Bysshe Shelley

Poetry lifts the veil from the hidden beauty of the world, and makes familiar objects be as if they were not familiar; it reproduces all that it represents, and the impersonations clothed in its Elysian light stand thenceforward, in the minds of those who have once contemplated them, as memorials of that gentle and exalted content which extends itself over all thought and actions with which it coexists. The great secret of morals is love; or a going out of our nature, and an identification of ourselves with the beautiful which exists in thought, action, or person, not our own. A man to be greatly good must imagine intensely and comprehensively; he must put himself in the place of another and of many others; the pains and pleasures of his species must become his own. The great instrument of moral good is the imagination; and poetry administers to the effect by acting upon the cause. Poetry enlarges the circumference of the imagination by replenishing it with thoughts of ever new delight, which have the power of attracting and assimilating to their own nature all other thoughts, and which form new intervals and interstices whose void forever craves fresh food. Poetry strengthens the faculty which is the organ of the moral nature of man, in the same manner as exercise strengthens a limb.

Poetry is indeed something divine. It is at once the centre and circumference of knowledge; it is that which comprehends all science, and that to which all science must be referred. It is at the same time the root and blossom of all other systems of thought; it is that from which all spring, and that which adorns all; and that which, if blighted, denies the fruit and the seed, and withholds from the barren world the nourishment and the succession of the scions of the tree of life. It is the perfect and consummate surface and bloom of all things; it is as the odour and the colour of the rose to the texture of the elements which compose it, as the form and splendour of unfaded beauty to the secrets of anatomy and corruption. What were virtue, love, patriotism, friendship; what were the scenery of this beautiful universe which we inhabit; what were our consolations on this side of the grave, and what were our aspirations beyond it,—if poetry did not ascend to bring light and fire from those eternal regions where the owl-winged faculty of calculation dare not ever soar?

Poetry is the record of the best and happiest moments of the happiest and best minds. We are aware of evanescent visitations of thought and feeling sometimes associated with place or person, sometimes regarding our own mind alone, and always arising unforeseen and departing unbidden, but elevating and delightful beyond all expression: so that even in the desire and the regret they leave, there cannot be but pleasure, participating as it does in the nature of its object. It is as it were the interpenetration of a diviner nature through our own; but its footsteps are like those of a wind over the sea, which the coming calm erases, and whose traces remain only as on the wrinkled sands which pave it. These and corresponding conditions of being are experienced principally by those of the most delicate sensibility and the most enlarged imagination; and the state of mind produced by them is at war with every base desire. The enthusiasm of virtue, love, patriotism, and friendship is essentially linked with such emotions; and whilst they last, self appears as what it is,—an atom to a universe. Poets are not only subject to these experiences as spirits of the most refined organisation, but they can colour all that they combine with the evanescent hue of this ethereal world; a word, a trait in the representation of a scene or a passion will touch the enchanted chord, and reanimate, in those who have ever experienced these emotions, the sleeping, the cold, the buried image of the past. Poetry thus makes immortal all that is best and most beautiful in the world; it arrests the vanishing apparitions which haunt the interlunations of life, and veiling them, or in language or in form, sends them forth among mankind, bearing sweet news of kindred joy to those with whom their sisters abide,—abide, because there is no portal of expression from the caverns of the spirit which they inhabit into the universe of things. Poetry redeems from decay the visitations of the divinity in man.

Abridged

SINCERITY THE SOUL OF ELOQUENCE
Goethe

How shall we learn to sway the minds of men
By eloquence?—to rule them, or persuade?—
Do you seek genuine and worthy fame?
Reason and honest feeling want no arts
Of utterance, ask no toil of elocution!
And, when you speak in earnest, do you need
A search for words? Oh! these fine holiday phrases,
In which you robe your worn-out commonplaces,
These scraps of paper which you crimp and curl
And twist into a thousand idle shapes,
These filigree ornaments, are good for nothing,—
Cost time and pains, please few, impose on no one;
Are unrefreshing as the wind that whistles,
In autumn, 'mong the dry and wrinkled leaves.
If feeling does not prompt, in vain you strive.
If from the soul the language does not come,

By its own impulse, to impel the hearts
Of hearers with communicated power,
In vain you strive, in vain you study earnestly!
Toil on forever, piece together fragments,
Cook up your broken scraps of sentences,
And blow, with puffing breath, a struggling light,
Glimmering confusedly now, now cold in ashes;
Startle the school-boys with their metaphors,—
And, if such food may suit your appetite,
Win the vain wonder of applauding children,—
But never hope to stir the hearts of men,
And mould the souls of many into one,
By words which come not native from the heart!

STANZAS ON FREEDOM

James Russell Lowell

Men! whose boast it is that ye
Come of fathers brave and free,
If there breathe on earth a slave,
Are ye truly free and brave?
If ye do not feel the chain,
When it works a brother's pain,
Are ye not base slaves indeed,
Slaves unworthy to be freed?

Women! who shall one day bear
Sons to breathe New England air,
If ye hear, without a blush,
Deeds to make the roused blood rush
Like red lava through your veins,
For your sisters now in chains,—
Answer! are ye fit to be
Mothers of the brave and free?

Is true Freedom but to break
Fetters for our own dear sake,
And, with leathern hearts, forget
That we owe mankind a debt?
NO! true freedom is to share
All the chains our brothers wear,
And, with heart and hand, to be
Earnest to make others free!

They are slaves who fear to speak
For the fallen and the weak;
They are slaves who will not choose
Hatred, scoffing, and abuse
Rather than in silence shrink
From the truth they needs must think;
They are slaves who dare not be
In the right with two or three.

WE MUST BE FREE OR DIE

William Wordsworth

It is not to be thought of that the flood
Of British freedom, which, to the open sea
Of the world's praise, from dark antiquity
Hath flowed, 'with pomp of waters, unwithstood,'
Roused though it be full often to a mood
Which spurns the check of salutary bands,
That this most famous Stream in bogs and sands
Should perish; and to evil and to good
Be lost for ever. In our halls is hung
Armoury of the invincible knights of old:
 We must be free or die, who speak the tongue
That Shakespeare spoke: the faith and morals hold
Which Milton held.—In everything we are sprung
Of Earth's first blood, have titles manifold.

THERE WAS A CHILD WENT FORTH [1]
Walt Whitman

There was a child went forth every day;
And the first object he look'd upon, that object he became;
And that object became part of him for the day, or a certain part of the day, or for many years, or stretching cycles of years.

The early lilacs became part of this child,
And grass, and white and red morning-glories, and white and red clover, and the song of the phoebe-bird,
And the Third-month lambs, and the sow's pink-faint litter, and the mare's foal, and the cow's calf,
And the noisy brood of the barn-yard, or by the mire of the pond-side,
And the fish suspending themselves so curiously below there— and the beautiful curious liquid,
And the water-plants with their graceful flat heads—all became part of him.

The field-sprouts of Fourth-month and Fifth-month became part of him;
Winter-grain sprouts, and those of the light-yellow corn, and the esculent roots of the garden,
And the apple-trees cover'd with blossoms, and the fruit afterward, and wood-berries, and the commonest weeds by the road;
And the school-mistress that pass'd on her way to the school,
And the friendly boys that pass'd—and the quarrelsome boys,
And the tidy and fresh-cheek'd girls—and the barefoot Negro boy and girl,

[1] From *Leaves of Grass* (Philadelphia: David McKay Company, 1900).

And all the changes of city and country, wherever he went . . .
Vehicles, teams, the heavy-plank'd wharves—the huge crossing
    at the ferries,
The village on the highlands, seen from afar at sunset—the
    river between,
Shadows, aureola and mist, the light falling on roof and gables
    of white or brown, two miles off,
The schooner near by, sleepily dropping down the tide—the
    little boat slack-tow'd astern,
The hurrying tumbling waves, quick-broken crests, slapping,
The strata of color'd clouds, the long bar of maroon-tint, away
    solitary by itself—the spread of purity, it lies motionless in,
The horizon's edge, the flying sea-crow, the fragrance of salt
    marsh and shore mud;
These became part of that child who went forth every day, and
    who now goes, and will always go forth every day.

THE HERO

Sir Henry Taylor

What makes a hero?—not success, not fame,
Inebriate merchants, and the loud acclaim
    Of glutted Avarice,—caps toss'd up in air,
    Or pen of journalist with flourish fair;
Bells peal'd, stars, ribbons, and a titular name—
    These, though his rightful tribute, he can spare;
His rightful tribute, not his end or aim,
    Or true reward; for never yet did these
    Refresh the soul, or set the heart at ease.

What makes a hero?—An heroic mind,
Express'd in action, in endurance prov'd.
    And if there be preëminence of right,
    Deriv'd through pain well suffer'd, to the **height**
Of rank heroic, 'tis to bear unmov'd,

Not toil, not risk, not rage of sea or wind,
Not the brute fury of barbarians blind,
  But worse—ingratitude and poisonous darts,
  Launch'd by the country he had serv'd and **lov'd**:

This, with a free, unclouded spirit pure,
This, in the strength of silence to endure,
  A dignity to noble deeds imparts
  Beyond the gauds and trappings of renown;
  This is the hero's complement and crown;
This miss'd, one struggle had been wanting still,
One glorious triumph of the heroic will,
  One self-approval in his heart of hearts.

WESTMINSTER ABBEY [1]

Joseph Addison

When I am in a serious humor, I very often walk by myself in Westminster Abbey; where the gloominess of the place and the use to which it is applied, with the solemnity of the building, and the condition of the people who lie in it, are apt to fill the mind with a kind of melancholy, or rather thoughtfulness, that is not disagreeable. I yesterday passed a whole afternoon in the churchyard, the cloisters, and the church, amusing myself with the tombstones and inscriptions that I met with in those several regions of the dead. Most of them recorded nothing else of the buried person, but that he was born upon one day, and died upon another, the whole history of his life being comprehended in those two circumstances, that are common to all mankind. I could not but look upon these registers of existence, whether of brass or marble, as a kind of satire upon the departed persons; who had left no other memorial of them, but that they were born and that they died. They put

[1] Friday, March 30, 1711.

me in mind of several persons mentioned in the battles of heroic poems, who have sounding names given them, for no other reason but that they may be killed, and are celebrated for nothing but being knocked on the head.

Upon my going into the church, I entertained myself with the digging of a grave; and saw in every shovel-full of it that was thrown up, the fragment of a bone or skull intermixt with a kind of fresh moldering earth, that some time or other had a place in the composition of an human body. Upon this, I began to consider with myself what innumerable multitudes of people lay confused together under the pavement of that ancient cathedral; how men and women, friends and enemies, priests and soldiers, monks and prebendaries, were crumbled amongst one another, and blended together in the same common mass; how beauty, strength, and youth, with old-age, weakness and deformity, lay undistinguished in the same promiscuous heap of matter.

After having thus surveyed this great magazine of mortality, as it were, in the lump; I examined it more particularly by the accounts which I found on several of the monuments which are raised in every quarter of that ancient fabric. Some of them were covered with such extravagant epitaphs, that, if it were possible for the dead person to be acquainted with them, he would blush at the praises which his friends have bestowed upon him. There are others so excessively modest, that they deliver the character of the person departed in Greek or Hebrew, and by that means are not understood once in a twelvemonth. In the poetical quarter, I found there were poets who had no monuments, and monuments which had no poets. I observed indeed that the present war had filled the church with many of these uninhabited monuments, which had been erected to the memory of persons whose bodies were perhaps buried in the plains of Blenheim, or in the bosom of the ocean.

I could not but be very much delighted with several modern epitaphs, which are written with great elegance of expression and justness of thought, and therefore do honor to the living as well as to the dead. As a foreigner is very apt to conceive an idea of the ignorance or politeness of a nation, from the turn of their public monuments and inscriptions, they should be submitted to the perusal of men of learning and genius, before they are put in execution. Sir Cloudesly Shovel's monument has very often given me great offense: Instead of the distinguishing character of that plain gallant man, he is represented on his tomb by the figure of a beau, dressed in long periwig, and reposing himself upon velvet cushions under a canopy of state. The inscription is answerable to the Monument; for instead of celebrating the many remarkable actions he had performed in the service of his country, it acquaints us only with the manner of his death, in which it was impossible for him to reap any honor. The Dutch, whom we are apt to despise for want of genius, shew an infinitely greater taste of antiquity and politeness in their buildings and works of this nature, than what we meet with in those of our own country. The monuments of their admirals, which have been erected at the public expense, represent them like themselves; and are adorned with rostral crowns and naval ornaments, with beautiful festoons of sea-weed, shells, and coral.

But to return to our subject. I have left the repository of our English kings for the contemplation of another day, when I shall find my mind disposed for so serious an amusement. I know that entertainments of this nature are apt to raise dark and dismal thoughts in timorous minds, and gloomy imaginations; but for my own part, though I am always serious, I do not know what it is to be melancholy; and can therefore take a view of nature in her deep and solemn scenes, with the same pleasure as in her most gay and delightful ones; by this means

I can improve myself with those objects, which others consider with terror. When I look upon the tombs of the great, every emotion of envy dies in me; when I read the epitaphs of the beautiful, every inordinate desire goes out; when I meet with the grief of parents upon a tomb-stone, my heart melts with compassion; when I see the tomb of the parents themselves, I consider the vanity of grieving for those whom we must quickly follow; when I see kings lying by those who deposed them, when I consider rival wits placed side by side, or the holy men that divided the world with their contests and disputes, I reflect with sorrow and astonishment on the little competitions, factions and debates of mankind. When I read the several dates of the tombs, of some that died yesterday, and some six hundred years ago, I consider that great day when we shall all of us be contemporaries, and make our appearance together.

SNOW-BOUND

John Greenleaf Whittier

The sun that brief December day
Rose cheerless over hills of gray,
And, darkly circled, gave at noon
A sadder light than waning moon.
Slow tracing down the thickening sky,
Its mute and ominous prophecy,
A portent seeming less than threat,
It sank from sight before it set.
A chill no coat, however stout,
Of homespun stuff could quite shut out,
 A hard, dull bitterness of cold,
That checked, mid-vein, the circling race
Of life-blood in the sharpened face,
 The coming of the snow-storm told.
The wind blew east; we heard the roar

Of Ocean on his wintry shore,
And felt the strong pulse throbbing there
Beat with low rhythm our inland air.

Meanwhile we did our nightly chores,—
Brought in the wood from out of doors,
Littered the stalls, and from the mows
Raked down the herd's-grass for the cows:
Heard the horse whinnying for his corn;
And, sharply clashing horn on horn,
Impatient down the stanchion rows
The cattle shake their walnut bows;
While, peering from his early perch
Upon the scaffold's pole of birch,
The cock his crested helmet bent
And down his querulous challenge sent.

Unwarmed by any sunset light
The gray day darkened into night,
So all night long the storm roared on:
The morning broke without a sun;
All day the hoary meteor fell;
And, when the second morning shone,
We looked upon a world unknown,
On nothing we could call our own.
Around the glistening wonder bent
The blue walls of the firmament,
No cloud above, no earth below,—
A universe of sky and snow!
The old familiar sights of ours
Took marvelous shapes; strange domes and towers
Rose up where sty or corn-crib stood,
Or garden-wall, or belt of wood;
A smooth white mound the brush-pile showed,
A fenceless drift what once was road;
The bridle-post an old man sat

With loose-flung coat and high cocked hat;
The well-curb had a Chinese roof;
And even the long sweep, high aloof,
In its slant splendor, seemed to tell
Of Pisa's leaning miracle.

All day the gusty north-wind bore
The loosening drift its breath before;
Beyond the circle of our hearth
No welcome sound of toil or mirth
Unbound the spell, and testified
Of human life and thought outside.
Shut in from all the world without,
We sat the clean-winged hearth about,
Content to let the north-wind roar
In baffled rage at pane and door.
What matter how the night behaved?
What matter how the north-wind raved?
Blow high, blow low, not all its snow
Could quench our hearth-fire's ruddy glow.
O Time and Change!—with hair as gray
As was my sire's that winter day,
How strange it seems, with so much gone
Of life and love, to still live on!
Ah, brother! only I and thou
Are left of all that circle now,—
The dear home faces whereupon
That fitful firelight paled and shone.
Henceforth, listen as we will,
The voices of that hearth are still;
Look where we may, the wide earth o'er
Those lighted faces smile no more.
We tread the paths their feet have worn,
　We sit beneath their orchard trees,
　We hear, like them, the hum of bees
And rustle of the bladed corn:

We turn the pages that they read,
    Their written words we linger o'er,
But in the sun they cast no shade,
No voice is heard, no sign is made,
    No step is on the conscious floor!
Yet Love will dream, and Faith will trust,
(Since He who knows our need is just,)
That somehow, somewhere, meet we must.
Alas for him who never sees
The stars shine through his cypress-trees!
Who, hopeless, lays his dead away,
Nor looks to see the breaking day
Across the mournful marbles play!
Who hath not learned, in hours of faith,
    The truth to flesh and sense unknown,
That Life is ever lord of Death,
    And Love can never lose its own!

Our mother, while she turned her wheel
Or run the new-knit stocking-heel,
Told how the Indian hordes came down
At midnight on Cocheco town.
Our uncle, innocent of books,
Was rich in lore of fields and brooks,
In moons and tides and weather wise,
He read the clouds as prophecies.
There, too, our elder sister plied
Her evening task the stand beside;
A full, rich nature, free to trust,
Truthful, and almost sternly just.

Brisk wielder of the birch and rule,
The master of the district school
Held at the fire his favored place,
Its warm glow lit a laughing face
Fresh-hued and fair, where scarce appeared

The uncertain prophecy of beard.
He teased the mitten-blinded cat,
Played cross-pins on my uncle's hat,
Sang songs, and told us what befalls
In classic Dartmouth's college halls.

At last the great logs, crumbling low,
Sent out a dull and duller glow,
The bull's-eye watch that hung in view,
Ticking its weary circuit through,
Pointed with mutely warning sign
Its black hand to the hour of nine.
That sign the pleasant circle broke;
My uncle ceased his pipe to smoke,
Knocked from its bowl the refuse gray,
And laid it tenderly away;
Then roused himself to safely cover
The dull red brands with ashes over.
And while, with care, our mother laid
The work aside, her steps she stayed
One moment, seeking to express
Her grateful sense of happiness
For food and shelter, warmth and health,
And love's contentment more than wealth,
With simple wishes . . .
That none might lack, that bitter night,
For bread and clothing, warmth and light.

Within our beds awhile we heard
The wind that round the gables roared,
With now and then a ruder shock,
Which made our very bedsteads rock.
We heard the loosened clapboards tost,
The board-nails snapping in the frost;
And on us, through the unplastered wall,
Felt the light sifted snow-flakes fall.

But sleep stole on, as sleep will do
When hearts are light and life is new;
Faint and more faint the murmurs grew,
Till in the summer-land of dreams
They softened to the sound of streams,
Low stir of leaves, and dip of oars,
And lapping waves on quiet shores.

Abridged

TO A SKYLARK

Percy Bysshe Shelley

Hail to thee, blithe Spirit!
  Bird thou never wert,
That from heaven, or near it,
  Pourest thy full heart
In profuse strains of unpremeditated **art**.

Higher still and higher
  From the earth thou springest
Like a cloud of fire;
  The blue deep thou wingest,
And singing still dost soar, and **soaring ever singest**.

In the golden lightning
  Of the sunken sun
O'er which clouds are brightening,
  Thou dost float and run,
Like an unbodied joy whose race is just begun.

The pale purple even
  Melts around thy flight;
Like a star of heaven
  In the broad daylight
Thou art unseen, but yet I hear thy shrill delight:

TO A SKYLARK

Keen as are the arrows
   Of that silver sphere,
Whose intense lamp narrows
   In the white dawn clear
Until we hardly see, we feel that it is there.

All the earth and air
   With thy voice is loud,
As, when night is bare,
   From one lonely cloud
The moon rains out her beams, and heaven is overflow'd.

What thou art we know not;
   What is most like thee?
From rainbow clouds there flow not
   Drops so bright to see
As from thy presence showers a rain of melody.

Like a poet hidden
   In the light of thought,
Singing hymns unbidden,
   Till the world is wrought
To sympathy with hopes and fears it heeded not:

Like a high-born maiden
   In a palace tower,
Soothing her love-laden
   Soul in secret hour
With music sweet as love, which overflows her bower:

Like a glow-worm golden
   In a dell of dew,
Scattering unbeholden
   Its aerial hue
Among the flowers and grass, which screen it from the view:

Like a rose embower'd
   In its own green leaves,
By warm winds deflower'd,
   Till the scent it gives
Makes faint with too much sweet these heavy-winged thieves.

Sound of vernal showers
   On the twinkling grass,
Rain-awaken'd flowers,
   All that ever was
Joyous, and clear, and fresh, thy music doth surpass.

Teach us, sprite or bird,
   What sweet thoughts are thine:
I have never heard
   Praise of love or wine
That panted forth a flood of rapture so divine.

Chorus hymeneal
   Or triumphal chaunt
Match'd with thine, would be all
   But an empty vaunt—
A thing wherein we feel there is some hidden want.

What objects are the fountains
   Of thy happy strain?
What fields, or waves, or mountains?
   What shapes of sky or plain?
What love of thine own kind? What ignorance of pain?

With thy clear keen joyance
   Languor cannot be:
Shadow of annoyance
   Never came near thee:
Thou lovest; but ne'er knew love's sad satiety;

Waking or asleep
   Thou of death must deem
Things more true and deep
   Than we mortals dream,
Or how could thy notes flow in such a crystal stream?

We look before and after,
   And pine for what is not:
Our sincerest laughter
   With some pain is fraught;
Our sweetest songs are those that tell of saddest thought.

Yet if we could scorn
   Hate, and pride, and fear;
If we were things born
   Not to shed a tear,
I know not how thy joy we ever should come near.

Better than all measures
   Of delightful sound,
Better than all treasures
   That in books are found,
Thy skill to poet were, thou scorner of the ground!

Teach me half the gladness
   That thy brain must know,
Such harmonious madness
   From my lips would flow
The world should listen then, as I am listening now!

WISDOM UNAPPLIED

Elizabeth Barrett Browning

If I were thou, O butterfly,
   And poised my purple wing to spy
   The sweetest flowers that live and die,

I would not waste my strength on those,
As thou,—for summer has a close,
And pansies bloom not in the snows.

If I were thou, O working bee,
And all that honey-gold I see
Could delve from roses easily,

I would not have it at man's door,
As thou,—that heirdom of my store
Should make him rich and leave me poor.

If I were thou, O eagle proud,
And screamed the thunder back aloud,
And faced the lightning from the cloud,

I would not build my eyrie-throne,
As thou,—upon a crumbling stone
Which the next storm may trample down.

If I were thou, O gallant steed,
With pawing hoof and dancing head,
And eye outrunning thine own speed,

I would not meeken to the rein,
As thou,—nor smooth my nostril plain
From the glad desert's snort and strain.

If I were thou, red-breasted bird,
With song at shut-up window heard,
Like Love's sweet Yes too long deferred,

I would not overstay delight,
As thou,—but take a swallow-flight
Till the new spring returned to sight.

While yet I spake, a touch was laid
Upon my brow, whose pride did fade
As thus, methought, an angel said,—

'If I were thou who sing'st this song,
Most wise for others, and most strong
In seeing right while doing wrong,

'I would not waste my cares, and choose,
As thou,—to seek what thou must lose,
Such gains as perish in the use.

'I would not work where none can win,
As thou,—halfway 'twixt grief and sin,
But look above and judge within.

'I would not let my pulse beat high,
As thou,—towards fame's regality,
Nor yet in love's great jeopardy.

'I would not champ the hard cold bit,
As thou,—of what the world thinks fit,
But take God's freedom, using it.

'I would not play earth's winter out,
As thou,—but gird my soul about,
And live for life past death and doubt.

'Then sing, O singer!—but allow,
Beast, fly and bird, called foolish now,
Are wise (for all thy scorn) as thou.'

THE PRINCESS PORCELAIN

Clara Morris

He had always been interested in the frail little thing. They were in the same row—the outer one—of the same oval bed that was crowded with fellow-Pansies, and he was quick to notice that by the gardener's carelessness the space between himself and his left-hand neighbor was wider than it should have been, a fact that annoyed him even then, and later became a source of real distress in his otherwise quiet life.

This little left-hand neighbor seemed to attract by her very weakness and slowness of growth. He, himself, came of a Dutch strain and showed it in his sturdy growth of stem and the body and velvet of his blossom. King of the Blacks he was called, and really he deserved his name, though one intensely "dark purple fellow" who had been called "Black" the summer before, remarked, somewhat maliciously, that "the title of the King of the Blacks could never pay *him* for going through life with a pinhead orange dot for an eye."

The King used sometimes to fear the little maid at his side would never reach maturity. If the sun were very strong, she shrank beneath the heat. If the rain fell, she would sometimes lie prostrate, and those were the times when the distance between them distressed him, for, as he often told her, he could and would have supported her, and at least partly sheltered her with his broader leaves, but as it was he could only help her with his advice. And when she at last formed her flower buds and a shower was imminent he would warn her to turn those delicate buds downward that the water might run off and so save the tenderly folded petals within from watery ruin.

Up to that time his feeling for her had been simply the tender affection one is apt to feel for the creature we help or protect, and he had often looked back with a bold, admiring orange eye at the smiling little mottled, banded Pansies, who had not hesitated one moment to nod at him,—for they are a generally coquettish tribe.

. . . . .

But one warm, still May morning all this was changed for the King of the Blacks, for there stood his slow-growing, frail neighbor holding up to his startled gaze the sweetest, tenderest, truest little face in all Pansydom. She was not brilliant nor velvet-blotched, nor yet banded, just a lovely porcelain blue of a perfectly even tint without markings of any kind, the pure color deepening into a violet eye with that speck of gold in the centre which, in a Pansy, answers to the pupil of a human eye.

Looking upon this innocent beauty the King of the Blacks was suddenly shaken by a great passion of love and longing. He realized in that moment that she held all the sweetness of life for him. For one moment he enjoyed the unalloyed bliss of his discovery; the next, alas! brought to his knowledge some of the tortures that invariably accompany true love. Was he, then, jealous? Of course! Who could see that small, fierce orange eye of his and doubt his jealousy—and goodness knows he had cause enough, but through no fault of little Porcelain Blue's, mind you! She adored him: was aquiver with love from the edge of her topmost petal to the tips of her threadlike roots.

But think of the maddening space between them! Do what they would they could not bridge it over. They looked and longed, and longed and looked, but only their sighs sweetly mingled. They knew neither embrace nor kiss.

The King of the Blacks was a sturdy fellow, and jealousy and disappointment made his temper prickly, and sometimes he wished many things of an unpleasant nature upon the gardener, whose carelessness had caused so much suffering. Often he cried out for a pest of mealy-bugs, or slugs, or snails to come upon his garden. Once he went so far as to wish moles to follow his footsteps beneath the lawn, but seeing how he had frightened Porcelain Blue he took that back, like the Dutch gentleman he really was.

But it was hard to see all the winged marauders buzzing around his gentle little sweetheart, offering her the tattered compliments they had offered to each floral feminine they had met that day. To see a great "bumble-bee" go blundering so heavily against her as to nearly knock her down! But, oh! worst of all, to see that Butterfly—that royally striped, banded, powdered, idiotic flirt masculine—to see him impudently clinging to shy little Porcelain Blue's shoulder, while he stole the precious nectar from the sweet flower lips that cried vainly for the King to drive him away.

. . . . .

No wonder he grew ill-tempered. He was so helpless. All he could do was to urge Porcelain Blue to call up her power of growing, and then to direct that growth toward him, while he cheered her up by calling her attention to the long arm he was forcing forward as rapidly as possible toward her, knowing well that the lady mistress of them all would much prefer his black, velvety blossoms to such a growth of leaf and stem.

Then, too, the King of the Blacks had much to endure from those about him. He had never concealed either his love or his distress, and there was much merriment at his expense among the flowers of his own bed and the insects that daily visited them.

One perfect morning, when all the world seemed made for love, the King of the Blacks felt his heart was breaking, little Porcelain Blue dropped and hung her head so sadly, while all the others were fairly asway with laughter. Just then, warm and sweet and strong, the West Wind came blowing. The romping, teasing, rowdy West Wind! Many a time had he chucked the

THE PRINCESS PORCELAIN

little one under the chin and set her petals into a wild, blue flutter, and now he paused a moment, disturbed at this sadness. Sadness in the path of the West Wind? Oh, no! he could not tolerate that. So back he drew a pace, gathered himself together, and then made a laughing rush upon the lovers, flinging with tender force young Porcelain Blue full upon the eager and clinging arms of the King of the Blacks. Then bumping their pretty faces together, he, rustling, fluttering, and waving, went on his merry way, leaving them to learn in peace the sweetness of the flower kiss. Porcelain Blue was so entangled in the strong arms of the King that she remained there, and if he found his Heaven in her sweet face she found hers in his gentle strength. And so happily they lived their little space and knew nothing but joy.

. . . . .

One early summer day the following year the mistress stood looking down with puzzled eyes upon a stranger in her great bed of saucy, wide-eyed beauties, in all their satiny, velvety gorgeousness. She knew them all by name. They were "Kings This," and "Queens That," and "Warrior So-and-So," and "French-Stained," and "German Blotched," and "Somebody's Royal Collection." But where did this stranger come from, here in the outer row of the big oval bed?

Down on his knees the gardener expatiated on the perfection of form and the firmness of texture to be found in this beautiful nameless blossom that was upheld so firmly by its sturdy stem.

"Pure porcelain blue, with markings that give it an almost human smile!" murmured the lady. "The markings of blackest velvet, and that great red-orange eye! Where have I seen that peculiar eye, and where that pure even tint of blue?

Why—!" and at the same moment the gardener struck his earth-stained hands together, exclaiming, "The King of the Blacks, ma'am!"

While his mistress cried, "Porcelain Blue!" and the gardener finished, "Hit's the offspring of them two plants, ma'am, has sure has you're halive, and she 'as no name, poor thing."

"Oh, yes, she has," smiled his mistress: "She is of Royal parentage and beautiful, and she is called The Princess Porcelain." And to herself she whispered, "Ah, love never dies! That is amply proved by the existence here of Princess Porcelain."

SEVEN TIMES TWO, ROMANCE
Jean Ingelow

You bells in the steeple, ring, ring out your changes
    How many soever they be,
And let the brown meadow lark's note as he ranges
    Come over, come over to me.

Yet birds' clearest carol by fall or by swelling
    No magical sense conveys,
And bells have forgotten their old art of telling
    The fortune of future days.

"Turn again, turn again," once they rang cheerily
    While a boy listened alone;
Made his heart yearn again, musing so wearily
    All by himself on a stone.

Poor bells! I forgive you; your good days are over,
    And mine, they are yet to be;
No listening, no longing shall aught, aught discover:
    You leave the story to me.

The foxglove shoots out of the green matted heather,
    And hangeth her hoods of snow;
She was idle, and slept till the sunshiny weather:
    O children take long to grow!

I wish, and I wish that the spring would go faster,
    Nor long summer bide so late;
And I could grow on like the foxglove and aster,
    For some things are ill to wait.

I wait for the day when dear hearts shall discover,
    While dear hands are laid on my head;
"The child is a woman, the book may close over,
    For all the lessons are said."

I wait for my story—the birds cannot sing it,
    Not one, as he sits on the tree;
The bells cannot ring it, but long years, O, bring it!
    Such as I wish it to be!

ORPHEUS

From KING HENRY VIII [1]

William Shakespeare

Orpheus with his lute made trees,
And the mountain-tops that freeze,
  Bow themselves, when he did sing:
To his music, plants and flowers
Ever sprung; as Sun and showers
  There had made a lasting Spring.

Everything that heard him play,
Even the billows of the sea,
  Hung their heads, and then lay by.

[1] Act III, Scene i.

In sweet music is such art,
Killing care and grief of heart
Fall asleep, or, hearing, die.

THE FUGITIVES
Percy Bysshe Shelley

I

The waters are flashing,
The white hail is dashing,
The lightnings are glancing,
The hoar-spray is dancing—
  Away!

The whirlwind is rolling,
The thunder is tolling,
The forest is swinging,
The minster bells ringing—
  Come away!

The earth is like Ocean,
Wreck-strewn and in motion:
Bird, beast, man and worm
Have crept out of the storm—
  Come away!

II

'Our boat has one sail,
And the helmsman is pale;—
A bold pilot I trow,
Who should follow us now,'—
  Shouted he—

And she cried: 'Ply the oar!
Put off gaily from shore!'—

THE FUGITIVES

As she spoke, bolts of death
Mixed with hail, specked their path
  O'er the sea.

And from isle, tower and rock,
The blue beacon-cloud broke,
And though dumb in the blast,
The red cannon flashed fast
  From the lee.

III

And 'Fear'st thou?' and 'Fear'st thou?'
And 'Seest thou?' and 'Hear'st thou?'
And 'Drive we not free
O'er the terrible sea,
  I and thou?'

One boat-cloak did cover
The loved and the lover—
Their blood beats one measure,
They murmur proud pleasure
  Soft and low;—

While around the lashed Ocean,
Like mountains in motion,
Is withdrawn and uplifted,
Sunk, shattered and shifted
  To and fro.

IV

In the court of the fortress
Beside the pale portress,
Like a bloodhound well beaten
The bridegroom stands, eaten
  By shame;

On the topmost watch-turret,
As a death-boding spirit,
Stands the gray tyrant father,
To his voice the mad weather
    Seems tame;

And with curses as wild
As e'er clung to child,
He devotes to the blast,
The best loveliest and last
    Of his name!

A CHILD'S DREAM OF A STAR
Charles Dickens

    There was once a child, and he strolled about a good deal, and thought of a number of things. He had a sister, who was a child too, and his constant companion. These two used to wonder all day long. They wondered at the beauty of the flowers; they wondered at the height and blueness of the sky; they wondered at the depth of the bright water; they wondered at the goodness and the power of GOD who made the lovely world.

    They used to say to one another, sometimes, Supposing all the children upon earth were to die, would the flowers, and the water, and the sky be sorry? They believed they would be sorry. For, said they, the buds are the children of the flowers, and the little playful streams that gambol down the hill-sides are the children of the water; and the smallest bright specks playing at hide and seek in the sky all night, must surely be the children of the stars; and they would all be grieved to see their playmates, the children of men, no more.

    There was one clear shining star that used to come out in the sky before the rest, near the church spire, above the graves. It was larger and more beautiful, they thought, than all the others, and every night they watched for it, standing hand in hand at a window. Whoever saw it first cried out, "I see the star!" And often they cried out both together, knowing so well when it would rise, and where.

But while she was still very young, oh very very young, the sister drooped, and came to be so very weak that she could no longer stand in the window at night; and then the child looked sadly out by himself, and when he saw the star, turned round and said to the patient pale face on the bed, "I see the star!"

But the time came all too soon when the child looked out alone, and when there was no face on the bed and when the star made long rays down towards him, as he saw it through his tears.

Now, these rays were so bright, and they seemed to make such a shining way from earth to Heaven, that when the child went to his solitary bed, he dreamed about the star; and dreamed that, lying where he was, he saw a train of people taken up that sparkling road by angels. And the star, opening, showed him a great world of light, where many more such angels waited to receive them.

All these angels, who were waiting, turned their beaming eyes upon the people who were carried up into the star; his sister's angel lingered near the entrance of the star, and said to the leader among those who had brought the people thither:

"Is my brother come?"

And he said, "No."

She was turning hopefully away, when the child stretched out his arms, and cried, "O, sister, I am here! Take me!" and then she turned her beaming eyes upon him, and it was night; and the star was shining in the room, making long rays down towards him as he saw it through his tears.

From that hour forth, the child looked out upon the star as on the home he was to go to, when his time should come.

He grew to be a young man, and was busy at his books when an old servant came to him and said:

"Thy mother is no more. I bring her blessing on her darling son!"

Again at night he saw the star, and all that former company. And he grew to be a man, whose hair was turning gray, and he was sitting in his chair by his fireside, heavy with grief, and with his face bedewed with tears, when the star opened once again.

Said his sister's angel to the leader: "Is my brother come?"

And he said, "Nay, but his maiden daughter."

And the man who had been the child saw his daughter, newly lost to him, a celestial creature among those three, and the star was shining.

Thus the child came to be an old man, and his once smooth face was wrinkled, and his steps were slow and feeble, and his back was bent. And one night as he lay upon his bed, his children standing round, he cried, as he had cried so long ago:

"I see the star! My age is falling from me like a garment, and I move towards the star as a child."

And the star was shining; and it shines upon his grave.

Abridged

HOW WE FOUGHT THE FIRE
Will Carlton

I

'Twas a drowsy night on Tompkins Hill;
The very leaves of the trees lay still;
The world was slumbering ocean deep;
And even the stars seemed half asleep,
And winked and blinked at the roofs below,
As yearning for morn, that they might go.

The streets as stolid and still did lie
As they would have done if streets could die;
The sidewalks stretched as quietly prone
As if a foot they had never known;
And not a cottage within the town
But looked as if it would fain lie down.
Away in the west a stacken cloud,
With white arms drooping and bare head bowed,
Was leaning against—with drowsy eye—
The dark-blue velveting of the sky.
      And that was the plight
      Things were in that night,
Before we were roused the foe to fight—
The foe so greedy and grand and bright—
      That plagued old Deacon Tompkins.

II

The Deacon lay on his first wife's bed,
His second wife's pillow beneath his head,
His third wife's coverlet o'er him wide,
His fourth wife slumbering by his side.
The parson visioned his Sunday's text,
And what he should hurl at Satan next;
The doctor a drowsy half-vigil kept,
Still studying, as he partly slept,
How men might glutton and tope and fly
In the face of Death, and still not die;
The lawyer dreamed that his clients meant
To club together and then present,
As proof that their faith had not grown dim,
A small bright silver hatchet to him;
The laborer such sound slumber knew,
He hadn't a dream the whole night through;
The ladies dreamed, but I can't say well
What 'tis they dream, for they never tell;
In short, such a general drowsy time

Had ne'er been known in that sleepy clime.
        As on the night
        Of clamor and fright,
We were roused the treacherous foe to fight—
The foe so greedy and grand and bright,
And carrying such an appetite—
        That plagued old Deacon Tompkins.

III

When all at once the old court-house bell
(Which had a voice like a maniac's yell),
Cried out, as if in its dim old sight
The judgment day had come in the night,
"Bang, whang, whang, bang, clang, dang, bang, **whang!**"
The poor old parcel of metal sang;
Whereat, from mansion, cottage, and shed,
Rose men and women as from the dead,
In different stages of attire,
And shouted, "The town is all afire!"
(Which came as near to being true
As some more leisurely stories do.)
They saw on the Deacon's house a glare,
And everybody hurried there,
And such a lot of visitors he
Had never before the luck to see.
The Deacon received these guests of night
In costume very simple and white,
And after a drowsy, scared "Ahem!"
He asked them what he could do for them.
"Fire! Fire!" they shouted; "your house's afire!"
And then, with energy sudden and dire,
They rushed through the mansion's solitudes,
And helped the Deacon to move his goods.
        And that was the sight
        We had that night,
When roused by the people who saw the light

Atop of the residence, cozy and white,
    Where lived old Deacon Tompkins.

IV

Ah! me! the way that they rummaged round!
Ah! me! the startling things they found!
No one with a fair idea of space
Would ever have thought that in one place
Were half the things, with a shout,
These neighborly burghers hustled out.
Came articles that the Deacon's wives
Had all been gathering all their lives;
Came furniture such as one might see
Didn't grow in the trunk of every tree.
A tall clock, centuries old, 'twas said,
Leaped out of a window, heels o'er head;
A veteran chair in which when new,
George Washington sat for a minute or two,
A bedstead strong as if in its lap
Old Time might take his terminal nap;
Dishes, that in meals long agone
The Deacon's fathers had eaten on;
Clothes, made of every cut and hue,
That couldn't remember when they were new;
A mirror, scatheless many a day,
Was promptly smashed in the regular way;
Old shoes enough, if properly thrown,
To bring good luck to all creatures known,
And children thirteen, more or less,
In varying plentitude of dress.
      And that was the sight
      We had that night,
When roused the terrible foe to fight,
Which blazed aloft to a moderate height,
And turned the cheeks of the timid white,
      Including Deacon Tompkins.

V

Lo! where the engines, reeking hot,
Dashed up to the interesting spot:
Came Number Two, "The City's Hope,"
Propelled by a line of men and rope,
And after them, on a spiteful run,
"The Ocean Billows," or Number One,
And soon the two, induced to play
By a hundred hands, were working away,
Until to the Deacon's flustered sight,
As he danced about in his robe of white,
It seemed as if, by the hand of Fate,
House-cleaning day were some two years late,
And with complete though late success
Had just arrived by the night express.
The "Ocean Billows" were at high tide,
And flung their spray upon every side;
The "City's Hope" were in perfect trim,
Preventing aught like an interim;
And a "Hook and Ladder Company" came
With hooks and poles and a long hard name,
And with an iconoclastic frown,
Were about to pull the whole thing down,
When some one raised the assuring shout,
"It's only the chimney a-burnin' out!"
Whereat, with a sense of injured trust,
The crowd went home in complete disgust.
Scarce one of those who, with joyous shout,
Assisted the Deacon moving out,
Refrained from the homeward-flowing din
To help the Deacon at moving in.
   And that was the plight
    At which, that night,
They left the Deacon, clad in white,
Who felt he was hardly treated right,

And used some words in the flickering light,
Not orthodox in their purport quite—
    Poor put-out Deacon Tompkins!

OUT OF THE CRADLE ENDLESSLY ROCKING [1]

Walt Whitman

Out of the cradle endlessly rocking,
Out of the mocking-bird's throat, the musical shuttle,
Out of the Ninth-month midnight,
Over the sterile sands and the fields beyond, where the child leaving his bed wandered alone, bare-headed, barefoot,
Down from the showered halo,
Up from the mystic play of shadows twining and twisting as if they were alive,
Out from the patches of briers and blackberries,
From the memories of the bird that chanted to me,
From your memories, sad brother, from the fitful risings and fallings I heard,
From under that yellow half-moon late-risen and swollen as if with tears,
From those beginning notes of yearning and love there in the mist,
From the thousand responses of my heart never to cease,
From the myriad thence-aroused words,
From the word stronger and more delicious than any,
From such as now they start the scene revisiting,
As a flock, twittering, rising, or overhead passing,
Borne hither, ere all eludes me, hurriedly,
A man, yet by these tears a little boy again,
Throwing myself on the sand, confronting the waves,
I, chanter of pains and joys, uniter of here and hereafter,
Taking all hints to use them, but swiftly leaping beyond them,
A reminiscence sing.

[1] From *Leaves of Grass* (Philadelphia: David McKay Company, 1900).

Once Paumanok,
When the lilac-scent was in the air and Fifth-month grass was
    growing,
Up this seashore in some briers,
Two feathered guests from Alabama, two together,
And their nest, and four light-green eggs spotted with brown,
And every day the he-bird to and fro near at hand,
And every day the she-bird crouched on her nest, silent, with
    bright eyes,
And every day I, a curious boy, never too close, never disturb-
    ing them,
Cautiously peering, absorbing, translating.

Shine! shine! shine!
Pour down your warmth, great sun!
While we bask, we two together.

Two together!
Winds blow south, or winds blow north,
Day come white, or night come black,
Home, or rivers and mountains from home,
Singing all time, minding no time
While we two keep together.

Till of a sudden,
Maybe killed, unknown to her mate,
One forenoon the she-bird crouched not on the nest,
Nor returned that afternoon, nor the next,
Nor ever appeared again,

And thenceforward all summer in the sound of the sea,
And at night under the full of the moon in calmer weather,
Over the hoarse surging of the sea,
Or flitting from brier to brier by day,
I saw, I heard at intervals the remaining one, the he-bird,
The solitary guest from Alabama.

Blow! blow! blow!
Blow up sea-winds along Paumanok's shore;
I wait and I wait till you blow my mate to me.

Yes, when the stars glisten'd,
All night long on the prong of a moss-scalloped stake,
Down almost amid the slapping waves,
Sat the lone singer wonderful causing tears.

He called on his mate,
He poured forth the meanings which I of all men know.

Yes, my brother, I know,—
The rest might not, but I have treasured every note,
For more than once dimly down to the beach gliding,
Silent, avoiding the moonbeams, blending myself with the shadows,
Recalling now the obscure shapes, the echoes, the sounds and sights after their sorts,
The white arms out in the breakers tirelessly tossing,
I, with bare feet, a child, the wind wafting my hair,
Listened long and long.

Listened to keep, to sing, now translating the notes,
Following you, my brother.

Soothe! soothe! soothe!
Close on its wave soothes the wave behind,
And again another behind embracing and lapping, every one close,
But my love soothes not me, not me.

Low hangs the moon, it rose late,
It is lagging— O I think it is heavy with love, with love.

O madly the sea pushes upon the land,
With love, with love.

O night! do I not see my love fluttering out among the breakers?
What is that little black thing I see there in the white?

Loud! loud! loud!
Loud I call to you, my love!

High and clear I shoot my voice over the waves,
Surely you must know who is here, is here,
You must know who I am, my love.
Low-hanging moon!
What is that dusky spot in your brown yellow?
O it is the shape, the shape of my mate!
O moon, do not keep her from me any longer.

Land! land! O land!
Whichever way I turn, O, I think you could give me my mate back again if you only would,
For I am almost sure I see her dimly whichever way I look.

O rising stars!
Perhaps the one I want so much will rise, will rise with some of you.

O throat! O trembling throat!
Sound clearer through the atmosphere!
Pierce the woods, the earth,
Somewhere listening to catch you must be the one I want.

Shake out carols!
Solitary here, the night's carols!
Carols of lonesome love! death's carols!
Carols under that lagging, yellow, waning moon!
O under that moon where she droops almost down into the sea!
O reckless despairing carols!

OUT OF THE CRADLE

But soft! sink low!
Soft! let me just murmur,
And do you wait a moment, you husky-noised sea,
For somewhere I believe I heard my mate responding to me,
So faint, I must be still, be still to listen,
But not altogether still, for then she might not come immediately to me.

Hither, my love!
Here I am! here!
With this just-sustained note I announce myself to you,
This gentle call is for you, my love, for you.

Do not be decoyed elsewhere:
That is the whistle of the wind, it is not my voice,
That is the fluttering, the fluttering of the spray,
Those are the shadows of leaves.

O darkness! O in vain!
O I am very sick and sorrowful.
O brown halo in the sky near the moon, drooping upon the sea!
O troubled reflection in the sea!
O throat! O throbbing heart!
And I singing uselessly! uselessly all the night.

O past! O happy life! O songs of joy!
In the air, in the woods, over fields,
Loved! loved! loved! loved! loved!
But my mate no more, no more with me!
We two together no more.

The aria sinking,
All else continuing, the stars shining,
The wind blowing, the notes of the bird continuous echoing,
With angry moans the fierce old mother incessantly moaning,
On the sands of Paumanok's shore gray and rustling,

The yellow half-moon enlarged, sagging down, drooping, the face of the sea almost touching,
The boy ecstatic, with his bare feet the waves, with his hair the atmosphere dallying,
The love in the heart long pent, now loose, now at last tumultuously bursting,
The aria's meaning, the ears, the Soul, swiftly depositing,
The strange tears down the cheeks coursing,
The colloquy there, the trio, each uttering,
The undertone, the savage old mother incessantly crying,
To the boy's Soul's questions sullenly timing, some drown'd secret hissing,
To the outsetting bard.

Demon or bird! (said the boy's soul)
Is it indeed toward your mate you sing? or is it really to me?
For I, that was a child, my tongue's use sleeping, now I have heard you,
Now in a moment I know what I am for, I awake,
And already a thousand singers, a thousand songs, clearer, louder and more sorrowful than yours,
A thousand warbling echoes have started to life within me, never to die.

O you singer solitary, singing by yourself, projecting me,
O solitary me listening, never more shall I cease perpetuating you,
Never more shall I escape, never more the reverberations,
Never more the cries of unsatisfied love be absent from me,
Never again leave me to be the peaceful child I was before what there in the night,
By the sea under the yellow and sagging moon,
The messenger there aroused, the fire, the sweet hell within,
The unknown want, the destiny of me,
O give me the clew! (it lurks in the night here somewhere)
O if I am to have so much, let me have more!

A word then, (for I will conquer it)
The word final, superior to all,
Subtle, sent up—what is it?—I listen;
Are you whispering it, and have been all the time, you sea-waves?
Is that it from your liquid rims and set sands?
Whereto answering, the sea,
Delaying not, hurrying not,
Whispered me through the night, and very plainly before daybreak,
Lisped to me the low and delicious word death,
And again death, death, death, death,
Hissing melodious, neither like the bird nor like my aroused child's heart,
But edging near as privately for me, rustling at my feet,
Creeping thence steadily up to my ears and laving me softly all over,
Death, death, death, death, death.

Which I do not forget,
But fuse the song of my dusky demon and brother,
That he sang to me in the moonlight on Paumanok's gray beach,
With the thousand responsive songs at random,
My own songs awaked from that hour,
And with them the key, the word up from the waves,
The word of the sweetest song and all songs,
That strong and delicious word which, creeping to my feet,
(Or like some old crone rocking the cradle, swathed in sweet garments, bending aside)
The sea whispered me.

THE VILLAGE PREACHER
Oliver Goldsmith

Near yonder copse where once the garden smiled,
And still where many a garden flower grows wild,
There, where a few torn shrubs the place disclose,
The village preacher's modest mansion rose.
A man he was to all the country dear,
And passing rich with forty pounds a year.
Remote from towns he ran his godly race,
Nor e'er had changed, or wished to change, his place;
Unskilful he to fawn, or seek for power,
By doctrines fashioned to the varying hour;
Far other aims his heart had learned to prize,
More bent to raise the wretched than to rise.
His house was known to all the vagrant train;
He chid their wanderings, but relieved their pain;
The long-remembered beggar was his guest,
Whose beard descending swept his aged breast;
The ruined spendthrift, now no longer proud,
Claimed kindred there, and had his claims allowed;
The broken soldier, kindly bade to stay,
Sat by his fire and talked the night away,—
Wept o'er his wounds, or, tales of sorrow done,
Shouldered his crutch and showed how fields were won.
Pleased with his guests the good man learned to glow,
And quite forgot their vices in their woe;
Careless their merits or their faults to scan,
His pity gave ere charity began.
Thus to relieve the wretched was his pride,
And e'en his failings leaned to virtue's side;
But, in his duty prompt at every call,
He watched and wept, he prayed and felt for all;
And, as a bird each fond endearment tries
To tempt its new-fledged offspring to the skies,

He tried each art, reproved each dull delay,
Allured to brighter worlds, and led the way.
Beside the bed where parting life was laid,
And sorrow, guilt, and pain by turns dismayed,
The reverend champion stood. At his control
Despair and anguish fled the struggling soul;
Comfort came down, the trembling wretch to raise,
And his last faltering accents whispered praise.
At church, with meek and unaffected grace,
His looks adorned the venerable place;
Truth from his lips prevailed with double sway,
And fools who came to scoff remained to pray.
The service past, around the pious man
With ready zeal each honest rustic ran;
E'en children followed, with endearing wile,
And plucked his gown, to share the good man's smile.
His ready smile a parent's warmth expressed;
Their welfare pleased him, and their cares distressed;
To them his heart, his love, his griefs were given,
But all his serious thoughts had rest in heaven.
As some tall cliff that lifts its awful form,
Swells from the vale, and midway leaves the storm,
Though round its breast the rolling clouds are spread,
Eternal sunshine settles on its head.

THE SPINNING-WHEEL SONG

John Francis Waller

Mellow the moonlight to shine is beginning;
Close by the window young Eileen is spinning;
Bent o'er the fire, her blind grandmother, sitting,
Is croaning, and moaning, and drowsily knitting.
"Eileen, achora, I hear some one tapping."
" 'T is the ivy, dear mother, against the glass flapping."
"Eileen, I surely hear somebody sighing."

" 'T is the sound, mother dear, of the summer wind dying."
Merrily, cheerily, noisily whirring,
Swings the wheel, spins the reel, while the foot's stirring;
Sprightly, and lightly, and airily ringing,
Thrills the sweet voice of the young maiden singing.

"What's that noise that I hear at the window, I wonder?"
" 'T is the little birds chirping the holly-bush under."
"What makes you be shoving and moving your stool on,
And singing all wrong that old song of 'The Coolun'?"
There's a form at the casement,—the form of her true love,—
And he whispers, with face bent, "I'm waiting for you, love:
Get up on the stool, through the lattice step lightly;
We'll rove in the grove while the moon's shining brightly."
Merrily, cheerily, noisily whirring,
Swings the wheel, spins the reel, while the foot's stirring;
Sprightly, and lightly, and airily ringing,
Thrills the sweet voice of the young maiden singing.

The maid shakes her head, on her lip lays her fingers,
Steals up from her seat,—longs to go, and yet lingers;
A frightened glance turns to her drowsy grandmother,
Puts one foot on the stool, spins the wheel with the other.
Lazily, easily, swings now the wheel round;
Slowly and lowly is heard now the reel's sound;
Noiseless and light to the lattice above her
The maid steps,—then leaps to the arms of her lover.
Slower, and slower, and slower the wheel swings;
Lower, and lower, and lower the reel rings;
Ere the reel and the wheel stop their ringing and moving,
Through the grove the young lovers by moonlight are roving.

FALSTAFF'S RECRUITS
From KING HENRY IV, Part II [1]
William Shakespeare

[NOTE: SIR JOHN FALSTAFF *has received a commission from the King to raise a company of soldiers to fight in the King's battles. After drafting a number of well-to-do farmers, who he knows will pay him snug sums of money, he proceeds to fill his company from the riff-raff of the country through which he passes.*

The scene is a village green before JUSTICE SHALLOW'S *house. The* JUSTICE *has received word from* SIR JOHN *that he is about to visit him, and desires him to call together a number of the villagers from which recruits may be selected.*

These villagers are now grouped upon the green, with JUSTICE SHALLOW *standing near.*

BARDOLPH, SIR JOHN FALSTAFF'S *corporal, enters and addresses* JUSTICE SHALLOW.]

BARDOLPH. Good morrow, honest gentlemen: I beseech you, which is Justice Shallow?
SHALLOW. I am Robert Shallow, sir; a poor esquire of this county, and one of the king's justices of the peace: what is your good pleasure with me?
BARDOLPH. My captain, sir, commends him to you; my captain, Sir John Falstaff, a tall gentleman, by heaven, and a most gallant leader.
SHALLOW. He greets me well, sir. I knew him a good backsword man. How doth the good knight? . . .
[*Enter* FALSTAFF.]
   Look, here comes good Sir John. Give me your good hand,

[1] Act III, Scene ii.

give me your worship's good hand; by my troth, you look well and bear your years very well: welcome, good Sir John.

FALSTAFF. I am glad to see you well, good Master Robert Shallow. . . . Fie! this is hot weather, gentlemen. Have you provided me here half a dozen sufficient men?

SHALLOW. Marry, have we, sir. Will you sit?

FALSTAFF. Let me see them, I beseech you.

SHALLOW. Where's the roll? where's the roll? where's the roll? Let me see, let me see, let me see. So, so, so, so, so, so, so, so, yea, marry, sir: Ralph Mouldy! Let them appear as I call; let them do so, let them do so. Let me see; where is Mouldy?

MOULDY. Here, an't please you.

SHALLOW. What think you, Sir John? a good-limbed fellow; young, strong, and of good friends.

FALSTAFF. Is thy name Mouldy?

MOULDY. Yea, an't please you.

FALSTAFF. 'T is the more time thou wert used.

SHALLOW. Ha, ha, ha! most excellent, i' faith! things that are mouldy lack use: very singular good! in faith, well said, Sir John, very well said. Shall I prick him, Sir John?

FALSTAFF. Yes, prick him.

MOULDY. I was pricked well enough before, an you could have let me alone: my old dame will be undone now for one to do her husbandry and her drudgery: you need not to have pricked me; there are other men fitter to go out than I. . . .

SHALLOW. Peace, fellow, peace; stand aside: know you where you are? For the other, Sir John: let me see: Simon Shadow!

FALSTAFF. Yea, marry, let me have him to sit under. He's like to be a cold soldier.

SHALLOW. Where's Shadow?

SHADOW. Here, sir.

FALSTAFF. Shadow, whose son art thou?

SHADOW. My mother's son, sir.

FALSTAFF'S RECRUITS

FALSTAFF. Thy mother's son! like enough, and thy father's shadow. . . . Shadow will serve for summer; prick him. . . .
SHALLOW. Thomas Wart!
FALSTAFF. Where's he?
WART. Here, sir.
FALSTAFF. Is thy name Wart?
WART. Yea, sir.
FALSTAFF. Thou art a very ragged wart.
SHALLOW. Shall I prick him down, Sir John?
FALSTAFF. It were superfluous; for his apparel is built upon his back and the whole frame stands upon pins: prick him no more.
SHALLOW. Ha, ha, ha! you can do it, sir; you can do it: I commend you well. Francis Feeble!
FEEBLE. Here, sir.
FALSTAFF. What trade art thou, Feeble?
FEEBLE. A woman's tailor, sir. . . .
FALSTAFF. Well, good woman's tailor! wilt thou make as many holes in an enemy's battle as thou hast done in a woman's petticoat?
FEEBLE. I will do my good will, sir: you can have no more.
FALSTAFF. Well said, good woman's tailor! Well said, courageous Feeble! thou wilt be as valiant as the wrathful dove or most magnanimous mouse. Prick the woman's tailor: well, Master Shallow; deep, Master Shallow.
FEEBLE. I would Wart might have gone, sir.
FALSTAFF. I would thou wert a man's tailor, that thou mightst mend him and make him fit to go. . . . Let that suffice, most forcible Feeble.
FEEBLE. It shall suffice, sir.
FALSTAFF. I am bound to thee, reverend Feeble. Who is next?
SHALLOW. Peter Bullcalf o' the green!
FALSTAFF. Yea, marry, let's see Bullcalf.

BULLCALF. Here, sir.

FALSTAFF. 'Fore God, a likely fellow! Come, prick me Bullcalf till he roar again.

BULLCALF. O Lord! good my lord captain,—

FALSTAFF. What, dost thou roar before thou art pricked?

BULLCALF. O Lord, sir, I'm a diseased man.

FALSTAFF. What disease hast thou?

BULLCALF. A terrible cold, sir, a cough, sir. . . .

FALSTAFF. Come, thou shalt go to the wars in a gown; we will have away thy cold. . . . Is here all?

SHALLOW. Here is two more called than your number; you must have but four here, sir; and so, I pray you, go in with me to dinner.

FALSTAFF. Come, I will go drink with you. . . .

[*Exeunt* FALSTAFF *and* JUSTICE SHALLOW.]

BULLCALF [*approaching* BARDOLPH]. Good Master Corporate Bardolph, stand my friend; and here's four Harry ten shillings in French crowns for you. In very truth, sir, I had as lief be hanged, sir, as go: and yet, for mine own part, sir, I do not care; but rather, because I am unwilling, and, for mine own part, have a desire to stay with my friends; else, sir, I did not care, for mine own part, so much.

BARDOLPH [*pocketing the money*]. Go to; stand aside. . . .

FEEBLE. By my troth, I care not.

Abridged

THE LEAP OF ROUSHAN BEG

Henry Wadsworth Longfellow

Mounted on Kyrat strong and fleet,
His chestnut steed with four white feet,
 Roushan Beg, called Kurroglou,
Son of the road, and bandit chief,

THE LEAP OF ROUSHAN BEG

Seeking refuge and relief,
  Up the mountain pathway flew.

Such was Kyrat's wondrous speed,
Never yet could any steed
  Reach the dust-cloud in his course.
More than maiden, more than wife,
More than gold and next to life
  Roushan the Robber loved his horse.

In the land that lies beyond
Erzeroum and Trebizond,
  Garden-girt his fortress stood;
Plundered khan, or caravan
Journeying north from Koordistan,
  Gave him wealth and wine and food.

Seven hundred and fourscore
Men at arms his livery wore,
  Did his bidding night and day.
Now, through regions all unknown,
He was wandering, lost, alone,
  Seeking without guide his way.

Suddenly the pathway ends,
Sheer the precipice descends,
  Loud the torrent roars unseen;
Thirty feet from side to side
Yawns the chasm; on air must ride
  He who crosses this ravine.

Following close in his pursuit,
At the precipice's foot,
  Reyhan the Arab of Orfah
Halted with his hundred men,
Shouting upward from the glen,
  "La Illah illa Allah!"

Gently Roushan Beg caressed
Kyrat's forehead, neck, and breast;
　　Kissed him upon both his eyes;
Sang to him in his wild way,
As upon the topmost spray
　　Sings a bird before it flies.

"O my Kyrat, O my steed,
Round and slender as a reed,
　　Carry me this peril through!
Satin housings shall be thine,
Shoes of gold, O Kyrat mine,
　　O thou soul of Kurroglou!

Kyrat, then, the strong and fleet,
Drew together his four white feet,
　　Paused a moment on the verge,
Measured with his eye the space,
And into the air's embrace
　　Leaped as leaps the ocean surge.

As the ocean surge o'er sand
Bears a swimmer safe to land,
　　Kyrat safe his rider bore;
Rattling down the deep abyss
Fragments of the precipice
　　Rolled like pebbles on a shore.

Roushan's tasselled cap of red
Trembled not upon his head,
　　Careless sat he and upright;
Neither hand nor bridle shook,
Nor his head he turned to look,
　　As he galloped out of sight.

Flash of harness in the air,
Seen a moment like the glare

Of a sword drawn from its sheath;
Thus the phantom horseman passed,
And the shadow that he cast
    Leaped the cataract underneath.

Reyhan the Arab held his breath
While this vision of life and death
    Passed above him. "Allahu!"
Cried he. "In all Koordistan
Lives there not so brave a man
    As this Robber Kurroglou!"

THE PERFECT ONE

Laurence Housman

Many years ago there lived in Persia a certain teacher and philosopher named Sabbah who seemed as a shining light to all who looked on him. His courtesy and dignity, his wisdom and humility, his imperturbability of temper, and his charity to all, won for him many followers; and among these there grew toward him so great a devotion that they could see in him nothing amiss. This, they said, was the perfect man whom all the world had been looking for. And because they found no flaw in his character and perceived no limitation in his wisdom, so far as things human were concerned, they called him "the perfect one," and fixing upon him the blind eye of imitation, but shutting upon him the eye of understanding, they sat daily at his feet and hearkened to his sayings; they spoke as he spoke and did as he did, hoping thereby to come in time to a like perfection.

So when, in the contemplation of deep things, the perfect one combed his beard with his fingers, they (such as had them) combed theirs, and those who had not, made combings in the air where presently their beards would be. And when he ate they ate, and when he fasted they fasted, and when he spat they spat, so as to be at one with him in all things appertaining to conduct. And they were happy in these things, and thought by discipline to come presently to the perfection wherein he seemed perfect.

So when, his hours of teaching being over (for he sat daily in the mosque and taught all that would hear him), he rose to return to his own house, those that doted on his example would rise and follow him; and where he trod they trod, and if he stayed to look on a piece of merchandise, or to handle a fabric and ask the price of it, they also would stay and look and handle and inquire. And because of these things they were a nuisance to the merchants, and the procession of the perfect one was imperfectly welcomed in the bazaars of that city. So presently the merchants would request the perfect one to go by other ways if he wished not to buy, but to go their way when buying was his intention; for when he bought then those that followed him bought also.

Now, every day when the perfect one reached his house thus accompanied and attended, he went in and shut the door, and they saw no more of him; and going sadly to their own homes, they wondered and questioned among themselves what he did when the door was shut, so that they also might do likewise, and by that much be nearer to perfection.

And this grew to be so great a debate among them that at last one, greatly daring, making himself spokesman for the rest, said:

"O Perfect One, when you go into your house and shut your door, so that we see no more of you, what is it that you do then? Let us know, that we also may do it and be perfect, as you are."

And the perfect one answered:

"I do many things. If I told you them all, you would not remember."

"Yet you may tell us the first thing," said he who spoke for the rest.

"The first thing?" said Sabbah; and musingly he combed his beard with his fingers, while all the rest did likewise. "The first thing that I do is to stand on my head and stick out my tongue and twiddle my toes, for I find great joy in it."

So that day when all his followers had parted from him and returned each to their own houses, they stood on their heads and stuck out their tongues and twiddled their toes, and found great joy in it.

"Now we be growing perfect," said they.

But the next day one of his followers said to him:

"O Perfect One, why do you do this thing? For though we find joy in it, we know not the celestial reason or the correspondency which makes it seem good."

And Sabbah answered:

"I will tell you first what I do, and I will tell you the reasons afterward."

So they said to him:

"O Perfect One, what is the next thing that you do?"

And Sabbah said:

"The next thing that I do? I tell my wife to beat me till I cry out for mercy."

So when his followers returned to their houses that day and had finished their first exercise in perfection, they told their wives to beat them till they cried out for mercy. And their wives did so.

The next day, a little crestfallen and sad, his followers came back to him, and one of them said:

"O Perfect One, after your wife has begun beating you, when do you cry out for mercy? There is a difference of opinion among us, and truly it matters."

Sabbah answered:

"I do not cry out for mercy."

At this answer they all looked much astonished and very sorry for themselves, and one who had come that day looking more crestfallen than the rest said:

"But I, Perfect One, have ten wives!"

Sabbah smiled on him.

"I have none," said Sabbah.

His followers sat and looked at him for a while in silence, then said one:

"O Perfect One, why have you done this?"

And the perfect one answered:

"When I go into my house and shut my door, then it is for the relief of being alone and quit of the mockery wherewith you mock me, pretending that I am perfect. It is for that, and to realize the more fully my own imperfection, that I stand on my head and twiddle my toes and stick out my tongue. Then I know that I am a fool. And that is the celestial reason and the correspondency which make me find joy in it.

"Then it is, because I know I am a fool, that I tell my wife to beat me until I cry out for mercy. And truly—and this shall be my last answer—the reason that I have no wife is because I am a wise man."

Then the perfect one arose from his place and went home, according to his custom; nor did any of his followers that time bear him company. But they gazed after him with the open eye of understanding, and, plucking out the blind eye of imitation, cast it from them, and went home full of thought how best to solve the domestic problem which there awaited them.

"Now I am at peace," said the perfect one, shutting his door.

SKIPPER IRESON'S RIDE

John Greenleaf Whittier

Of all the rides since the birth of time,
Told in story or sung in rhyme,—
On Apuleius's Golden Ass,
Or one-eyed Calendar's horse of brass,
Witch astride of a human back,
Islam's prophet on Al-Borak,—
The strangest ride that ever was sped
Was Ireson's, out from Marblehead!
  Old Floyd Ireson, for his hard heart,
    Tarred and feathered and carried in a cart
      By the women of Marblehead!

Body of turkey, head of owl,
Wings adroop like a rained-on fowl,
Feathered and ruffled in every part,
Skipper Ireson stood in the cart.
Scores of women, old and young,
Strong of muscle and glib of tongue,
Pushed and pulled up the rocky lane,
Shouting and singing the shrill refrain:
  "Here's Flud Oirson, fur his horrd horrt,
    Torr'd an' futherr'd an' corr'd in a corrt
      By the women o' Morble'ead!"

Wrinkled scolds with hands on hips,
Girls in bloom of cheek and lips,
Wild-eyed, free-limbed, such as chase
Bacchus round some antique vase,
Brief of skirt, with ankles bare,
Loose of kerchief and loose of hair,
With conch shells blowing and fish horns' twang,

Over and over the Maenads sang:
    "Here's Flud Oirson, fur his horrd horrt,
    Torr'd an' futherr'd an' corr'd in a corrt
        By the women o' Morble'ead!"

Small pity for him!—He sailed away
From a leaky ship in Chaleur Bay,—
Sailed away from a sinking wreck,
With his own town's people on her deck!
"Lay by! lay by!" they called to him.
Back he answered, "Sink or swim!
Brag of your catch of fish again!"
And off he sailed through the fog and rain!
    Old Floyd Ireson, for his hard heart,
    Tarred and feathered and carried in a cart
        By the women of Marblehead!

Fathoms deep in dark Chaleur
That wreck shall lie forevermore,
Mother and sister, wife and maid,
Looked from the rocks of Marblehead
Over the moaning and rainy sea,—
Looked for the coming that might not be!
What did the winds and the sea birds say
Of the cruel captain who sailed away?—
    Old Floyd Ireson, for his hard heart,
    Tarred and feathered and carried in a cart
        By the women of Marblehead.

Through the street, on either side,
Up flew windows, doors swung wide;
Sharp-tongued spinsters, old wives gray,
Treble lent the fish horn's bray.
Sea-worn grandsires, cripple-bound,
Hulks of old sailors run aground,
Shook head, and fist, and hat, and cane,

And cracked with curses the hoarse refrain:
"Here's Flud Oirson, fur his horrd horrt,
Torr'd an' futherr'd an' corr'd in a corrt
   By the women o' Morble'ead!"

Sweetly along the Salem road
Bloom of orchard and lilac showed.
Little the wicked skipper knew
Of the fields so green and the sky so blue.
Riding there in his sorry trim,
Like an Indian idol glum and grim,
Scarcely he seemed the sound to hear
Of voices shouting, far and near:
   "Here's Flud Oirson, fur his horrd horrt,
   Torr'd an' futherr'd an' corr'd in a corrt
      By the women o' Morble'ead!"

"Hear me, neighbors!" at last he cried,—
"What to me is this noisy ride?
What is the shame that clothes the skin
To the nameless horror that lives within?
Waking or sleeping, I see a wreck,
And hear a cry from a reeling deck!
Hate me and curse me,—I only dread
The hand of God and the face of the dead!"
   Said old Floyd Ireson, for his hard heart,
   Tarred and feathered and carried in a cart
      By the women of Marblehead!

Then the wife of the skipper lost at sea
Said, "God has touched him! why should we!"
Said an old wife mourning her only son,
"Cut the rogue's tether and let him run!"
So with soft relentings and rude excuse,
Half scorn, half pity, they cut him loose,
And gave him a cloak to hide him in,

And left him alone with his shame and sin.
Poor Floyd Ireson for his hard heart,
Tarred and feathered and carried in a cart
By the women of Marblehead!

From ROMEO AND JULIET [1]
William Shakespeare

MERCUTIO. O, then, I see, Queen Mab hath been with you.
She is the fairy midwife; and she comes
In shape no bigger than an agate-stone
On the fore-finger of an alderman,
Drawn with a team of little atomies
Athwart men's noses as they lie asleep.
Her chariot is an empty hazel-nut,
Made by the joiner squirrel or old grub,
Time out o' mind the fairies' coachmakers:
Her wagon-spokes made of long spinner's legs;
The cover, of the wings of grasshoppers;
The traces, of the smallest spider's web;
The collars, of the moonshine's watery beams;
Her whip, of cricket's bone; the lash, of film;
Her wagoner, a small grey-coated gnat.
And in this state, she gallops night by night
Through lovers' brains, and then they dream of love;
O'er courtiers' knees, that dream on curtsies straight;
O'er lawyers' fingers, who straight dream on fees;
O'er ladies' lips, who straight on kisses dream:
Sometimes she gallops o'er a courtier's nose,
And then dreams he of smelling out a suit;
And sometimes comes she with a tithe-pig's tail
Tickling a parson's nose that lies asleep,
Then dreams he of another benefice:
Sometimes she driveth o'er a soldier's neck,

[1] Act I, Scene iv.

And then dreams he of cutting foreign throats,
Of breaches, ambuscadoes, Spanish blades,
Of healths five-fathom deep; and then anon
Drums in his ear, at which he starts, and wakes;
And, being thus frighted, swears a prayer or two,
And sleeps again.

LONGING FOR HOME
Jean Ingelow

A song of a boat:—
   There was once a boat on a billow:
Lightly she rocked to her port remote:
And the foam was white in her wake like snow,
And her frail mast bowed when the breeze would blow.
   And bent like a wand of willow.

I shaded mine eyes one day when a boat
   Went curtseying over the billow,
I marked her course till a dancing mote
She faded out on the moonlit foam,
And I stayed behind in the dear loved home:
   And my thoughts all day were about the boat,
   And my dreams upon the pillow.

I pray you hear my song of a boat,
   For it is but short:—
My boat, you shall find none fairer afloat,
   In river or port.
Long I looked out for the lad she bore,
   On the open desolate sea,
And I think he sailed to the heavenly shore,
   For he came not back to me—
        Ah me!

A song of a nest:—
There was once a nest in a hollow:
Down in the mosses and knot-grass pressed,
Soft and warm, and full to the brim—
Vetches leaned over it purple and dim,
With buttercup buds to follow.

I pray you hear my song of a nest,
For it is not long:—
You shall never light, in a summer quest
The bushes among—
Shall never light on a prouder sitter,
A fairer nestful, nor ever know
A softer sound than their tender twitter,
That wind-like did come and go.

I had a nestful once of my own,
Ah happy, happy I!
Right dearly I loved them: but when they were grown
They spread out their wings to fly—
O, one after one they flew away
Far up to the heavenly blue,
To the better country, the upper day,
And—I wish I was going too.

I pray you, what is the nest to me,
My empty nest?
And what is the shore where I stood to see
My boat sail down to the west?
Can I call that home where I anchor yet,
Though my good man has sailed?
Can I call that home where my nest was set,
Now all its hope hath failed?
Nay, but the port where my sailor went,
And the land where my nestlings be:

There is the home where my thoughts are sent,
The only home for me—
Ah me!

NAAMAN AND GEHAZI
II *Kings* 5

Now Naaman, captain of the host of the king of Syria, was a great man with his master, and honorable, because by him the Lord had given deliverance unto Syria: he was also a mighty man in valor, but he was a leper. And the Syrians had gone out by companies, and had brought away captive out of the land of Israel a little maid; and she waited on Naaman's wife.

And she said unto her mistress, "Would God my Lord were with the prophet that is in Samaria! for he would recover him of his leprosy."

And one went in, and told his lord, saying, Thus and thus said the maid that is of the land of Israel.

And the king of Syria said, "Go to, go, and I will send a letter unto the king of Israel."

And he departed, and took with him ten talents of silver, and six thousand pieces of gold, and ten changes of raiment. And he brought the letter to the king of Israel, saying, "Now when this letter is come unto thee, behold, I have therewith sent Naaman my servant to thee, that thou mayest recover him of his leprosy."

And it came to pass, when the king of Israel had read the letter, that he rent his clothes, and said, "Am I God, to kill and to make alive, that this man doth send unto me to recover a man of his leprosy? Wherefore consider, I pray you, and see how he seeketh a quarrel against me."

And it was so, when Elisha the man of God had heard that

the king of Israel had rent his clothes, that he sent to the king, saying, "Wherefore hast thou rent thy clothes? Let him come now to me, and he shall know that there is a prophet in Israel."

So Naaman came with his horses and his chariot, and stood at the door of the house of Elisha. And Elisha sent a messenger unto him saying, "Go and wash in Jordon seven times, and thy flesh shall come again to thee, and thou shalt be clean."

But Naaman was wroth, and went away, and said, "Behold, I thought, he will surely come out to me and call on the name of the Lord his God, and strike his hand over the place, and recover the leper. Are not Abana and Pharpar, rivers of Damascus, better than all the waters of Israel? May I not wash in them and be clean?"

So he turned and went away in a rage.

And his servants came near, and spake unto him, and said, "My father, if the prophet had bid thee do some great thing, wouldst thou not have done it? How much rather, then, when he saith to thee, 'Wash, and be clean'?"

Then went he down, and dipped himself seven times in Jordan, according to the saying of the man of God; and his flesh came again like unto the flesh of a little child, and he was clean.

And he returned to the man of God, he and all his company, and came, and stood before him: and he said, "Behold, now I know that there is no God in all the earth, but in Israel: now therefore, I pray thee, take a blessing of thy servant."

But he said, "As the Lord liveth, before whom I stand, I will receive none."

And he urged him to take it; but he refused.

And Naaman said, "Shall there not, then, I pray thee, be given to thy servant two mules' burden of earth? for thy servant will henceforth offer neither burnt offering nor sacrifice unto other gods, but unto the Lord. In this thing the Lord pardon thy servant, that when my master goeth into the house of Rimmon to worship there, and he leaneth upon my hand, and I bow myself in the house of Rimmon: when I bow down myself in the house of Rimmon, the Lord pardon thy servant in this thing."

And he said unto him, "Go in peace."

So he departed from him a little way.

But Gehazi, the servant of Elisha the man of God, said, "Behold, my master hath spared Naaman this Syrian, in not receiving at his hands that which he brought; but as the Lord liveth, I will run after him and take somewhat of him."

So Gehazi followed after Naaman. And when Naaman saw him running after him, he lighted down from the chariot to meet him, and said, "Is all well?"

And he said, "All is well. My master hath sent me, saying, 'Behold, even now there be come to me from Mount Ephraim two young men of the sons of the prophets: give them, I pray thee, a talent of silver, and two changes of garments.'"

And Naaman said, "Be content, take two talents." And he urged him, and bound two talents of silver in two bags, with two changes of garments, and laid them upon his two servants; and they bare them before him. And when he came to the tower, he took them from their hands, and bestowed them in the house: and he let the men go, and they departed. But he went in, and stood before his master.

And Elisha said unto him, "Whence comest thou, Gehazi?"

And he said, "Thy servant went no whither."

And he said unto him, "Went not mine heart with thee, when the man turned again from his chariot to meet thee? Is it a time to receive money, and to receive garments, and oliveyards, and vineyards, and sheep, and oxen, and menservants, and maidservants? The leprosy therefore of Naaman shall cleave unto thee, and unto thy seed forever."

And he went out from his presence a leper, as white as snow.

THE OWL AND THE PUSSY-CAT
Edward Lear

    The Owl and the Pussy-Cat went to sea
        In a beautiful pea-green boat:
    They took some honey and plenty of money
        Wrapped up in a five-pound note.
    The Owl looked up to the stars above,
        And sang to a small guitar,
    "O lovely Pussy, O Pussy, my love,
        What a beautiful Pussy you are,
            You are,
            You are,
    What a beautiful Pussy you are!"

    Pussy said to the Owl, "You elegant fowl,
        How charmingly sweet you sing!
    Oh, let us be married; too long we have tarried:
        But what shall we do for a ring?"
    They sailed away, for a year and a day,
        To the land where the bong-tree grows;
    And there in a wood a Piggy-wig stood,
        With a ring at the end of his nose,
            His nose,
            His nose,
    With a ring at the end of his nose.

    "Dear Pig, are you willing to sell for one shilling
        Your ring?" Said the Piggy, "I will."

So they took it away, and were married next day
  By the Turkey who lives on the hill.
They dined on mince and slices of quince,
  Which they ate with a runcible spoon;
And hand in hand, on the edge of the sand,
  They danced by the light of the moon,
      The moon,
      The moon,
  They danced by the light of the moon.

SPRING SONG

From As You Like It

William Shakespeare

It was a lover and his lass,
  With a hey, and a ho, and a hey nonino,
That o'er the green corn-field did pass,
  In the spring time, the only pretty ring time,
When birds do sing, hey ding a ding, ding;
Sweet lovers love the spring.

Between the acres of the rye,
  With a hey, and a ho, and a hey nonino,
These pretty country folks would lie,
  In the spring time, the only pretty ring time,
When birds do sing, hey ding a ding, ding;
Sweet lovers love the spring.

This carol they began that hour,
  With a hey, and a ho, and a hey nonino,
How that a life was but a flower
  In the spring time, the only pretty ring time,
When birds do sing, hey ding a ding, ding;
Sweet lovers love the spring.

And therefore take the present time,
   With a hey, and a ho, and a hey nonino,
For love is crownèd with the prime
   In the spring time, the only pretty ring time,
When birds do sing, hey ding a ding, ding;
Sweet lovers love the spring.

SPINNING

Helen Hunt Jackson

Like a blind spinner in the sun,
   I tread my days;
I know that all the threads will run
   Appointed ways;
I know each day will bring its task,
And, being blind, no more I ask.

I know not now the use or name
   Of that I spin;
I only know that some one came,
   And laid within
My hand the thread, and said, "Since you
Are blind, but one thing you can do."

Sometimes the threads so rough and fast
   And tangled fly,
I know wild storms are sweeping past,
   And fear that I
Shall fall; but dare not try to find
A safer place, since I am blind.

I know not why, but I am sure
   That tint and place,
In some great fabric to endure
   Past time and race

My threads will have; so from the first,
Though blind, I never felt accurst.

I think, perhaps, this trust has sprung
   From one short word
Said over me when I was young,—
   So young, I heard
It, knowing not that God's name signed
My brow, and sealed me His, though blind.

But whether this be seal or sign
   Within, without,
It matters not. The bond divine
   I never doubt.
I know he set me here, and still,
And glad, and blind, I wait His will;

But listen, listen, day by day,
   To hear their tread
Who bear the finished web away,
   And cut the thread;
And bring God's message in the sun,
"Thou poor blind spinner, work is done."

THE SKELETON IN ARMOR

Henry Wadsworth Longfellow

"Speak! speak! thou fearful guest!
Who, with thy hollow breast
Still in rude armor drest,
   Comest to daunt me!
Wrapt not in Eastern balms,
But with thy fleshless palms
Stretched, as if asking alms,
   Why dost thou haunt me?"

Then from those cavernous eyes
Pale flashes seemed to rise,
As when the Northern skies
   Gleam in December;
And, like the water's flow
Under December's snow,
Came a dull voice of woe
   From the heart's chamber.

"I was a Viking old!
My deeds, though manifold,
No Skald in song has told,
   No Saga taught thee!
Take heed that in thy verse
Thou dost the tale rehearse,
Else dread a dead man's curse;
   For this I sought thee.

"Far in the Northern Land,
By the wild Baltic's strand,
I, with my childish hand,
   Tamed the gerfalcon;
And, with my skates fast bound,
Skimmed the half-frozen Sound
That the poor whimpering hound
   Trembled to walk on.

"Oft to his frozen lair
Tracked I the grisly bear,
While from my path the hare
   Fled like a shadow;
Oft through the forest dark
Followed the were-wolf's bark,
Until the soaring lark
   Sang from the meadow.

THE SKELETON IN ARMOR

"But when I older grew,
Joining a corsair's crew,
O'er the dark sea I flew
   With the marauders.
Wild was the life we led;
Many the souls that sped,
Many the hearts that bled,
   By our stern orders.

"Many a wassail-bout
Wore the long Winter out;
Often our midnight shout
   Set the cocks crowing,
As we the Berserk's tale
Measured in cups of ale,
Draining the oaken pail
   Filled to o'erflowing.

"Once as I told in glee
Tales of the stormy sea,
Soft eyes did gaze on me,
   Burning yet tender;
And as the white stars shine
On the dark Norway pine,
On that dark heart of mine
   Fell their soft splendor.

"I wooed the blue-eyed maid,
Yielding, yet half afraid,
And in the forest's shade
   Our vows were plighted.
Under its loosened vest
Fluttered her little breast,
Like birds within their nest
   By the hawk frighted.

"Bright in her father's hall
Shields gleamed upon the wall,
Loud sang the minstrels all,
　　Chanting his glory;
When of old Hildebrand
I asked his daughter's hand,
Mute did the minstrels stand
　　To hear my story.

"While the brown ale he quaffed,
Loud then the champion laughed,
And as the wind gusts waft
　　The sea foam brightly,
So the loud laugh of scorn,
Out of those lips unshorn,
From the deep drinking horn
　　Blew the foam lightly.

"She was a Prince's child,
I but a Viking wild,
And though she blushed and smiled,
　　I was discarded!
Should not the dove so white
Follow the sea mew's flight?
Why did they leave that night
　　Her nest unguarded?

"Scarce had I put to sea,
Bearing the maid with me,—
Fairest of all was she
　　Among the Norsemen!—
When on the white sea strand,
Waving his armed hand,
Saw we old Hildebrand,
　　With twenty horsemen.

THE SKELETON IN ARMOR

"Then launched they to the blast,
Bent like a reed each mast,
Yet we were gaining fast,
   When the wind failed us;
And with a sudden flaw
Came round the gusty Skaw,
So that our foe we saw
   Laugh as he hailed us.

"And as to catch the gale
Round veered the flapping sail,
'Death!' was the helmsman's hail,
   'Death without quarter!'
Midships with iron keel
Struck we her ribs of steel;
Down her black hulk did reel
   Through the black water!

"As with his wings aslant,
Sails the fierce cormorant,
Seeking some rocky haunt,
   With his prey laden,
So toward the open main,
Beating to sea again,
Through the wild hurricane,
   Bore I the maiden.

"Three weeks we westward bore,
And when the storm was o'er,
Cloudlike we saw the shore
   Stretching to leeward;
There for my lady's bower
Built I the lofty tower,
Which, to this very hour,
   Stands looking seaward.

"There lived we many years;
Time dried the maiden's tears;
She had forgot her fears,
　　She was a mother;
Death closed her mild blue eyes;
Under that tower she lies;
Ne'er shall the sun arise
　　On such another.

"Still grew my bosom then,
Still as a stagnant fen!
Hateful to me were men,
　　The sunlight hateful!
In the vast forest here,
Clad in my warlike gear,
Fell I upon my spear,
　　Oh, death was grateful!

"Thus, seamed with many scars,
Bursting these prison bars,
Up to its native stars
　　My soul ascended!
There from the flowing bowl
Deep drinks the warrior's soul,
Skoal! to the Northland! skoal!"
　　Thus the tale ended.

Scene from MACBETH [1]

William Shakespeare

MACBETH. Go bid thy mistress, when my drink is ready,
She strike upon the bell. Get thee to bed.—
[*Exit* SERVANT.]

[1] Act II, Scene i (in part) and Scene ii.

Is this a dagger which I see before me,
The handle toward my hand? Come, let me clutch thee:—
I have thee not, and yet I see thee still.
Art thou not, fatal vision, sensible
To feeling as to sight? or art thou but
A dagger of the mind, a false creation,
Proceeding from the heat-oppressèd brain?
I see thee yet, in form as palpable
As this which now I draw.
Thou marshal'st me the way that I was going;
And such an instrument I was to use,—
Mine eyes are made the fools o' the other senses,
Or else worth all the rest: I see thee still,
And on thy blade and dudgeon gouts of blood,
Which was not so before.—There's no such thing:
It is the bloody business which informs
Thus to mine eyes.—Now o'er the one-half-world
Nature seems dead, and wicked dreams abuse
The curtain'd sleep; now witchcraft celebrates
Pale Hecate's offerings; and wither'd Murder,
Alarum'd by his sentinel, the wolf,
Whose howl's his watch, thus with his stealthy pace,
With Tarquin's ravishing strides, toward his designs
Moves like a ghost.—Thou sure and firm-set earth,
Hear not my steps, which way they take, for fear
The very stones prate of my whereabout,
And take the present horror from the time,
Which now suits with it.—Whiles I threat, he lives:

| | Words to the heat of deeds too cold breath gives. [*A bell rings.*]
I go, and it is done; the bell invites me.
Hear it not, Duncan; for it is a knell
That summons thee to Heaven or to Hell.
[*Exit.*] |
|---|---|
| LADY MACBETH. | [*entering*]. That which hath made them drunk hath made me bold;
What hath quench'd them, hath given me fire.
—Hark!—Peace!
It was the owl that shriek'd the fatal bellman,
Which gives the stern's good-night. He is about it;
The doors are open; and the surfeited grooms
Do mock their charge with snores. I have drugg'd their possets,
That death and nature do contend about them,
Whether they live or die. |
| MACBETH. | [*within*]. Who's there?—what, ho! |
| LADY MACBETH. | Alack! I am afraid they have awak'd,
And 'tis not done:—the attempt, and not the deed,
Confounds us.—Hark!—I laid their daggers ready;
He could not miss them.—Had he not resembled
My father as he slept, I had done 't.—My husband! [*Enter* MACBETH.] |
MACBETH.	I have done the deed. Didst thou not hear a noise?
LADY MACBETH.	I heard the owl scream, and the cricket cry. Did you not speak?
MACBETH.	When?
LADY MACBETH.	Now.
MACBETH.	As I descended?
LADY MACBETH.	Ay.

MACBETH. Hark!—
            Who lies i' the second chamber?
LADY MACBETH.   Donalbain.
MACBETH. This is a sorry sight. [*Looking at his hands.*]
LADY MACBETH. A foolish thought, to say a sorry sight.
MACBETH. There's one did laugh in his sleep, and one cried, "Murder!"
That they did wake each other: I stood and heard them;
But they did say their prayers, and address'd them
Again to sleep.
LADY MACBETH.   There are two lodged together.
MACBETH. One cried "God bless us!" and "Amen," the other;
As they had seen me, with these hangman's hands.
Listening their fear, I could not say, "Amen,"
When they did say, "God bless us!"
LADY MACBETH.   Consider it not so deeply.
MACBETH. But wherefore could not I pronounce, "Amen"?
I had most need of blessing, and "Amen"
Stuck in my throat.
LADY MACBETH.   These deeds must not be thought
After these ways; so, it will make us mad.
MACBETH. Methought I heard a voice cry, "Sleep no more!
Macbeth does murder sleep! the innocent sleep;
Sleep, that knits up the ravell'd sleave of care,
The death of each day's life, sore labor's bath,
Balm of hurt minds, great nature's second course,
Chief nourisher in life's feast—
LADY MACBETH.   What do you mean?

MACBETH.　　　　　Still it cried, "Sleep no more!" to all the house:
"Glamis hath murder'd sleep, and therefore Cawdor
Shall sleep no more; Macbeth shall sleep no more!"
LADY MACBETH. Who was it that thus cried? Why, worthy thane,
You do unbend your noble strength, to think
So brain-sickly of things. Go, get some water,
And wash this filthy witness from your hand.—
Why did you bring these daggers from the place?
They must lie there: go, carry them; and smear
The sleepy grooms with blood.
MACBETH.　　　　　　　　　　I'll go no more:
I am afraid to think what I have done;
Look on 't again I dare not.
LADY MACBETH.　　　　　　　Infirm of purpose!
Give me the daggers: the sleeping and the dead
Are but as pictures: 'tis the eye of childhood
That fears a painted devil. If he do bleed,
I'll gild the faces of the grooms withal,
For it must seem their guilt.
[*Exit. Knocking within.*]
MACBETH.　　　　　　　Whence is that knocking?
How is 't with me, when every noise appals me?
What hands are here? Ha! They pluck out mine eyes!
Will all great Neptune's ocean wash this blood
Clean from my hand? No; this my hand will rather
The multitudinous seas incarnadine,
Making the green one red. [*Re-enter* LADY MACBETH.]
LADY MACBETH. My hands are of your color, but I shame

	To wear a heart so white. [*Knock.*] I hear a knocking
	At the south entry:—retire we to our chamber:
	A little water clears us of this deed:
	How easy it is then! Your constancy
	Hath left you unattended.—[*Knocking.*] Hark, more knocking.
	Get on your night-gown, lest occasion call us,
	And show us to be watchers. Be not lost
	So poorly in your thoughts.
MACBETH.	To know my deed, 'twere best not know myself. [*Knock.*]
	Wake Duncan with thy knocking. I would thou couldst!

NICHOLAS NICKLEBY LEAVING THE YORKSHIRE SCHOOL

Charles Dickens

The poor creature, Smike, paid bitterly for the friendship of Nicholas Nickleby; all the spleen and ill humor that could not be vented on Nicholas were bestowed on him. Stripes and blows, stripes and blows, morning, noon and night, were his penalty for being compassionated by the daring new master. Squeers was jealous of the influence which the said new master soon acquired in the school, and hated him for it; Mrs. Squeers had hated him from the first; and poor Smike paid heavily for all.

One night he was poring hard over a book, vainly endeavoring to master some task which a child of nine years could have conquered with ease, but which to the brain of the crushed boy of nineteen was a hopeless mystery. Nicholas laid his hand upon his shoulder. "I can't do it."

"Do not try. You will do better, poor fellow, when I am gone."

"Gone? Are you going?"

"I cannot say. I was speaking more to my own thoughts than to you. I shall be driven to that at last! The world is before me, after all."

"Is the world as bad and dismal as this place?"

"Heaven forbid. Its hardest, coarsest toil is happiness to this."

"Should I ever meet you there?"

"Yes,"—willing to soothe him.

"No! no! Should I—say I should be sure to find you."

"You would, and I would help and aid you, and not bring fresh sorrow upon you, as I have done here."

The boy caught both his hands, and uttered a few broken sounds which were unintelligible. Squeers entered at the moment, and he shrunk back into his old corner.

Two days later, the cold feeble dawn of a January morning was stealing in at the windows of the common sleeping-room.

"Now, then," cried Squeers, from the bottom of the stairs, "are you going to sleep all day up there?"

"We shall be down directly, sir."

"Down directly! Ah! you had better be down directly, or I'll be down upon some of you in less time than directly. Where's that Smike?"

Nicholas looked round. "He is not here, sir."

"Don't tell me a lie. He is."

Squeers bounced into the dormitory, and swinging his cane in the air ready for a blow, darted into the corner where Smike usually lay at night. The cane descended harmlessly. There was nobody there.

"What does this mean? Where have you hid him?"

"I have seen nothing of him since last night."

"Come, you won't save him this way. Where is he?"

"At the bottom of the nearest pond, for anything I know."

In a fright, Squeers inquired of the boys whether any one of them knew anything of their missing school-mate. There was a general hum of denial, in the midst of which one shrill voice was heard to say—as indeed everybody thought—

"Please, sir, I think Smike's run away, sir."

"Ha! who said that?"

Squeers made a plunge into the crowd, and caught a very little boy. "You think he has run away, do you, sir?"

"Yes, please, sir."

"And what reason have you to suppose that any boy would run away from this establishment? Eh?"

The child raised a dismal cry by way of answer, and Squeers beat him until he rolled out of his hands.

"There! Now if any other boy thinks Smike has run away, I shall be glad to have a talk with him." Profound silence.

"Well, Nickleby, you think he has run away, I suppose?"

"I think it extremely likely."

"Maybe you know he has run away?"

"I know nothing about it."

"He didn't tell you he was going, I suppose?"

"He did not. I am very glad he did not, for then it would have been my duty to tell you."

"Which no doubt you would have been sorry to do?"

"I should, indeed."

Mrs. Squeers now hastily made her way to the scene of action. "What's all this here to-do? What on earth are you talking to him for, Squeery? The cow-house and stables are locked up, so Smike can't be there; and he's not downstairs anywhere. Now, if you takes the chaise and goes one road, and I borrows Swallow's chaise and goes t'other, one or other of us is moral sure to lay hold of him."

The lady's plan was put in execution without delay, Nicholas remaining behind in a tumult of feeling. Death, from want and exposure, was the best that could be expected from the prolonged wandering of so helpless a creature. Nicholas lingered on, in restless anxiety, picturing a thousand possibilities, until the evening of the next day, when Squeers returned alone.

"No news of the scamp!"

Another day came, and Nicholas was scarcely awake when he heard the wheels of a chaise approaching the house. It stopped, and the voice of Mrs. Squeers was heard, ordering a glass of spirits for somebody, which was in itself a sufficient sign that something extraordinary had happened. Nicholas hardly dared look out of the window, but he did so, and the first object that met his eyes was the wretched Smike, bedabbled with mud and rain, haggard and worn and wild.

"Lift him out," said Squeers. "Bring him in, bring him in."

"Take care," cried Mrs. Squeers. "We tied his legs under the apron, and made 'em fast to the chaise, to prevent him giving us the slip again."

With hands trembling with delight, Squeers loosened the cord; and Smike more dead than alive, was brought in and locked up in a cellar, until such a time as Squeers should deem it expedient to operate upon him.

The news that the fugitive had been caught and brought back ran like wildfire through the hungry community, and expectation was on tiptoe all the morning. In the afternoon, Squeers, having refreshed himself with his dinner and an extra libation or so, made his appearance, accompanied by his amiable partner, with a fearful instrument of flagellation, strong, supple, wax-ended and new.

"Is every boy here?" Every boy was there.

"Each boy keep his place. Nickleby! go to your desk, sir." There was a curious expression in the usher's face; but he took his seat, without opening his lips in reply. Squeers left the room, and shortly afterward returned, dragging Smike by the collar—

or rather by that fragment of his jacket which was nearest the place where his collar ought to have been.

"Now what have you got to say for yourself? Stand a little out of the way, Mrs. Squeers; I've hardly got room enough."

"Spare me, sir!"

"Oh, that's all you've got to say, is it? Yes, I'll flog you within an inch of your life, and spare you that."

One cruel blow had fallen on him, when Nicholas Nickleby cried "Stop!"

"Who cried 'Stop!'"

"I did. This must not go on."

"Must not go on!"

"No! Must not! Shall not! I will prevent it! You have disregarded all my quiet interference in this miserable lad's behalf; you have returned no answer to the letter in which I begged forgiveness for him, and offered to be responsible that he would remain quietly here. Don't blame me for this public interference. You have brought it upon yourself, not I."

"Sit down, beggar!"

"Wretch, touch him again at your peril! I will not stand by and see it done. My blood is up, and I have the strength of ten such men as you. By Heaven! I will not spare you, if you drive me on! I have a series of personal insults to avenge, and my indignation is aggravated by the cruelties practised in this cruel den. Have a care, or the consequences will fall heavily upon your head!"

Squeers, in a violent outbreak, spat at him, and struck him a blow across the face. Nicholas instantly sprung upon him, wrested his weapon from his hand, and, pinning him by the throat, beat the ruffian till he roared for mercy. He then flung him away with all the force he could muster, and the violence of his fall precipitated Mrs. Squeers over an adjacent form; Squeers, striking his head against the same form in his descent, lay at his full length on the ground, stunned and motionless.

Having brought affairs to this happy termination, and having ascertained to his satisfaction that Squeers was only stunned, and not dead,—upon which point he had had some unpleasant doubts at first,—Nicholas packed up a few clothes in a small valise, and finding that nobody offered to oppose his progress, marched boldly out by the front door, and struck into the road. Then such a cheer arose as the walls of Dotheboys Hall had never echoed before, and would never respond to again. When the sound had died away, the school was empty; and of the crowd of boys not one remained.

DAYBREAK

Henry Wadsworth Longfellow

A wind came up out of the sea,
And said, "O, mists, make room for me."

It hailed the ships, and cried, "Sail on,
Ye mariners, the night is gone."

And hurried landward far away,
Crying, "Awake! it is the day."

It said unto the forest, "Shout!
Hang all your leafy banners out!"

It touched the wood bird's folded wing,
And said, "O bird, awake and sing."

And o'er the farms, "O chanticleer,
Your clarion blow; the day is near."

It whispered to the fields of corn,
"Bow down, and hail the coming morn."

It shouted through the belfry tower,
"Awake, O bell! proclaim the hour."

It crossed the churchyard with a sigh,
And said, "Not yet! in quiet lie."

TAMPA ROBINS

Sidney Lanier

The robin laughed in the orange tree:
"Ho, windy North, a fig for thee:
While breasts are red and wings are bold
And green trees wave us globes of gold,
   Time's scythe shall reap but bliss for me
   —Sunlight, song, and the orange tree.

Burn, golden gloves in leady sky,
My orange planets: crimson I
Will shine and shoot among the spheres
(Blithe meteor that no mortal fears)
   And thrid the heavenly orange tree
   With orbits bright of minstrelsy.

If that I hate wild winter's spite—
The gibbet trees, the world in white,
The sky but gray wind over a grave—
Why should I ache, the season's slave?
   I'll sing from the top of the orange tree,
   Gramercy, winter's tyranny.

I'll south with the sun, and keep my clime;
My wing is king of the summer time;
My breast to the sun his torch shall hold;
And I'll call down through the green and gold,
   Time, take thy scythe, reap bliss for me,
   Bestir thee under the orange tree."

THE TIME I'VE LOST IN WOOING

Thomas Moore

The time I've lost in wooing,
In watching and pursuing
The light that lies
In woman's eyes,
Has been my heart's undoing.

Tho' wisdom oft has sought me,
I scorn'd the lore she brought me,
My only books
Were woman's looks,
And folly's all they taught me.

Her smile when Beauty granted,
I hung with gaze enchanted,
Like him the sprite
Whom maids by night
Oft meet in glen that's haunted.

Like him, too, Beauty won me;
But when the spell was on me,
If once their ray
Was turn'd away,
O! winds could not outrun me.

And are those follies going?
And is my proud heart growing
Too cold or wise
For brilliant eyes
Again to set it glowing?

No—vain, alas! th' endeavor
From so sweet to sever;—
Poor Wisdom's chance
Against a glance
Is now as weak as ever.

AUNT MELISSY ON BOYS
John T. Trowbridge

I hain't nothin' agin' boys, as sich. They're a necessary part o' creation, I s'pose—like a good many disagreeable things! But deliver me! I'd ruther bring up a family of nine gals, any day in the year, with cats an' dogs throw'd in, than one boy.

Gittin' fishhooks into their jacket-pockets, to stick in yer fingers washin'-days! Gals don't carry fishhooks in their jacket-pockets. Tearin' their trousis a-climbin' fences! perfec'ly reckless! an' then, patch! patch!

Kiverin' the floor with whiddlin's soon as ever you've got nicely slicked up! an' then down must come the broom an' dustpan agin; an' I remember once, when I kep' house for Uncle Amos, I hed the Dorkis S'iety to tea, an' I'd been makin' a nice dish of cream-toast, an' we was waitin' for the minister—blessed soul! he mos' gener'ly dropped in to tea when the S'iety met, an' he never failed when 'twas to our house, he was so fond o' my cream-toast—an' bimeby he come in, an' when everybody was ready, I run and ketched up the things from the kitchen hairth, where I'd left 'em to keep warm, an' put 'em ontew the table, and we drawed up our chairs, an' got quiet, an' I never noticed anything was out o' the way, till bimeby, jes's the minister—blessed soul!—was a-askin' the blessin', I kind o' opened one corner of my eye to see how the table looked—for I prided myself on my table—when I declare to goodness, if

I didn't think I should go right through the top of the house! For there was the great, splendid, elegant, nice dish o' cream-toast, stuccoted all over with pine whiddlin's! right between the blazin' candles Lucindy'd put on jes' as we was a-settin' down.

Ye see, I'd poured the cream over the toast the last thing when I set it by the fire, an' never noticed Hezekier in the corner a-whiddlin' out his canew—I should say canoo! Why, that 'air cream-toast was like a foamin' cataract kivered by a fleet of canews, where the whiddlin's was curled up on't, capsized, stickin' up eendways an' every which way, enough to make a decent housekeeper go intew fits! An' I thought I should!

I shet my eyes, an' tried to keep my mind ontew things speritooal, but I couldn't for my life think of anything but the pesky whiddlin's in the toast, an' how was I ever goin' to snatch it off'm the table an' out of sight, the minute the blessin' was through, an' 'fore the minister—blessed soul!—or anybody had their eyes open to the material things; for right ontew the tail of the Amen, ye know, comp'ny will kind o' look 'round, hopeful and comf'table, to see what creatur' comforts is put afore 'em.

But I watched my chance.

I knowed perty well the way he mos' gener'ly allers tapered off, an' soon's ever that long-hankered-for Amen come out, I jumped like a cat at a mouse, had that 'air toast off'm the table, whisked it into the pantry, picked the whiddlin's out with my thumb-an'-finger, give that Hezekier a good smart box on the ear, as a foretaste of what was in store for him when the comp'ny was gone, an' had it back ontew the table agin, all serene an' beautiful, only I noticed Miss Smith,—she's got eyes like a lynx, an' she was dreffle jealous of my housekeepin',—she'd seen suthin'! she looked awful queer an' puzzled! an' I was mortified tew death when the minister—blessed soul!—a-eatin' of his slice, took suthin' tough out of his mouth, and laid it careful under the side of his plate. He was a wonderful perlite man, an' not a soul in the world 'sides me an' him ever 'spected he'd been chorrin' ontew a pine whiddlin'!

That's jest a specimint o' that 'air Hezekier. His excuse allers was, he didn't mean ter dew it. Once his pa give him about tew quarts o' seed-corn in a bucket, an' told him to put it to soak—his pa gener'ly soaked his seed-corn for plantin'; he said it come up so much quicker. Hezekier, he took the bucket, but he was tew lazy to git any water, so he jest ketched up the fust thing come handy, which happened to be a jug o' rum, an' poured it all into the corn, an' then went to flyin' his kite.

Wal, that afternoon, his pa was a-goin' through the woodshed, an' he kep' snuffin', snuffin', till bimeby says he "Melissy," says he, "what under the canopy ye been doin' with rum?" says he. Of course I hadn't been doin' nothin' with rum, only smellin' on't for the last half hour—I detest the stuff!—but we put our noses together an' follered up the scent, and there was that corn!

"Now, Amos," says I, "I hope to gracious goodness you'll give that boy a good tunin'—for he's jest sufferin' for it!" says I.

"No, I ain't!" says Hezekier. "I shall be sufferin' if ye give it tew me!" says he. "I seen pa drinkin' out o' the jug, an' thought 'twa'n't nothin' but water!" says he.

An' his pa jest kinder winked to me, an' scolded and threatened a little, an' then drove off to town, tellin' Hezekier to toe the mark an' jest look sharp arter things, or he'd give it to him.

Wal, Hezekier was perty quiet that arternoon, which I noticed it, for gener'ly, if he wa'n't makin' a noise to drive ye distracted, ye might be sure he was up to some wus mischief; an' bimeby think says I to myself, think says I; "Now what under the canopy can that Hezekier be up tew now!" think says I; for I hadn't heerd him blow his squawker, nor pound on a tin pan, nor pull the cat's tail, nor touch off his cannon, nor bounce his ball agin' the house, nor screech, nor break a glass, nor nothin', for all of five minutes; an' I was a-wonderin', when perty soon he comes into the house of his own accord, a-lookin' kinder scaret and meechin'; an' says he, "Aunt Melissy," says he, "I'm a-feared there's suthin' the matter with them 'air turkeys."

"The turkeys!" says I. "What in the name of goodness can be the matter with them?"

"I don'o'," says he; "but I guess ye better come out an' look."

And I did go out an' look! an' there behind the woodshed was all them seven turkeys, the hull caboodle of 'em, ol' gobbler an' all, keeled over and stretched out on the ground, a sight to behold!

"Massy goodness sakes alive! What's been an' gone an' killed off all the turkeys?"

"I don'o', 'thout it's suthin' they've et."

"Et!" says I. "What you been givin' on 'em to eat? fer goodness' sakes!"

"Nothin', only that corn that was sp'ilt for plantin'; I tho't 'twas too bad to have it all wasted, so I fed it to the turkeys."

"Fed it to the turkeys! An' you've jest killed 'em, every blessed one! An' what'll yer pa say now dew you s'pose?"

"I didn't mean ter do it."

"I'd didn't mean ter yet, if ye was my boy!" says I. "Now ketch hold and help me pick their feathers off an' dress 'em for market, fust thing—for that's all the poor critters is good for now—so much for yer plaguy nonsense!"

He sprung tew perty smart, for once, an' Lucindy she helped, an we jest stripped them 'air turkeys jest as naked as any fowls ever ye see, 'fore singein—all but their heads, an' I was jest a-goin' to cut off the old gobbler's—I'd got it ontew the choppin' block, an' raised the ax, when he kinder give a wiggle, an' squawked!

Jest then Lucindy, she spoke up: "Oh, Aunt Melissy! there's one a-kickin'!" I jest dropped that 'air gobbler an' the ax an'

looked, an' there was one or tew more a-kickin' by that time; for if you'll believe me, not one o' them turkeys was dead at all, only dead drunk from the rum in the corn! an' it wa'n't many minutes 'fore every one o' them poor, naked, ridic'lous critters was up, staggerin' 'round, lookin' dizzy an' silly enough, massy knows! While that Hezekier! he couldn't think o' nothin' else to dew, but jest to keel over on the grass an' roll an' kick an' screech, like all possessed! For my part, I couldn't see nothin' to laugh at. I pitied the poor naked, tipsy things, an' set to work that very arternoon, a-makin' little jackets for 'em to wear; an' then that boy had to go intew coniptions agin, when he seen 'em with their jackets on. An' if you'll believe it, his pa, he laughed tew—so foolish! An' jes' said to Hezekier: "Didn't ye know no better 'n to go an' give corn soaked in rum to the turkeys?" says he, an' then kinder winked to me out o' t'other side of his face; an' that's every speck of a whippin' that boy got!
Abridged.

THE WAY TO SING

Helen Hunt Jackson

The birds must know. Who wisely sings
    Will sing as they;
The common air has generous wings,
    Songs make their way.
No messenger to run before,
    Devising plan;
No mention of the place or hour
    To any man;
No waiting till some sound betrays
    A listening ear;
No different voice, no new delays,
    If steps draw near.

"What bird is that? Its song is good."
   And eager eyes
Go peering through the dusky wood,
   In glad surprise.
Then late at night, when by his fire
   The traveller sits,
Watching the flame grow brighter, higher,
   The sweet song flits
By snatches through his weary brain
   To help him rest;
When next he goes that road again,
   An empty nest
On leafless bough will make him sigh,
   "Ah me! last spring
Just here I heard, in passing by,
   That rare bird sing!"

But while he sighs, remembering
   How sweet the song,
The little bird on tireless wing,
   Is borne along
In other air, and other men
   With weary feet,
On other roads, the simple strain
   Are finding sweet.
The birds must know. Who wisely sings
   Will sing as they;
The common air has generous wings,
   Songs make their way.

MERLIN AND THE GLEAM

Alfred Tennyson

O young Mariner,
You from the haven

Under the sea-cliff,
You that are watching
The gray Magician
With eyes of wonder,
I am Merlin,
And I am dying,
I am Merlin
Who follow The Gleam.

Mighty the Wizard
Who found me at sunrise
Sleeping, and woke me
And learned me magic!
Great the Master,
And sweet the Magic,
When over the valley,
In early summers,
Over the mountain,
On human faces,
And all around me,
Moving to melody,
Floated The Gleam.

Once at the croak of a Raven who crost it,
A barbarous people,
Blind to the Magic,
And deaf to the melody,
Snarled at and cursed me.
The light retreated,
The landskip darkened,
The melody deadened;
The Master whispered,
"Follow The Gleam."

Then to the melody,
Over a wilderness

Gliding, and glancing at
Elf of woodland,
Gnome of the cavern,
Griffin and Giant,
And dancing Fairies
In desolate hollows,
And wraiths of the mountain,
And rolling of dragons
By warble of water,
Or cataract music
Of falling torrents,
Flitted The Gleam.

Down from the mountain
And over the level,
And streaming and shining on
Silent river,
Silvery willow,
Pasture and plowland,
Innocent maidens,
Garrulous children,
Homestead and harvest,
Reaper and gleaner,
And rough-ruddy faces
Of lowly labor,
Glided The Gleam—

Then, with a melody
Stronger and statelier,
Led me at length
To the city and palace
Of Arthur the king;
Touched at the golden
Cross of the churches,
Flashed on the Tournament,
Flickered and bickered

From helmet to helmet,
And last on the forehead
Of Arthur the blameless
Rested The Gleam.

Clouds and darkness
Closed upon Camelot;
Arthur had vanished
I knew not whither,
The king who loved me
And cannot die;
For out of the darkness
Silent and slowly
The Gleam, that had waned to a wintry glimmer
On icy fallow
And faded forest,
Drew to the valley
Named of the shadow,
And slowly brightening
Out of the glimmer,
And slowly moving again to the melody
Yearningly tender,
Fell on the shadow,
No longer shadow,
But clothed with The Gleam.

And broader and brighter
The Gleam flying onward,
Wed to the melody,
Sang through the world;
And slower and fainter,
Old and weary,
But eager to follow,
I saw, whenever
In passing it glanced upon
Hamlet or city,

That under the Crosses
The dead man's garden,
The mortal hillock,
Would break into blossom;
And so to the land's
Last limit I came—
And can no longer,
But die rejoicing,
For through the Magic
Of Him the Mighty,
Who taught me in childhood,
There on the border
Of boundless Ocean,
And all but in Heaven
Hovers The Gleam.

Not of the sunlight,
Not of the moonlight,
Not of the starlight!
O young Mariner,
Down to the haven,
Call your companions,
Launch your vessel,
And crowd your canvas,
And, ere it vanishes
Over the margin,
After it, follow it,
Follow The Gleam.

From ROMEO AND JULIET [1]

William Shakespeare

ROMEO: He jests at scars, that never felt a wound.
[JULIET *appears above at a window.*]

[1] Act II, Scene ii.

But, soft! what light through yonder window **breaks?**
It is the east, and Juliet is the sun.
Arise, fair sun, and kill the envious moon,
Who is already sick and pale with grief,
That thou, her maid, art far more fair than she:
Be not her maid, since she is envious;
Her vestal livery is but sick and green,
And none but fools do wear it: cast it off.
It is my lady; oh, it is my love!
Oh that she knew she were!
She speaks, yet she says nothing: what of that?
Her eye discourses, I will answer it.—
I am too bold, 't is not to me she speaks:
Two of the fairest stars in all the heaven,
Having some business, do entreat her eyes
To twinkle in their spheres till they return.
What if her eyes were there, they in her head?
The brightness of her cheek would shame those **stars,**
As daylight doth a lamp; her eyes in heaven
Would through the airy region stream so bright
That birds would sing and think it were not night.
As silver-voiced; her eyes as jewel-like,
And cased as richly; in face another Juno;
Who starves the ears she feeds, and makes them **hungry**
The more she gives them speech.

CONTENTMENT

Oliver Wendell Holmes

Little I ask; my wants are few;
   I only wish a hut of stone,
(A *very plain* brown stone will do,)
   That I may call my own;—
And close at hand is such a one,
In yonder street that fronts the sun.

Plain food is quite enough for me;
    Three courses are as good as ten;—
If Nature can subsist on three,
    Thank Heaven for three. Amen!
I always thought cold victual nice;—
My *choice* would be vanilla-ice.

I care not much for gold or land;—
    Give me a mortgage here and there,—
Some good bank-stock, some note of hand,
    Or trifling railroad share,—
I only ask that Fortune send
A *little* more than I shall spend.

Honors are silly toys, I know,
    And titles are but empty names;
I would, *perhaps,* be Plenipo,—
    But only near St. James;
I'm very sure I should not care
To fill our Gubernator's chair.

Jewels are baubles; 'tis a sin
    To care for such unfruitful things;—
One good-sized diamond in a pin,—
    Some, *not so large,* in rings,—
A ruby, and a pearl, or so,
Will do for me;—I laugh at show.

My dame should dress in cheap attire;
    (Good, heavy silks are never dear;)—
I own perhaps I *might* desire
    Some shawls of true Cashmere,—
Some marrowy crapes of China silk,
Like wrinkled skins on scalded milk.

CONTENTMENT

I would not have the horse I drive
   So fast that folks must stop and stare;
An easy gait—two forty-five—
   Suits me; I do not care;—
Perhaps, for just a *single spurt,*
Some seconds less would do no hurt.

Of pictures, I should like to own
   Titians and Raphaels three or four,—
I love so much their style and tone,—
   One Turner, and no more,
(A landscape,—foreground golden dirt,—
The sunshine painted with a squirt.)

Of books but few,—some fifty score
   For daily use, and bound for wear;
The rest upon an upper floor;—
   Some *little* luxury *there*
Of red morocco's gilded gleam
And vellum rich as country cream.

Busts, cameos, gems,—such things as these,
   Which others often show for pride,
I value for their power to please,
   And selfish churls deride;—
One Stradivarius, I confess,
Two Meerschaums, I would fain possess.

Wealth's wasteful tricks I will not learn,
   Nor ape the glittering upstart fool;—
Shall not carved tables serve my turn,
   But *all* must be of buhl?
Give grasping pomp its double share,—
I ask but *one* recumbent chair.

Thus humble let me live and die,
  Nor long for Midas' golden touch;
If Heaven more generous gifts deny,
  I shall not miss them *much*,—
Too grateful for the blessing lent
Of simple tastes and mind content!

DRIFTING

Thomas Buchanan Read

  My soul to-day
  Is far away,
Sailing the Vesuvian Bay;
  My winged boat,
  A bird afloat,
Swings round the purple peaks remote:—

  Round purple peaks
  It sails, and seeks
Blue inlets and their crystal creeks,
  Where high rocks throw,
  Through deeps below,
A duplicated golden glow.

  Far, vague, and dim,
  The mountains swim;
While on Vesuvius' misty brim,
  With outstretched hands,
  The gray smoke stands
O'erlooking the volcanic lands.

. . . . .

  I heed not if
  My rippling skiff
Float swift or slow from cliff to cliff;

DRIFTING

    With dreamful eyes
     My spirit lies
Under the walls of Paradise.

      . . . . .

    Over the rail
     My hand I trail
Within the shadow of the sail,
     A joy intense,
     The cooling sense
Glides down my drowsy indolence.

    With dreamful eyes
     My spirit lies
Where Summer sings and never dies,—
     O'erveiled with vines
     She glows and shines
Among her future oil and wines.

      . . . . .

    The fisher's child,
     With tresses wild,
Unto the smooth, bright sand beguiled,
     With glowing lips
     Sings as she skips,
Or gazes at the far-off ships.

    Yon deep bark goes
     Where traffic blows,
From lands of sun to lands of snows;—
     This happier one,
     Its course is run
From lands of snow to lands of sun.

    O happy ship,
     To rise and dip,
With the blue crystal at your lip!

O happy crew,
  My heart with you
Sails, and sails, and sings anew!

No more, no more
  The worldly shore
Upbraids me with its loud uproar!
  With dreamful eyes
  My spirit lies
Under the walls of Paradise!

Abridged

THE VISION OF SIR LAUNFAL
James Russell Lowell

PRELUDE TO PART FIRST

Over his keys the musing organist,
  Beginning doubtfully and far away,
First lets his fingers wander as they list,
  And builds a bridge from Dreamland for his lay:
Then, as the touch of his loved instrument
  Gives hope and fervor, nearer draws his theme,
First guessed by faint auroral flushes sent
  Along the wavering vista of his dream.

  Not only around our infancy
  Doth heaven with all its splendors lie;
  Daily, with souls that cringe and plot,
  We Sinais climb and know it not.

Over our manhood bend the skies;
  Against our fallen and traitor lives
The great winds utter prophecies;
  With our faint hearts the mountain strives;
Its arms outstretched, the druid wood

Waits with its benedicte;
And to our age's drowsy blood
   Still shouts the inspiring sea.

Earth gets its price for what Earth gives us;
   The beggar is taxed for a corner to die in,
The priest hath his fee who comes and shrives us,
   We bargain for the graves we lie in;
At the devil's booth are all things sold,
Each ounce of dross costs its ounce of gold;
   For a cap and bells our lives we pay,
Bubbles we buy with a whole soul's tasking:
   'T is heaven alone that is given away,
'T is only God may be had for the asking;
No price is set on the lavish summer;
June may be had by the poorest comer.

And what is so rare as a day in June?
   Then, if ever, come perfect days;
Then Heaven tries earth if it be in tune,
   And over it softly her warm ear lays;
Whether we look, or whether we listen,
We hear life murmur, or see it glisten;
Every clod feels a stir of might,
   An instinct within it that reaches and towers,
And, groping blindly above it for light,
   Climbs to a soul in grass and flowers;
The flush of life may well be seen
   Thrilling back over hills and valleys;
The cowslip startles in meadows green,
   The buttercup catches the sun in its chalice,
And there's never a leaf nor a blade too mean
   To be some happy creature's palace;
The little bird sits at his door in the sun,
   Atilt like a blossom among the leaves,
And lets his illumined being o'errun

With the deluge of summer it receives;
His mate feels the eggs beneath her wings,
And the heart in her dumb breast flutters and sings;
He sings to the wide world, and she to her nest,—
In the nice ear of Nature which song is the best?

Now is the high-tide of the year,
   And whatever of life hath ebbed away
Comes flooding back with a ripply cheer,
   Into every bare inlet and creek and bay;
Now the heart is so full that a drop overfills it,
We are happy now because God wills it;
No matter how barren the past may have been,
'T is enough for us now that the leaves are green;
We sit in the warm shade and feel right well
How the sap creeps up and the blossoms swell;
We may shut our eyes, but we cannot help knowing
That skies are clear and grass is growing;
The breeze comes whispering in our ear,
That dandelions are blossoming near,
   That maize has sprouted, that streams are flowing,
That the river is bluer than the sky,
That the robin is plastering his house hard by;
And if the breeze kept the good news back
For other couriers we should not lack;
   We could guess it all by yon heifer's lowing,—
And hark! how clear bold chanticleer,
Warmed with the new wine of the year,
   Tells all in his lusty crowing!

Joy comes, grief goes, we know not how;
Everything is happy now,
   Everything is upward striving;
'T is as easy now for the heart to be true
As for the grass to be green or skies to be blue,—
'T is the natural way of living:

Who knows whither the clouds have fled?
    In the unscarred heaven they leave no wake;
And the eyes forget the tears they have shed,
    The heart forgets its sorrow and ache;
The soul partakes the season's youth,
    And the sulphurous rifts of passion and woe
Lie deep 'neath a silence pure and smooth,
    Like burnt-out craters healed with snow.
What wonder if Sir Launfal now
Remembered the keeping of his vow?

Part First

I

"My golden spurs now bring to me,
    And bring to me my richest mail,
For to-morrow I go over land and sea
    In search of the Holy Grail;
Shall never a bed for me be spread,
Nor shall a pillow be under my head,
Till I begin my vow to keep;
Here on the rushes will I sleep,
And perchance there may come a vision true
Ere day create the world anew."
    Slowly Sir Launfal's eyes grew dim,
    Slumber fell like a cloud on him,
And into his soul the vision flew.

II

The crows flapped over by twos and threes,
In the pool drowsed the cattle up to their knees,
    The little birds sang as if it were
    The one day of summer in all the year,
And the very leaves seemed to sing on the trees:
The castle alone in the landscape lay

Like an outpost of winter, dull and gray:
'T was the proudest hall in the North Countree,
And never its gates might opened be,
Save to lord or lady of high degree;
Summer besieged it on every side,
But the churlish stone her assaults defied;
She could not scale the chilly wall,
Though around it for leagues her pavilions tall
Stretched left and right,
Over the hills and out of sight;
   Green and broad was every tent,
   And out of each a murmur went
Till the breeze fell off at night.

III

The drawbridge dropped with a surly clang,
And through the dark arch a charger sprang,
Bearing Sir Launfal, the maiden knight,
In his gilded mail, that flamed so bright
It seemed the dark castle had gathered all
Those shafts the fierce sun had shot over its wall
   In his siege of three hundred summers long,
And, binding them all in one blazing sheaf,
   Had cast them forth: so, young and strong,
And lightsome as a locust-leaf,
Sir Launfal flashed forth in his maiden mail,
To seek in all climes for the Holy Grail.

IV

It was morning on hill and stream and tree,
   And morning in the young knight's heart;
Only the castle moodily
Rebuffed the gifts of the sunshine free,
   And gloomed by itself apart;
The season brimmed all other things up
Full as the rain fills the pitcher-plant's cup.

V

As Sir Launfal made morn through the darksome gate,
    He was 'ware of a leper, crouched by the same,
Who begged with his hand and moaned as he sate;
    And a loathing over Sir Launfal came;
The sunshine went out of his soul with a thrill,
    The flesh 'neath his armor 'gan shrink and crawl,
And midway its leap his heart stood still
    Like a frozen waterfall;
For this man, so foul and bent of stature,
Rasped harshly against his dainty nature,
And seemed the one blot on the summer morn,—
So he tossed him a piece of gold in scorn.

VI

The leper raised not the gold from the dust:
"Better to me the poor man's crust,
Better the blessing of the poor,
Though I turn me empty from his door;
That is no true alms which the hand can hold;
He gives only the worthless gold
    Who gives from a sense of duty;
But he who gives but a slender mite,
And gives to that which is out of sight,
    That thread of the all-sustaining Beauty
Which runs through all and doth all unite,—
The hand cannot clasp the whole of his alms,
The heart outstretches its eager palms,
For a god goes with it and makes it store
To the soul that was starving in darkness before."

PRELUDE TO PART SECOND

Down swept the chill wind from the mountain peak,
    From the snow five thousand summers old;
On open wold and hilltop bleak
    It had gathered all the cold,

And whirled it like sleet on the wanderer's cheek;
It carried a shiver everywhere
From the unleafed boughs and pastures bare;
The little brook heard it and built a roof
'Neath which he could house him, winter-proof;
All night by the white stars' frosty gleams
He groined his arches and matched his beams;
Slender and clear were his crystal spars
As the lashes of light that trim the stars:
He sculptured every summer delight
In his halls and chambers out of sight;
Sometimes his tinkling waters slipt
Down through a frost-leaved forest-crypt,
Long, sparkling aisles of steel-stemmed trees
Bending to counterfeit a breeze;
Sometimes the roof no fretwork knew
But silvery mosses that downward grew;
Sometimes it was carved in sharp relief
With quaint arabesques of ice-fern leaf;
Sometimes it was simply smooth and clear
For the gladness of heaven to shine through, and here
He had caught the nodding bulrush-tops
And hung them thickly with diamond drops,
That crystalled the beams of moon and sun,
And made a star of every one:
No mortal builder's most rare device
Could match this winter-palace of ice;
'T was as if every image that mirrored lay
In his depths serene through the summer day,
Each fleeting shadow of earth and sky,
   Lest the happy model should be lost,
Had been mimicked in fairy masonry
   By the elfin builders of the frost.

Within the hall are song and laughter,
   The cheeks of Christmas glow red and jolly,

And sprouting is every corbel and rafter
　　With lightsome green of ivy and holly;
Through the deep gulf of the chimney wide
Wallows the Yule-log's roaring tide;
The broad flame-pennons droop and flap
　　And belly and tug as a flag in the wind;
Like a locust shrills the imprisoned sap,
　　Hunted to death in its galleries blind;
And swift little troops of silent sparks,
　　Now pausing, now scattering away as in fear,
Go threading the soot-forest's tangled darks
　　Like herds of startled deer.

But the wind without was eager and sharp,
Of Sir Launfal's gray hair it makes a harp,
　　And rattles and wrings
　　The icy strings,
Singing, in dreary monotone,
A Christmas carol of its own,
　　Whose burden still, as he might guess,
　　Was "Shelterless, shelterless, shelterless!"
The voice of the seneschal flared like a torch
As he shouted the wanderer away from the porch,
And he sat in the gateway and saw all night
　　The great hall-fire, so cheery and bold,
　　Through the window-slits of the castle old,
Build out its piers of ruddy light
Against the drift of the cold.

Part Second

I

There was never a leaf on bush or tree,
The bare boughs rattled shudderingly;
The river was dumb and could not speak,

For the weaver Winter its shroud had spun;
A single crow on the tree-top bleak
From his shining feathers shed off the cold sun;
Again it was morning, but shrunk and cold,
As if her veins were sapless and old,
And she rose up decrepitly
For a last dim look at earth and sea.

II

Sir Launfal turned from his own hard gate,
For another heir in his earldom sate;
An old, bent man, worn out and frail,
He came back from seeking the Holy Grail;
Little he recked of his earldom's loss,
No more on his surcoat was blazoned the cross,
But deep in his soul the sign he wore,
The badge of the suffering and the poor.

III

Sir Launfal's raiment thin and spare
Was idle mail 'gainst the barbed air,
For it was just at the Christmas time;
So he mused, as he sat, of a sunnier clime,
And sought for a shelter from cold and snow
In the light and warmth of long-ago;
He sees the snake-like caravan crawl
O'er the edge of the desert, black and small,
Then nearer and nearer, till, one by one,
He can count the camels in the sun,
As over the red-hot sands they pass
To where, in its slender necklace of grass,
The little spring laughed and leapt in the shade,
And with its own self like an infant played,
And waved its signal of palms.

IV

"For Christ's sweet sake, I beg an alms";
The happy camels may reach the spring,
But Sir Launfal sees only the grewsome thing,
The leper, lank as the rain-blanched bone,
That cowers beside him, a thing as lone
And white as the ice-isles of Northern seas
In the desolate horror of his disease.

V

And Sir Launfal said, "I behold in thee
An image of Him who died on the tree;
Thou also hast had thy crown of thorns,
Thou also hast had the world's buffets and scorns,
And to thy life were not denied
The wounds in the hands and feet and side;
Mild Mary's Son, acknowledge me;
Behold, through him, I give to thee!"

VI

Then the soul of the leper stood up in his eyes
    And looked at Sir Launfal, and straightway he
Remembered in what a haughtier guise
    He had flung an alms to leprosie,
When he girt his young life up in gilded mail
And set forth in search of the Holy Grail.
The heart within him was ashes and dust;
He parted in twain his single crust,
He broke the ice on the streamlet's brink,
And gave the leper to eat and drink,
'T was a mouldy crust of coarse brown bread,
    'T was water out of a wooden bowl,—
Yet with fine wheaten bread was the leper fed,
    And 't was red wine he drank with his thirsty soul.

VII

As Sir Launfal mused with a downcast face
A light shone round about the place;
The leper no longer crouched at his side,
But stood before him glorified,
Shining and tall and fair and straight
As the pillar that stood by the Beautiful Gate,—
Himself the Gate whereby men can
Enter the temple of God in Man.

VIII

His words were shed softer than leaves from the pine,
And they fell on Sir Launfal as snows on the brine,
That mingle their softness and quiet in one
With the shaggy unrest they float down upon;
And the voice that was softer than silence said,
"Lo, it is I, be not afraid!
In many climes, without avail,
Thou hast spent thy life for the Holy Grail;
Behold, it is here,—this cup which thou
Didst fill at the streamlet for me but now;
This crust is My body broken for thee,
This water His blood that died on the tree;
The Holy Supper is kept, indeed,
In whatso we share with another's need;
Not what we give, but what we share,
For the gift without the giver is bare;
Who gives himself with his alms feeds three,
Himself, his hungering neighbor, and Me."

IX

Sir Launfal awoke as from a swound:
"The Grail in my castle here is found!
Hang my idle armor up on the wall,
Let it be the spider's banquet-hall;

He must be fenced with stronger mail
Who would seek and find the Holy Grail."

x

The castle gate stands open now,
   And the wanderer is welcome to the hall
As the hangbird is to the elm-tree bough;
   No longer scowl the turrets tall,
The summer's long siege at last is o'er;
When the first poor outcast went in at the door,
She entered with him in disguise,
And mastered the fortress by surprise;
There is no spot she loves so well on ground,
She lingers and smiles there the whole year round:
The meanest serf on Sir Launfal's land
Has hall and bower at his command;
And there's no poor man in the North Countree
But is lord of the earldom as much as he.

THE STAGE-COACH

Charles Dickens

  When the coach came round at last, with "London" blazoned in letters of gold upon the boot, it gave Tom such a turn, that he was half disposed to run away. But he didn't do it; for he took his seat upon the box instead, and looking down upon the four grays, felt as if he were another gray himself, or, at all events, a part of the turn-out; and was quite confused by the novelty and splendor of his situation.

  And really it might have confused a less modest man than Tom to find himself sitting next to that coachman; for of all the swells that ever flourished a whip, professionally, he might have been elected emperor. He didn't handle his gloves like another man, but put them on—even when he was standing on the pavement, quite detached from the coach—as if the four grays were, somehow or other, at the ends of the fingers. It was the same with his hat. He did things with his hat, which nothing but an unlimited knowledge of horses and the wildest freedom of the road could ever have made him perfect in. Valuable little parcels were brought to him with particular instructions, and he pitched them into his hat, and stuck it on again, as if the laws of gravity did not admit of such an event as its being knocked off or blown off, and nothing like an accident could befall it. The guard too! Seventy breezy miles a day were written in his very whiskers. His manners were a canter; his conversation a round trot. He was a fast coach upon a downhill turnpike road; he was all pace. A wagon couldn't have moved slowly, with that guard and his key-bugle on the top of it.

These were all foreshadowings of London, Tom thought, as he sat upon the box, and looked about him. Such a coachman and such a guard never could have existed between Salisbury and any other place; the coach was none of your steady-going, yokel coaches, but a swaggering, rakish, dissipated, London coach; up all night, and lying by all day, and leading a terrible life. It cared no more for Salisbury than if it had been a hamlet. It rattled noisily through the best streets, defied the cathedral, took the worst corners sharpest, went cutting in everywhere, making everything get out of its way; and spun along the open country-road, blowing a lively defiance out of its key-bugle, as its last glad parting legacy.

It was a charming evening. Mild and bright. And even with the weight upon his mind which arose out of the immensity and uncertainty of London, Tom could not resist the captivating sense of rapid motion through the pleasant air. The four grays skimmed along, as if they liked it quite as well as Tom did; the bugle was in as high spirits as the grays; the coachman chimed in sometimes with his voice; the wheels hummed cheerfully in unison; the brass-work on the harness was an orchestra of little bells; and thus they went clinking, jingling, rattling smoothly on, the whole concern, from the buckles of the leaders' coupling-reins to the handle of the hind boot, was one great instrument of music.

Yoho! past hedges, gates, and trees; past cottages and barns, and people going home from work. Hoho! past donkey-chaises, drawn aside into the ditch, and empty carts with rampant horses, whipped up at a bound upon the little water-course, and held by struggling carters close to the five-barred gate, until the coach had passed the narrow turning in the road. Yoho! by churches dropped down by themselves in quiet nooks, with rustic burial-grounds about them, where the graves are green, and daisies sleep—for it is evening—on the bosoms of the dead. Yoho! past streams, in which the cattle cool their feet, and where the rushes grow; past paddock-fences, farms, and rick-yards; past last year's stacks, cut, slice by slice, away, and showing, in the waning light, like ruined gables, old and brown. Yoho! down the pebbly dip, and through the merry water-splash, and up at a canter to the level road again. Yoho! Yoho!

Yoho! among the gathering shades; making of no account the deep reflections of the trees, but scampering on through light and darkness, all the same, as if the light of London, fifty miles away, were quite enough to travel by, and some to spare. Yoho! beside the village green, where cricket-players linger yet, and every little indentation made in the fresh grass by bat or wicket, ball or player's foot, sheds out its perfume on the night. Away with four fresh horses from the Bald-faced Stag, where topers congregate about the door admiring; and the last team, with traces hanging loose, go roaming off towards the pond, until observed and shouted after by a dozen throats, while volunteering boys pursue them. Now with the clattering of hoofs and striking out of fiery sparks, across the old stone bridge, and down again into the shadowy road, and through the open gate, and far away, away, into the wold. Yoho!

See the bright moon! High up before we know it: making the earth reflect the objects on its breast like water. Hedges, trees, low cottages, church steeples, blighted stumps and flourishing young slips, have all grown vain upon the sudden, and mean to contemplate their own fair images till morning. The poplars yonder rustle, that their quivering leaves may see themselves upon the ground. Not so the oak; trembling does not become *him;* and he watches himself in his stout old burly steadfastness, without the motion of a twig. The moss-grown gate, ill-poised upon its creaking hinges, crippled and decayed, swings to and fro before its glass like some fantastic dowager; while our own ghostly likeness travels on. Yoho! Yoho! through ditch and brake, upon the ploughed land and the smooth, along the steep hillside and steeper wall, as if it were a phantom-hunter.

Clouds too! And a mist upon the hollow! Not a dull fog that hides it, but a light airy gauze-like mist, which in our eyes of modest admiration gives a new charm to the beauties it is spread before: as real gauze has done ere now, and would again, so please you, though we were the Pope. Yoho! Why, now we travel like the moon herself. Hiding this minute in a grove of trees, next minute in a patch of vapor; emerging now upon our broad clear course; withdrawing now, but always dashing on, our journey is a counterpart of hers. Yoho! A match against the moon!

The beauty of the night is hardly felt, when day comes leaping up. Yoho! Two stages and the country roads are almost changed to a continuous street. Yoho! past market gardens, rows of houses, villas, crescents, terraces, and squares; past wagons, coaches, carts; past early workmen, late stragglers, drunken men, and sober carriers of loads; past brick and mortar in its every shape; and in among the rattling pavements, where a jaunty-seat upon a coach is not so easy to preserve! Yoho! down countless turnings, and through countless mazy ways, until an old inn-yard is gained, and Tom Pinch, getting down, quite stunned and giddy, is in London.

INDIRECTION
Richard Realf

Fair are the flowers and the children, but their subtle suggestion is fairer;
Rare is the roseburst of dawn, but the secret that clasps it is rarer;
Sweet the exultance of song, but the strain that precedes it is sweeter;
And never was poem yet writ, but the meaning outmastered the meter.

Never a daisy that grows, but a mystery guideth the growing;
Never a river that flows, but a majesty scepters the flowing;
Never a Shakespeare that soared, but a stronger than he did enfold him,
Nor ever a prophet foretells, but a mightier seer hath foretold him.

Back of the canvas that throbs, the painter is hinted and hidden;
Into the statue that breathes, the soul of the sculptor is bidden;
Under the joy that is felt, lie the infinite issues of feeling;
Crowning the glory revealed, is the glory that crowns the revealing.

Great are the symbols of being, but that which is symboled is greater;
Vast the create and beheld, but vaster the inward creator;
Back of the sound broods the silence, back of the gift stands the giving;

Back of the hand that receives thrill the sensitive nerves of receiving.

Space is as nothing to spirit, the deed is outdone by the doing;
The heart of the wooer is warm, but warmer the heart of the wooing;
And up from the pits where these shiver, and up from the heights where those shine,
Twin voices and shadows swim starward, and the essence of life is divine.

THE TRUE BALLAD OF THE KING'S SINGER
Helen Hunt Jackson

The king rode fast, the king rode well,
   The royal hunt went loud and gay,
A thousand bleeding chamois fell
   For royal sport that day.

When sunset turned the hills all red,
   The royal hunt went still and slow;
The king's great horse with weary tread
   Plunged ankle-deep in snow.

Sudden a strain of music sweet,
   Unearthly sweet, came through the wood;
Up sprang the king, and on both feet
   Straight in his saddle stood.

"Now, by our lady, be it bird,
   Or be it man or elf who plays,
Never before my ears have heard
   A music fit for praise!"

Sullen and tired, the royal hunt
   Followed the king, who tracked the song,

THE BALLAD OF THE SINGER

Unthinking, as is royal wont,
   How hard the way and long.

Stretched on a rock the shepherd lay
   And dreamed and piped, and dreamed and sang,
And careless heard the shout and bay
   With which the echoes rang.

"Up, man! the king!" the hunters cried.
   He slowly stood, and, wondering,
Turned honest eyes from side to side:
   To him, each looked like king.

Strange shyness seized the king's bold tongue;
   He saw how easy to displease
This savage man who stood among
   His courtiers, so at ease.

But kings have silver speech to use
   When on their pleasure they are bent;
The simple shepherd could not choose;
   Like one in dream he went.

O hear! O hear! The ringing sound
   Of twenty trumpets swept the street,
The king a minstrel now has found,
   For royal music meet.

With cloth of gold, and cloth of red,
   And woman's eyes the place is bright.
"Now, shepherd, sing," the king has said,
   "The song you sang last night!"

One faint sound stirs the perfumed air,
   The courtiers scornfully look down;
The shepherd kneels in dumb despair,
   Seeing the king's dark frown.

The king is just; the king will wait.
    "Ho, guards! let him be gently led,
Let him grow used to royal state,—
    To being housed and fed."

All night the king unquiet lay,
    Racked by his dream's presentiment;
Then rose in haste at break of day,
    And for the shepherd sent.

"Ho now, thou beast, thou savage man,
    How sound thou sleepest, not to hear!"
They jeering laughed, but soon began
    To louder call in fear.

They wrenched the bolts; unrumpled stood
    The princely bed all silken fine,
Untouched the plates of royal food,
    The flask of royal wine!

The costly robes strewn on the floor,
    The chamber empty, ghastly still;
The guards stood trembling at the door,
    And dared not cross the sill.

All night the sentinels their round
    Had kept. No man woud pass that way.
The window dizzy high from ground;
    Below, the deep moat lay.

They crossed themselves. "The foul fiend lurks
    In this," they said. They did not know
The miracles sweet Freedom works,
    To let her children go.

THE BALLAD OF THE SINGER

It was the fiend himself who took
   That shepherd's shape to pipe and sing;
And every man with terror shook,
   For who would tell the king!

The heads of men all innocent
   Rolled in the dust that day;
And east and west the bloodhounds went,
   Baying their dreadful bay;

Safe on a snow too far, too high,
   For scent of dogs or feet of men,
The shepherd watched the clouds sail by,
   And dreamed and sang again;

And crossed himself, and knelt and cried,
   And kissed the holy Edelweiss,
Believing that the fiends had tried
   To buy him with a price.

The king rides fast, the king rides well;
   The summer hunts go loud and gay;
The courtiers, who this tale can tell,
   Are getting old and gray.

But still they say it was a fiend
   That took a shepherd's shape to sing,
For still the king's heart is not weaned
   To care for other thing.

Great minstrels come from far and near,
   He will not let them sing or play,
But waits and listens still to hear
   The song he heard that day.

THE CHAMBERED NAUTILUS
Oliver Wendell Holmes

This is the ship of pearl, which, poets feign,
    Sails the unshadowed main,—
    The venturous bark that flings
On the sweet summer wind its purpled wings
In gulfs enchanted, where the Siren sings,
    And coral reefs lie bare,
Where the cold sea-maids rise to sun their streaming hair.

Its webs of living gauze no more unfurl;
    Wrecked is the ship of pearl!
    And every chambered cell,
Where its dim dreaming life was wont to dwell,
As the frail tenant shaped his growing shell,
    Before thee lies revealed,—
Its irised ceiling rent, its sunless crypt unsealed!

Year after year beheld the silent toil
    That spread his lustrous coil;
    Still, as the spiral grew,
He left the past year's dwelling for the new,
Stole with soft step its shining archway through,
    Built up its idle door,
Stretched in his last-found home, and knew the old no more.

Thanks for the heavenly message brought by thee,
    Child of the wandering sea,
    Cast from her lap, forlorn!
From thy dead lips a clearer note is born
Than ever Triton blew from wreathed horn!
    While on mine ear it rings,
Through the deep caves of thought I hear a voice that sings—

Build thee more stately mansions, O my soul,
  As the swift seasons roll!
  Leave thy low-vaulted past!
Let each new temple, nobler than the last,
Shut thee from heaven with a dome more vast,
  Till thou at length art free,
Leaving thine outgrown shell by life's unresting sea!

JESUS AND THE BLIND MAN
John 9:1–21, 24–38

And as Jesus passed by, he saw a man which was blind from his birth. And his disciples asked him, saying, Master, who did sin, this man, or his parents, that he was born blind? Jesus answered, Neither hath this man sinned, nor his parents: but that the works of God should be made manifest in him. I must work the works of him that sent me, while it is day: the night cometh, when no man can work. As long as I am in the world, I am the light of the world. When he had thus spoken, he spat on the ground, and made clay of the spittle, and he anointed the eyes of the blind man with the clay, and said unto him, Go, wash in the pool of Siloam. He went his way therefore, and washed, and came seeing.

The neighbours therefore, and they which before had seen him that he was blind, said, Is not this he that sat and begged? Some said, This is he: others said, He is like him: but he said, I am he. Therefore said they unto him, How were thine eyes opened? He answered and said, A man that is called Jesus made clay, and anointed mine eyes, and said unto me, Go to the pool of Siloam, and wash: and I went and washed, and I received sight. Then said they unto him, Where is he? He said, I know not.

They brought to the Pharisees him that aforetime was blind,

And it was the sabbath day when Jesus made the clay, and opened his eyes. Then again the Pharisees also asked him how he had received his sight. He said unto them, He put clay upon mine eyes, and I washed, and do see. Therefore said some of the Pharisees, This man is not of God, because he keepeth not the sabbath day. Others said, How can a man that is a sinner do such miracles? And there was a division among them. They say unto the blind man again, What sayest thou of him, that he hath opened thine eyes? He said, He is a prophet.

But the Jews did not believe concerning him, that he had been blind, and received his sight, until they called the parents of him that had received his sight. And they asked them, saying, Is this your son, who ye say was born blind? how then doth he now see? His parents answered them and said, We know that this is our son, and that he was born blind; but by what means he now seeth, we know not; or who hath opened his eyes, we know not: he is of age; ask him; he shall speak for himself. . . .

Then again called they the man that was blind, and said unto him, Give God the praise: we know that this man is a sinner. He answered and said, Whether he be a sinner or not, I know not: one thing I know, that, whereas I was blind, now I see. Then said they to him again, What did he to thee? how opened he thine eyes? He answered them, I have told you already, and ye did not hear: wherefore would ye hear it again? will ye also be his disciples? Then they reviled him, and said, Thou art his disciple; but we are Moses' disciples. We know that God spake unto Moses: as for this fellow, we know not from whence he is. The man answered and said unto them, Why herein is a marvellous thing, that ye know not from whence he is, and yet he hath opened mine eyes. Now we know that God heareth not sinners: but if any man be a worshipper of God, and doeth his will, him he heareth. Since the world began was it not heard that any man opened the eyes of one that was born blind. If this man were not of God, he could do nothing. They answered and said unto him, Thou wast altogether born in sin, and dost thou teach us? And they cast him out.

Jesus heard that they had cast him out; and when he had found him, he said unto him, Dost thou believe on the Son of God? He answered and said, Who is he, Lord, that I might believe on him? And Jesus said unto him, Thou hast both seen him, and it is he that talketh with thee. And he said, Lord, I believe. And he worshipped him.

LOVE'S COURAGE

The Romance of Robert and Elizabeth Barrett Browning As Revealed Through Their Poetry and Letters [1]

A Lecture-Recital Adapted by

Sara Lowrey

In his poem, "One Word More," Robert Browning stated:

> God be thanked, the meanest of his creatures
> Boasts two soul-sides; one to face the world with,
> One to show a woman when he loves her!

In January of 1845, two letters were exchanged that marked the beginning of one of the world's most famous correspondences. The first, postmarked "New Cross, Surrey," was from Robert Browning—a vigorous, handsome young man who became the toast of Society upon the publication of his poem, "Paracelsus." The vigor and depth of his poetry, his patrician features, his graceful carriage, and his splendid figure contributed to his charm. He soon became known as a favorite "diner-out."

The second letter, post marked "50 Wimpole Street" was from Elizabeth Barrett Barrett—a slender, fragile recluse—

[1] *The Letters of Robert Browning and Elizabeth Barrett Barrett* (New York and London: Harper and Brothers, 1902), Vols. I and II.

no longer young—who was completely apart from society. An invalid since an injury to her spine in childhood, a lonely genius wasting away in a gloomy house under the tyrannical rule of a father whose harsh disciplines were as erratic and fanatical as his prejudice against marriage—she had only one outlet for her imagination: literature—reading and writing poetry, and corresponding with literary figures of the day.

Her interest in contemporary poets was her first introduction to Robert Browning. Her appreciation of him is recorded in her poem "Lady Geraldine's Courtship" where she said of him:

> . . . . Or from Browning
> Some Pomegranate, which if cut deep down the middle,
> Shows a heart within, blood-tinctured, of veined humanity.

Browning's heart swelled with pride at these gracious words from the mysterious poetess whose writing was already widely known. Wishing to express his gratitude, he asked a friend, Mr. Robert Kenyon—her cousin—about the possibility of meeting Miss Barrett. Mr. Kenyon replied that she was an invalid and saw no one, but agreed that she would be pleased to receive a letter from a fellow poet.

This first letter of Robert Browning's was an open, impulsive expression of gratitude, and of enthusiastic appreciation, ending,

> I love your verses with all my heart, dear Miss Barrett. The fresh strange music, the affluent language, the exquisite pathos, and true, new, brave thought; but in this addressing myself to you, your own self, and for the first time, my feeling rises altogether. I do, as I say, love these books with all my heart, and I love you, too.

Elizabeth Barrett's feelings rose also, and her pulse raced with excitement; but she replied with the discipline of an artist and the restraint of her thirty-eight years:

January 11, 1845

I thank you, dear Mr. Browning, from the bottom of my heart. You meant to give me pleasure by your letter—and even if the object had not been answered, I ought still to thank you. But it is thoroughly answered. Such a letter from such a hand! Sympathy is dear—very dear to me: but the sympathy of a poet, and of such a poet, is the quintessence of sympathy to me!

On January 28, 1845 Browning wrote:

If you hate writing me as I hate writing to nearly everybody, I pray you never write— God Knows—I do not know what will help me more than hearing from you—and therefore if you do not so very much hate it, I know I *shall* hear from you.

Elizabeth replied on February 3, 1845:

Why how could I hate to write to you, dear Mr. Browning? Everybody likes writing to somebody, and it would be strange and contradictory if I were not always delighted both to hear from you and to write to you; this talking upon paper being as good a social pleasure as another. As for me, I have done most of my talking by post of late years—as people shut up in dungeons take up with scrawling mottoes on the walls. Not that I write to many in the way of regular correspondence, but there are a few who will write, and be written to by me without a sense of injury. Dear Miss Mitford, for instance, has filled a large drawer in this room with delightful letters, heart-warm and soul-warm . . . driftings of nature (if sunshine could drift like snow).

I write this to you to show how I can have pleasure in

letters, and never think them too long, nor too frequent, if you will only promise to treat me as a comrade—taking no thought for your sentences (nor for mine), nor for your badd spelling (nor for mine), and if you agree to send me a thought whenever you are in the mind for it, and with as little ceremony and less legibility than you would think it necessary to employ toward your printer—why, then I I am ready to sign and seal the contract, and to rejoice in being "articled" as your correspondent. Only don't let us have any constraint. Don't be civil to me when you feel rude, nor yielding when you are perverse.

See how out of the world I am! But you will find me an honest man on the whole; and we have great sympathies in common, and I am inclined to look up to you in many things, and to learn as much of everything as you will teach me. On the other hand, you must prepare yourself to forebear and to forgive—will you? While I throw off the ceremony, I hold the faster to kindness. Need I assure you that I shall always hear with the deepest interest every word you will say to me of what you are doing or about to do? I think—if I may dare to name myself with you in the poetic relation—that we both have high views of the Art we follow, and steadfast purpose in the pursuit of it, and that we should not, either of us, be likely to be thrown from the course, by the casting of any Atalanta-ball of speedy popularity. But I do not know, I cannot guess whether you are liable to be pained deeply by hard criticisms and cold neglect, such as original writers, like yourself, are too often exposed to—or whether the love of Art is enough for you, and the exercise of Art the filling joy of your life.

Browning evidently followed her instructions to some degree. In his answer to her he said:

I don't dare—yet I will—ask can you read this? I could write a little better, but not so fast. Do you keep writing just as you do now!

These early letters were long and concerned mostly with literary friendships and their art, the word *Art* being always capitalized. One day, however, Elizabeth wrote to explain her pet name "Ba":

> We are famous in this house for what is called nicknames, and I am never called anything else except by the *nom de paix* proving, as Mr. Kenyon says, that I am just 'half a baby'—no more nor less; and in fact the name has that precise definition.

One day Ba wrote:

> The mission of Art, like that of Religion, is to make the rugged paths straight and the wilderness to blossom as the rose—at least it seems so to me.

On February 17, 1845, Elizabeth wrote:

> The pursuit of an Ideal acknowledged by the mind, will draw and concentrate the powers of the mind—and Art you know, is a jealous god and demands the whole of man or woman. I cannot conceive of a sincere artist who is also a careless one—though one may have a quicker hand than another, in general,—and though all are liable to vicissitudes in the degree of facility—and to entanglements in the machinery, notwithstanding every degree of facility. You may write twenty lines one day—or three like Euripides in three days—and a hundred lines in one more day—

and yet on the hundred, may have been expended as much good work as on the twenty and the three. And also, as you say, the lamp is trimmed behind the wall—and the act of utterance is the evidence of foregone study still more than it is the occasion to study. The deep interest with which I read all that you had the kindness to write to me of yourself, you trust me for, as I find it hard to express it. It is sympathy in one way, and interest every way. And now, see! Although you proved to me with admirable logic that, for reasons which you know and reasons which you don't know, I couldn't possibly know anything about you; I really did understand of you before I was told, exactly what you told me! Yes, I did indeed. I felt sure that as a poet you fronted the future—and that your chief works, in your own apprehension were to come. But I do not, you say, know yourself— You! I only know your abilities and faculties. Well, then, teach me yourself— You! In fact, you have not written the Robert Browning poem yet— your rays fall obliquely rather than directly straight. I see you only in your moon. Do tell me all of yourself that you can and will.

And indeed Mr. Browning did write much of himself. He also wrote of the weather. On Wednesday Morning, February 26, 1845, he wrote:

Real warm Spring, dear Miss Barrett, and the birds know it; and in the Spring I shall see you, surely see you—for when did I once fail to get whatever I had set my heart upon?

She answered:

Yes, but, dear Mr. Browning, I want the spring according to the new 'style'—(mine!), and not the old one of you and the rest of the poets. To me, unhappily, the snowdrop is much the same as the snow—it feels as cold underfoot—and I have grown sceptical about 'the voice of the turtle'; the east wind blows so loud. A little later comes my spring; and indeed after such severe weather, from which I have just escaped with my life, I may thank it for coming at all. How happy you are, to be able to listen to the 'birds' without the commentary of the east wind, which, like other commentaries, spoils the music.

Is it true that your wishes fulfil themselves? And when they do, are they not bitter to your taste—do you not wish them unfulfilled? Oh, this life, this life! There is comfort in it, they say, and I almost believe—but the brightest place in the house, is the leaning out of the window—at least, for me.

Ever faithfully yours,
E. B. B.

On March 1, 1845, Browning wrote:

Dear Miss Barrett,—I seem to find of a sudden—surely I knew of it before—anyhow, I do find now, that with the octaves on octaves of quite new golden strings you enlarged the compass of my life's harp with, there is added, too, such a tragic chord, that which you touched so gently, in the beginning of your letter I got this morning. But if my truest heart's wishes avail, as they have hitherto done, you shall laugh at East winds yet, as I do!

She answered:

March 5, 1845

But I did not mean to strike a 'tragic chord'; dear Mr. Browning, indeed I did not! Sometimes one's melancholy will be uppermost and sometimes one's mirth,—the world goes round, you know—and I suppose that in that letter of mine the melancholy took the turn. It is well to fly towards the light, even where there may be some fluttering and bruising of wings against the windowpanes, is it not?

Mr. Browning suggested in one letter that Elizabeth sometimes took her own good time in writing; and:

You think that I 'unconsciously exaggerate what you are to me.' Now, you don't know what that is,—nor can I very well tell you.

She replied:

March 20, 1845

Whenever I delay to write to you, dear Mr. Browning, it is not, be sure, that I take my 'own good time,' but submit to my own bad time. It was kind of you to wish to know how I was, and not unkind of me to suspend my answer to your question—for indeed, I have not been very well, nor have had much heart for saying so. I will indeed see you when the warm weather has revived me a little. If you think that I shall not like to see you, you are wrong, for all your learning. But I shall be afraid of you at first— though I am not, in writing thus. You are Paracelsus, and I am a recluse, with nerves that have been all broken on the rack, and now hang loosely—quivering at a step or breath.

When in one of his letters he almost demanded that she see him, Elizabeth was overcome with nervousness and hesitance. She had more faith in the written than in the spoken word, and more than an invalid's normal timidity in the presence of strange faces. Her answer to his request was in the form of a warning:

> There is nothing to see in me, nor to hear in me. If my poetry is worth anything, it is the flower of me—the rest of me is nothing but a root fit for the ground and darkness.

Robert suggested that he might be permitted to judge that for himself. He wrote re-assuringly:

> You are the most entirely lovable creature I ever dreamed might perhaps be in a better world.

His first gift was a yellow rose from his mother's garden. Ba was amused, for she knew, if he did not, that the yellow rose was the symbol of infidelity. "Come Tuesday at Three," she wrote.

He came. He was announced by Arabel. Browning was tense with anticipation and excitement; Elizabeth was nervous and fearful, but her sense of humor came to their rescue. The awkward moment dissolved in the warmth of her smile. At tea-time the visitor departed, but as Miss Barrett expressed it later:

> When you came, you never went away.

Robert hurried home to write her a letter, stating that he had fallen deeply in love with her. She was at first dumbfounded, then pleased; and not many weeks after, she realized that her admiration of the poet was in reality love for the man. Inconceivable as it was that he should love her, she was happy. In the first of her now famous "Sonnets from the Portuguese" she wrote:

> I thought once how Theocritus had sung
> Of the sweet years, the dear and wished-for years,
> Who each one in a gracious hand appears

To bear a gift for mortals, old or young:
And, as I mused it in his antique tongue,
I saw, in gradual vision through my tears,
The sweet, sad years, the melancholy years,
Those of my own life, who by turns had flung
A shadow across me. Straightway I was 'ware,
So weeping, how a mystic Shape did move
Behind me, and drew me backward by the hair;
And a voice said in mastery, while I strove,—
'Guess now who holds thee'—'Death,' I said. But there
The silver answer rang,—'Not Death, but Love!'

With the daily exchange of letters—sometimes twice daily—and weekly visits from Robert Browning, life for Elizabeth Barrett took on new meaning. In Browning's mind a plan was forming. Here was a woman who shared his devotion to poetry —who understood him—who sympathized with him—who loved him, as he loved her. Why should her invalidism stand as an insurmountable obstacle to the beauty of life together?

In June 1845, he proposed marriage. She sorrowfully refused. Her feelings were expressed in sonnets:

III

Unlike are we, unlike, O princely Heart!
Unlike our uses and our destinies.
Our ministering two angels look surprise
On one another, as they strike athwart
Their wings in passing. Thou, bethink thee, art
A guest for queens to social pageantries,
With gages from a hundred brighter eyes
Than tears, even, can make mine, to play thy part
Of chief musician. What hast thou to do
With looking from the lattice-lights at me,
A poor, tired, wandering singer, singing through
The dark, and leaning up a cypress tree?
The chrism is on thine head,—on mine, the dew,—
And Death must dig the level where these agree.

IV

Thou hast thy calling to some palace-floor,
Most gracious singer of high poems! Where
The dancers will break footing, from the care
Of watching up thy pregnant lips for more.
And dost thou lift this house's latch, too poor
For hand of thine? and canst thou think and bear
To let thy music drop here unaware
In folds of golden fullness at my door?
Look up and see the casement broken in,
The bats and owlets builders in the roof!
My cricket chirps against thy mandolin.
Hush, call no echo up in further proof
Of desolation! There's a voice within
That weeps . . . as thou must sing . . . alone, aloof.

VIII

What can I give thee back, O liberal
And princely giver, who hast brought the gold
And purple of thine heart, unstained, untold,
And laid them on the outside of the wall
For such as I to take or leave withal,
In unexpected largesse? Am I cold,
Ungrateful, that for these most manifold
High gifts, I render nothing back at all?
Not so; not cold,—but very poor instead.
Ask God who knows. For frequent tears have run
The colors from my life, and left so dead
And pale a stuff, it were not fitly done
To give the same as pillow to thy head.
Go farther! let it serve to trample on.

IX

Can it be right to give what I can give?
To let thee sit beneath the fall of tears
As salt as mine, and hear the sighing years
Re-sighing on my lips renunciative

Through those infrequent smiles which fail to live
For all thy adjurations? O my fears,
For this can scarce be right! We are not peers,
So to be lovers; and I own, and grieve,
That givers of such gifts as mine are, must
Be counted with the ungenerous. Out, alas!
I will not soil thy purple with my dust,
Nor breathe my poison on thy Venice-glass,
Nor give thee any love—which were unjust.
Beloved, I only love thee!—let it pass.

VI

Go from me. Yet I feel that I shall stand
Henceforward in thy shadow. Nevermore
Alone upon the threshold of my door
Of individual life, I shall command
The uses of my soul, nor lift my hand
Serenely in the sunshine as before,
Without the sense of that which I forbore—
Thy touch upon the palm. The widest land
Doom takes to part us, leaves thy heart in mine
With pulses that beat double. What I do
And what I dream include thee, as the wine
Must taste of its own grapes. And when I sue
God for myself, He hears that name of thine,
And sees within my eyes the tears of two.

Yet these thoughts were concealed from Robert Browning for many years. Elizabeth's letter of refusal stated that he must never mention such things again. If he *did* (and she underscored the line heavily) *"I must not—I will not see you again!"* She advised him to burn the letter which she sent back to him, and he did.

For three months he obeyed her, and soon he was calling twice a week, carrying flowers. His agitation is suggested in one of her letters. "The flowers look beautiful though you put their heads into the water instead of their feet." This friendship was a tonic of happiness for Elizabeth whose health improved rapidly. In October she wrote:

> Do I stand?—do I walk? Yes!—most uprightly. I walk upright everyday. Do I go out? No, never!

But by spring of 1846 she was going out. On Sunday, June 22, she wrote:

> Think of my having left Flush behind me fast asleep. He dashes at the door in the most peremptory way, and nearly throws me backward when I open it, with his leaping-up-joy—if it is not rather his reproach.
>
> Now I am here all alone, except Flush—sitting, leaning against the open window with my feet curled up, and, at them, Flush curled up too; and I writing on my knee. How did you get home? How are you, dearest? And your mother? tell me of her, and of you! You always, you know (do you know) leave your presence with me in the flowers; and, as the lilies unfold, of course I see more and more of you in each apocalypse. Still the Saturday's visit is the worst of all to come to an end, as always I feel. In the first place stands Sunday, like a wall without a door in it. No letter! Monday is a good day and makes up a little, but it does not prevent Tuesday and Wednesday following—more intervening days than between the other meetings—or so it seems.

On Saturday June 27, 1846, she wrote:

> I walked longer today than usual. How strong you make me, you who make me happy!

Robert started calling Ba by her pet name immediately upon hearing it. It was more than a year before she was able to call him, "Robert." One day he wrote:

". . . Dearest—dearest, you did once, one time only, call me by my name, Robert; and though it was to bid, 'Robert not to talk extravagances' (your very words) still the name so spoken became what it never had been before to me. I am never called by any pet name, nor abbreviation, here at home or elsewhere. Oh it is one of my incommunicable advantages to have a Ba of my own, and call her so—indeed yes, my Ba! I write 'Dearest,' and 'Most dearest,' but it all ends in 'Ba'—and the 'my' is its framework,—its surrounding arm—Ba . . . my own Ba! 'Robert' is in Saxon 'famous in council,' so let him give a proof of his quality in counselling you to hold your good, happy inspiration about Italy . . ."

Ba answered:

No, No! Indeed I never did. If you heard me say 'Robert,' it was on a stair-landing in the house of dreams—never anywhere else! Why how could you fancy such a thing? Wasn't it rather your own disquieted conscience which spoke instead of me, saying 'Robert, don't be extravagant.' Yes, just the speech that is for a 'good uneasy' discerning conscience—and you took it for my speech! 'Don't be extravagant.' I may certainly have said. Both I and the conscience might have said so obvious a thing.

Ah—and now I have got the name, shall I have courage to say it? Tell me, best councellor! I like it better than any other name, though I never spoke it with my own lips—I never called any one by such a name.

The next day she wrote:

Quite you make me laugh by your positiveness about the name-calling. Well—if ever I did such a thing it was in a moment of unconsciousness, all the more surprising, that even to my own soul, in the lowest spirit-whisper, I have not been in the habit of saying 'Robert,' speaking of you. You have only been the One. No word ever stood for you. The idea admitted of no representative. Still such very positive people must be right, of course—they always are! Some day I expect to hear you say and swear that you saw me fly out of one window and fly in another, oh my 'famous in council.'

Am I laughing? Am I crying? Who can tell. But I am not teasing, . . . *Robert!*

Robert was not inattentive to Flush, the chaperon. He bore flowers for Ba and cakes for Flush. But Flush was afraid of trousers, and returned Robert's kindness with snarls and snaps. He even sank his teeth into Robert's ankles once or twice, but the poet, smiling happily, insisted that it was nothing. After one of these incidents Ba wrote:

Ah Flush, Flush! He did not hurt you really? You will forgive him for me? The truth is that he hates all unpetticoated people, and that though he does not hate you, he has a certain distrust of you, which any outward sign, such as the umbrella, reawakens. But if you had seen how sorry and ashamed he was yesterday! I slapped his ears and told him that he never should be loved again; and he sat on the sofa with his eyes fixed on me all the time I did the flowers, with an expression of quite despair in his face. At last I said, 'If you are good, Flush, you may come and say that you are sorry,' on which he dashed across the room and, trembling all over, kissed first one of my hands and then another, and put up his paws to be shaken, and looked into my face with such beseeching eyes that you would certainly have forgiven him just as I did. It is not savageness; if he once loved you, you might pull his ears or his tail, and take a bone out of his mouth even, and he would not bite you. He has no savage caprices like other dogs and men I have known.

Writing of Flush, in my uncle comes, and then my cousin, and then my aunt—by relays! And now it is nearly four and this letter may be too late for the post which reaches you irregularly. So provoked I am! But I shall write again tonight, you know.

Robert answered:

Oh poor Flush, do you think I do not love and respect him for his jealous supervision—his slowness to know another, having once known you? All my apprehension is that, in the imaginations downstairs, he may very well unconsciously play the part of the dog that is heard to 'bark violently' while something dreadful takes place. Yet I do not sorrow over his slapped ears, as if they ever pained him very much, you dear Ba.

And tomorrow I shall see you. Are you, can you be really 'better' after I have seen you?

In a Sonnet Ba had written:

XX

Belovèd, my Belovèd, when I think
That thou wast in the world a year ago,
What time I sat alone here in the snow
And saw no footprint, heard the silence sink
No moment at thy voice, but, link by link,
Went counting all my chains as if that so
They never could fall off at any blow
Struck by thy possible hand,—why, thus I drink
Of life's great cup of wonder! Wonderful,
Never to feel thee thrill the day or night

With personal act or speech,—nor ever cull
Some prescience of thee with the blossoms white
Thou sawest growing! Atheists are so dull,
Who cannot guess God's presence out of sight.

Ba occasionally expressed the fear that Robert's love might fade. In a sonnet she wrote:

XIV

If thou must love me, let it be for nought
Except for love's sake only. Do not say
'I love her for her smile—her look—her way
Of speaking gently,—for a trick of thought
That falls in well with mine, and certes brought
A sense of pleasant ease on such a day—'
For these things in themselves, Belovèd, may
Be changed, or change for thee,—and love, so wrought,
May be unwrought so. Neither love me for
Thine own dear pity's wiping my cheeks dry,—
A creature might forget to weep, who bore
Thy comfort long, and lose thy love thereby!
But love me for love's sake, that evermore
Thou mayst love on, through love's eternity.

On Wednesday morning, July 15, 1846, Ba wrote:

At dinner my aunt said to Papa . . . I have not seen Ba all day,—and when I went to her room, to my astonishment a gentleman was sitting there.' 'Who was that?' said Papa's eyes to Arabel. 'Mr. Browning called here today,' she answered, 'and Ba bowed her head' continued my aunt, 'as if she meant to signify to me that I was not to come in.' 'Oh,' cried Henrietta, 'that must have been a mistake of yours. Perhaps she meant just the contrary.' 'You should have gone in,' said Papa, 'and seen the poet.'

In speaking too of your visit this morning, Stormy said

to her,—'Oh Mr. Browning is a great friend of Ba's. He comes here twice a week. Is it twice a week or once, Arabel?'

By the way I made quite clear to Flush that you left the cakes, and they were graciously received indeed.

When Ba mentioned that her health might force her to go to Italy for the winter, Robert was enthusiastic. He came to his visits primed with information about that beloved country. Ba's letters give evidence that by the middle of July they were planning more than calls in Italy. In a letter postmarked July 17 she wrote

> We must be humble and beseeching afterwards at least, and try to get forgiven—poor Papa! I have turned it over and over in my mind, whether it would be less offensive, less shocking to him, if an application were made first. If I were strong, I think I should incline to it at all risks— but at it is,—it might, would, probably,—take away the power of action from me altogether. We should be separated, you see, from that moment—hindered from writing, hindered from meeting—and I could evade nothing. Then the positive disobedience might be a greater offense than the unauthorized act. I shut my eyes in terror sometimes. May God direct us to the best.

By July 23, 1846, plans seem to have become crystallized for an elopement. Ba wrote:

> Perhaps in the days to come we shall look back on these days as covetable things. Will you do so, because you were loved in them as a beginning, or because you were free? I shall look back on these days gratefully and gladly, because the good in them has overcome the evil, for the first time in days of mine.

One extravagance I had intended to propose to you—but it shall be exactly as you like, and I hesitate a little as I begin to speak of it. I have thought of taking Wilson with me—for a year, say, until I should be stronger perhaps and wiser—rather less sublimely helpless and impotent than I am now. But if you would rather it were otherwise, be honest and say so, and let me alter my thoughts at once. But I fear that I cannot leave this house with the necessary number of shoes and pocket handkerchiefs, without help from somebody. Now whoever helps me, will suffer through me. Besides if I left Wilson behind, she would be turned into the street before sunset. Would it be right and just of me to permit it? Consider! I must manage a sheltering ignorance for my poor sisters, at the last.

Wilson is attached to me, I believe—and, in all the discussions about Italy, she has professed herself willing to 'go anywhere in the world with me.'

Robert answered:

My dearest—dearest,—you might go to Italy without shoes,—or feet to wear them for aught I know, since you may have wings, but without your Wilson, or someone in her capacity, you—no— She cannot be dispensed with! It is most fortunate, most providential that Wilson is inclined to go— I am very happy; for a new servant, even with the best disposition, would never be able to anticipate your wants and wishes.

In a letter postmarked Sunday, August 3rd, Ba wrote:

Dearest, Papa came into the room at about seven, before he went to dinner— I was lying on the sofa and had on a white dressing gown, to get rid of the strings—so oppressive the air was, for all the purifications of lightning. He looked a little as if the thunder had passed into him and said, 'Has this been your costume since the morning, pray?'

'Oh no,' I answered, 'Only just now, because of the heat.'

'Well,' he resumed, with a still graver aspect, (so displeased he looked, dearest!) 'it appears that *that man* has spent the whole day with you.' To which I replied as quietly as I could that you had several times meant to go away, but that the rain would not let you,—and there the colloquy ended. Brief enough,—but it took my breath away. . . .

Shall you dare come of Tuesday after all? He will be out. If he is not—if my aunt should not be—if a new obstacle should occur,—you shall hear on Tuesday. At any rate I shall write.

If things should go smoothly, however, I want to say one word, once for all, in relation to them. Once or twice you have talked as if a change were to take place in your life through marrying—whereas I do beg you to keep in mind that not a pebble in the path changes, nor is pushed aside because of me. If you should make me feel myself in the way, should I like it, do you think? And how could I disturb a single habit or manner of yours—as an unmarried man—though being within call—I? The best of me is, that I am really very quiet and not difficult to content—having not been spoilt by an excess of prosperity even in little things. It will be prosperity in the greatest, if you seem to be happy—believe that, and leave all the rest. You will go out just as you do now,—when you choose, and as a matter of course, and without need of a word,—you will be precisely as you are now in everything, lord of the house-door-key, and of your own ways.

Robert answered:

Oh the comfort you are to me, Ba,—the perpetual blessing and sustainment! And what a piece of you, how instinct with you, this letter is! I will not try to thank you, but my whole life shall.

A biographer suggests that the conduct of these intense lovers was most circumspect; we find, however, the word "kiss" mentioned frequently in Robert's later letters. Ba expressed her feelings in a sonnet:

XXXVIII

First time he kissed me, he but only kissed
The fingers of this hand wherewith I write:
And ever since, it grew more clean and white,
Slow to world-greetings, quick with its 'Oh, list,'
When angels speak. A ring of amethyst
I could not wear here, plainer to my sight,
Than that first kiss. The second passed in height
The first, and sought the forehead, and half missed,
Half falling on the hair. O beyond meed!
That was the chrism of love, which love's own crown,
With sanctifying sweetness, did precede.
The third upon my lips was folded down
In perfect, purple state; since when, indeed,
I have been proud and said, 'My love, my own!'

On Sunday Morning, August 24, 1846, Ba wrote:

While I am writing, comes in Arabel with such a face. My brother had been talking, talking to me. Stormy suddenly touched her and said,—'Is it true that there is an engagement between Mr. Browning and Ba?' She was taken unaware, but had just power to say, 'You had better ask them, if you want to know. What nonsense, Storm.' 'Well,' he resumed, 'I'll ask Ba when I go upstairs.'

George was by, looking as grave as if antedating his judgeship. Think how frightened I was, Robert,—expecting them upstairs every minute,—for all my brothers come here on Sunday, all together. But they came, and not a single word was said—not on that subject—and I talked on every other in a sort of hurried way, I was so frightened.

The one great heartache, now, was her father, who no doubt was growing suspicious and hence decided to take his family away from London. On September 10, 1846, Ba wrote:

Dearest, this night, an edict has gone out, and George is tomorrow to be on his way to take a house for a month either at Dover, Reigate, Tunbridge. . . . Papa 'did not mind which,' he said, and 'you may settle it among you'—!! —but he 'must have this house empty for a month in order to its cleaning'—we are to go therefore and not delay.

Now!—what can be done? It is possible that the absense may be longer than for a month, indeed it is probable. I am embarrassed to the utmost degree as to the best path to take. If we are taken away on Monday . . . what then?

Hastily written letters give us a rather complete story of events leading to a dramatic climax.

Robert to Elizabeth, Thursday morning, 12 o'clock:

On returning I find your note,—We must be married directly, and go to Italy. I will go for a license today, and we can be married on Saturday. I will call tomorrow at Three and arrange everything with you.

On Saturday, September 12, 1846, Elizabeth walked to Marlebone Church where she was married to Robert Browning. She was sustained by thoughts that she later put into words:

> In the emotion and confusion there was yet room in me for one thought which was not a feeling. I thought that of the many, many women who have stood, and to the same end, there where I stood; not one, perhaps, since that building was a church, had had reasons strong as mine for an absolute trust and devotion towards the man she married,—not one!

Ba returned to Wimpole Street immediately after her marriage. On the following day she wrote:

> I sit in a dream, when left to myself. I cannot believe, or understand. Oh, but in all this difficult, embarrassing, and painful situation, I feel happy and exulting to belong to you, past every opposition, out of sight of every will of man —none can put us assunder now, at least. Beseech for me the indulgence of your father and mother, and ask your sister to love me. I feel so as if I had slipped down over the wall and into somebody's garden. I feel ashamed. To be grateful and affectionate to them all, while I live, is all that I can do, and it is too much a matter of course to need to be promised. Promise it, however, for your own Ba, whom you made so happy with the dear letter last night.
>
> I did hate so, to have to take off the ring! You will have to take the trouble of putting it on again, some day!

Robert answered:

> My family all love you, dearest. You cannot conceive my Father and Mother's childlike faith in Goodness—and my sister is very quick of apprehension—so as to seize the true point of the case at once.

Elizabeth wrote on Monday Evening:

There seems so much to do, that I am frightened to look towards the heap of it. The letters, the letters! I am paralysed when I think of having to write such words as . . 'Papa, I am married; I hope you will not be too displeased.' Ah, poor Papa! To the utmost he will be angry, —he will cast me off. Well, there is no comfort in such thoughts. How I felt tonight when I saw him at seven o'clock for the first time since the event of Saturday! He spoke kindly too, and asked me how I was. Once I heard of his saying of me that I was 'the purest woman he ever knew'—which made me smile at the moment, or laugh, I believe, outright; because I understood perfectly what he meant by that—that I had not troubled him with the iniquity of love affairs, or any impropriety of seeming to think about being married. But now the whole sex will go down to perdition. See the effect of my wickedness! 'Those women!'

But we will submit, dearest. I will put myself under his feet, to be forgiven a little—enough to be taken up again in his arms. I love him—he is my father. He has good and high qualities after all; he is my father, above all. And you, because you are so generous and tender to me, will let me, you say, and help me to try to win back the alienated affection—for he will wish that I had died years ago! For the storm will come and endure. And at last, perhaps, he will forgive us—it is my hope.

On Wednesday she wrote:

Dearest, the general departure from this house takes place on Monday—and the house at Little Bookham is six miles from the railroad, and a mile and a half from where a coach runs. Now you are to judge. Certainly if I go with you on Saturday I shall not have half the letters written. Still I may certainly write the *necessary* letters and do the others on the road.

Wilson and I have a light box and a carpet bag between us. Have you a friend, someone to whose house they might be sent?—or could they go directly to the railroad office—and what office? In that case they should have your name on them, should they not?

Now think for me, ever dearest.

Robert answered:

Take nothing you can leave—but secure our letters. I will take out a passport.

All this in such haste! Bless you, my dearest, dearest, Ba.

In a sonnet Ba wrote:

XXVIII

My letters! all dead paper, mute and white!
And yet they seem alive and quivering
Against my tremulous hands, which loose the string
And let them drop down on my knee tonight.
This said,—he wished to have me in his sight
Once, as a friend; this fixed a day in spring
To come and touch my hand . . . a simple thing,
Yet I wept for it!—this, the paper's light—
Said *Dear, I love thee;* and I sank and quailed
As if God's future thundered on my past.
This said, *I am thine*—and so its ink has paled
With lying at my heart that beat too fast.

And this . . . O love, thy words have ill availed
If, what this said, I dared repeat at last!

In a letter she wrote:

At from half-past three to four, then,—four will not, I suppose be too late. I will not write more—I cannot. By tomorrow at this time I shall have you only, to love me,—my beloved!

You only! As if one said 'God only.' And we shall have Him beside, I pray of Him.

Is this my last letter to you, ever dearest? Oh—if I loved you less—a little, little less.

Do you pray for me tonight, Robert? Pray for me, and love me, that I may have courage,—feeling both.

Your own Ba

P. S.
The boxes are safely sent. Wilson has been perfect to me. And I calling her 'timid,' and afraid of her timidity! I begin to think that none are so bold as the timid when they are fairly roused.

Edward-Moulton-Barrett never permitted Elizabeth to return home—never spoke to her—never wrote to her, nor read her letters to him. They were returned to her years later with the seals unbroken. But the sunshine of Italy and the devotion of her husband gave Ba fifteen years of happiness. With pen and ink she expressed her devotion to Robert in words of highest ecstasy:

XLIII

How do I love thee? Let me count the ways.
I love thee to the depth and breadth and height
My soul can reach, when feeling out of sight
For the ends of Being and ideal Grace;

I love thee to the level of every day's
Most quiet need, by sun and candlelight.
I love thee freely, as men strive for Right;
I love thee purely, as they turn from Praise.
I love thee with the passion put to use
In my old griefs, and with my childhood's faith.
I love thee with a love I seemed to lose
With my lost saints,—I love thee with the breath,
Smiles, tears, of all my life! and if God choose,
I shall but love thee better after death.

Robert, in fewer words, but with all the sincerity of his being, said, "I am all gratitude, and all pride. My life is in thy dearest little hand."

In a sonnet Ba had said:

XXVI

I lived with visions for my company
Instead of men and women, years ago,
And found them gentle mates, nor thought to know
A sweeter music than they played to me.
But soon their trailing purple was not free
Of this world's dust, their lutes did silent grow,
And I myself grew faint and blind below
Their vanishing eyes. Then THOU didst come, to be
Belovèd, what they *seemed*. Their shining fronts
Their songs, their splendors (better, yet the same,
As river-water hallowed into fonts),
Met in thee, and from out thee overcame
My soul with satisfaction of all wants:
Because God's gifts put man's best dreams to shame.

After their marriage, Ba grew stronger. Robert boasted about her strength to anyone who would listen. She wrote a friend:

I have to tell him that he really must not go telling everyone how his wife walked here with him or walked there with him, as if a wife with two feet were a miracle in nature.

Their home in Italy became a mecca for the literary: Dickens, Thackeray, Hans Christian Andersen, Nathaniel Hawthorne, Alfred Tennyson, Leigh Hunt, Isa Blagden, were among the many who enjoyed the hospitality of the Brownings.

Robert and Elizabeth soon began writing again—each inspiring the other. One morning, as Robert stood at the window, Ba slipped into the room, thrust a manuscript into his hand, and was gone before he could turn to question her. Wondering, he began to read aloud, but as he continued the words faded into a whisper. He was seeing for the first time Elizabeth Barrett's Sonnets, which told the story of the progress of her love.

> Guess now who holds thee—'Death!' I said. But there
> The silver answer rang: 'Not Death, but Love!'

He turned to the next piece of paper, and saw there "Rejection":

> I will not soil thy purple with my dust,
> Nor breathe my poison on my Venice-glass,
> Nor give thee any love—which were unjust.
> Beloved, I only love thee! Let it pass.

Another page, and there, at last, "Submission":

> Yet, love, mere love, is beautiful indeed
> And worthy of acceptation. Fire is bright
> Let temple burn, or flax; an equal light
> Leaps in the flame from cedar plank or weed;

> And love is fire. And when I say at need
> I love thee—Mark—I love thee!—in thy sight
> I stand transfigured, glorified aright,
> With conscience of the new rays that proceed
> Out of my face toward thine.

Soon his eyes came across heart-satisfying lines of "Avowel":

> Men could not part us with their worldly jars,
> Nor the seas change us, nor the tempests bend;
> Our hands would touch for all the mountain-bars,—
> And heaven being rolled between us at the end,
> We should but vow the faster for the stars.

His exaltation was highest in her expression of "Eternal Love":

> I love thee with the breath,
> Smiles, tears, of all my life: and if God choose,
> I shall but love thee better after death.

Completing the manuscript, he rushed to Ba to tell her of his joy and pride. When he found her, neither could speak a word. These were the poems Ba had begun after his first letter, and which she had promised he might someday read. She had written them without thought of publication, but as Browning said later:

> I dared not reserve to myself the finest sonnets written in any language since Shakespeare.

The title, *Sonnets from the Portuguese,* was suggested by Robert, who, because of her dark coloring, frequently called her "my little Portuguese."
Once he had written:

Dearest, I believed in your glorious genius and knew it for a true star from the moment I saw it; long before I had the blesssing of knowing it was my star, with my fortune and futurity in it.

He expressed this thought in a poem, "My Star":

> All I know of a certain star
> Is, it can throw (like the angled spar)
> Now a dart of red, now a dart of blue
> Till my friends have said they would fain see, too
> My star that dartles the red and the blue!
> Then it stops like a bird; like a flower, hangs furled:
> They must solace themselves with the Saturn above it.
> What matter to me if their star is a world:
> Mine has opened its soul to me; therefore I love it.

Perhaps his greatest tribute to her was written many years after her death, "Prospice" (see page 203).

THE GETTYSBURG ADDRESS
Abraham Lincoln
[*Delivered at the Dedication of the National Cemetery, November 19, 1863*]

Fourscore and seven years ago our fathers brought forth on this continent a new nation, conceived in liberty, and dedicated to the proposition that all men are created equal.

Now we are engaged in a great civil war, testing whether that nation, or any nation so conceived and so dedicated, can long endure. We are met on a great battlefield of that war. We have come to dedicate a portion of that field as a final resting place for those who here gave their lives that that nation might live. It is altogether fitting and proper that we should do this.

But, in a larger sense, we cannot dedicate—we cannot consecrate—we cannot hallow—this ground. The brave men, living and dead, who struggled here, have consecrated it far above our poor power to add or detract. The world will little note nor long remember what we say here, but it can never forget what they did here. It is for us, the living, rather, to be dedicated here to the unfinished work which they who fought here have thus far so nobly advanced. It is rather for us to be here dedicated to the great task remaining before us—that from these honored dead we take increased devotion to that cause for which they gave the last full measure of devotion; that we here highly resolve that these dead shall not have died in vain; that this nation, under God, shall have a new birth of freedom; and that government of the people, by the people, for the people, shall not perish from the earth.

DOVER BEACH

Matthew Arnold

The sea is calm tonight.
The tide is full, the moon lies fair
Upon the straits;—on the French coast the light
Gleams and is gone; the cliffs of England stand,
Glimmering and vast, out in the tranquil bay.
Come to the window, sweet is the night-air!
Only, from the long line of spray
Where the sea meets the moon-blanched land,
Listen! you hear the grating roar
Of pebbles which the waves draw back, and fling,
At their return, up the high strand,
Begin, and cease, and then again begin,
With tremulous cadence slow, and bring
The eternal note of sadness in.

Sophocles long ago
Heard it on the Aegean, and it brought
Into his mind the turbid ebb and flow
Of human misery; we
Find also in the sound a thought,
Hearing it by this distant northern sea.

The Sea of Faith
Was once, too, at the full, and round earth's shore
Lay like the folds of a bright girdle furled.
But now I only hear
Its melancholy, long, withdrawing roar,
Retreating, to the breath
Of the night-wind, down the vast edges drear
And naked shingles of the world.
Ah, love, let us be true
To one another! for the world, which seems
To lie before us like a land of dreams,
So various, so beautiful, so new,
Hath really neither joy, nor love, nor light,
Nor certitude, nor peace, nor help for pain;
And we are here as on a darkling plain
Swept with confused alarms of struggle and flight,
Where ignorant armies clash by night.

SUMMER STORM

James Russell Lowell

  Untremulous in the river clear,
Toward the sky's image, hangs the imaged bridge;
  So still the air that I can hear
The slender clarion of the unseen midge;
  Out of the stillness, with a gathering creep,
Like rising wind in leaves, which now decreases,
Now lulls, now swells, and all the while increases,

SUMMER STORM

The huddling trample of a drove of sheep
Tilts the loose planks, and then as gradually ceases
    In dust on the other side; life's emblem deep,
A confused noise between two silences,
Finding at last in dust precarious peace.
On the wide marsh the purple-blossomed grasses
    Soak up the sunshine; sleeps the brimming tide,
Save when the wedge-shaped wake in silence passes
    Of some slow water-rat, whose sinuous glide
Wavers the sedge's emerald shade from side to side;
But up the west, like a rock-shivered surge,
    Climbs a great cloud edged with sun-whitened spray;
Huge whirls of foam boil toppling o'er its verge,
    And falling still it seems, and yet it climbs alway.

    Suddenly all the sky is hid
    As with the shutting of a lid,
One by one great drops are falling
    Doubtful and slow,
    Down the pane they are crookedly crawling,
    And the wind breathes low;
Slowly the circles widen on the river,
    Widen and mingle, one and all;
Here and there the slenderer flowers shiver,
    Struck by an icy rain-drop's fall.

Now on the hills I hear the thunder mutter,
    The wind is gathering in the west;
The upturned leaves first whiten and flutter,
    Then droop to a fitful rest;
Up from the stream with sluggish flap
    Struggles the gull and floats away;
Nearer and nearer rolls the thunder-clap,—
    We shall not see the sun go down to-day:
Now leaps the wind on the sleepy marsh,
    And tramples the grass with terrified feet,

The startled river turns leaden and harsh.
You can hear the quick heart of the tempest beat.

Look! look! that livid flash!
And instantly follows the rattling thunder,
As if some cloud-crag, split asunder,
Fell, splintering with a ruinous crash,
On the earth, which crouches in silence under;
And now a solid gray wall of rain
Shuts off the landscape, mile by mile;
For a breath's space I see the blue wood again,
And ere the next heart-beat, the wind-hurled pile,
That seemed but now a league aloof,
Bursts crackling o'er the sun-parched roof;
Against the windows the storm comes dashing,
Through tattered foliage the hail tears crashing,
The blue lightning flashes,
The rapid hail clashes,
The white waves are tumbling,
And, in one baffled roar,
Like the toothless sea mumbling
A rock-bristled shore,
The thunder is rumbling
And crashing and crumbling,—
Will silence return nevermore?

Hush! Still as death,
The tempest holds his breath
As from a sudden will;
The rain stops short, but from the eaves
You see it drop, and hear it from the leaves,
All is so bodingly still;
Again, now, now, again
Plashes the rain in heavy gouts,
The crinkled lightning
Seems ever brightening,

   And loud and long
Again the thunder shouts
   His battle-song,—
   One quivering flash,
   One wildering crash,
Followed by silence dead and dull,
   As if the cloud, let go,
   Leapt bodily below
To whelm the earth in one mad overthrow,
   And then a total lull.

   Gone, gone, so soon!
  No more my half-crazed fancy there,
   Can shape a giant in the air,
  No more I see his streaming hair,
 The writhing portent of his form;—
   The pale and quiet moon
  Makes her calm forehead bare,
 And the last fragments of the storm,
Like shattered rigging from a fight at sea,
Silent and few, are drifting over me.

THE SINGER'S HILLS

Helen Hunt Jackson

He dwelt where level lands lay low and drear,
Long stretches of waste meadow pale and sere,
With dull seas languid tiding up and down,
Turning the lifeless sands from white to brown,—
Wide barren fields for miles and miles, until
The pale horizon walled them in, and still
No lifted peak, no slope, not even mound
To raise and cheer the weary eye was found.
From boyhood up and down these dismal lands,
And pacing to and fro the barren sands,
And always gazing, gazing seaward, went

The Singer. Daily with the sad winds blent
His yearning voice.
                    "There must be hills," he said,
"I know they stand at sunset rosy red,
And purple in the dewy shadowed morn;
Great forest trees like babes are rocked and borne
Upon their breasts, and flowers like jewels shine
Around their feet, and gold and silver line
Their hidden chambers, and great cities rise
Stately where their protecting shadow lies,
And men grow brave and women are more fair
'Neath higher skies, and in the clearer air!"
One day thus longing, gazing, lo! in awe
Made calm by ecstasy, he sudden saw,
Far out to seaward, mountain peaks appear,
Slow rising from the water pale and clear.
Purple and azure, there they were, as he
Had faithful yearning visions they must be;
Purple and azure and bright rosy red,
Like flashing jewels, on the sea they shed
Their quenchless light.
                    Great tears ran down
The Singer's cheeks, and through the busy town,
And all across the dreary meadow lands,
And all along the dreary lifeless sands,
He called aloud, "Ho! tarry! tarry ye!
Behold those purple mountains in the sea!"
The people saw no mountains!
            .   "He is mad,"
They careless said, and went their way and had
No farther thought of him.
                    And so, among
His fellows' noisy, idle, crowding throng,
The Singer walked, as strangers walk who speak
A foreign tongue and have no friend to seek.
And yet the silent joy which filled his face

Sometimes their wonder stirred a little space,
And following his constant seaward look,
One wistful gaze they also seaward took.
One day the Singer was not seen. Men said
That as the early day was breaking red,
He rowed far out to sea, rowed swift and strong,
Toward the spot where he had gazed so long.
Then all the people shook their heads, and went
A little sadly, thinking he had spent
His life in vain, and sorry they no more
Should hear his sweet mad songs along their shore.
But when the sea with sunset hues was dyed,
A boat came slowly drifting with the tide,
Nor oar nor rudder set to turn or stay,
And on the crimson deck the Singer lay.
"Ah, he is dead," some cried. "No! he but sleeps,"
Said others, "Madman that he is, joy keeps
Sweet vigils with him now."
      The light keel grazed
The sands; alert and swift the Singer raised
His head, and with red cheeks and eyes aflame
Leaped out, and shouted loud, and called by name
Each man, and breathlessly his story told.
"Lo, I have landed on the hills of gold!
See, these are flowers, and these are fruits, and these
Are boughs from off the giant forest trees;
And these are jewels which lie loosely there,
And these are stuffs which beauteous maidens wear!"
And staggering he knelt upon the sands
As laying burdens down.
      But empty hands
His fellows saw, and passed on smiling. Yet,
The ecstasy in which his face was set
Again smote on their hearts with sudden sense
Of half involuntary reverence.
And some said, whispering, "Alack, is he

The madman? Have ye never heard there be
Some spells which make men blind?
         And thenceforth they
More closely watched the Singer day by day,
Till finally they said, "He is not mad.
There be such hills, and treasure to be had
For seeking there! We too without delay
Will sail."
    And of the men who sailed that day,
Some found the purple mountains in the sea,
Landed, and roamed their treasure countries free,
And drifted back with brimming laden hands.
Walking along the lifeless silent sands,
The Singer, gazing ever seaward, knew,
Well knew the odors which the soft wind blew
Of all the fruits and flowers and boughs they bore.
Standing with hands stretched eager on the shore,
When they leaped out, he called, "Now God be praised,
Sweet comrades, were they then not fair?"
            Amazed,
And with dull scorn, the other men who brought
No treasures, found no mountains, and saw nought
In these men's hands, beheld them kneeling low,
Lifting, shouting, and running to and fro
As men unlading argosies whose freight
Of gorgeous things bewildered by its weight.

 Tireless the great years waxed; the great years waned;
Slowly the Singer's comrades grew and gained
Till they were goodly number.
        No man's scorn
Could hurt or hinder them. No pity born
Of it could make them blush, or once make less
Their joy's estate; and as for loneliness
They knew it not.
      Still rise the magic hills,

Purple and gold and red; the shore still thrills
With fragrance when the sunset winds begin
To blow and waft the subtle odors in
From treasure laden boats that drift, and bide
The hours and moments of the wave and tide,
Laden with fruits and boughs and flowers rare,
And jewels such as monarchs do not wear,
And costly stuffs which dazzle on the sight,
Stuffs wrought for purest virgin, bravest knight;
And men with cheeks all red, and eyes aflame,
And hearts that call to hearts by brothers' name,
Still leap out on the silent lifeless sands,
And staggering with over-burdened hands
Joyous lay down the treasures they have brought,
While smiling, pitying, the world sees nought!

A NIGHT AMONG THE PINES
Robert Louis Stevenson

Night is a dead monotonous period under a roof; but in the open world it passes lightly, with its stars and dews and perfumes, and the hours are marked by changes in the face of Nature. What seems a kind of temporal death to people choked between walls and curtains, is only a light and living slumber to the man who sleeps a-field. All night long he can hear Nature breathing deeply and freely; even as she takes her rest, she turns and smiles; and there is one stirring hour unknown to those who dwell in houses, when a wakeful influence goes abroad over the sleeping hemisphere, and all the outdoor world are on their feet. It is then that the cock first crows, not this time to announce the dawn, but like a cheerful watchman speeding the course of night. Cattle awake on the meadows; sheep break their fast on dewy hillsides, and change to a new lair among the ferns; and houseless men, who have lain down with the fowls, open their dim eyes and behold the beauty of the night.

At what inaudible summons, at what gentle touch of Nature, are all these sleepers thus recalled in the same hour to life? Do the stars rain down an influence, or do we share some thrill of mother earth below our resting bodies?

When that hour came to me among the pines, I wakened thirsty. My tin was standing by me half full of water. I emptied it at a draught; and feeling broad awake after this internal cold aspersion, sat upright to make a cigarette. The stars were clear, coloured, and jewel-like, but not frosty. A faint silvery vapour stood for the Milky Way. All around me the black fir-points stood upright and stock-still.

A faint wind, more like a moving coolness than a stream of air, passed down the glade from time to time; so that even in my great chamber the air was being renewed all night long. I thought with horror of the inn. I have not often enjoyed a more serene possession of myself, nor felt more independent of material aids. The outer world, from which we cower into our houses, seemed after all a gentle habitable place; and night after night a man's bed, it seemed, was laid and waiting for him in the fields, where God keeps an open house.

Abridged.

THE LOTUS EATERS

Alfred Tennyson

There is sweet music here that softer falls
Than petals from blown roses on the grass,
Or night-dews on still waters between walls
Of shadowy granite, in a gleaming pass;
Music that gentlier on the spirit lies,
Than tir'd eyelids upon tir'd eyes;
Music that brings sweet sleep down from the blissful skies.
Here are cool mosses deep,

And thro' the moss the ivies creep,
And in the stream the long-leaved flowers weep,
And from the craggy ledge the poppy hangs in sleep.

Why are we weigh'd upon with heaviness,
And utterly consumed with sharp distress,
While all things else have rest from weariness?
All things have rest: why should we toil alone,
We only toil, who are the first of things,
And make perpetual moan,
Still from one sorrow to another, thrown;
Nor ever fold our wings,
And cease from wanderings,
Nor steep our brows in slumber's holy balm;
Nor hearken what the inner spirit sings,
"There is no joy but calm!"
Why should we only toil, the roof and crown of things?

. . . . .

How sweet it were, hearing the downward stream,
With half-shut eyes ever to seem
Falling asleep in a half-dream!
To dream and dream, like yonder amber light,
Which will not leave the myrrh-bush on the height;
To hear each other's whisper'd speech;
Eating the Lotus day by day,
To watch the crisping ripples on the beach,
And tender curving lines of creamy spray;
To lend our hearts and spirits wholly
To the influence of mild-minded melancholy;
To muse and brood and live again in memory,
With those old faces of our infancy
Heap'd over with a mound of grass,
Two handfuls of white dust, shut in an urn of brass!

Abridged.

SONGS

From WILLIAM TELL [1]
Schiller

FISHER BOY [*singing in his boat*].

The clear smiling lake woo'd to bathe in its deep,
A boy on its green shore had laid him to sleep;
  Then heard he a melody
   Flowing and soft,
  And sweet as when angels
   Are singing aloft.
And as thrilling with pleasure he wakes from his rest,
The waters are murmuring over his breast;
  And a voice from the deep cries,
   "With me thou must go;
  I charm the young shepherd,
   I lure him below."

HERDSMAN [*singing on the mountains*].

  Farewell, ye green meadows,
   Farewell, sunny shore,
  The herdsman must leave you,
   The summer is o'er.
We go to the hills, but you'll see us again,
 When the cuckoo is calling, and wood-notes are gay,
When flow'rets are blooming in dingle and plain,
 And the brooks sparkle up in the sunshine of May.
  Farewell, ye green meadows,
   Farewell, sunny shore,
  The herdsman must leave you,
   The summer is o'er.

[1] Act I, Scene i.

CHAMOIS HUNTER [*appearing on the top of a cliff*].

On the heights peals the thunder, and trembles the bridge;
The huntsman bounds on by the dizzying ridge.
  Undaunted he hies him
   O'er ice-covered wild,
  Where leaf never budded,
   Nor spring ever smiled;
And beneath him an ocean of mist, where his eye
No longer the dwellings of man can espy;
  Through the parting clouds only
   The earth can be seen,
  Far down 'neath the vapor
   The meadows of green.

SHADOWS OF BIRDS

Helen Hunt Jackson

In darkened air, alone with pain,
I lay. Like links of heavy chain
The minutes sounded, measuring day,
And slipping lifelessly away.
Sudden across my silent room
A shadow darker than its gloom
Swept swift; a shadow slim and small
Which poised and darted on the wall,
And vanished quickly as it came;
A shadow, yet it lit like flame;
A shadow, yet I heard it sing,
And heard the rustle of its wing,
Till every pulse with joy was stirred;
It was the shadow of a bird!

Only the shadow! Yet it made
Full summer everywhere it strayed;
And every bird I ever knew

Back and forth in the summer flew;
And breezes wafted over me
The scent of every flower and tree;
Till I forgot the pain and gloom
And silence of my darkened room.
Now, in the glorious open air,
I watch the birds fly here and there;
And wonder, as each swift wing cleaves
The sky, if some poor soul that grieves
In lonely, darkened, silent walls
Will catch the shadow as it falls!

BEWARE!

From the German

Henry Wadsworth Longfellow

I know a maiden fair to see,
  Take care!
She can both false and friendly be,
  Beware! Beware!
  Trust her not,
She is fooling thee!

She has two eyes, so soft and brown,
  Take care!
She gives a side-glance and looks down,
  Beware! Beware!
  Trust her not,
She is fooling thee!

And she has hair of a golden hue,
  Take care!
And what she says it is not true,
  Beware! Beware!
  Trust her not,
She is fooling thee!

She has a bosom as white as snow,
    Take care!
She knows how much it is best to show,
    Beware! Beware!
    Trust her not,
She is fooling thee!

She gives thee a garland woven fair,
    Take care!
It is a fool's-cap for thee to wear,
    Beware! Beware!
    Trust her not,
She is fooling thee!

WAKEN, LORDS AND LADIES GAY!

Sir Walter Scott

Waken, lords and ladies gay!
On the mountain dawns the day,
All the jolly chase is here,
With hawk and horse, and hunting-spear!
Hounds are in their couples yelling,
Hawks are whistling, horns are knelling.
Merrily, merrily mingle they,
Waken, lords and ladies gay.

Waken, lords and ladies gay!
The mist has left the mountains gray,
Springlets in the dawn are streaming,
Diamonds on the brake are gleaming;
And foresters have busy been
To track the buck in thicket green;
Now we come to chant our lay,
Waken, lords and ladies gay!

Louder, louder, chant the lay;
Waken, lords and ladies gay.
Tell them youth, and mirth, and glee,
Run a course as well as we;
Time, stern huntsman, who can baulk,
Staunch as hound, and fleet as hawk?
Think of this, and rise with day,
Gentle lords and ladies gay.
Waken, lords and ladies gay.

POEM OF JOYS [1]

Walt Whitman

O the joy of my spirit! It is uncaged! It darts like lightning!
It is not enough to have this globe, or a certain time—I will have thousands of globes, and all time.

O the joy of that vast elemental sympathy which only the human Soul is capable of generating and emitting in steady and limitless floods.

O the joy of increase, growth, recuperation,
The joy of soothing and pacifying—the joy of concord and harmony.

. . . . .

O the joy of my Soul leaning poised on itself—receiving identity through materials, and loving them—observing characters, and absorbing them;
O my Soul, vibrated back to me, from them—from facts, sight, hearing, touch, my phrenology, reason, articulation, comparison, memory, and the like;
O the real life of my senses and flesh, transcending my senses and flesh;

[1] From *Leaves of Grass* (Philadelphia: David McKay Company, 1900).

O my body, done with materials—my sight, done with my material eyes;
O what is proved to me this day, beyond cavil, that it is not my material eyes which finally see,
Nor my material body which finally loves, walks, laughs, shouts, embraces, procreates.

O to realize space!
The plenteousness of all—that there are no bounds;
To emerge, and be of the sky—of the sun and moon, and the flying clouds, as one with them.
O, while I live, to be the ruler of life—not a slave,
To meet life as a powerful conqueror,
No fumes—no ennui—no more complaints or scornful criticisms.

O the joy of suffering!
To struggle against great odds! to meet enemies undaunted!
To be entirely alone with them! to find how much I can stand!
To look strife, torture, prison, popular odium, death, face to face!
To mount the scaffold! to advance to the muzzles of guns with perfect nonchalance!
To be indeed a God!

O the joy of a manly self-hood!
Personality—to be servile to none—to defer to none—not to any tyrant, known or unknown,
To walk with erect carriage, a step springy and elastic,
To look with calm gaze, or with a flashing eye,
To speak with a full and sonorous voice, out of a broad chest,
To confront with your personality all the other personalities of the earth.

POEM OF THE ROAD [1]

Walt Whitman

Afoot and light-hearted I take to the open road,
Healthy, free, the world before me,
The long brown path before me, leading wherever I choose.

Still here I carry my old delicious burdens,
I carry them, men and women—I carry them with me wherever I go,
I swear it is impossible for me to get rid of them,
I am filled with them, and I will fill them in return.

You air that serves me with breath to speak!
You objects that call from diffusion my meanings and give them shape!
You light that wraps me and all things in delicate equable showers!
You animals moving serenely over the earth!
You birds that wing yourselves through the air! you insects!
You sprouting growths from the farmers' fields! you stalks and weeds by the fences!
You paths worn in the irregular hollows by the roadsides!
I think you are latent with curious existences—you are so dear to me.

The earth expanding right hand and left hand,
The picture alive, every part in its best light,
The music falling in where it is wanted, and stopping where it was not wanted,
The cheerful voice of the public road—the gay fresh sentiment of the road.

[1] From *Leaves of Grass* (Philadelphia: David McKay, 1900).

POEM OF THE ROAD

I think heroic deeds were all conceived in the open air,
I think I could stop here myself, and do miracles,
I think whatever I meet on the road I shall like, and whoever beholds me shall like me,
I think whoever I see must be happy.

From this hour, freedom!
From this hour I ordain myself loosed of limits and imaginary lines,
Going where I list—my own master, total and absolute,
Listening to others, and considering well what they say,
Pausing, searching, receiving, contemplating,
Gently, but with undeniable will, divesting myself of the holds that would hold me.

I inhale great draughts of air,
The east and the west are mine, and the north and the south are mine.

I am larger than I thought,
I did not know I held so much goodness.

All seems beautiful to me,
I can repeat over to men and women, You have done such good to me, I would do the same to you.

I will recruit for myself and you as I go,
I will scatter myself among men and women as I go,
I will toss the new gladness and roughness among them;
Whoever denies me, it shall not trouble me,
Whoever accepts me, he or she shall be blessed, and shall bless me.

Here is the test of wisdom,
Wisdom is not finally tested in schools,
Wisdom cannot be passed from one having it, to another not having it,

Wisdom is of the Soul, is not susceptible of proof, is its own
    proof,
Applies to all stages and objects and qualities, and is content,
Is the certainty of the reality and immortality of things, and
    the excellence of things;
Something there is in the float of the sight of things that pro-
    vokes it out of the Soul.

Allons! Whoever you are, come travel with me!
Travelling with me, you find what never tires.

The earth never tires,
The earth is rude, silent, incomprehensible at first—Nature is
    rude and incomprehensible at first;
Be not discouraged—keep on—there are divine things, well
    enveloped,
I swear to you there are divine things more beautiful than words
    can tell.

Abridged

THE TIGER

William Blake

Tiger, tiger, burning bright
In the forests of the night,
What immortal hand or eye
Could frame thy fearful symmetry?

In what distant deeps or skies
Burnt the fire of thine eyes?
On what wings dare he aspire?
What the hand dare seize the fire?

And what shoulder and what art
Could twist the sinews of thy heart?
And, when thy heart began to beat,
What dread hand and what dread feet?

What the hammer? What the chain?
In what furnace was thy brain?
What the anvil? What dread grasp
Dare its deadly terrors clasp?

When the stars threw down their spears,
And water'd heaven with their tears,
Did He smile His work to see?
Did He who made the lamb make thee?

Tiger, tiger, burning bright
In the forests of the night,
What immortal hand or eye
Dare frame thy fearful symmetry?

OTHELLO'S DEFENCE

From OTHELLO [1]

William Shakespeare

Most potent, grave, and reverend signiors,
My very noble and approved good masters,
That I have ta'en away this old man's daughter,
It is most true; true, I have married her;
The very head and front of my offending,
Hath this extent, no more.
                      Rude am I in speech
And little bless'd with the set phrase of peace;
For since these arms of mine had seven years' pith,
Till now some nine moons wasted, they have used
Their dearest action in the tented field;
And little of this great world can I speak,
More than pertains to feats of broil or battle;
And therefore little shall I grace my cause,
On speaking for myself. Yet, by your gracious patience

---

[1] Act I, Scene iii.

I will a round unvarnished tale deliver,
Of my whole course of love; what drugs, what charms,
What conjuration, and what mighty magic
(For such proceedings I'm charged withal),
I won his daughter with.

. . . . .

Her father loved me; oft invited me;
Still questioned me the story of my life,
From year to year; the battles, sieges, fortunes
That I have pass'd.
I ran it through, even from my boyish days,
To the very moment that he bade me tell it:
Wherein I spoke of most disastrous chances,
Of moving accidents, by flood and field;
Of hair-breadth 'scapes in the imminent deadly breach;
Of being taken by the insolent foe,
And sold to slavery; of my redemption thence,
And with it all my travel's history.

. . . . .

These things to hear,
Would Desdemona seriously incline;
But still the house affairs would draw her thence;
Which ever as she could with haste despatch,
She'd come again, and with a greedy ear
Devour up my discourse; which I observing,
Took once a pliant hour; and found good means
To draw from her a prayer of earnest heart,
That I would all my pilgrimage dilate,
Whereof by parcels she had something heard,
But not attentively. I did consent.
And often did beguile her of her tears,
When I did speak of some distressful stroke,
That my youth suffered. My story being done,

She gave me for my pains a world of sighs;
She swore—in faith, 'twas strange, 'twas passing strange;
'Twas pitiful, 'twas wondrous pitiful;
She wished she had not heard it; yet she wished
That Heaven had made her such a man.
                                          She thank'd me;
And bade me if I had a friend that loved her,
I should teach him how to tell my story,
And that would woo her. On this hint, I spake;
She loved me for the dangers I had pass'd;
And I loved her, that she did pity them.
This only is the witchcraft I have used.

MR. PICKWICK ENGAGES A MAN SERVANT

From THE PICKWICK PAPERS

Charles Dickens

Mr. Pickwick's apartments in Goswell Street, although on a limited scale, were not only of a very neat and comfortable description, but peculiarly adapted for the residence of a man of his genius and observation. His sitting-room was the first floor front, his bed-room the second floor front; and thus, whether he were sitting at his desk in his parlor, or standing before the dressing-glass in his dormitory, he had an equal opportunity of contemplating human nature in all the numerous phases it exhibits, in that not more populous than popular thoroughfare. His landlady, Mrs. Bardell—the relict and sole executrix of a deceased customhouse officer—was a comely woman of bustling manners and agreeable appearance, with a natural genius for cooking, improved by study and long practice, into an exquisite talent. There were no children, no servants, no fowls. The only other inmates of the house were a large man and a small boy; the first a lodger, the second a production of Mrs. Bardell's. The large man was always home precisely at ten o'clock at night, at which hour he regularly condensed himself into the limits of a dwarfish French bedstead in the back parlor; and the infantine sports and gymnastic exercises of Master Bardell were exclusively confined to the neighboring pavements and gutters. Cleanliness and quiet reigned throughout the house; and in it Mr. Pickwick's will was law.

To any one acquainted with these points of the domestic economy of the establishment, and conversant with the admirable regulation of Mr. Pickwick's mind, his appearance and behavior on this morning would have been most mysterious and unaccountable. He paced the room to and fro with hurried steps, popped his head out of the window at intervals of about three minutes each, constantly referred to his watch, and exhibited many other manifestations of impatience very unusual with him. It was evident that something of great importance was in contemplation, but what that something was, not even Mrs. Bardell herself had been enabled to discover.

"Mrs. Bardell," said Mr. Pickwick, at last, as that amiable female approached the termination of a prolonged dusting of the apartment—

"Sir," said Mrs. Bardell.

"Your little boy is a very long time gone."

"Why it's a good long way to the Borough, sir," remonstrated Mrs. Bardell.

"Ah, very true, so it is," and Mr. Pickwick relapsed into silence, and Mrs. Bardell resumed her dusting.

"Mrs. Bardell," said Mr. Pickwick, at the expiration of a few minutes.

"Sir," said Mrs. Bardell again.

"Do you think it a much greater expense to keep two people, than to keep one?"

"La, Mr. Pickwick," said Mrs. Bardell, coloring up to the very border of her cap, as she fancied she observed a species of matrimonial twinkle in the eyes of her lodger; "La, Mr. Pickwick, what a question!"

"Well, but *do* you?"

"That depends—" said Mrs. Bardell, approaching the duster very near to Mr. Pickwick's elbow, which was planted on the table—"That depends a good deal upon the person, you know, Mr. Pickwick; and whether it's a saving and careful person, sir."

"That's very true, but the person I have in my eye (here he looked very hard at Mrs. Bardell) I think possesses these qualities; and has, moreover, a considerable knowledge of the world, and a great deal of sharpness, Mrs. Bardell; which may be of material use to me."

"La, Mr. Pickwick," said Mrs. Bardell, the crimson rising to her cap-border again.

"I do," said Mr. Pickwick, growing energetic, as was his wont in speaking of a subject which interested him, "I do, indeed; and to tell you the truth, Mrs. Bardell, I have made up my mind."

"Dear me, sir," exclaimed Mrs. Bardell.

"You'll think it very strange now, that I never consulted you about this matter, and never even mentioned it, till I sent your little boy out this morning—eh?"

Mrs. Bardell could only reply by a look. She had long worshipped Mr. Pickwick at a distance, but here she was, all at once, raised to a pinnacle to which her wildest and most extravagant hopes had never dared to aspire. Mr. Pickwick was going to propose—a deliberate plan, too—sent her little boy to the Borough, to get him out of the way—how thoughtful—how considerate!

"Well, what do you think?" said Mr. Pickwick.

"Oh, Mr. Pickwick, you're very kind, sir," said Mrs. Bardell, trembling with agitation.

"It'll save you a good deal of trouble, won't it?" said Mr. Pickwick.

"Oh, I never thought anything of the trouble, sir, and, of course, I should take more trouble to please you then, than ever; but it is kind of you, Mr. Pickwick, to have so much consideration for my loneliness."

"Ah, to be sure, I never thought of that. When I am in town, you'll always have somebody to sit with you. To be sure, so you will."

"I'm sure I ought to be a very happy woman. Oh you kind good playful dear," said Mrs. Bardell; and without more ado, she rose from her chair, and flung her arms round Mr. Pickwick's neck, with a cataract of tears and a chorus of sobs.

"Bless my soul," cried the astonished Mr. Pickwick;—"Mrs. Bardell—my good woman—dear me, what a situation—pray consider—Mrs. Bardell, don't—if anybody should come—"

"Oh, let them come, I'll never leave you—dear, kind, good soul;" and, with these words, Mrs. Bardell clung the tighter.

"Mercy upon me," said Mr. Pickwick, struggling violently, "I hear somebody coming up the stairs. "Don't, don't, there's a good creature, don't." But entreaty and remonstrance were alike unavailing; for Mrs. Bardell had fainted in Mr. Pickwick's arms; and before he could gain time to deposit her on a chair, Master Bardell entered the room, ushering in Mr. Tupman, Mr. Winkle, and Mr. Snodgrass.

Mr. Pickwick was struck motionless and speechless. He stood with his lovely burden in his arms, gazing vacantly on the countenances of his friends, without the slightest attempt at recognition or explanation. They, in their turn, stared at him; and Master Bardell, in his turn, stared at everybody.

The astonishment of the Pickwickians was so absorbing, and the perplexity so extreme, that they might have remained in exactly the same relative situations until the suspended animation of the lady was restored, had it not been for a most beautiful and touching expression of filial affection on the part of her youthful son. Clad in a tight suit of corduroy, spangled with brass buttons of a very considerable size, he at first stood at the door astounded and uncertain; but by degrees, the impression that his mother must have suffered some personal damage, pervaded his partially developed mind, and considering Mr. Pickwick as the aggressor, he set up an appalling and semi-earthly kind of howling, and butting forward with his head, commenced assailing that immortal gentleman about the back and legs, with such blows and pinches as the strength of his arm, and the violence of his excitement allowed.

"Take this little villain away," said the agonized Mr. Pickwick, "he's mad."

"What *is* the matter?" said the three tongue-tied Pickwickians.

"I don't know," replied Mr. Pickwick, pettishly. "Take away the boy" (here Mr. Winkle carried the interesting boy, screaming and struggling, to the further end of the apartment). "Now, help me lead this woman down stairs."

"Oh, I am better now," said Mrs. Bardell, faintly.

"Let me lead you down stairs," said the ever gallant Mr. Tupman.

"Thank you, sir—thank you," exclaimed Mrs. Bardell, hysterically. And down stairs she was led accordingly, accompanied by her affectionate son.

"I cannot conceive—" said Mr. Pickwick when his friend returned—"I cannot conceive what has been the matter with that woman. I had merely announced to her my intention of keeping a man servant, when she fell into the extraordinary paroxysm in which you found her. Very extraordinary thing. Placed me in such an extremely awkward situation."

"Very," was the reply of his followers, as they coughed slightly, and looked dubiously at each other.

This behavior was not lost upon Mr. Pickwick. He remarked their incredulity. They evidently suspected him.

"There is a man in the passage now," said Mr. Tupman.

"It's the man I spoke to you about," said Mr. Pickwick, "I sent for him to the Borough this morning. Have the goodness to call him up, Snodgrass."

Mr. Snodgrass did as he was desired; and Mr. Samuel Weller forthwith presented himself.

"Oh—you remember me, I suppose?" said Mr. Pickwick.

"I should think so," replied Sam, with a patronizing wink. "Queer start that 'ere, but he was one too many for you, warn't he? Up to snuff and a pinch or two over—eh?"

"Never mind that matter now," said Mr. Pickwick hastily, "I want to speak to you about something else. Sit down."

"Thank'ee, sir," said Sam. And down he sat without further bidding, having previously deposited his old white hat on the landing outside the door. "Ta'nt a werry good 'un to look at," said Sam, "but it's an astonishin' 'un to wear; and afore the brim went, it was a werry handsome tile. How's ever it's lighter without it, that's one thing, and every hole lets in some air, that's another—wentilation gossamer I calls it." On the delivery of this sentiment, Mr. Weller smiled agreeably upon the assembled Pickwickians.

"Now with regard to the matter on which I, with the concurrence of these gentlemen, sent for you," said Mr. Pickwick.

"That's the pint, sir," interposed Sam; "out with it, as the father said to the child, wen he swallowed a garden."

"We want to know, in the first place," said Mr. Pickwick, "whether you have any reason to be discontented with your present situation."

"Afore I answers that 'ere question, gen'lm'n," replied Mr.

Weller, "*I* should like to know, in the first place, whether you're a goin' to purwide me with a better."

A sunbeam of placid benevolence played on Mr. Pickwick's features as he said, "I have half made up my mind to engage you myself."

"Have you, though?" said Sam.

Mr. Pickwick nodded in the affirmative.

"Wages?" inquired Sam.

"Twelve pounds a year," replied Mr. Pickwick.

"Clothes?"

"Two suits."

"Work?"

"To attend upon me; and travel about with me and these gentlemen here."

"Take the bill down," said Sam, emphatically, "I'm let to a single gentleman, and the terms is agreed upon."

"You accept the situation?" inquired Mr. Pickwick.

"Cert'nly," replied Sam. "If the clothes fits me half as well as the place, they'll do."

"You can get a character of course?" said Mr. Pickwick.

"Ask the landlady o' the White Hart about that, sir," replied Sam.

"Can you come this evening?"

"I'll get into the clothes this minute, if they're here," said Sam with great alacrity.

"Call at eight this evening," said Mr. Pickwick; "and if the inquiries are satisfactory, they shall be provided."

With the single exception of one amiable indiscretion, in which an assistant housemaid had equally participated, the history of Mr. Weller's conduct was so very blameless, that Mr. Pickwick felt fully justified in closing the engagement that very evening. With the promptness and energy which characterized not only the public proceedings, Mr. Weller was furnished with a grey coat with the P.C. button, a black hat with a cokade to it, a pink striped waistcoat, light breeches and gaiters, and a variety of other necessaries, too numerous to recapitulate.

"Well," said that suddenly-transformed individual, as he took his seat on the outside of the Eatanswill coach next morning; "I wonder whether I'm meant to be a footman, or a groom, or a gamekeeper, or a seedsman. I looks like a sort of compo of every one on 'em. Never mind; there's change of air, plenty to see, and little to do; and all this suits my complaint uncommon; so long life to the Pickwicks, says I!"

Abridged

MR. PICKWICK IS SUED FOR BREACH OF PROMISE
From The Pickwick Papers
Charles Dickens

Mr. Pickwick would in all probability have gone on for some time, had not the entrance of Sam, with a letter, caused him to break off in his eloquent discourse. He passed his handkerchief across his forehead, took off his spectacles, wiped them, and put them on again; and his voice had recovered its wonted softness of tone when he said:

"What have you there, Sam?"

"Called at the Post-office just now, and found this here letter, as had laid there for two days," replied Mr. Weller. "It's sealed with a vafer, and directed in round hand."

"I don't know this hand," said Mr. Pickwick, opening the letter. "Mercy on us! what's this? It must be a jest—it—it—can't be true."

"What's the matter?" was the general inquiry.

"Nobody dead, is there?" said Wardle, alarmed at the horror in Mr. Pickwick's countenance.

Mr. Pickwick made no reply, but, pushing the letter across

the table, and desiring Mr. Tupman to read it aloud, fell back in his chair with a look of vacant astonishment quite alarming to behold.

Mr. Tupman, with a trembling voice, read the letter.

Freeman's Court, Cornhill,
August 28th, 1830.

Bardell against Pickwick.

Sir,

Having been instructed by Mrs. Martha Bardell to commence an action against you for a breach of promise of marriage, for which the plaintiff lays her damages at fifteen hundred pounds, we beg to inform you that a writ has been issued against you in this suit in the Court of Common Pleas; and request to know, by return of post, the name of your attorney in London, who will accept service thereof.

We are, Sir,
Your obedient servants,
Dodson and Fogg.

Mr. Samuel Pickwick.

There was something so impressive in the mute astonishment with which each man regarded his neighbor, and every man regarded Mr. Pickwick, that all seemed afraid to speak. The silence was at length broken by Mr. Tupman.

"Dodson and Fogg," he repeated mechanically.

"Bardell and Pickwick," said Mr. Snodgrass, musing.

"Peace of mind and happiness of confiding females," murmured Mr. Winkle, and with an air of abstraction.

"It's a conspiracy," said Mr. Pickwick at length recovering the power of speech; "a base conspiracy between these two grasping attorneys, Dodson and Fogg. Mrs. Bardell would never do it;—she hasn't the heart to do it;—she hasn't the case to do it. Ridiculous—ridiculous."

"Of her heart," said Wardle, with a smile, "you should certainly be the best judge. I don't wish to discourage you, but I should certainly say that, of her case, Dodson and Fogg are far better judges than any of us can be."

"It's a vile attempt to extort money," said Mr. Pickwick.

"I hope it is," said Wardle, with a short, dry cough.

"Who ever heard me address her in any way but that in which a lodger would address his landlady?" continued Mr. Pickwick, with great vehemence. "Who ever saw me with her? Not even my friends here—"

"Except on one occasion," said Mr. Tupman.

Mr. Pickwick changed color.

"Ah," said Mr. Wardle, "well, that's important. There was nothing suspicious then, I suppose?"

Mr. Tupman glanced timidly at his leader. "Why," said he, "there was nothing suspicious; but—I don't know how it happened, mind—she certainly was reclining in his arms."

"Gracious powers!" ejaculated Mr. Pickwick, as the recollection of the scene in question struck forcibly upon him; "what a dreadful instance of the force of circumstances! So she was—so she was."

"And our friend was soothing her anguish," said Mr. Winkle, rather maliciously.

"So I was," said Mr. Pickwick. "I won't deny it. So I was."

"Hallo!" said Wardle; "for a case in which there's nothing suspicious, this looks rather queer—eh, Pickwick? Ah, sly dog—sly dog!" and he laughed till the glasses on the side-board rang again.

"What a dreadful conjunction of appearances!" exclaimed Mr. Pickwick, resting his chin upon his hands. "Winkle—Tupman—I beg your pardon for the observations I made just now. We are all the victims of circumstances, and I the greatest." With this apology Mr. Pickwick buried his head in his hands, and ruminated; while Wardle measured out a regular circle of nods and winks, addressed to the other members of the company.

"I'll have it explained, though," said Mr. Pickwick, raising his head and hammering the table. "I'll see this Dodson and Fogg! I'll go to London tomorrow."

"Not tomorrow," said Wardle; "you're too lame."

"Well, then, next day."

"Next day is the first of September, and you're pledged to ride out with us, as far as Sir Geoffrey Manning's grounds, at all events, and to meet us at lunch, if you don't take the field."

"Well, then, the day after," said Mr. Pickwick; "Thursday.—Sam!"

"Sir," replied Mr. Weler.

"Take two places outside to London, on Thursday morning, for yourself and me."

"Werry well, sir."

Mr. Weller left the room, and departed slowly on his errand with his hands in his pockets, and his eyes fixed on the ground.

"Rum feller, the hemperor," said Mr. Weller, as he walked slowly up the street. "Think o' his making up to that 'ere Mrs. Bardell—vith a little boy, too! Always the vay vith these here old 'uns, hows'ever, as is such steady goers to look at. I didn't think he'd ha' done it, though—I didn't think he'd ha' done it!" Moralizing in this strain, Mr. Samuel Weller bent his steps towards the booking-office.

Abridged

THE PIED PIPER OF HAMELIN
Robert Browning

Hamelin Town's in Brunswick,
By famous Hanover city;
The river Weser, deep and wide,

Washes its wall on the southern side;
A pleasanter spot you never spied;
But, when begins my ditty,
Almost five hundred years ago,
To see the townsfolk suffer so
From vermin, was a pity.

Rats!
They fought the dogs and killed the cats,
And bit the babies in the cradles,
And ate the cheeses out of the vats,
And licked the soup from the cooks' own ladles,
Split open the kegs of salted sprats,
Made nests inside men's Sunday hats,
And even spoiled the women's chats
By drowning their speaking
With shrieking and squeaking
In fifty different sharps and flats.

At last the people in a body
To the Town Hall came flocking:
" 'T is clear," cried they, "our Mayor's a noddy;
And as for our Corporation—shocking
To think we buy gowns lined with ermine
For dolts that can't or won't determine
What's best to rid us of our vermin!
You hope, because you're old and obese,
To find in the furry civic robe ease?
Rouse up, sirs! Give your brains a racking
To find the remedy we're lacking,
Or, sure as fate, we'll send you packing!"
At this the Mayor and Corporation
Quaked with a mighty consternation.

An hour they sat in council;
At length the Mayor broke silence:
"For a guilder I'd my ermine gown sell,

I wish I were a mile hence!
It's easy to bid one rack one's brain—
I'm sure my poor head aches again,
I've scratched it so, and all in vain.
Oh for a trap, a trap, a trap!"
Just as he said this, what should hap
At the chamber-door but a gentle tap?
"Bless us," cried the Mayor, "what's that?"
(With the Corporation as he sat,
Looking little though wondrous fat;
Nor brighter was his eye, nor moister
Than a too-long-opened oyster,
Save when at noon his paunch grew mutinous
For a plate of turtle green and glutinous)
"Only a scraping of shoes on the mat?
Anything like the sound of a rat
Makes my heart go pit-a-pat!"

"Come in!"—the Mayor cried, looking bigger:
And in did come the strangest figure!
His queer long coat from heel to head
Was half of yellow and half of red,
And he himself was tall and thin,
With sharp blue eyes, each like a pin,
And light loose hair, yet swarthy skin,
No tuft on cheek nor beard on chin,
But lips where smiles went out and in;
There was no guessing his kith and kin:
And nobody could enough admire
The tall man and his quaint attire.
Quoth one: "It's as my great-grandsire,
Starting up at the Trump of Doom's tone,
Had walked this way from his painted tombstone!"

He advanced to the council-table;
And, "Please your honors," said he, "I'm able,

By means of a secret charm, to draw
All creatures living beneath the sun,
That creep or swim or fly or run,
After me so as you never saw!
And I chiefly use my charm
On creatures that do people harm.
The mole and toad and newt and viper;
And people call me the Pied Piper."
(And here they noticed round his neck
A scarf of red and yellow stripe,
To match with his coat of the self-same cheque;
And at the scarf's end hung a pipe;
And his fingers, they noticed, were ever straying
As if impatient to be playing
Upon this pipe, as low it dangled
Over his vesture so old-fangled.)
"Yet," said he, "poor piper as I am,
In Tartary I freed the Cham,
Last June, from his huge swarms of gnats;
I eased in Asia the Nizam
Of a monstrous brood of vampire-bats:
And as for what your brain bewilders,
If I can rid your town of rats
Will you give me a thousand guilders?"
"One? fifty thousand!"—was the exclamation
Of the astonished Mayor and Corporation.

Into the street the Piper stept,
Smiling first a little smile,
As if he knew what magic slept
In his quiet pipe the while;
Then, like a musical adept,
To blow the pipe his lips he wrinkled,
And green and blue his sharp eyes twinkled,
Like a candle-flame where salt is sprinkled;
And ere three shrill notes the pipe uttered,

You heard as if an army muttered;
And the muttering grew to a grumbling;
And the grumbling grew to a mighty rumbling;
And out of the houses the rats came tumbling.
Great rats, small rats, lean rats, brawny rats,
Brown rats, black rats, gray rats, tawny rats,
Grave old plodders, gay young friskers,
Fathers, mothers, uncles, cousins,
Cocking tails and pricking whiskers,
Families by tens and dozens,
Brothers, sisters, husbands, wives—
Followed the Piper for their lives.
From street to street he piped advancing,
And step for step they followed dancing,
Until they came to the river Weser,
Wherein all plunged and perished!
—Save one who, stout as Julius Caesar,
Swam across and lived to carry
 (As he, the manuscript he cherished)
To Rat-land home his commentary:
Which was, "At the first shrill notes of the pipe,
I heard a sound as of scraping tripe,
And putting apples, wondrous ripe,
Into a cider-press's gripe,
And a moving away of pickle-tub-boards,
And a leaving ajar of conserve-cupboards,
And a drawing the corks of train-oil-flasks,
And a breaking the hoops of butter-casks:
And it seemed as if a voice
 (Sweeter far than by harp or by psaltery
Is breathed) called out, 'Oh rats, rejoice!
The world is grown to one vast drysaltery!
So munch on, crunch on, take your nuncheon,
Breakfast, supper, dinner, luncheon!"
And just as a bulky sugar-puncheon,
All ready staved, like a great sun shone

Glorious scarce an inch before me,
Just as methought it said, 'Come, bore me!'
—I found the Weser rolling o'er me."

You should have heard the Hamelin people
Ringing the bells till they rocked the steeple.
"Go," cried the Mayor, "and get long poles,
Poke out the nests and block up the holes!
Consult with carpenters and builders,
And leave in our town not even a trace
Of the rats!"—when suddenly, up the face
Of the Piper perked in the market-place
With a, "First, if you please, my thousand guilders!"

A thousand guilders! The Mayor looked blue;
So did the Corporation too.
For council dinners made rare havoc
With Claret, Moselle, Vin-de-Grave, Hock;
And half the money would replenish
Their cellar's biggest butt with Rhenish.
To pay this sum to a wandering fellow
With a gypsy coat of red and yellow!
"Beside," quoth the Mayor with a knowing wink,
"Our business was done at the river's brink;
We saw with our eyes the vermin sink,
And, what's dead can't come to life, I think,
So, friend, we're not the folks to shrink
From the duty of giving you something for drink,
And a matter of money to put in your poke;
But as for the guilders, what we spoke
Of them, as you very well know, was in joke,
Beside, our losses have made us thrifty,
A thousand guilders! Come, take fifty!"

The Piper's face fell, and he cried,
"No trifling! I can't wait, beside!

I've promised to visit by dinner time
Bagdat, and accept the prime
Of the Head-Cook's pottage, all he's rich in,
For having left, in the Caliph's kitchen,
Of a nest of scorpions no survivor:
With him I proved no bargain-driver,
With you, don't think I'll bate a stiver!
And folks who put me in a passion
May find me pipe after another fashion."
"How?" cried the Mayor, "D'ye think I brook
Being worse treated than a Cook?
Insulted by a lazy ribald
With idle pipe and vesture piebald?
You threaten us, fellow? Do your worst,
Blow your pipe there till you burst!"

Once more he stept into the street,
And to his lips again
Laid his long pipe of smooth straight cane;
And ere he blew three notes (such sweet
Soft notes as yet musician's cunning
Never gave the enraptured air)
There was a rustling that seemed like a bustling
Of merry crowds justling at pitching and hustling;
Small feet were pattering, wooden shoes clattering,
Little hands clapping and little tongues chattering,
And, like fowls in a farm-yard when barley is scattering,
Out came the children running.
All the little boys and girls,
With rosy cheeks and flaxen curls,
And sparkling eyes and teeth like pearls,
Tripping and skipping, ran merrily after
The wonderful music with shouting and laughter.

The Mayor was dumb, and the Council stood
As if they were changed into blocks of wood,

Unable to move a step, or cry
To the children merrily skipping by,
—Could only follow with the eye
That joyous crowd at the Piper's back.
But how the Mayor was on the rack,
And the wretched Council's bosoms beat,
As the Piper turned from the High Street
To where the Weser rolled its waters
Right in the way of their sons and daughters!
However, he turned from South to West,
And to Koppelberg Hill his steps addressed,
And after him the children pressed;
Great was the joy in every breast.
"He never can cross that mighty top!
He's forced to let the piping drop.
And we shall see our children stop."
When, lo, as they reached the mountain-side,
A wondrous portal opened wide,
As if a cavern was suddenly hollowed;
And the piper advanced and the children followed,
And when all were in to the very last,
The door in the mountain-side shut fast.
Did I say all? No! One was lame,
And could not dance the whole of the way;
And in after years, if you would blame
His sadness, he was used to say,—
"It's dull in our town since my playmates left!
I can't forget that I'm bereft
Of all the pleasant sights they see,
Which the Piper also promised me.
For he led us, he said, to a joyous land,
Joining the town and just at hand,
Where waters gushed and fruit-trees grew
And flowers put forth a fairer hue,
And everything was strange and new;
The sparrows were brighter than peacocks here

And their dogs outran our fallow deer,
And honey-bees had lost their stings,
And horses were born with eagle's wings:
And just as I became assured
My lame foot would be speedily cured,
The music stopped and I stood still,
And found myself outside the hill,
Left alone against my will,
To go now limping as before,
And never hear of that country more!"

Alas, alas for Hamelin!
There came into many a burgher's pate
A text which says that heaven's gate
Opes to rich at as easy rate
As the needle's eye takes a camel in!
The Mayor sent East, West, North and South
To offer the Piper, by word of mouth,
Wherever it was men's lot to find him,
Silver and gold to his heart's content,
If he'd only return the way he went
And bring the children behind him.
But when they saw 'twas a lost endeavor,
And Piper and dancers were gone forever,
They made a decree that lawyers never
Should think their records dated duly
If, after the day of the month and year,
These words did not as well appear,
"And so long after what happened here
On the Twenty-second of July,
Thirteen hundred and seventy-six:"
And the better in memory to fix
The place of the children's last retreat,
They called it, The Pied Piper's Street—
Where anyone playing on pipe or tabor
Was sure for the future to lose his labor.

Nor suffered they hostelry or tavern
To shock with mirth a street so solemn
But opposite the place of the cavern
They wrote the story on a column.
And on the great church-window painted
The same, to make the world acquainted
How their children were stolen away,
And there it stands to this very day.
And I must not omit to say
That in Transylvania there's a tribe
Of alien people who ascribe
The outlandish ways and dress
On which their neighbors lay such stress,
To their fathers and mothers having risen
Out of some subterraneous prison
Into which they were trepanned
Long time ago in a mighty band
Out of Hamelin town in Brunswick land,
But how or why, they don't understand.

So, Willy, let me and you be wipers
Of scores out with all men—especially pipers!
And, whether they pipe us free from rats or from mice,
If we've promised them aught, let us keep our promise!

EACH AND ALL

Ralph Waldo Emerson

Little thinks, in the field, yon red-cloaked clown,
Of thee from the hill-top looking down;
The heifer that lows in the upland farm,
Far heard, lows not thine ear to charm;
The sexton, tolling his bell at noon,
Deems not that great Napoleon
Stops his horse, and lists with delight,

Whilst his files sweep round yon Alpine height;
Nor knowest thou what argument
Thy life to thy neighbor's creed has lent.
All are needed by each one;
Nothing is fair or good alone.

I thought the sparrow's note from heaven,
Singing at dawn on the alder-bough;
I brought him home, in his nest, at even;
He sings the song, but it pleases not now,
For I did not bring home the river and sky;—
He sang to my ear,—they sang to my eye.

The delicate shells lay on the shore;
The bubbles of the latest wave
Fresh pearls to their enamel gave;
And the bellowing of the savage sea
Greeted their safe escape to me.
I wiped away the weeds and foam,
I fetched my sea-born treasures home;
But the poor, unsightly, noisome things
Had left their beauty on the shore,
With the sun, and the sand, and the wild **uproar**.

The lover watched his graceful maid,
As 'mid the virgin train she strayed,
Nor knew her beauty's best attire
Was woven still by the snow-white choir.
At last she came to his hermitage,
Like the bird from the woodlands to the **cage**;—
The gay enchantment was undone,
A gentle wife, but fairy none.

Then I said, "I covet truth;
Beauty is unripe childhood's cheat;
I leave it behind with the games of **youth**."

As I spoke, beneath my feet
The ground-pine curled its pretty wreath,
Running over the club-moss burrs;
I inhaled the violet's breath;
Around me stood the oaks and firs;
Pine-cones and acorns lay on the ground;
Over me soared the eternal sky,
Full of light and of deity;
Again I saw, again I heard,
The rolling river, the morning bird;—
Beauty through my senses stole;
I yielded myself to the perfect whole.

HOW THE KING LOST HIS CROWN
John T. Trowbridge

The King's men, when he had slain the boar,
Strung him aloft on the fisher's oar,
And, two behind, and two before,
In triumph bore him along the shore.
"An oar!" says the King; "'tis a trifle! why
Did the fisher frown and the good wife sigh?"
"A trifle, sire!" was the Fool's reply;
"Then frown or laugh who will: for I,
Who laugh at all and am only a clown,
    Will never more laugh at trifles!"

A runner next day leaped down the sand,
And launched a skiff from the fisher's strand;
For he cried, "An army invades the land!
The passes are seized on either hand!
And I must carry my message straight
Across the lake to the castle gate!"
The castle he neared, but the waves were great,
The fanged rocks foamed like jaws of Fate;

And lacking an oar the boat went down.
    The Furies laugh at trifles.

The swimmer against the waves began
To strive, as a valiant swimmer can.
"Methinks," said the Fool, " 'twere no bad plan
If succor were sent to the drowning man!"
To succor a perilled pawn instead,
The monarch moving his rook ahead—
Bowed over the chessmen, white and red—
Gave "check"—then looked on the lake and said,
"The boat is lost, the man will drown!"
    O King, beware of trifles!

To the lords and mirthful dames the bard
Was trolling his latest song; the guard
Were casting dice in the castle yard;
And the captains all were drinking hard,
Then came the chief of the halberdiers,
And told to the King's astounded ears:
"An army on every side appears!
An army with banners and bows and spears!
They have gained the wall and surprised the town!"
    Our fates are woven of trifles!

The red usurper reached the throne;
The tidings over the realm were blown;
And, flying to alien lands alone
With a trusty few, the King made moan,
But long and loudly laughed the clown:
"We broke the oar and the boat went down,
And so the messenger chanced to drown;
The messenger lost, we lost the town;
And the loss of the town has cost a crown;
    And all these things are trifles!"

THE PATRIOT
Robert Browning

It was roses, roses, all the way,
    With myrtle mixed in my path like mad:
The house-roofs seemed to heave and sway,
    The church-spires flamed, such flags they had,
A year ago on this very day.

The air broke into a mist with bells,
    The old walls rocked with the crowd and cries.
Had I said, "Good folk, mere noise repels—
    But give me your sun from yonder skies!"
They had answered, "And afterward, what else?"

Alack, it was I who leaped at the sun
    To give it my loving friends to keep!
Naught man could do, have I left undone:
    And you see my harvest, what I reap
This very day, now a year is run.

There's nobody on the house-tops now—
    Just a palsied few at the windows set;
For the best of the sight is, all allow,
    At the Shambles' Gate—or, better yet,
By the very scaffold's foot, I trow.

I go in the rain, and more than needs,
    A rope cuts both my wrists behind;
And I think, by the feel, my forehead bleeds,
    For they fling, whoever has a mind,
Stones at me for my year's misdeeds.

Thus I entered, and thus I go!
    In triumphs, people have dropped down dead.
"Paid by the world, what dost thou owe
    Me?"—God might question; now instead,
'Tis God shall repay: I am safer so.

WHEN THE TIDE COMES IN
Helen Hunt Jackson

When the tide comes in,
At once the shore and sea begin
   Together to be glad.
   What the tide has brought
No man has asked, no man has sought:

   What other tides have had
   The deep sand hides away;
The last bit of the wrecks they wrought
   Was burned up yesterday.

   When the tide goes out,
The shore looks dark and sad with doubt.
   The landmarks are all lost.
   For the tide to turn
Men patient wait, men restless yearn.
   Sweet channels they have crossed,
   In boats that rocked with glee,
Stretch now bare stony roads that burn
   And lead away from sea.

   When the tide comes in
In heart, at once the hearts begin
   Together to be glad.
   What the tide has brought
They do not care, they have not sought.
   All joy they ever had
   The new joy multiplies;
All pain by which it may be bought
   Seems paltry sacrifice.

When the tide goes out,
The hearts are wrung with fear and doubt;
All trace of joy seems lost.
Will the tide return?
In restless questioning they yearn,
With hands unclasped, uncrossed.
They weep, on separate ways.
Ah! darling, shall we ever learn
Love's tidal hours and days?

LINCOLN'S ANNUAL MESSAGE TO CONGRESS, DECEMBER 3, 1861

It is not needed nor fitting here that a general argument be made in favor of popular institutions; but there is one point, with its connections, not so hackneyed as most others, to which I ask a brief attention. It is the effort to place capital on an equal footing with, if not above, labor, in the structure of government. It is assumed that labor is available only in connection with capital; that nobody labors unless somebody else, owning capital, somehow by the use of it induces him to labor. This assumed, it is next considered whether it is best that capital shall hire laborers, and thus induce them to work by their own consent, or buy them, and drive them to it without their consent. Having proceeded thus far, it is naturally concluded that all laborers are either hired laborers or what we call slaves. And, further, it is assumed that whoever is once a hired laborer is fixed in that condition for life.

Now, there is no such relation between capital and labor as assumed, nor is there any such thing as a free man being fixed for life in the condition of a hired laborer. Both of these assumptions are false, and all inferences from them are groundless.

Labor is prior to, and independent of, capital. Capital is

only the fruit of labor, and could never have existed if labor had not first existed. Labor is the superior of capital, and deserves much the higher consideration. Capital has its rights, which are as worthy of protection as any other rights. Nor is it denied that there is, and probably always will be, a relation between labor and capital producing mutual benefits. The error is in assuming that the whole labor of the community exists within that relation. A few men own capital, and that few avoid labor themselves, and with their capital hire or buy another few to labor for them. A large majority belong to neither class—neither work for others nor have others working for them. In most of the Southern states a majority of the whole people, of all colors, are neither slaves nor masters; while in the Northern a large majority are neither hirers nor hired. Men with their families—wives, sons, and daughters—work for themselves, on their farms, in their houses, and in their shops, taking the whole product to themselves, and asking no favors of capital on the one hand, nor of hired laborers or slaves on the other. It is not forgotten that a considerable number of persons mingle their own labor with capital—that is, they labor with their own hands and also buy or hire others to labor for them; but this is only a mixed and not a distinct class. No principle stated is disturbed by the existence of this mixed class.

Again, as has already been said, there is not, of necessity, any such thing as the free hired laborer being fixed to that condition for life. Many independent men everywhere in these states, a few years back in their lives, were hired laborers. The prudent, penniless beginner in the world labors for wages awhile, saves a surplus with which to buy tools or land for himself, then labors on his own account another while, and at length hires another beginner to help him. This is the just and generous and prosperous system which opens the way to all—gives hope to all, and consequent energy and progress and improvement of condition to all. No men living are more worthy to be trusted than those who toil up from poverty—none less inclined to take or touch aught which they have not honestly earned. Let them beware of surrendering a political power which they already possess, and which, if surrendered, will surely be used to close the door of advancement against such as they, and to fix new disabilities and burdens upon them, till all of liberty shall be lost.

THE PRESENT CRISIS

James Russell Lowell

When a deed is done for Freedom, through the broad earth's
    aching breast
Runs a thrill of joy prophetic, trembling on from east to west,
And the slave, where'er he cowers, feels the soul within him
    climb
To the awful verge of manhood, as the energy sublime
Of a century bursts full-blossomed on the thorny stem of Time.

Through the walls of hut and palace shoots the instantaneous
    throe,
When the travail of the Ages wrings earth's systems to and fro;
At the birth of each new Era, with a recognizing start,
Nation wildly looks at nation, standing with mute lips apart,
And glad Truth's yet mightier man-child leaps beneath the
    Future's heart.

· · · · ·

For mankind are one in spirit, and an instinct bears along,
Round the earth's electric circle, the swift flash of right or
    wrong;
Whether conscious or unconscious, yet Humanity's vast frame

Through its ocean-sundered fibres feels the gush of joy or shame;—
In the gain or loss of one race all the rest have equal claim.

Once to every man and nation comes the moment to decide,
In the strife of Truth with Falsehood, for the good or evil side;
Some great cause, God's new Messiah, offering each the bloom or blight,
Parts the goats upon the left hand, and the sheep upon the right,
And the choice goes by forever 'twixt that darkness and that light.

. . . . .

Backward look across the ages and the beacon-moments see,
That, like peaks of some sunk continent, jut through Oblivion's sea:
Not an ear in court or market for the low foreboding cry
Of those Crises, God's stern winnowers, from whose feet earth's chaff must fly;
Never shows the choice momentous till the judgment hath passed by.

Careless seems the great Avenger; history's pages but record
One death-grapple in the darkness 'twixt old systems and the Word;
Truth forever on the scaffold, Wrong forever on the throne,—
Yet that scaffold sways the future, and, behind the dim unknown,
Standeth God within the shadow, keeping watch above his own.

. . . . .

Then to side with Truth is noble when we share her wretched crust,
Ere her cause bring fame and profit, and 'tis prosperous to be just;

Then it is the brave man chooses, while the coward stands aside,
Doubting in his abject spirit, till his Lord is crucified,
And the multitude make virtue of the faith they had denied.

Count me o'er earth's chosen heroes,—they were souls that stood alone,
While the men they agonized for hurled the contumelious stone,
Stood serene, and down the future saw the golden beam incline
To the side of perfect justice, mastered by their faith divine,
By one man's plain truth to manhood and to God's supreme design.

· · · · ·

For Humanity sweeps onward: where to-day the martyr stands,
On the morrow crouches Judas with the silver in his hands;
Far in front the cross stands ready and the crackling fagots burn,
While the hooting mob of yesterday in silent awe return
To glean up the scattered ashes into History's golden urn.

'Tis as easy to be heroes as to sit the idle slaves
Of a legendary virtue carved upon our father's graves,
Worshippers of light ancestral make the present light a crime;—
Was the Mayflower launched by cowards, steered by men behind their time?
Turn those tracks toward Past or Future, that makes Plymouth Rock sublime?

· · · · ·

They have rights who dare maintain them; we are traitors to our sires,
Smothering in their holy ashes Freedom's new-lit altar-fires;
Shall we make their creed our jailer? Shall we, in our haste to slay,

From the tombs of the old prophets steal the funeral lamps
 away
To light up the martyr-fagots round the prophets of to-day?

New occasions teach new duties; Time makes ancient good
 uncouth;
They must upward still, and onward, who would keep abreast
 of Truth;
Lo, before us gleam her camp-fires; we ourselves must Pilgrims
 be,
Launch our Mayflower and steer boldly through the desperate
 winter sea,
Nor attempt the Future's portal with the Past's blood-rusted
 key.

Abridged.

GIVE ME THE SPLENDID SILENT SUN [1]

Walt Whitman

Give me the splendid silent sun with all his beams full-dazzling,
Give me juicy autumnal fruit ripe and red from the orchard,
Give me a field where the unmowed grass grows,
Give me an arbor, give me the trellised grape,
Give me fresh corn and wheat, give me serene-moving animals
 teaching content,
Give me nights perfectly quiet as on high plateaus west of the
 Mississippi, and I looking up at the stars,
Give me odorous at sunrise a garden of beautiful flowers where
 I can walk undisturbed,
Give me for marriage a sweet-breathed woman of whom I
 should never tire,
Give me a perfect child, give me, away aside from the noise of
 the world, a rural domestic life,
Give me to warble spontaneous songs recluse by myself, for
 my own ears only,

[1] From *Leaves of Grass* (Philadelphia: David McKay Company, 1900).

Give me soltitude, give me Nature, give me again O Nature
your primal sanities!

These demanding to have them, (tired with ceaseless excitement, and racked by the war-strife)
These to procure incessantly asking, rising in cries from my heart,
While yet incessantly asking still I adhere to my city
Day upon day and year upon year, O city, walking your streets,
Where you hold me enchained a certain time refusing to give me up,
Yet giving to make me glutted, enriched of soul, you give me forever faces;
(O I see what I ought to escape, confronting, reversing my cries,
I see my own soul trampling down what it asked for.)

Keep your splendid silent sun,
Keep your woods, O Nature, and the quiet places by the woods,
Keep your fields of clover and timothy, and your cornfields and orchards,
Keep the blossoming buckwheat fields where the Ninth-month bees hum;
Give me faces and streets—give me these phantoms incessant and endless along the trottoirs!
Give me interminable eyes—give me women—give me comrades and lovers by the thousand!
Let me see new ones every day—let me hold new ones by the hand every day!
Give me such shows—give me the streets of Manhattan!
Give me Broadway, with the soldiers marching—give me the sound of the trumpets and drums!
(The soldiers in companies or regiments—some starting away flushed and reckless,
Some, their time up, returning with thinned ranks, young, yet very old, worn, marching, noticing nothing;)
Give me the shores and wharves heavy-fringed with black ships!

O such for me! O an intense life, full to repletion and varied!
The life of the theatre, bar-room, huge hotel, for me!
The saloon of the steamer! The crowded excursion for me! The torchlight procession!
The dense brigade bound for the war, with high-piled military wagons following;
People, endless, streaming, with strong voices, passions, pageants,
Manhattan streets with their powerful throbs, with beating drums as now,
The endless and noisy chorus, the rustle and clank of muskets (even the sight of the wounded),
Manhattan crowds, with their turbulent musical chorus!
Manhattan faces and eyes forever for me.

ODE

ON INTIMATIONS OF IMMORTALITY FROM RECOLLECTIONS OF EARLY CHILDHOOD

William Wordsworth

There was a time when meadow, grove and stream,
    The earth, and every common sight,
      To me did seem
    Appareled in celestial light,
The glory and the freshness of a dream.
It is not now as it hath been of yore;—
    Turn wheresoe'er I may,
      By night or day,
The things which I have seen I now can see no more.

    The rainbow comes and goes,
    And lovely is the rose,
    The moon doth with delight
Look round her when the heavens are bare,
    Waters on a starry night

Are beautiful and fair;
The sunshine is a glorious birth;
But yet I know, where'er I go,
That there hath past away a glory from the earth.

Now, while the birds thus sing a joyous song,
And while the young lambs bound
As to the tabor's sound,
To me alone there came a thought of grief:
A timely utterance gave that thought relief,
And I again am strong:
The cataracts blow their trumpets from the steep;
No more shall grief of mine the season wrong;
I hear the echoes through the mountains throng,
The winds come to me from the fields of sleep,
And all the earth is gay;
Land and sea
Give themselves up to jollity,
And with the heart of May
Doth every beast keep holiday;—
Thou child of joy,
Shout round me, let me hear thy shouts, thou happy shepherd-boy!

Ye blessèd creatures, I have heard the call
Ye to each other make; I see
The heavens laugh with you in your jubilee;
My heart is at your festival,
My head hath its coronal,
The fulness of your bliss, I feel—I feel it all.
Oh evil day! if I were sullen
While earth herself is adorning,
This sweet May-morning,
And the children are culling
On every side,
In a thousand valleys far and wide,

Fresh flowers; while the sun shines warm,
And the babe leaps up on his mother's arm:—
  I hear, I hear, with joy I hear!
  —But there's a tree, of many, one,
A single field which I have looked upon,
Both of them speak of something that is gone:
  The pansy at my feet
  Doth the same tale repeat:
Whither is fled the visionary gleam?
Where is it now, the glory and the dream?

Our birth is but a sleep and a forgetting:
The soul that rises with us, our life's Star,
  Hath had elsewhere its setting,
   And cometh from afar:
  Not in entire forgetfulness,
  And not in utter nakedness,
But trailing clouds of glory do we come
  From God, who is our home:
Heaven lies about us in our infancy!
Shades of the prison-house begin to close
  Upon the growing boy,
But he beholds the light, and whence it flows
  He sees it in his joy;
The Youth, who daily farther from the east
  Must travel, still is nature's priest,
  And by the vision splendid
  Is on his way attended;
At length the man perceives it die away,
And fade into the light of common day.

Earth fills her lap with pleasures of her own;
Yearnings she hath in her own natural kind,
And even with something of a mother's mind,
  And no unworthy aim,
  The homely nurse doth all she can

To make her foster-child, her inmate man,
    Forget the glories he hath known,
And that imperial palace whence he came.

Behold the child among his new-born blisses,
A six years' darling of a pigmy size!
See, where 'mid work of his own hand he lies,
Fretted by sallies of his mother's kisses,
With light upon him from his father's eyes!
See, at his feet, some little plan or chart,
Some fragment from his dream of human life,
Shaped by himself with newly-learnèd art;
    A wedding or a festival,
    A mourning or a funeral,
      And this hath now his heart,
    And unto this he frames his song:
      Then will he fit his tongue
To dialogues of business, love, or strife;
    But it will not be long
    Ere this be thrown aside,
    And with new joy and pride
The little actor cons another part;
Filling from time to time his 'humorous stage'
With all the persons, down to palsied age,
That life brings with her in her equipage;
    As if his whole vocation
    Were endless imitation.

Thou, whose exterior semblance doth belie
    Thy soul's immensity;
Thou best philosopher, who yet dost keep
Thy heritage, thou eye among the blind,
That, deaf and silent, read'st the eternal deep,
Haunted for ever by the eternal mind,—
    Mighty prophet! Seer blest!
    On whom those truths do rest,

Which we are toiling all our lives to find,
In darkness lost, the darkness of the grave;
Thou, over whom thy immortality
Broods like the day, a master o'er a slave,
A presence which is not to be put by;
Thou little child, yet glorious in the might
Of heaven-born freedom on thy being's height,
Why with such earnest pains dost thou provoke
The years to bring the inevitable yoke,
Thus blindly with thy blessedness at strife?
Full soon thy Soul shall have her earthly freight,
Heavy as frost, and deep almost as life!

    Oh joy! that in our embers
    Is something that doth live,
    That nature yet remembers
    What was so fugitive!
The thought of our past years in me doth breed
Perpetual benediction: not indeed
For that which is most worthy to be blest;
Delight and liberty, the simple creed
Of childhood, whether busy or at rest,
With new-fledged hope still fluttering in his breast:—
    Not for these I raise
    The song of thanks and praise;
    But for those obstinate questionings
    Of sense and outward things,
    Fallings from us, vanishings;
    Blank misgivings of a creature
Moving about in worlds not realized,
High instincts before which our mortal nature
Did tremble like a guilty thing surprised:
    But for those first affections,
    Those shadowy recollections,
  Which, be they what they may,
Are yet the fountain light of all our day,

Are yet a master light of all our seeing;
  Uphold us, cherish, and have power to make
Our noisy years seem moments in the being
Of the eternal silence: truths that wake,
    To perish never;
Which neither listlessness, nor mad endeavor,
    Nor man nor boy,
Nor all that is at enmity with joy,
Can utterly abolish or destroy!
      Hence in a season of calm weather
      Though inland far we be,
Our Souls have sight of that immortal sea
    Which brought us hither,
    Can in a moment travel thither,
And see the children sport upon the shore,
And hear the mighty waters rolling evermore.

Then sing, ye birds, sing, sing a joyous song!
    And let the young lambs bound
    As to the tabor's sound!
We in thought will join your throng,
    Ye that pipe and ye that play,
Ye that through your hearts to-day
    Feel the gladness of the May!
What though the radiance which was once so bright
Be now for ever taken from my sight,
  Though nothing can bring back the hour
Of splendor in the grass, of glory in the flower;
    We will grieve not, rather find
    Strength in what remains behind;
    In the primal sympathy
    Which having been must ever be;
    In the soothing thoughts that spring
    Out of human suffering;
    In the faith that looks through death,
In years that bring the philosophic mind.

And O, ye fountains, meadows, hills, and groves,
Forebode not any severing of our loves!
Yet in my heart of hearts I feel your might;
I only have relinquished one delight
To live beneath your more habitual sway.
I love the brooks which down their channels fret,
Even more than when I tripped lightly as they;
The innocent brightness of a new-born day
    Is lovely yet;
The clouds that gather round the setting sun
Do take a sober coloring from an eye
That hath kept watch o'er man's mortality.
Another race hath been, and other palms are won.
Thanks to the human heart by which we live,
Thanks to its tenderness, its joys, and fears,
To me the meanest flower that blows can give
Thoughts that do often lie too deep for tears.

SELF-RELIANCE

Ralph Waldo Emerson

    To believe your own thought, to believe that what is true for you in your private heart, is true for all men—that is genius. Speak your latent conviction and it shall be the universal sense; for always the inmost becomes the outmost,—and our first thought is rendered back to us by the trumpets of the Last Judgment. Familiar as the voice of the mind is to each, the highest merit we ascribe to Moses, Plato, and Milton, is that they set at naught books and traditions, and spoke not what men, but what *they* thought. A man should learn to detect and watch that gleam of light which flashes across his mind from within, more than the lustre of the firmament of bards and sages. Yet he dismisses without notice his thought, because it is his. In every work of genius we recognize our own rejected thoughts: they come back to us with a certain alienated majesty. Great works of art have no more affecting lesson for us than this. They teach us to abide by our spontaneous impression with good-humored inflexibility then most when the whole cry of voices is on the other side. Else, to-morrow a stranger will say with masterly good sense precisely what we have thought and felt all the time, and we shall be forced to take with shame our own opinion from another.

There is a time in every man's education when he arrives at the conviction that envy is ignorance; that imitation is suicide; that he must take himself for better, for worse, as his portion; that though the wide universe is full of good, no kernel of nourishing corn can come to him but through his toil bestowed on that plot of ground which is given to him to till. The power which resides in him is new in nature, and none but he knows what that is which he can do, nor does he know until he has tried. Not for nothing one face, one character, one fact makes much impression on him, and another none. It is not without preëstablished harmony, this sculpture in the memory. The eye was placed where one ray should fall, that it might testify of that particular ray. . . . We but half express ourselves, and are ashamed of that divine idea which each of us represents. It may be safely trusted as proportionate and of good issues, so it be faithfully imparted, but God will not have his work made manifest by cowards. . . . A man is relieved and gay when he has put his heart into his work and done his best; but what he has said or done otherwise, shall give him no peace. It is a deliverance which does not deliver. In the attempt his genius deserts him; no muse befriends; no invention, no hope.

Trust thyself: every heart vibrates to that iron string. Accept the place the divine Providence has found for you; the society of your contemporaries, the connection of events. Great men have always done so and confided themselves childlike to the genius of their age, betraying their perception that the Eternal was stirring at their heart, working through their hands, predominating in all their being.

And we are now men, and must accept in the highest mind the same transcendent destiny; and not pinched in a corner, not cowards fleeing before a revolution, but redeemers and benefactors, pious aspirants to be noble clay. Under the Almighty effort let us advance on Chaos and the Dark.

THE LOVER'S RESOLUTION
George Wither

Shall I, wasting in despair,
Die because a woman's fair:
Or make pale my cheeks with care,
'Cause another's rosy are?
Be she fairer than the day,
Or the flowery meads in May!
  If she be not so to me,
  What care I how fair she be?

Should my heart be grieved or pined,
'Cause I see a woman kind?
Or a well disposed nature
Joined with a lovely feature?
Be she meeker, kinder than
Turtle dove, or pelican!
  If she be not so to me,
  What care I how kind she be?

Shall a woman's virtues move
Me to perish for her love?
Or her well deserving known,

Make me quite forget mine own?
Be she with that goodness blest
Which may gain her, name of best!
   If she be not such to me,
   What care I how good she be?

'Cause her fortune seems too high,
Shall I play the fool, and die?
Those that bear a noble mind,
Where they want of riches find,
Think 'What, with them, they would do
That, without them, dare to woo!'
   And unless that mind I see,
   What care I though great she be?

Great, or good, or kind, or fair,
I will ne'er the more despair!
If she love me (this believe!)
I will die, ere she shall grieve!
If she slight me, when I woo,
I can scorn, and let her go!
   For if she be not for me,
   What care I for whom she be?

THE FINALITIES OF EXPRESSION [1]

Hamilton Wright Mabie

Socrates seems to most of us an eminently wholesome character, incapable of corrupting the youth, although adjudged guilty of that grave offence, and altogether a man to be trusted and honoured. And the tradition of Xantippe adds our sympathy to our faith. But Carlyle evidently distrusted Socrates, for he says of him, reproachfully, that he was "terribly at ease

[1] From *My Study Fire,* by Hamilton Wright Mabie. Reprinted by permission of the publishers, Dodd, Mead and Company, Inc.

in Zion." It is quite certain that neither within Zion nor outside its walls was Carlyle at ease. No sweating smith ever groaned more at his task than did this greatest of modern English literary artists. He fairly grovelled in toil, bemoaning himself and smiting his fellow-man in sheer anguish of spirit; producing his masterpieces to an accompaniment of passionate but unprofane curses on the conditions under which, and the task upon which, he worked. This, however, was the artisan, not the artist, side of the great writer; it was the toil-worn, unrelenting Scotch conscience astride his art and riding it at times as Tam o' Shanter spurred his gray mare, Meg, on the ride to Kirk Alloway. Socrates, on the other hand, is always at ease and in repose. His touch on the highest themes is strong and sure, but light almost as air. There seems to be no effort about his morality, no self-consciousness in his piety, no strain in his philosophy. The man and his words are in perfect harmony, and both seem to be a natural flowering and fulfilment of the higher possibilities of life. Uncouth as he was in person, there was a strange and compelling beauty in this unconventional teacher; for the expression both of his character and of his thought was wholly in the field of art. He was an artist just as truly as Phidias or Pericles or Plato; one, that is, who gave the world not the processes but the results of labour; for grace, as George Macdonald somewhere says, is the result of forgotten toil. Socrates had his struggles, but what the world saw and heard was the final and harmonious achievement; it heard the finished speech, not the orator declaiming on the beach with pebbles in his mouth; it saw the completed picture, not the artist struggling with those obdurate patches of colour about which Hamerton tells us. When the supreme moment and experience came, Socrates was calm amid his weeping friends, and died with the quiet assurance of one to whom death was so entirely incidental that any special agitation would seem to exaggerate its importance; and exaggeration is intolerable in art.

This bit of vital illustration may suggest a deeper view of art than that which we habitually take, and a view which may make us for a moment conscious of the loss which modern life sustains in having lost so largely the art spirit. Men degenerate without a strong grasp on morality, but they grow deformed and unhappy without art. For art is as truly the final expression of perfect character as of perfect thought, and beauty is as much a quality of divinity as righteousness. When goodness gets beyond self-consciousness, when the love of man for God becomes as genuine and simple and instinctive as the love of a child for its father, both goodness and love become beautiful. Beauty is the final form of all pure activities, and truth and righteousness do not reach their perfect stage until they take on beauty. Struggle is heroic, and our imaginations are deeply moved by it, but struggle is only a means to an end, and to rest in it and glorify it is to exalt the process above the consummation. We need beauty just as truly as we need truth, for it is as much a part of our lives. A beautiful character, like a beautiful poem or statue, becomes a type or standard; it brings the ideal within our vision, and, while it fills us with a divine discontent, satisfies and consoles us. The finalities of character and of art restore our vision of the ends of life, and, by disclosing the surpassing and thrilling beauty of the final achievement, reconcile us to the toil and anguish which go before it. The men and women are few who would not gladly die if they might do one worthy thing perfectly.

The conscience of most English-speaking people has been trained in the direction of morality, but not in the direction of beauty. We hold ourselves with painful solicitude from all contact with that which corrupts or defiles, but we are absolutely unscrupulous when it comes to colour and form and proportion. We are studious not to offend the moral sense, but we do not hesitate to abuse the aesthetic sense. We fret at political corruption, and at long intervals we give ourselves the trouble of getting rid of it; but we put up public buildings which may well make higher intelligences than ours shudder at such an uncovering of our deformity. We insist on decent compliance with the law, but we ruthlessly despoil a beautiful landscape and stain a fair sky, as if these acts were not flagrant violations of the order of the universe. The truth is, our consciences are like our tastes; they are only half trained. They operate directly and powerfully on one side of our lives, and on the other they are dumb and inactive.

An intelligent conscience insists on a whole life no less than on a clean one; it exacts obedience, not to one set of laws, but to law; it makes us as uncomfortable in the presence of a neglected opportunity as in the presence of a misused one. It is not surprising that men are restless under present conditions; there is a squalor in many manufacturing and mining countries which eats into the soul,—an ugliness that hurts the eye and makes the heart ache. Blue sky and green grass cry out at such profanation, and it is not strange that the soul of the man who daily faces that hideous deformity of God's fair world grows savage and that he becomes a lawbreaker like his employer. For lawbreaking is contagious, and he who violates the wholesome beauty of the world lets loose a spirit which will not discriminate between general and particular property, between the landscape and the private estates which compose it. The culprit who defaces a picture in a public gallery meets with condign punishment, but the man who defaces a lovely bit of nature, a living picture set in the frame of a golden day, goes unwhipped of justice; for we are as yet only partly educated, and civilization ends abruptly in more than one direction.

The absence of the corrective spirit of art is seen in the

obtrusiveness of much of our morality and religion; we formulate and methodise so much that ought to be spontaneous and free. The natural key is never out of harmony with the purest strains of which the soul is capable, but we distrust it to such an extent that much of the expression of religious life is in an unnatural key. We are afraid of simple goodness, and are never satisfied until we have cramped it into some conventional form and substituted for the pure inspiration a well-contrived system of mechanism; for the Psalms we are always substituting the Catechism, and in all possible ways translating the deep and beautiful poetry of the spiritual life into the hard prose of ecclesiasticism and dogmatism. The perfect harmony of the life and truth of the divinest character known to men teaches a lesson which we have yet to learn. If the words of Christ and those of any catechism are set in contrast, the difference between the crudity of provisional statements and the divine perfection of the finalities of truth and life is at once apparent. We have learned in part the lesson of morality, but we have yet to learn the lesson of beauty. We have not learned it because in our moral education we have stopped short of perfection; for the purest and highest morality becomes a noble form of art.

WORK AND CONTEMPLATION

Elizabeth Barrett Browning

The woman singeth at her spinning-wheel
A pleasant chant, ballad or barcarole;
She thinketh of her song, upon the whole,
Far more than of her flax; and yet the reel
Is full, and artfully her fingers feel
With quick adjustment, provident control,
The lines—too subtly twisted to unroll—

Out to a perfect thread. I hence appeal
To the dear Christian church—that we may do
Our Father's business in these temples mirk,
Thus, swift and steadfast; thus, intent and strong;
While thus, apart from toil, our souls pursue
Some high, calm, spheric tune, and prove our work
The better for the sweetness of our song.

From THE PRAIRIES

(1832)

William Cullen Byrant

These are the gardens of the Desert, these
The unshorn fields, boundless and beautiful,
For which the speech of England has no name—
The Prairies. I behold them for the first,
And my heart swells while the dilated sight
Takes in the encircling vastness. Lo, they stretch
In airy undulations, far away,
As if the Ocean, in his gentlest swell,
Stood still, with all his rounded billows fixed
And motionless forever. Motionless?
No, they are all unchained again: The clouds
Sweep over with their shadows, and, beneath,
The surface rolls and fluctuates to the eye;
Dark hollows seem to glide along and chase
The sunny ridges. Breezes of the South,
Who toss the golden and the flame-like flowers,
And pass the prairie-hawk that, poised on high,
Flaps his broad wings, yet moves not, ye have played
Among the palms of Mexico and vines
Of Texas, and have crisped the limpid brooks
That from the fountains of Sonora glide
Into the calm Pacific: have ye fanned
A nobler or a lovelier scene than this?

Man hath no part in all this glorious work:
The hand that built the firmament hath heaved
And smoothed these verdant swells, and sown their slopes
With herbage, planted them with island groves,
And hedged them round with forests. Fitting floor
For this magnificent temple of the sky,
With flowers whose glory and whose multitude
Rival the constellations! The great heavens
Seem to stoop down upon the scene in love—
A nearer vault, and of a tenderer blue,
Than that which bends above our Eastern hills.

A CHRISTMAS CAROL

Charles Dickens

Marley was dead, to begin with. There is no doubt whatever about that. The register of his burial was signed by the clergyman, the clerk, the undertaker, and the chief mourner. Scrooge signed it. And Scrooge's name was good upon 'Change for anything he chose to put his hand to.

Old Marley was as dead as a door-nail.

Scrooge knew he was dead. Of course he did. How could it be otherwise? Scrooge and he had been partners for I do not know how many years. Scrooge was his sole executor, his sole administrator, his sole assignee, residuary legatee, his sole friend, his sole mourner.

Scrooge never painted out old Marley's name, however. There it yet stood, years afterwards, above the warehouse door, —SCROOGE AND MARLEY. The firm was known as Scrooge and Marley. Sometimes people new to the business called Scrooge Scrooge, and sometimes Marley. He answered to both names. It was all the same to him.

Oh! But he was a tight-fisted hand at the grindstone, was

Scrooge! a squeezing, wrenching, grasping, scraping, clutching, covetous old sinner! External heat and cold had little influence on him. No warmth could warm, no cold could chill him. No wind that blew was bitterer than he, no falling snow was more intent upon its purpose, no pelting rain less open to entreaty.

Nobody ever stopped him on the streets to say, with gladsome looks, "My dear Scrooge, how are you? When will you come to see me?" No beggars implored him to bestow a trifle, no children asked him what it was o'clock, no man or woman ever once in all his life inquired the way to such and such a place, of Scrooge.

Once upon a time—of all the good days in the year, upon a Christmas eve—old Scrooge sat busy in his counting-house. It was cold, bleak, biting, foggy weather; and the city clocks had only just gone three, but it was quite dark already.

The door of Scrooge's counting-house was open, that he might keep his eye upon his clerk, who in a dismal little cell beyond, a sort of tank, was copying letters. Scrooge had a very small fire, but the clerk's fire was so very much smaller that it looked like one coal. But he couldn't replenish it, for Scrooge kept the coal-box in his room; and so surely as the clerk came in with the shovel the master predicted that it would be necessary for them to part. Wherefore the clerk put on his white comforter, and tried to warm himself at the candle; in which effort, not being a man of strong imagination, he failed.

"A merry Christmas, Uncle!" cried a cheerful voice. It was the voice of Scrooge's nephew, who came upon him so quickly that this was the first intimation that Scrooge had of his approach.

"Bah! humbug!"

"Christmas a humbug, Uncle! You don't mean that I am sure!"

"I do. Out upon merry Christmas! Keep Christmas in your own way and let me keep it in mine."

"Keep it! But you don't keep it."

"Let me leave it alone, then. Much good may it do you! Much good has it ever done you!"

"Don't be angry, Uncle. Come! Dine with us to-morrow."

Scrooge said that he would see him—yes, indeed, he did. He went the whole length of the expression, and said that he would see him in that extremity first.

"But why? why?"

"Why did you get married?"

"Because I fell in love."

"Because you fell in love. Good afternoon!"

"Nay, Uncle, but you never came to see me before that happened. Why give it as a reason for not coming now?"

"Good afternoon!"

"A merry Christmas, Uncle."

"Good afternoon!"

"And a Happy New Year!"

"Good afternoon!"

The hour of shutting up the counting-house had arrived. With an ill-will Scrooge, dismounting from his stool, tacitly admitted the fact to the expectant clerk in the tank, who instantly snuffed his candle out, and put on his hat.

"You'll want all day to-morrow, I suppose?"

"If quite convenient, sir."

"It's not convenient, and it's not fair. If I was to stop half a crown for it, you'd think yourself mightily ill-used, I'll be bound?"

"Yes, sir."

"And yet you don't think me ill-used, when I pay a day's wages for no work."

"It's only once a year, sir!"

"A poor excuse for picking a man's pocket every twenty-fifth of December! But I suppose you must have the whole day. Be here all the earlier next morning."

Scrooge took his melancholy dinner in his usual melancholy tavern; then went home to bed. He lived in chambers that had once belonged to his deceased partner. They were a gloomy suite of rooms. The building was old enough now, and dreary enough; for nobody lived in it but Scrooge.

Scrooge put on his dressing-gown and slippers and his nightcap and sat down before the very low fire to take his gruel.

As he threw his head back in the chair, his glance happened to rest upon a bell, that hung in the room, and communicated, for some purpose now forgotten, with a chamber in the highest story of the building. It was with great astonishment, and with a strange inexplicable dread, that, as he looked, he saw this bell begin to ring. Soon it rang out loudly, and so did every bell in the house.

This was succeeded by a clanking noise, deep down below. Then he heard the noise much louder, on the floors below; then coming up the stairs; then coming straight towards his door.

It came on through the heavy door, and a spectre passed into the room before his eyes. And upon its coming in the dying flame leaped up, as though it cried out, "I know him! Marley's ghost!"

"How now!" said Scrooge, caustic and cold as ever. "What do you want with me?"

"Much!"—Marley's voice, no doubt about it!

"Who are you?"

"Ask me who I was."

"Who were you, then?"

"In life I was your partner, Jacob Marley."

"Dreadful apparition, why do you trouble me? Why do spirits walk the earth, and why do they come to me?"

"It is required of every man, that the spirit within him should walk abroad among his fellowmen, and travel far and wide; and if that spirit goes not forth in life, it is condemned to do so after death. My spirit—mark me!—in life my spirit never roved beyond the narrow limits of our money-changing hole; and weary journeys lie before me!"

"Seven years dead. And traveling all the time? You travel fast?"

"On the wings of the wind."

"You might have got over a great quantity of ground in seven years."

"O blind man, blind man! Not to know that no space of regret can make amends for one life's opportunities misused! Yet I was like this man!"

"But you were always a good man of business, Jacob."

"Business! Mankind was my business. I am here to warn you that you have yet a chance to escape my fate. A chance and hope of my procuring, Ebenezer."

"You were always a good friend to me, thank'ee!"

"You will be haunted by three spirits."

"Is that the chance and hope you mentioned, Jacob? I—I think I'd rather not."

"Without these visits you cannot hope to shun the path I tread. Look to see me no more; and look that, for your own sake, you remember what has passed between us!"

It walked backward from him; and every step it took, the window raised itself a little, so that when the apparition reached it, it was wide open; and the spirit floated out upon the air and disappeared.

When Scrooge awoke, it was so dark, that he could scarcely

distinguish the transparent window from the opaque walls of his chamber, until suddenly the church clock tolled a deep, dull, hollow, melancholy ONE.

Light flashed up in the room upon the instant, and the curtains of the bed were drawn aside by a strange figure.

"Are you the spirit, sir, whose coming was foretold to me?"

"I am!"

"Who and what are you?"

"I am the ghost of Christmas past."

"Long past?"

"No. Your past."

"What brings you here?"

"Your welfare. Rise and walk with me."

"I am a mortal and liable to fall."

"Bear but a touch of my hand there," said the Spirit, laying it upon his heart, "and you shall be upheld in more than this."

As the words were spoken, they passed through the wall, and stood in the busy thoroughfares of the city. It was made plain enough by the dressing of the shops that here, too, it was Christmas time.

The ghost stopped at a certain warehouse door, and asked Scrooge if he knew it.

"Know it! I was apprenticed here!"

They went in. At sight of an old gentleman in a Welsh wig, Scrooge cried in great excitement, "Why, it's old Fezziwig! Bless his heart, it's Fezziwig, alive again!"

Old Fezziwig laid down his pen, and looked up at the clock which pointed to the hour of seven. He rubbed his hands; adjusted his capacious waistcoat; laughed all over himself, from his shoes to his organ of benevolence; and called out in a comfortable, oily, rich, fat jovial voice: "Yoho, there! Ebenezer! Dick!"

A living and moving picture of Scrooge's former self, a young man, came briskly in, accompanied by his fellow-'prentice.

"Yoho, my boys!" said Fezziwig. "No more work to-night. Christmas eve, Dick. Christmas, Ebenezer! Let's have the shutters up, before a man can say Jack Robinson! Clear away, my lads, and let's have lots of room here!"

Clear away! There was nothing they wouldn't have cleared away, with old Fezziwig looking on. It was done in a minute. Every movable was packed off, as if it were dismissed from public life forevermore; the floor was swept and watered, the lamps were trimmed, fuel was heaped upon the fire; and the warehouse was as snug and warm and dry and bright a ball-room as you would desire to see upon a winter's night.

In came a fiddler with a music-book, and went up to the lofty desk, and made an orchestra of it, and tuned like fifty stomach aches. In came Mrs. Fezziwig, one vast substantial smile. In came the three Miss Fezziwigs, beaming and lovable. In came the six young followers whose hearts they broke. In came all the young men and women employed in the business. In came the housemaid, with her cousin the baker. In came the cook, with her brother's particular friend the milkman. In they all came one after another; some shyly, some boldly, some gracefully, some awkwardly, some pushing, some pulling; in they all came, anyhow and everyhow. Away they all went, twenty couples at once; hands half round and back again the other way; down the middle and up again; round and round in various stages of affectionate grouping; old top couple always turning up in the wrong place; new top couple starting off again as soon as they got there; all top couples at last, and not a bottom one to help them. When this result was brought about, old Fezziwig, clapping his hands to stop the dance, cried out, "Well done!" and the fiddler plunged his hot face into a pot of porter especially provided for that purpose.

There were more dances and there were forfeits, and more dances, and there was cake, and there was a great piece of Cold Roast, and there was a great piece of Cold Boiled, and there were mince-pies, and plenty of beer. But the great effect of the evening came when they struck up "Sir Roger de Coverley." Then old Fezziwig stood out to dance with Mrs. Fezziwig. Top couple, too; with a good stiff piece of work cut out for them; three or four and twenty pair of partners; people who were not to be trifled with; people who *would* dance, and had no notion of walking.

But if they had been twice as many,—four times,—old Fezziwig would have been a match for them and so would Mrs. Fezziwig. As to *her*, she was worthy to be his partner in every sense of the term. A positive light seemed to issue from Fezziwig's calves. They shone in every part of the dance. You couldn't have predicted, at any time, what would become of them next. And when old Fezziwig and Mrs. Fezziwig had gone through the dance,—advance and retire, turn your partner, bow and curtsey, corkscrew, thread the needle and back again to your place,—Fezziwig "cut" so deftly, that he appeared to wink with his legs.

When the clock struck eleven this domestic ball broke up. Mr. and Mrs. Fezziwig took their stations on either side of the door, and, shaking hands with every person individually as he or she went out, wished him or her a Merry Christmas. When everybody had retired but the two 'prentices, they did the same to them; and thus the cheerful voices died away, and the lads were left to their beds, which were under a counter in the back shop.

"A small matter," said the ghost, "to make these silly folks so full of gratitude. He has spent but a few pounds of your mortal money; three or four, perhaps. Is that so much that he deserves this praise?"

"It isn't that," said Scrooge, "it isn't that, Spirit. He has the power to render us happy or unhappy; to make our service light or burdensome; a pleasure or a toil. Say that his power lies in words and looks; in things so light and insignificant that it is impossible to add and count them up: what then? The happiness is as great as though it cost a fortune."

He felt the Spirit's glance, and stopped.

"What is the matter?"

"Nothing in particular. I should like to be able to say a word or two to my clerk just now. That's all."

"My time grows short, quick!"

This was not addressed to Scrooge, or to anyone whom he could see, for he immediately found himself in his own bedroom. He had barely time to reel to bed before he sank into a heavy sleep.

Scrooge awoke in his own bedroom. There was no doubt of that. But it and his own adjoining sitting-room, into which he shuffled in his slippers, were brilliant with a great light, and in easy state upon a couch there sat a Giant glorious to see, who bore a glowing torch, in shape not unlike Plenty's horn, and who raised it high to shed its light on Scrooge as he came peeping round the door.

"Come in—come in! and know me better, man. I am the Ghost of Christmas Present. Look upon me!"

"Spirit, conduct me where you will. I went forth last night on compulsion, and I learnt a lesson which is working now. To-night, if you have aught to teach me, let me profit by it."

"Touch my robe!"

Scrooge did as he was told, and held it fast.

The room and its contents vanished instantly, and they stood in the city streets upon a snowy Christmas morning.

Scrooge and the Ghost passed on, invisible, straight to Scrooge's clerk; and on the threshold of the door the Spirit smiled, and stopped to bless Bob Cratchit's dwelling with the sprinkling of the torch. Think of that! Bob had but fifteen "bob" a week himself; he pocketed on Saturdays but fifteen copies of his Christian name; and yet the Ghost of Christmas Present blessed his four-roomed house!

Then up rose Mrs. Cratchit, dressed out but poorly in a twice-turned gown, but brave in ribbons, which are cheap and make a goodly show for sixpence; and she laid the cloth assisted by Belinda Cratchit, second of her daughters, also brave in ribbons; while Master Peter Cratchit plunged a fork into the saucepan of potatoes. Two smaller Cratchits, boy and girl, came tearing in, screaming that outside the baker's they had smelt the goose, and known it for their own; and, basking in luxurious thoughts of sage and onion, these young Cratchits danced about the table.

"What has ever got your precious father?" said Mrs. Cratchit. "And your brother, Tiny Tim! And Martha warn't as late last Christmas Day by half an hour!"

"Here's Martha, mother! Hurrah, there's such a goose, Martha!"

"Why, bless your heart alive, my dear, how late you are!"

"We'd a deal of work to finish up last night, and had to clear away this morning, mother."

"Well, never mind, so long as you are come. Sit ye down before the fire, my dear, and have a warm, God bless ye!"

"No, no! There's father coming home from church," cried the two young Cratchits. "Hide, Martha, hide!"

So Martha hid herself, and in came little Bob, the father, with at least three feet of comforter, exclusive of the fringe, hanging down before him; and his threadbare clothes darned up and brushed, to look seasonable; and Tiny Tim upon his shoulder. Alas for Tiny Tim, he bore a little crutch, and had his limbs supported by an iron frame!

"Why, where's our Martha?"

"Not coming!"

"Not coming?"

"No!"

"Not coming upon Christmas Day!"

Martha did not like to see him disappointed, if it were only a joke; so she came out prematurely from behind the closet door, and ran into his arms, while the two young Cratchits hustled Tiny Tim, and bore him off into the wash-house, that he might hear the pudding singing in the copper.

"And how did little Tim behave?" said Mrs. Cratchit.

"As good as gold, and better!"

His active little crutch was heard upon the floor, and back came Tiny Tim before another word was spoken.

And now all set to work with a will to get dinner ready. Mrs. Cratchit made the gravy hissing hot; Master Peter mashed the potatoes with incredible vigor; Miss Belinda sweetened up the apple-sauce; Martha dusted the hot plates; the two young Cratchits set chairs for everybody. At last the dishes were set on and grace was said. It was succeeded by a breathless pause, as Mrs. Cratchit, looking slowly all along the carving knife, prepared to plunge it into the breast; but when she did, and when the long-expected gush of stuffing issued forth, one murmur of delight arose all round the board, and even Tiny Tim, excited by the two young Cratchits, beat on the table with the handle of his knife, and feebly cried, Hurrah!

There never was such a goose. Its tenderness and flavor, size and cheapness, were the themes of universal admiration. Eked out by apple-sauce and mashed potatoes, it was a sufficient dinner for the whole family; indeed, as Mrs. Cratchit said with great delight (surveying one small atom of a bone upon the dish), they hadn't ate it all at last! Yet every one had had enough, and the youngest Cratchits in particular were steeped in sage and onions to the eyebrows. But now, the plates being changed by Miss Belinda, Mrs. Cratchit left the room alone, —too nervous to bear witnesses,—to take the pudding up and bring it in.

Suppose it should not be done enough! Suppose it should break in the turning out! Suppose somebody should have got over the wall of the back yard, and stolen it, while they were merry with the goose,—a supposition at which the two young Cratchits became livid! All sorts of horrors were supposed.

Hallo! A great deal of steam! The pudding was out of the copper. A smell like a washing-day! That was the cloth. A smell like an eating-house and a pastry-cook's next door to each other, with a laundress next door to that! That was the pudding! In half a minute Mrs. Cratchit entered,—flushed but smiling proudly,—with the pudding, like a speckled cannon ball, so hard and firm, blazing in half of half a quartern of ignited brandy, and bedight with Christmas holly stuck into the top.

O, a wonderful pudding! Bob Cratchit said, and calmly too, that he regarded it as the greatest success achieved by Mrs. Cratchit since their marriage. Mrs. Cratchit said that now the weight was off her mind she would confess she had had her doubts about the quantity of flour. Everybody had something to say about it, but nobody thought it was at all a small pudding for a large family. Any Cratchit would have blushed to hint at such a thing.

At last the dinner was done, the cloth was cleared, the hearth swept, and the fire made up. Then all the family drew around the hearth, in what Bob Cratchit called a circle. Then Bob proposed:

"A merry Christmas to us all, my dears. God bless us!"

Which all the family re-echoed.

"God bless us every one!" said Tiny Tim, the last of all.

Scrooge raised his head speedily on hearing his own name.

"Mr. Scrooge!" said Bob: "I'll give you Mr. Scrooge, the Founder of the Feast!"

"The Founder of the Feast indeed!" cried Mrs. Cratchit, reddening.

"My dear, the children! Christmas Day!"

"I'll drink his health for your sake and the day's, not for his. Long life to him! A merry Christmas and a happy New Year!"

The mention of the name cast a dark shadow on the party, which was not dispelled for full five minutes. After it had passed away, they were ten times merrier than before, from mere relief.

It was a great surprise to Scrooge, as this scene vanished, to hear a hearty laugh. It was a much greater surprise to Scrooge to recognize it as his own nephew's, and to find himself in a bright, dry, gleaming room, with the Spirit standing smiling at his side, and looking at the same nephew.

"He said that Christmas was a humbug, as I live! He believed it, too."

"More shame for him, Fred!" said Scrooge's niece, indignantly.

"He's a comical old fellow, that's the truth; and not so pleasant as he might be. However, his offences carry their own punishment, and I have nothing to say against him. Who suffers by his ill whims? Himself, always! He won't come and dine with us. What's the consequence? He don't lose much of a dinner."

"Indeed, I think he loses a very good dinner!" said Scrooge's niece. Everybody else said the same, and they must be allowed to be competent judges, because they had just had dinner, and were clustered round the fire by lamplight.

Then there was music, and after the music there were games, and Scrooge's nephew proposed a game called Yes and No, where Scrooge's nephew had to think of something, and the rest must find out what, he answering to their questions only yes or no, as the case was. The fire of questioning to which he was exposed elicited from him that he was thinking of an animal, a live animal, rather a disagreeable animal, a savage animal, an animal that growled and grunted sometimes, and talked sometimes, and lived in London, and walked about the streets, and wasn't made a show of, and wasn't led by anybody, and didn't live in a menagerie, and was never killed in a market, and was not a horse, or an ass, or a cow, or a bull, or a tiger, or a dog, or a pig, or a cat, or a bear. At every new question put to him, this nephew burst into a fresh roar of laughter, and was so inexpressibly tickled that he was obliged to get up off the sofa and stamp. At last one cried out:

"I have found it! I know what it is, Fred! I know what it is."

"What is it?"

"It's your uncle Scro-o-o-ge!"

Which it certainly was. Admiration was the universal sentiment, though some objected that the reply to "Is it a bear?" ought to have been "Yes."

Uncle Scrooge had imperceptibly become so gay and light of heart that he would have drunk to the company in an inaudible speech. But the whole scene passed off in the breath of the last word spoken by his nephew, and he and the Spirit were again upon their travels.

Suddenly, as they stood together in an open place, the bell struck twelve and Scrooge was alone. He saw the Ghost no more.

As the last stroke of twelve ceased to vibrate, Scrooge beheld a solemn Phantom, draped and hooded, coming like a mist along the ground towards him.

"Lead on! lead on! The night is waning fast, and it is precious time to me, I know. Lead on, Ghost of Christmas Yet To Come!"

They scarcely seemed to enter the city; for the city rather seemed to spring up about them. But there they were in the heart of it; on 'Change, amongst the merchants.

The spirit stopped beside one little group of business men. Scrooge advanced and listened.

"No," said a fat man, "I don't know much about it either way. I only know he is dead."

"When did he die?"

"Last night, I believe."

"Why, what was the matter with him? I thought he'd never die!"

"God knows," said the fat man with a yawn.

"What has he done with his money?"

"I haven't heard; company, perhaps. He hasn't left it to me. That's all I know. By, by!"

They left this busy scene, and went into an obscure part of town, to a low shop where iron, old rags, bottles were bought. A gray-haired rascal of great age sat smoking his pipe.

Scrooge and the Phantom came into the presence of this man just as a woman with a heavy bundle slunk into the shop. But she had scarcely entered, when another woman, similarly laden, came in too; and she was closely followed by a man in faded black.

They all three burst out laughing and the first to enter cried: "Let the charwoman alone to be the first; let the laundress alone to be the second; and let the undertaker's man alone to be the third. Look here, old Joe, here's a chance! If we haven't all three met here without meaning it!"

"What have you got to sell?"

"What odds then! what odds, Mrs. Dilber?" said the other

woman. "Every person has a right to take care of himself. *He* always did! Who's the worse for the loss of a few things like these? Not a dead man, I suppose."

"No, indeed, ma'am."

"If he wanted to keep 'em after he was dead, a wicked old screw, why wasn't he natural in his life-time? If he had been, he'd have had somebody to look after him when he was struck with Death, instead of lying gasping out his last there, alone by himself."

"It's the truest word that ever was spoke, it's a judgment on him."

"Open that bundle, Joe, and let me know the value of it."

Joe went down on his knees for the greater convenience of opening the bundle, and dragged out a large and heavy roll of some dark stuff.

"What do you call this? Bed-curtains!"

"Ah! Bed-curtains! Don't drop that oil upon the blankets, now."

"*His* blankets?"

"Whose else do you think? He isn't likely to take cold without 'em, I dare say."

Scrooge listened to this dialogue in horror.

"Spirit, I see, I see. The case of this unhappy man might be my own. My life ends that way, now. Merciful Heaven, what is this!"

The scene changed, and now he almost touched a bare, uncurtained bed. On it, unwatched, unwept, uncared for, was the body of this plundered, unknown man.

"Spirit, let me see some tenderness connected with death, or this dark chamber, Spirit, will be forever present to me."

The Ghost conducted him to poor Bob Cratchit's house,—the dwelling he had visited before,—and found the mother and children seated around the fire.

Quiet. Very quiet. The noisy little Cratchits were as still as statues in one corner, and sat looking up at Peter, who had a book before him. The mother and her daughters were engaged in needlework. But surely they were very quiet!

" 'And he took a child and set him in the midst of them.' "

Where had Scrooge heard those words? He had not dreamed them. The boy must have read them out, as he and the Spirit crossed the threshold. Why did he not go on?

The mother laid her work upon the table and put her hand up to her face.

"The color hurts my eyes," she said.

The color? Ah, poor Tiny Tim!

"I wouldn't show weak eyes to your father when he comes home for the world. It must be near his time."

"Past it rather," Peter answered, shutting up his book. "But I think he has walked a little slower than he used, these last few evenings."

"I have known him walk with—I have known him walk with Tiny Tim upon his shoulder, very fast indeed."

"And so have I, often!"

"But he was very light to carry, and his father loved him so that it was no trouble—no trouble. And there is your father at the door."

She hurried out to meet him; and little Bob and his comforter—he had need of it, poor fellow—came in. His tea was ready for him on the hob, and they all tried who should help him to it most. Then the two young Cratchits got upon his knees and laid each child a little cheek against his face, as if they said, "Don't mind it, father. Don't be grieved!"

Bob was very cheerful with them, and spoke pleasantly to all the family. He looked at the work upon the table, and praised the industry and speed of Mrs. Cratchit and the girls. They would be done long before Sunday.

"Sunday! You went to-day, then, Robert?"

"Yes, my dear, I wish you could have gone. It would have done you good to see how green a place it is. But you'll see it often. I promised him I would walk there on a Sunday. My little child!"

He broke down all at once.

"Spectre," said Scrooge, "something informs me that our parting moment is at hand. I know it, but I do not know how. Tell me what man that was, with the covered face, whom we saw lying dead?"

The Ghost of Chrismas Yet To Come conveyed him to a dismal, wretched, ruinous churchyard.

The Spirit stood among the graves, and pointed down to One.

Scrooge crept toward it, trembling as he went; and, following the finger, read upon the stone of the neglected grave his own name,—EBENEZER SCROOGE.

"Am I that man who lay upon the bed? No, Spirit! O no, no! Spirit! hear me! I am not the man I was. I will not be the man I must have been but for this intercourse. Why show me this if I am past all hope? Assure me that I yet may change these shadows you have shown me by an altered life. O tell me I may sponge away the writing on this stone!"

Holding up his hands in one last prayer to have his fate reversed, he saw an alteration in the Phantom's hood and dress. It shrunk, collapsed, and dwindled down into a bedpost. Yes, and the bedpost was his own, the room was his own. Best and happiest of all, the Time before him was his own, to make amends in! The church bells were ringing out the lustiest peals he had ever heard. Running to the window, he opened it, and put his head out. No fog, no mist, no night; clear, bright, stirring, golden day.

"What's to-day?" cried Scrooge, calling downward to a boy

in Sunday clothes, who perhaps had loitered in to look about him.

"Eh?"

"What's to-day, my fine fellow?"

"To-day! Why, Christmas Day!"

"It's Christmas Day! I haven't missed it. Hallo, my fine fellow!"

"Hallo!"

"Do you know the poulterer's, in the next street but one, at the corner?"

"I should hope I did."

"An intelligent boy! A remarkable boy! Do you know whether they have sold the prize turkey that was hanging up there? Not the little prize turkey,—the big one?"

"What, the one as big as me?"

"What a delightful boy! It's a pleasure to talk to him. Yes, my buck!"

"It's hanging there now."

"Is it? Go and buy it, and tell 'em to bring it here, that I may give them the direction where to take it. Come back with the man and I'll give you a shilling. Come back with him in less than five minutes and I'll give you half a crown!"

The boy was off like a shot.

"I'll send it to Bob Cratchit's! He sha'n't know who sends it. It's twice the size of Tiny Tim!"

The hand in which he wrote the address was not a steady one; but write it he did, somehow, and went down stairs to open the street door, ready for the coming of the turkey.

It *was* a turkey! He never could have stood upon his legs, that bird. He would have snapped 'em short off in a minute, like sticks of sealing wax.

Scrooge dressed himself "all in his best," and at last got out into the streets. The people were by this time pouring forth,

A CHRISTMAS CAROL

and walking with his hands behind him, Scrooge regarded every one with a delighted smile. He looked so irresistibly pleasant that three or four good-humored fellows said, "Good morning, sir! A merry Christmas to you!" And Scrooge said often afterwards, that, of all the blithe sounds he had ever heard, those were the blithest in his ears.

In the afternoon he turned his steps towards his nephew's house. He passed the door a dozen times before he had the courage to go up and knock. But he made a dash and did it.

"Is your master at home, my dear?"

"Yes, sir."

"Where is he, my love?"

"He's in the dining-room, sir, along with mistress."

"He knows me and I'll step right in there, my dear.—Fred!"

"Why, bless my soul, who's that?"

"It's I, your uncle Scrooge. I have come to dinner. Will you let me in?"

Let him in! It is a mercy he didn't shake his arm off. Nothing could be heartier. His niece looked just the same. So did every one else. Wonderful party, wonderful games, wonderful unanimity, won-derful happiness!

But he was early at the office the next morning. O, he was early there. If he could only be there first and catch Bob Cratchit coming late! That was the thing he had set his heart upon.

And he did it. The clock struck nine. No Bob. A quarter past. No Bob. Bob was full eighteen minutes and a half behind the time. Scrooge sat with his door wide open, that he might see him come in. Bob's hat was off before he opened the door, his comforter too. He was on his stool in a jiffy, driving away with his pen, as if he were trying to overtake Nine O'clock.

"Hallo!" growled Scrooge, in his accustomed voice, as near

as he could feign it. "What do you mean by coming here at this time of the day?"

"I am sorry, sir, I am behind my time."

"You are? Yes. I think you are. Step this way, if you please."

"It's only once a year, sir. It shall not be repeated. I was making rather merry yesterday, sir."

"Now, I'll tell you what, my friend. I am not going to stand this sort of thing any longer. And therefore," Scrooge continued, leaping from his stool and giving Bob such a dig in the waistcoat that he staggered back into the tank again,—"and therefore I am about to raise your salary!"

Bob trembled.

"A merry Christmas, Bob! A merry Christmas, Bob, my good fellow, merrier than I have given you for many a year! I'll raise your salary, and endeavor to assist your struggling family, and we will discuss your affairs this very afternoon, over a Christmas bowl of smoking bishop, Bob! Make up the fires, and buy a second coal-scuttle before you dot another i, Bob Cratchit!"

Scrooge was better than his word. He did all and infinitely more; and to Tiny Tim who did *not* die, he became a second father. He became as good a friend, as good a master, and as good a man as the good old city knew, or any other good old city, town, or borough in the good old world. Some people laughed to see the alteration in him; but his own heart laughed, and that was quite enough for him.

It was always said of him, that he knew how to keep Christmas well if any man alive possessed the knowledge.

May that be truly said of us, and all of us! And so, as Tiny Tim observed, God Bless Us, Every One!

Abridged.

THE END OF THE PLAY

William Makepeace Thackeray

The play is done—the curtain drops,
    Slow falling to the prompter's bell;
A moment yet the actor stops,
    And looks around, to say farewell.
It is an irksome word and task;
    And when he's laughed and said his say,
He shows, as he removes the mask,
    A face that's anything but gay.

One word, ere yet the evening ends:
    Let's close it with a parting rhyme,
And pledge a hand to all young friends,
    As fits the merry Christmas time;
On life's wide scene you, too, have parts,
    That fate ere long shall bid you play;
Good-night!—with honest gentle hearts
    A kindly greeting go alway!

Good-night!—I'd say the griefs, the joys,
    Just hinted in this mimic page,
The triumphs and defeats of boys,
    Are but repeated in our age;
I'd say your woes were not less keen,
    Your hopes more vain, than those of **men**,
Your pangs or pleasures of fifteen
    At forty-five played o'er again.

I'd say we suffer and we strive
    Not less nor more as men than **boys**,
With grizzled beards at forty-five,
    As erst at twelve in corduroys,
And if, in time of sacred youth,

We learned at home to love and pray,
Pray heaven that early love and truth
    May never wholly pass away.

And in the world, as in the school,
    I'd say how fate may change and shift,
The prize be sometimes with the fool,
    The race not always to the swift;
The strong may yield, the good may fall,
    The great man be a vulgar clown
The knave be lifted over all,
    The kind cast pitilessly down.

Who knows the inscrutable design?
    Blessed be he who took and gave!
Why should your mother, Charles, not mine,
    Be weeping at her darling's grave?
We bow to heaven that willed it so,
    That darkly rules the face of all,
That sends the respite or the blow,
    That's free to give or to recall.

This crowns his feast with wine and wit—
    Who brought him to that mirth and state?
His betters, see, below him sit,
    Or hunger hopeless at the gate.
Who bade the mud from Dives' wheel
    To spurn the rags of Lazarus?
Come, brother, in that dust we'll kneel,
    Confessing heaven that ruled it thus.

So each shall mourn, in life's advance,
    Dear hopes, dear friends, untimely killed,
Shall grieve for many a forfeit chance,
    And longing passion unfulfilled.
Amen!—whatever fate be sent,

Pray God the heart may kindly glow,
Although the head with cares be bent,
And whitened with the winter snow.

Come wealth or want, come good or ill,
Let young and old accept their part,
And bow before the awful will,
And bear it with an honest heart.
Who misses or who wins the prize—
Go, lose or conquer as you can;
But if you fail, or if you rise,
Be each, pray God, a gentleman.

A gentleman, or old or young!
(Bear kindly with my humble lays;)
The sacred chorus first was sung
Upon the first of Christmas days;
The shepherds heard it overhead—
The joyful angels raised it then:
Glory to heaven on high, it said,
And peace on earth to gentle men!

My song, save this, is little worth;
I lay the weary pen aside,
And wish you health, and love, and mirth,
As fits the solemn Christmas-tide.
As fits the holy Christmas birth,
Be this, good friends, our carol still:
Be peace on earth, be peace on earth,
To men of gentle will.

ODE TO THE WEST WIND
Percy Bysshe Shelley

I

O, wild West Wind, thou breath of Autumn's being,
Thou, from whose unseen presence the leaves dead
Are driven, like ghosts from an enchanter fleeing,

Yellow, and black, and pale, and hectic red,
Pestilence-stricken multitudes: O, thou,
Who chariotest to their dark wintry bed

The winged seeds, where they lie cold and low,
Each like a corpse within its grave, until
Thine azure sister of the spring shall blow

Her clarion o'er the dreaming earth, and fill
(Driving sweet buds like flocks to feed in air)
With living hues and odors plain and hill:

Wild Spirit, which art moving everywhere;
Destroyer and preserver; hear, O, hear!

II

Thou on whose stream, 'mid the steep sky's commotion,
Loose clouds like earth's decaying leaves are shed,
Shook from the tangled boughs of Heaven and Ocean,

Angels of rain and lightning: there are spread
On the blue surface of thine airy surge,
Like the bright hair uplifted from the head

Of some fierce Mænad, even from the dim verge
Of the horizon to the zenith's height
The locks of the approaching storm. Thou dirge

ODE TO THE WEST WIND

Of the dying year, to which this closing night
Will be the dome of a vast sepulcher,
Vaulted with all thy congregated might

Of vapors, from whose solid atmosphere
Black rain, and fire, and hail will burst: O hear!

III

Thou who didst waken from his summer dreams
The blue Mediterranean, where he lay,
Lulled by the coil of his crystalline streams,

Besides a pumice isle in Baiæ's Bay.
And saw in sleep old palaces and towers
Quivering within the wave's intenser day,

All overgrown with azure moss and flowers
So sweet, the sense faints picturing them! Thou
For whose path the Atlantic's level powers

Cleave themselves into chasms, while far below
The sea-blooms and the oozy woods which wear
The sapless foliage of the ocean, know

Thy voice, and suddenly grow gray with fear,
And tremble and despoil themselves: O hear!

IV

If I were a dead leaf thou mightest bear;
If I were a swift cloud to fly with thee;
A wave to pant beneath thy power, and share

The impulse of thy strength, only less free
Than thou, O, uncontrollable! If even
I were as in my boyhood, and could be

The comrade of thy wanderings over heaven,
As then, when to outstrip thy skiey speed
Scarce seemed a vision; I would ne'er have striven

As thus with thee in prayer in my sore need.
Oh! Lift me as a wave, a leaf, a cloud!
I fall upon the thorns of life! I bleed!

A heavy weight of hours has chained and bowed
One too like thee: tameless, and swift, and proud.

V

Make me thy lyre, even as the forest is:
What if my leaves are falling like its own!
The tumult of thy mighty harmonies

Will take from both a deep, autumnal tone,
Sweet though in sadness. Be thou, spirit fierce,
My spirit! Be thou me, impetuous one!

Drive my dead thoughts over the universe
Like withered leaves to quicken a new birth!
And, by the incantation of this verse,

Scatter, as from an unextinguished hearth
Ashes and sparks, my words among mankind!
Be through my lips to unawakened earth

The trumpet of a prophecy! O, wind,
If Winter comes, can Spring be far behind?

A MAN'S A MAN FOR A' THAT

Robert Burns

Is there, for honest poverty,
   That hings his head, an' a' that?

The coward slave, we pass him by,
  We dare be poor for a' that!
    For a' that, an' a' that,
      Our toils obscure, an' a' that;
      The rank is but the guinea's stamp;
        The man's the gowd for a' that.

What tho' on hamely fare we dine,
  Wear hodden-gray, an' a' that;
Gie fools their silks, and knaves their wine,
  A man's a man for a' that.
    For a' that, an' a' that,
      Their tinsel show, an' a' that,
      The honest man, tho' e'er sae poor,
        Is king o' men for a' that.

You see yon birkie, ca'd a lord,
  Wha struts, an' stares, an' a' that;
Tho' hundreds worship at his word,
  He's but a coof for a' that.
    For a' that, an' a' that,
      His riband, star, an' a' that,
      The man o' independent mind,
        He looks and laughs at a' that.

A prince can mak a belted knight,
  A marquis, duke, an a' that;
But an honest man's aboon his might,
  Guid faith he mauna fa' that!
    For a' that, an' a' that,
      Their dignities, an' that,
      The pith o' sense, an' pride o' worth,
        Are higher rank than a' that.

Then let us pray that come it may,
  As come it will for a' that,

That sense and worth, o'er a' the earth,
   May bear the gree, an' a' that.
      For a' that, an' a' that,
         It's coming yet, for a' that,
      That man to man, the warld o'er,
         Shall brothers be for a' that.

From THE RUBÁIYÁT OF OMAR KHAYYÁM
Edward Fitzgerald

Why, if the Soul can fling the dust aside,
And naked on the air of Heaven ride,
   Wer't not a shame—wer't not a shame for him
In this clay carcase crippled to abide?

'Tis but a tent where takes his one-day's rest
A Sultan to the realm of Death addrest;
   The Sultan rises, and the dark Ferrash
Strikes, and prepares it for another guest.

And fear not lest existence closing your
Account, and mine, should know the like no more;
   The Eternal Saki from that bowl has poured
Millions of bubbles like us, and will pour.

When you and I behind the veil are past,
Oh, but the long, long while the world shall last,
   Which of our coming and departure heeds
As the Seven Seas should heed a pebble-cast.

A moment's halt—a momentary taste
Of Being from the well amid the waste—
   And lo!—the phantom caravan has reached
The Nothing it set out from— Oh, make haste!

The Moving Finger writes; and, having writ,
Moves on: nor all your Piety nor Wit

Shall lure it back to cancel half a Line
Nor all your Tears wash out a Word of it.

. . . . .

Yet ah, that Spring should vanish with the rose!
That Youth's sweet-scented manuscript should close!
    The nightingale that in the branches sang,
Ah, whence, and whither flown again, who knows!

Would but the desert of the fountain yield
One glimpse—if dimly, yet indeed, revealed,
    To which the fainting traveler might spring,
As springs the trampled herbage of the field!

Would but some winged Angel ere too late
Arrest the yet unfolded roll of fate,
    And make the stern Recorder otherwise
Enregister, or quite obliterate!

Ah, Love! could you and I with him conspire
To grasp this sorry Scheme of Things entire,
    Would not we shatter it to bits—and then
Re-mold it nearer to the heart's desire!

BY THE WAY [1]

Hamilton Wright Mabie

How much of what is best and pleasantest in life comes to us by the way! The artist forms great plans and sets about great achievements, but when he comes to the hour of realization he discovers that the personal reward has come mainly by the way. The applause of which he dreamed, the fame for which he hoped, bring small satisfaction; the joy of the work was largely in the doing of it, and was taken in the long days of toil and the

[1] From *My Study Fire*, by Hamilton Wright Mabie. Reprinted by permission of the publishers, Dodd, Mead and Company, Inc.

brief times of rest which were part of the great undertaking. To the man or woman who looks forward from the heights of youth life seems to be an artistic whole, which can be completely shaped by the will, and wrought out with perfection of detail in the repose and silence of the workshop. In that glowing time the career of a great man appears to be so symmetrical, so rounded, so complete, that it seems to be a veritable work of art, thought out and executed without hindrance, and with the co-operation of all the great forces. Nights of rest and days of work, uninterrupted and cumulative, with bursts of applause widening and deepening as the years go by, with fame adding note after note to her hymn of praise,—is not this the dream of young ambition as it surveys the field from the place of preparation?

The ideal is not an ignoble one, but it falls far short of the great reality in range and effort. There is an artistic harmony in a great life; but it is not a conscious beauty deliberately evoked by a free hand bent only on the illustration of its skill; it is a beauty born of pain, self-sacrifice, and arduous surrender to the stern conditions of success. A bit of fancy lightly inspires the singer, and as lightly borrows the wings of verse; a great vision of the imagination demands years and agonies. A bit of verse, such as serves for the small currency of poetry, runs off the pen on a convenient scrap of paper; a great poem involves a deep movement of human life,—something vast, profound, mysterious. A great life is a work of art of that noble order in which a man surrenders himself to the creative impulse, and becomes the instrument of a mightier thought and passion than he consciously originates. There is a deep sense in which we make our careers, but there is a deeper sense in which our careers are made for us. The greater the man the greater the influences that play upon him and centre in him; it is more a question of what he shall receive than of what he shall do.

His life-work is wrought out in no well-appointed *atelier,* barred against intrusion, enfolded in silence; the task must be accomplished in the great arena of the world, jostled by crowds, beaten upon by storms, broken in upon by all manner of interruptions. The artist does not stand apart from his work, surveying its progress from hour to hour, and with a skilful hand bringing his thought in ever clearer view; for the work is done, not by, but within him; his aspiring soul, passionate heart, and eager mind are the substance upon which the tools of the graver work. Death and care, disease and poverty, do not wait afar off, awed by greatness and enthralled by genius; the door is always open to them, and they are often familiar companions. The work of a great life is always accomplished with toil, self-sacrifice, and with incessant intrusions from without; it is often accomplished amid bitter sorrows and under the pressure of relentless misfortune.

Yet these things, that break in upon the artistic mood and play havoc with the artistic poise, make the life-work immeasurably nobler and richer; the reality differs from the ideal of youth in being vaster, and therefore more difficult and painful of attainment. The easy achievement, always well in hand, and executed in the quiet of reposeful hours, gives place to the sublime accomplishment wrought out amid the uproar of the world and under the pressure of the sorrow and anguish which are a part of every human lot. The toil is intense, prolonged, and painful because it is to be imperishable; there is a divine element in it, and the work takes on a form of immortality. The little time which falls to the artist here is inadequate to the greatness of his task; the applause, small or great, which accompanies his toil is but a momentary and imperfect recognition of what has been done with strength and beauty. It is pleasant when men see what one has done, but the real satisfaction is the consciousness that something worthy of being seen has been accomplished. The rewards of great living are not external things, withheld until the crowning hour of success arrives; they come by the way,—in the consciousness of growing power and worth, of duties nobly met, and work thoroughly done. To the true artist, working always in humility and sincerity, all life is a reward, and every day brings a deeper satisfaction. Joy and peace are by the way.

Appendix A

SYLLABUS FOR A COLLEGE COURSE IN INTERPRETATIVE READING

> Shared experience is the greatest of human goods.
> *John Dewey*

> Genuinely to share at one's best level is to be what the physicians call healthy, the economists secure, the educators understanding, and the psychiatrists mature.[1]
> *Jerome Nathanson*

OBJECTIVES   This course is planned to help the student to develop:
1. The ability to interpret the meaning of literature and to communicate it to an audience.
2. Understanding of basic principles of art and their application to the oral interpretation of literature.
3. Creative thinking through vicariously experiencing literature.
4. Habits of intelligent and appreciative listening.
5. The ability to evaluate his own work and that of his classmates; to give and to take constructive criticism.
6. Freedom and balance through emotional awareness and control.
7. A basis for more effective living through:
    (a) habits of reading for erudition, adjustment, and enjoyment.
    (b) skills for vocational effectiveness in a business or profession.
    (c) skills for worthy use of leisure time.

INTRODUCTION   For adequate progress in interpretative reading the student must work for both erudition and adjustment. Erudition may be thought of as knowledge plus awareness, information plus understanding, learning so assimilated that it seems a part of one's natural endowment.

Erudition in interpretative reading is developed through class experiences, study of the textbook, observation, parallel reading, and listening, and through appraising these experiences in written and oral reports.

---

[1] Jerome Nathanson, "John Dewey: American Radical," *The Nation,* October 22, 1949. Vol. 169, p. 392.

Adjustment in interpretative reading is adjustment to the total speech situation. It is sometimes called skill, which according to the dictionary is "the ability to use one's knowledge effectively."

Adjustment, or skill, is developed through practice guided by sound principles. Some of this practice will take place during the class hour; much of it should be outside of class in preparation for class experiences. New ways should be mastered for personal enrichment as well as for effective reading. One may feel foolish reading aloud to an imaginary audience, yet sincere practice when one is alone can pay big dividends. The student is fortunate who finds someone to listen to his practice: a child, wife, husband, parent, or friend. Students in one university found it rewarding to read to a blind lady who needed companionship and intellectual stimulation.

PARALLEL READING Freedom of choice in parallel reading and freedom to make one's own selection for oral reading is desirable. Parallel reading should clarify and extend understanding of the principles of the textbook. General order for parallel reading:

I. Books which give understanding of and motivation to the study of literature.
II. Books in oral interpretation, dramatic art, speech fundamentals, voice and diction.
III. Books on aesthetics, philosophy of art, psychology, social science and education.
IV. (*a*) Collections of literature for selection of material for classroom oral reading.
(*b*) Background material for a complete understanding of selections.

WRITTEN REPORTS should be handed in periodically. These reports may be an informal sharing of student response to parallel reading, listening to readers on platform, phonograph, radio, or television.

UNITS FOR CLASS WORK A unit may take a few days or several weeks.

UNIT I: INTRODUCTORY LECTURE AND DISCUSSION

Read and discuss, "Foreword," "To the Student," and Chapter I.

UNIT II: IMAGERY, Chapter II

1. Study the principles and practice the examples.
2. Observe examples of sense perception in everyday experiences. Prepare to tell class about experiences of various types of imagery.

Supplementary: Read chapters on imagery from psychology, literature, dramatic art, etc.

Culmination of Unit: Select a piece of literature from the anthology section of the textbook or from some other source. Analyze it for imagery. Prepare to read it to the class, concentrating on the various types of imagery. Work for successful experience in reading with imagery as a technique of thinking. Observe use of imagery by classmates.

UNIT III: BODILY ACTION, Chapter III

1. Study and practice principles and techniques of bodily action.
2. Observe some person's actions that you may pantomime him. Write:
    (a) Name or descriptive title of person.
    (b) General characteristics observed: build, posture, carriage.
    (c) Mannerisms: Head movements, facial expression, hand gestures, etc.
    (d) Brief outline of pantomime giving details in narrative order.
3. Practice pantomime to retain general characteristics and communicate incident through bodily action.

Supplementary: Read chapters on bodily action in other speech textbooks, psychology, dance, physical education, dramatic art, etc.

Culmination of Unit: Select a piece of literature and analyze it for motor and organic imagery. Prepare to read it with abandon, sensing actions. In the beginning do not be afraid of acting and overdoing as a means to vital reading.

UNIT IV: DRAMATIC TIMING, Chapter IV

1. Study pause, tempo and rhythm as elements of dramatic timing.
2. Practice reading examples in Chapter IV according to instructions.
3. Observe timing elements in everyday life: Prepare to tell class about observations of pause and tempo as related to mood or situation, rhythm of action, rhythm of character, etc.
4. Select passages of literature as illustrations of rhythm of action. Read them with literal actions timing the actions to the words.
5. Practice choral reading, Chapter X.

Supplementary:

1. Listen to phonograph records and analyze elements of timing.
2. Read discussions of elements of timing in textbooks on speech, oral interpretation, dramatic art, English literature, etc.

Culmination of Unit: Select a piece of literature and analyze it for elements of timing, studying the uses of pause, the need of variety in tempo, and the possible use of the five ways of finding and following the rhythm. Practice for class reading and observe how techniques of timing aid in vicarious experience of literature.

UNIT V: STRUCTURE, Chapter V

1. Study and practice: build, topping, contrast, word emphasis as elements of structure.
2. Draw diagrams of builds on paper, the blackboard, in the air as you build practice material.
3. Study sonnets for structure. They are short and the whole may be diagramed to show the relation of parts to the whole.
4. Practice builds and topping with another student, casting scene from "The School for Scandal," observing builds and drops within individual speeches and within portions shared by two characters.
5. Practice choral reading. See "Adding and Subtracting Voices," Chapter X.
6. State the central thought, or dominant unity of poems, scenes, stories, or plays you have read.

Supplementary:

1. Listen to phonograph records and analyze variations in pitch patterns.
2. Read discussions of elements of structure in books on literature, speech, dramatic art, etc.
3. Listen to the radio and observe pitch patterns which are varied and those which are monotonous. (A sports announcer describing a football game builds and drops from eagerness to share vital experiences.)

Culmination of Unit: Select a piece of literature and analyze it for various types in structure, drawing diagrams of builds, octave drops, etc. Underline key words. State in one sentence the central thought or dominant unity. Practice bodily action and timing and observe relation to structure. Concentration on imagery should help you in your reading to give precedence to spirit over form. Do not worry, however, if at first the reading is artificial; you should learn how to avoid artificiality later; your next unit will deal with that problem. This unit emphasizes the development of an oral form in accord with the structure of the writing, and in accord with the life experience suggested.

UNIT VI: ILLUSION, Chapter VI

Study this chapter thoughtfully: Can you recall experiences which illustrate the principles: crystalization, illusion of the first time, restraint with abandon, aesthetic distance?

1. Practice a piece of material you have read for class exercises and capture, if you can, the "illusion of the first time." (Meditate on

APPENDIX 583

the statement of Antoine de Saint Exupery: "Illumination is vision: granted suddenly to the spirit after long and gradual preparation." You will be better able to practice the principles of illusion if you review material read before than if you select new material for this unit. A careful artist gives due attention to form, then, reworks for spontaneity, for the illusion of the first time.)

Supplementary: Re-read Chapter I. Read books on aesthetics, the philosophy of art, the study of literature, etc.

Culmination of Unit: Review the literature you used in the culmination of Units II, III, IV, and V. Practice to apply all techniques studied thus far *plus* the principle of illusion.

UNIT VII: Voice, Chapter VII

1. Study and practice the principles applying all techniques studied thus far. Motor imagery is fundamental to support of tones; organic imagery is fundamental to tone color.
2. Practice choral reading, Chapter X.

Supplementary:

1. Listen to phonograph records and analyze diction and voice characteristics: tone color, melody, etc.
2. Read chapters on voice in other speech textbooks. Analyze your own needs and practice exercises designed to correct your particular faults.

Culmination of Unit: Analyze a piece of literature for tone color, inflection, diction, etc. Practice to read it to the class using all techniques studied including "the illusion of the first time."

UNIT VIII: Backgrounds and Introductions, Chapter IX

1. Read Chapters IX and XI for ideas on selection and arrangement of material.
2. Prepare a piece of literature for class reading.
   (a) Study it carefully and read from whatever sources needed for adequate background.
   (b) Write a paper giving details of study for background.
   (c) Select from this background that which is needed for audience understanding and write an introduction to be given extemporaneously when selection is read to the class.
3. Select a scene from Shakespeare and adapt it for class reading. Read the entire play as background from which ideas for introduction may be taken.

Culmination of Unit: Select several passages of literature which are related in *theme*. Arrange them in an effective order. Write an introduction and write transitions between passages. Suggested themes: peace, love, friendship, immortality, Thanksgiving, Mother's Day, etc.

UNIT IX: INTERPRETATION OF MEANING, Chapter IX

Note: It is obvious that you have been working on the interpretation of meaning since Unit II when you used imagery as a technique of thinking. You are now ready to consider some special problems in interpreting the author's meaning.

1. Study the chapter and the selections for what you think they mean. Look up obscure words in dictionaries and encyclopedias. Write a paper answering these questions:
   (*a*) Which of the two interpretations of the word *glad* (page 203) do you accept, and why?
   (*b*) What is Browning's answer to the question "Fear Death?" Study the entire poem, "Prospice," for the answer.
   (*c*) Write the story of "Meeting at Night" and "Parting at Morning." (There is a precept for effective speech preparation which says, "Think yourself empty; then read yourself full"—think about the author's meaning until you have emptied yourself of all ideas concerning your judgment of his meaning, then read what others have said about it.)
2. Analyze the other material in this chapter and practice for effective communication of meaning.

Culmination of Unit: Select a piece of literature which is challenging because of its profundity. Analyze it for the author's meaning. Write a paper giving details of your method of finding the meaning including interpretations found in notes or commentaries.

UNIT X: PROGRAMS

Monotony can be avoided and student interest sustained by varied programs posted on the bulletin board several weeks in advance. For example:

Scene from Shakespeare (6 minutes)	Mary Brown
Short Story (10 minutes)	John Hughes
Great Poem (8 minutes)	Adrian Hope
Theme Program (10 minutes)	Agnes Allen
Rhythm (3 minutes)	Oliver Walker
Scene from Modern Play (10 minutes)	Marvin Black
Nonsense Poem (3 minutes)	Horace Nolan
Poem of Choice (4 minutes)	James Miller

Appendix B

SUGGESTED MATERIAL FOR SUPPLEMENTARY READING & REFERENCE

ABNEY, Louise, *Choral Speaking Arrangements for High Schools* (Boston: Expression Company, 1937).

ANDERSON, Virgil A., *Training the Speaking Voice* (New York: Oxford University Press, 1942).

BATES, Gladys, and KOY, Helena, *Literature for Interpretation* (Boston: Expression Company, 1939).

BOLESLAVSKI, Richard, *Acting, The First Six Lessons* (New York: Theater Arts Inc., 1933).

BOSWORTH, Halliam, *Technique of Dramatic Art* (New York: The Macmillan Company, 1937).

BROWN, H. A., and HELTMAN, H. J., eds., *Let's Read Together Poems*, (Evanston, Illinois: Row, Peterson and Company, 1949).

BUTCHER, Samuel H., *Aristotle's Theory of Poetry and the Fine Arts* (New York: The Macmillan Company, 1920).

CLARK, S. H., and BABCOCK, M. M., *Interpretation of the Printed Page* (New York: Prentice-Hall, Inc., 1941).

CRAFTON, Allen, and ROYER, Jessica, *Self Expression Through the Spoken Word* (New York: Thomas Y. Crowell Company, 1928).

COMPERE, Moiree, *Living Literature for Oral Interpretation* (New York: Appleton-Century-Crofts, Inc., 1949).

CROCKER, L. G., and EICH, L. M., *Oral Reading* (New York: Prentice-Hall, Inc., 1947).

CROCKER, C., FIELDS, V. A., and BROOMALL, W., *Taking the Stage* (New York: Pitman Publishing Corporation, 1939).

CUNNINGHAM, C. C., *Making Words Come Alive* (Dubuque, Iowa: William C. Brown Company, 1951).

CUNNINGHAM, C. C., *Literature as a Fine Art* (New York: Thomas Nelson and Sons, 1941).

CURRY, S. S., *Browning and the Dramatic Monologue* (Boston: Expression Company, 1908).

CURRY, S. S., *The Province of Expression* (Boston: Expression Company, 1891, 1917).

DARROW, Anne, *Phonetic Study in Folk Speech and Broken English* (Boston: Expression Company, 1937).
DE BANKE, Cecile, *The Art of Choral Speaking* (Boston: Baker's Plays, 1937).
DEWEY, John, *Art as Experience* (New York: Minton, Balch and Company, 1935).
DOLMAN, John, Jr., *The Art of Acting* (New York: Harper and Brothers, 1949).
DOLMAN, John, Jr., *The Art of Play Production* (New York: Harper and Brothers, 1946).
DREW, Alfred, and BARRY, Robinson, *A Commentary on Prose and Verse Speaking* (Boston: Baker's Plays, 1933).
DUDLEY, Louise, *The Study of Literature* (Boston: Houghton Mifflin Company, 1928).
EASTMAN, Max, *The Enjoyment of Poetry* (New York: Charles Scribner's Sons, 1918).
ENFIELD, Gertrude, *Verse Choir Technique* (Boston: Expression Company, 1937).
FAIRBANKS, Grant, *Practical Voice Practice* (New York: Harper and Brothers, 1944).
FARMA, William J., *Prose, Poetry and Drama for Oral Interpretation*, 1st, 2nd Series (New York: Harper and Brothers, 1930, 1936).
FLACCUS, Louis W., *The Spirit and Substance of Art* (New York: Prentice-Hall, Inc., 1938).
FOGERTY, Elsie, *The Speaking of English Verse* (New York: E. P. Dutton and Company, Inc., 1923).
GRIGGS, Edward H., *The Philosophy of Art* (New York: Orchard Hill Press, 1937).
GRIM, Harriet E., *Practical Voice Training* (New York: Appleton-Century-Crofts, Inc., 1948).
GUGGENHEIMER, R. H., *Creative Vision in Artist and Audience* (New York: Harper and Brothers, 1950).
GULLAN, Marjorie, *The Speech Choir* (New York: Harper and Brothers, 1950).
GULLAN, Marjorie, and SANSOM, C., *Poet Speaks,* 4th Edition (London: Methuen Company, 1951).
HAHN, Lomas, and VANDRAEGEN, *Basic Voice Training for Speech* (New York: McGraw-Hill Book Company, Inc., 1952).
HAMM, Agnes Curran, *Choral Speaking Techniques* (Milwaukee: Tower Press, 1951).
H'DOUBLER, Margaret, *Dance: A Creative Art Experience* (New York: Appleton-Century-Crofts, Inc., 1940).

APPENDIX

HICKS, Helen G., *The Reading Chorus* (New York: Noble & Noble, 1939).
HERMAN, L. H., and HERMAN, M. S., *Manual of Foreign Dialects* (New York: Ziff-Davis Publishing Company, 1943).
JOHNSON, Gertrude E., *Dialects for Oral Interpretation* (New York: Appleton-Century-Crofts, Inc., 1922).
JOHNSON, GERTRUDE E., *Modern Literature for Oral Interpretation* (New York: Appleton-Century-Crofts, Inc., 1930).
JOHNSON, Gertrude E., *Studies in the Art of Interpretation* (New York: Appleton-Century-Crofts, Inc., 1940).
KAPLAN, M. A., *Radio and Poetry* (New York: Columbia University Press, 1949).
KENYON, J. S. and KNOTT, T. A., *A Pronouncing Dictionary of American English* (Springfield, Mass.: G. & C. Merriam Company, 1944).
KEPPIE, Elizabeth, *The Teaching of Choric Speech* (Boston: Expression Company, 1931).
KERFOOT, J. B., *How to Read* (Boston: Houghton Mifflin Company, 1916).
KRAPP, G. P., *Pronunciation of Standard English in America* (New York: Oxford University Press, 1919).
LANGFELD, Herbert S., *The Aesthetic Attitude* (New York: Harcourt Brace and Company, Inc., 1920).
LEE, Charlotte, *Oral Interpretation* (Boston: Houghton Mifflin Company, 1952).
LEE, Harold Newton, *Perception and Aesthetic Value* (New York: Prentice-Hall, Inc., 1938).
LYMAN, R. L., *The Mind at Work* (New York: Scott, Foresman and Company, 1924).
McLEAN, Margaret P., *Good American Speech* (New York: E. P. Dutton and Company, Inc., 1952).
McLEAN, Margaret P., *Oral Interpretation of Forms of Literature* (New York: E. P. Dutton and Company, Inc., 1942).
MORGAN, Lucia C., *Voice and Diction Drill Books for Students in Speech* (Dubuque, Iowa: William C. Brown Company, 1951).
NICHOLS, Wallace B., *The Speaking of Poetry* (Boston: Expression Company, 1937).
PARRISH, W. M., *Reading Aloud* (New York: Thomas Nelson & Sons, 1941).
QUILLER-COUCH, Sir Arthur T., *On the Art of Reading* (Cambridge: The Cambridge University Press, 1924).
ROBINSON, Marion P., and THURSTON, Rozetta L., *Poetry Arranged for the Speaking Choir* (Boston: Expression Company, 1936).
ROBBS, Mary Margaret, *Oral Interpretation of Literature* (New York: H. W. Wilson Company, 1941).

SANTAYANA, George, *The Interpretation of Poetry* (New York: Charles Scribner's Sons, 1936).

SARRETT and FOSTER, *Basic Principles of Speech* (Boston: Houghton Mifflin Company, 1946).

SELDEN, Samuel, *First Steps in Acting* (New York: Appleton-Century-Crofts, Inc., 1947).

SMITH, Charles A., *What Can Literature Do for Me?* (Garden City: Doubleday, Page, and Company, 1924).

STANISLAVSKI, Constantin, *My Life in Art* (Boston: Little, Brown & Company, 1938).

SUTTON, Vida R., *Seeing and Hearing America* (Boston: Expression Company, 1936).

SWANN, Mona, *An Approach to Choral Speech* (Boston, Expression Company, 1934).

TALLCOTT, Rollo, *The Art of Acting and Public Reading* (Indianapolis: The Bobbs-Merrill Company, 1922).

TASSIN, A., *The Oral Study of Literature* (New York: Alfred A. Knopf, 1929).

TOROSSIN, Aram, *A Guide to Aesthetics* (Stanford, Calif.: Stanford University Press, 1937).

VAN DUSEN, C. R., *Training the Voice for Speech* (New York: McGraw-Hill Book Company, Inc., 1952).

WALSH, Gertrude, *Sing Your Way to Better Speech* (New York: E. P. Dutton and Company, Inc., 1947).

WOOLBERT, C. H., and NELSON, S. E., *Art of Interpretative Speech* (New York: Appleton-Century-Crofts, Inc., 1934).

YOUNG, Stark, *Theatre Practice* (New York: Charles Scribner's Sons, 1935).

INDEX

Authors' names are printed in CAPITALS AND SMALL CAPITALS.
Titles are printed in *italics*.
Subject-matter is printed in usual upper and lower case.

Abandon, 175
ABBOTT, WALDO (quoted), 286
Abnegation, 154
ABNEY, LOUISE (quoted), 257
Acting, vii, 222
ADAMS, GEORGE MATTHEW (quoted), xiv
Adding and subtracting voices, 280
ADDISON, JOSEPH, 330
Aesthetic distance, 176
Afton Water, 93
ALDRICH, THOMAS BAILEY, 118
ANDERSEN, HANS CHRISTIAN, 313
Annual Message to Congress, Lincoln's, 1861, 524
Antiphonal reading, 262
Appreciation, 228
ARNOLD, MATTHEW, 477
Arrangement of literature for radio, 300
Art, 15
As You Like It (from), 113, 389
Attitudes, 17, 218
Auditory images, 37
Aunt Melissy on Boys, 409
Author's meaning, the, 202

Backgrounds, 234
BEAUMONT, FRANCIS, 193
BEDDOES, THOMAS LOVELL, 82
Bee and the Flower, The, 185

Belovèd, my Belovèd When I Think, 462
Beware!, 490
BIBLE, 37, 79, 262, 385, 445
BLACK, AGNES KNOX (quoted), 238
BLAKE, WILLIAM, 496
Bodily Action, 46
Bonie Doon, 130
BOTTOMLY, GORDON (quoted), 254
Break, Break, Break, 67
BRONTÈ, CHARLOTTE (quoted), 44
Brook, The (from), 102
BROWNING, ELIZABETH BARRETT, 53, 63, 266, 341, 447-475, 544
BROWNING, ROBERT, 52, 96, 109, 137, 147, 172, 203, 204, 205, 208, 223, 227, 447-476, 509, 522
BRYANT, WILLIAM CULLEN, 545
Build, 136
BULWER-LYTTON, EDWARD, 36, 59
BURNS, ROBERT, 93, 105, 130, 572
BUTCHER, SAMUEL HENRY (quotation), 24
By the Way, 575

Cadence, 103
Can It Be Right to Give, 457
CARLILE, JOHN S. (quoted), 285, 292
CARLTON, WILL, 354
Central thought, 165
Chambered Nautilus, The, 444

INDEX

Characters, Interpretation of, 71
Character angles, 72
Character rhythms, 114
CHENEY, JOHN VANCE, 263
Child and Boatman, 115
Child's Dream of a Star, A, 352
Child's Laughter, A, 37
Choral reading, 254
Christmas Carol, A, 546
Christmas Night in the Quarters (from), 126
CLARK, S. H. (quoted), 80
Clear and Cool, 261
CLEMENS, SAMUEL (MARK TWAIN), 73
Climax, 135
Comic sense, 88
Connotation, 28, 200
Consciousness of technique, 61
Contentment, 419
Contrast, 146
Core of Speech Training, vi
CORSON, HIRAM (quoted), 14
CRANE, FRANK (quoted), 231
CRAWSHAW, W. H. (quoted), 249
Creative reading, 13
Crescendo and diminuendo, 139
Criticism, xiv
CROCKER, CHARLOTTE (quoted), 124
CROWELL, GRACE NOLL (cited), 198
Crystallization, 169
CUNNINGHAM, CORNELIUS (quotation), 100
Cyrano de Bergerac (from), 90, 112

DAUDET, ALPHONSE, 307
David Copperfield, (scene from), 127
Day, 96
Daybreak, 406
DE BANKE, CÉCILE (quoted), 255

DE MAUPASSANT, GUY, 212
Defence of Poetry, The, 323
DELSARTE (quoted), 134
Denotative meaning, 28
Destruction of Pompeii, The, 36
Diagrams, 137-140, 151-153
Dialect, 124-133
Diamond Necklace, The, 212
DICKENS, CHARLES, 54, 127, 352, 401, 435, 499, 506, 546
Diction, 193
Directing choral reading, 258
Dissertation upon Roast Pig, A, 41
DOBIE, J. FRANK, 39
DOLMAN, JOHN (quoted), 176
Dominant unity, 166
Dover Beach, 477
Dramatic pause, 83
Dramatic timing, 77
Drifting, 422
Drinking Song, 277
DRYDEN, JOHN, 278
DUDLEY, LOUISE (quoted), 31, 32
DUNLAP, KNIGHT (quoted), 30

Each and All, 518
Eagle, The, 113
EASTMAN, MAX (quoted), 56
Echo, 160
Elementary School, The, ix
ELIOT, GEORGE (quoted), 26
EMERSON, RALPH WALDO, 518, 537
Emotion, 55
Empathy, 62
Emphasis, 155, 157, 164
End of the Play, The, 567
Explorer, The (from), 139

Falstaff's Recruits, 369
FERBER, EDNA, 42
Finalities of Expression, The, 540
First Time He Kissed Me, 467

INDEX

First Snow-Fall, The, 36
FITHIAN, GEORGE W. (quoted), 306
FITZGERALD, EDWARD, 574
Flexibility, 182
FOGERTY, ELSIE (quoted), 104
Fountain, The, 94
Freedom, Stanzas on, 326
From a Railway Carriage, 153
FROST, ROBERT (quoted), 112, 236
Fugitives, The, 350

Gettysburg Address, The, 476
Give Me the Splendid Silent Sun, 529
GOETHE, 325
Go from Me, Yet I Feel, 458
GOLDSMITH, OLIVER, 366
GRIMM, HARRIET (quoted), 250
Gustatory images, 41

Hamlet (from), 113, 136, 153, 173
HAMPDEN, WALTER (quoted), 171
Harp That Once Through Tara's Halls, The, 82
HARRIS, JOEL CHANDLER (quoted), 126
HARTE, BRET, 81
HAYES, ROLAND (quoted), 51
HEDGES, M. M. (quoted), 3
HELM, MACKINLEY (quoted), 51
Hero, The, 329
HOLMES, OLIVER WENDELL, 419, 444
HOLSTEIN, MARK (quoted), 56
Home-Thoughts from Abroad, 227
HOOD, THOMAS, 96, 163
House and the Brain, The (from), 59
Housman, A. E. (quoted), 56
HOUSMAN, LAURENCE, 375
How Do I Love Thee, 472
How Green Was My Valley, (from), 43
How the King Lost His Crown, 520
How They Brought the Good News from Ghent to Aix, 109
How Tom Sawyer Whitewashed the Fence, 73
How We Fought the Fire, 354

I Lived with Visions, 473
If Thou Must Love Me, 463
I Remember, I Remember, 96
I Thought Once How Theocritus, 455
I Wandered Lonely as a Cloud, 34
I Was Born An American, 185
Idylls of the King, The, 231
Illusion, 168
Illusion of the first time, 171
Imagination, 20, 30, 233
Indirection, 439
Individuality, 16
Inflection, 188
INGELOW, JEAN, 115, 348, 383
Inscription, 138
Intellectual humor, 86
Interclausal relations, 207
Interpretation of meaning, 197
Introductions, 241

JACKSON, HELEN HUNT, 390, 413, 440, 481, 489, 523
Jane Eyre, (from), 44
Jaques' Seven Ages of Man, 113
Jesus and the Blind Man, 445
Journey for Margaret, (from), 38
Joys, Poem of, 492
Juliet's Dilemma, 220
Julius Caesar (from), 302

KEATS, JOHN, 61
KERFOOT, J. B. (quoted), 31, 234
King Henry IV (from), 369
King Henry VIII (from), 349

592 INDEX

King Lear's Defiance, 186
Kings Bow Their Heads, 117
KINGSLEY, CHARLES, 149, 261
KIPLING, RUDYARD, 139, 161
Kitchen Clock, The, 263

Lady Macbeth's Preparation, 205
L'Allegro, 95
LAMB, CHARLES, 41
LANGFELD (quoted), 65
Language, 196
Language study, x
LANIER, SIDNEY, 407
Last Lesson, The, 307
Leap of Roushan Beg, The, 372
LEAR, EDWARD, 388
Lecture Recital, The, 251, 447
Letters, Browning, 447-476
LINCOLN, ABRAHAM, 98, 476, 524
Line around, a, 277
List for choral reading, 282
Little Man and Little Soul, 162
LLEWELLYN, RICHARD (quoted), 43
Location, Sense of, 68
LONGFELLOW, HENRY WADSWORTH, 77, 107, 372, 391, 406, 490
Longing for Home, 383
Lotus Eaters, The (from), 59, 486
Love Among the Ruins, 147
Lover's Resolution, The, 539
Love's Courage, 447
LOWE, ROBERT LIDDELL, 117
LOWELL, AMY (quoted), 99, 170
LOWELL, JAMES RUSSELL, 36, 38, 94, 326, 424, 478, 526
LYMAN, R. L. (quoted), 169
Lyrical Ballads, Preface, 208
LYTTON, EDWARD, BULWER-, 36, 59

MABIE, HAMILTON WRIGHT, 2, 174, 197, 236, 540, 575

Macbeth (from), 41, 205, 396
MCGILL, EARLE (quoted), 289
MACLEISH, ARCHIBALD (quoted), 240
MALLORY, LOUIS A. (quoted), 166, 288
Man's a Man for A' That, A, 572
MASEFIELD, JOHN (quoted), 168, 246
MAUGHAM, W. SOMERSET, 41
Meaning of Words, 200
Meeting at Night, 204
Melody, 187
Merlin and the Gleam, 414
Message to Congress, Lincoln's Annual, 1861, 524
Meter, 158
MILTON, JOHN, 95
Mr. Pickwick Engages a Man Servant, 499
Mr. Pickwick Is Sued for Breach of Promise, 506
Modest Wit, A, 88
Moon and Sixpence, The (from), 41
MOORE, THOMAS, 82, 104, 162, 192, 408
MORRIS, CLARA, 343
Motor sense, 49
Musical Instrument, A, 53
My Heart's in the Highlands, 105
My Last Duchess, 223
My Letters! All Dead Paper, 471
My Star, 476

Naaman and Gehazi, 385
New approach, a, xiii
New ideas versus old, 160
Nicholas Nickleby Leaving the Yorkshire School, 401
Night Among the Pines, A, 485
Nijinsky, Romolo (quoted), 46, 66
Novel, the, 249

INDEX

O. HENRY (SIDNEY PORTER), 40, 112
Objective methods of finding the rhythm, 102
Ode on Intimations of Immortality, 531
Ode to a Nightingale, (from), 61
Ode to the West Wind, 570
Off Stage, 69, 70, 71
On Stage, 69, 70, 71
Old Clock on the Stairs, The (from), 107
Old Man Talking in His Sleep, An, 117
Olfactory Images, 40
On the Life Of Man, 193
Open-mindedness, 230
Orator Puff, 192
Organic senses, 57
Originality, 21
Orpheus, 349
Othello (from), 84, 156, 497
Out of the Cradle Endlessly Rocking, 359
Owl, The, 161
Owl and the Pussy Cat, The, 388
Ozymandias, 35

PARRISH, WAYLAND MAXFIELD (quoted), 98, 218
Parting at Morning, 205
Patriot, The, 522
Pause, 78
Pause for comedy, 84
Peculiar Treasure, A (from), 42
Perdita Singing, To (from), 38
Perfect One, The, 375
Personal Values, vi
PETERS, KEN (KENNETH FAGERLIN) (quoted), 293
PHELPS, WILLIAM LYON (quoted), xvi, 8, 9
Philippians 4:8, 79
PHILLIPS, ARTHUR EDWARD (quotation), 302

Pickup within the phrase, 80
Pickwick Papers (from), 54, 499, 506
Pickwickians on Ice, The, 54
Pied Piper of Hamelin, The, 509
Pippa Passes (from), 96, 137
Pit and The Pendulum, The (from), 44
Planes, 137
POE, EDGAR ALLEN, 44
Poem of Joys, 492
Poem of the Road, 494
Polarity, 150
PORTER, SIDNEY (O. HENRY), 40, 112
Posture, 49
POWERS, LELAND (quoted), 20
Prairies, The, 545
Present Crisis, The, 526
Princess, The (from), 260
Princess Porcelain, The, 343
Professional Reading, viii
Public Speaking, vii
Programs, 243
Projecting thought, 65
Prospice, 203
Psalm XIX, 37
Psalm XXIV, 262
Punctuation, 189

Rabbi Ben Ezra (from), 208
Radio, xi, 285
RARIG, F. M. (quoted), 13
READ, THOMAS BUCHANAN, 422
Reading club, radio, 293
REALF, RICHARD, 439
Recital plans, 246
Refrains, 265
Relief, 141
Relieving Guard, 81
Remember This One?, 307, 313
Report on radio experiment, 294
Reserve, 145
Restraint, 172

Rhyme of the Duchess May, The, 266
Rhythm, 97
Road, Poem of The, 494
Romance of a Busy Broker, The, (from), 40
Romeo and Juliet, 220, 382, 418
ROSSETTI, CHRISTINA GEORGINA, 75, 154
ROSTAND, EDMOND, 90, 112
Rubáiyát of Omar Khayyám, The (from), 574
RUSSELL, IRWIN, 126

Sailor Boy, A, 225
SAPIR, EDWARD (quoted), 20
SARETT, LEW (quoted), 48
Saul (from), 52
Scansion, 103
SCHILLER, 488
School for Scandal, The (from), 142
Scope of interpretative reading, 23
SCOTT, SIR WALTER, 491
SEABURY, DAVID (quoted), 45
Self-discipline, 22
Self-Reliance, 537
Sensation, 30
Set of Turquoise, The, 118
Seven Times Two, Romance, 348
Shadows of Birds, 489
SHAKESPEARE, WILLIAM, 84, 113, 136, 151, 153, 156, 173, 184, 186, 205, 220, 302, 349, 369, 382, 389, 396, 418, 497
SHELLEY, PERCY BYSSHE, 35, 323, 338, 350, 570
SHERIDAN, RICHARD BRINSLEY, 142, 277
Short story series, 307, 313
Sight images, 32
Silent reading, 26
SIMON, CLARENCE (quoted), 57

Sincerity, the Soul of Eloquence, 325
Singer's Hills, The, 481
Skeleton in Armor, The, 391
Skipper Ireson's Ride, 379
Snow-Bound, 333
Snow Man, The, 313
Social Responsibility, x
Song for St. Cecilia's Day, 278
Song of Myself (from), 60
Song of Slaves in the Desert, 281
Song of the Shirt, The, 163
Songs (from William Tell), 488
Sonnets From the Portuguese, 455, 456, 457, 458, 462, 463, 467, 471, 472, 473
Speech Correction, xi
Speech patterns, 151
Spinning, 390
Spinning-Wheel Song, The, 367
Splendour Falls, The, 260
Spring Song, 389
Stage-Coach, The, 435
STANISLAVSKI, CONSTANTINE (quotation), 20
Stanzas on Freedom, 326
STEVENSON, ROBERT LOUIS, 105, 153, 485
Stress and meter, 158
Structure, 134
Subordination, 155
Suggestiveness, 210
Summer Storm, The, 478
Supplementary reading, Appendix B, 585
Sweet and Low, 108
SWINBURNE, ALGERNON CHARLES, 37
Syllabus for a College Course, 579

Tactile images, 42
Talent, xvi
Taming of the Shrew, The (from), 151

INDEX

Tampa Robins, 407
TAYLOR, SIR HENRY, 329
Technique in interpretative reading, 17
Technique of angles, 72
Technique of thinking, 26
Tempo, 91
TENNYSON, ALFRED, 59, 67, 102, 108, 113, 130, 161, 185, 186, 225, 231, 234, 260, 414, 486
Texan, In England, A (from), 39
Textbook, The, xii
THACKERAY, WILLIAM MAKEPEACE, 567
There Was a Child Went Forth, 328
Those Evening Bells, 104
Thou Hast Thy Calling to Some Palace Floor, 457
Three part division, 278
Tiger, The, 496
Time I've Lost in Wooing, The, 408
Timeliness, 302
Timing, 77, 305
To a Skylark (SHELLEY), 338
To a Skylark (WORDSWORTH), 154
To Perdita, Singing, 38
To Sea! To Sea!, 82
To the Student, 3
To the Teacher, v
Tomorrow, 130
Tone color, 183
Tone copying, 190
Topping, 140
TROWBRIDGE, JAMES T., 409, 520
True Ballad of the King's Singer, The, 440
TWAIN, MARK (SAMUEL CLEMENS), 73

Unison reading, 259
Unity and emphasis, 164
Universality, 301

Unlike Are We, O Princely Heart, 456
Up-Hill, 75

Village Preacher, The, 366
Vision of Sir Launfal, The, 424
Voice, 179
Voice Spoke Out of the Skies, A, 186
Voices, 191

Waken, Lords and Ladies Gay, 491
WALLER, JOHN FRANCIS, 367
Way to Sing, The, 413
We Must Be Free or Die, 327
WEAVER, ANDREW THOMAS (quotation), 27, 92, 182
WEBSTER, DANIEL, 185
Westminster Abbey, 330
What Can I Give Thee Back, 457
When in Disgrace with Fortune and Men's Eyes, 184
When the Tide Comes in, 523
WHIPPLE, JAMES (quoted), 304
WHITE, W. L. (quoted), 38
WHITMAN, WALT, 60, 179, 191, 196, 328, 359, 492, 494, 529
WHITTIER, JOHN G., 281, 333, 379
Whole, the, xv, 19, 179
WILIE, MAX (quoted), 301
William Tell (from), 488
Wind, The, 105
Wisdom Unapplied, 341
WISE, C. M. (quoted), 194
WITHER, GEORGE, 539
WOOLBERT, CHARLES (quoted), 26
WORDSWORTH, WILLIAM, 34, 154, 202, 208, 327, 531
Work and Contemplation, 544
World Is Too Much with Us, The, 202

Year's at the Spring, The, 137
Young and Old, 149